The Metaphysical Society

The Metaphysical Society

VICTORIAN MINDS IN CRISIS, 1869-1880

Alan Willard Brown

OCTAGON BOOKS

A DIVISION OF FARRAR, STRAUS AND GIROUX

New York 1973

Reprinted 1973
by special arrangement with Columbia University Press

OCTAGON BOOKS
A DIVISION OF FARRAR, STRAUS & GIROUX, INC.
19 Union Square West
New York, N. Y. 10003

Library of Congress Cataloging in Publication Data

Brown, Alan Willard, 1910-
The Metaphysical Society.

Reprint of the ed. published by Columbia University Press, New York.

Originally presented as the author's thesis, Columbia University.

Bibliography: p.
1. Metaphysical Society, London.

B11.M4B7 1973 110'.6'2421 73-8422
ISBN 0-473-91008-1

Manufactured by Braun-Brumfield, Inc.
Ann Arbor, Michigan

Printed in the United States of America

TO BEATRICE

Preface

THE MOST PLEASANT task in the writing of any book is to give thanks and express gratitude for the many kindnesses and gracious gestures which have on all sides helped to ease the writer's difficulties. My first and greatest debt is to Miss Diana Russell, daughter of Lord Arthur Russell, who has made available to me a full photographic record on microfilm of her nearly complete set of the Papers of the Metaphysical Society. The speed and skill with which John Johnson of the University Press, Oxford, arranged for the photography during some of the darkest days of the war also deserves grateful mention, as does the willingness of the Bodleian Library to permit the photographing of several papers in their collection which were not in Miss Russell's. Mr. W. D. Paden of the University of Kansas generously put into my hands a volume containing thirteen of the Society's Papers and other printed documents relative to the Society's dissolution, formerly belonging to Sir Frederick Pollock; one of these papers is not in any other collection known to me. Mrs. Frewen Lord, daughter of Sir James Knowles, courteously loaned me a printed proof of a part of the Minute Book of the Society, formerly in her father's possession. She also went to considerable trouble in an effort, unfortunately unsuccessful, to locate the present owner of the Minute Book itself.

Among those in England who have been most helpful in answering inquiries and giving information are: R. Nicol Cross, the Principal of Manchester College, Oxford, and Raymond V. Holt, the Librarian; A. Esdaile and H. Thomas, of the British Museum Library; Sir John Pollock, son of Sir Frederick Pollock; Ethel Sidgwick, niece of Henry Sidgwick; my uncle, the late Dr. John A. Hutton, until recently editor of the *British Weekly;* and several officers of the Bodleian Library at Oxford. The courtesy and willing coöperation of these men and women once more puts an American student greatly in England's debt.

The staffs of many libraries helped me in making the fullest use of their facilities. I am especially grateful to the Columbia University Library, the Harvard College Library, and the New York Public Library, where I did most of my reading and research. I am also deeply indebted to the libraries of the University of Vermont and of Middlebury College for permitting me, during several summers spent on Lake Champlain, to borrow freely from their splendid files of Victorian periodicals. I must thank, too, the Yale University Library, the Congressional Library, and the University of Chicago Library for their courtesies to a wandering student. I have made intensive use of some of the manuscript materials in the Pierpont Morgan Library in New York, and in the Huntington Library in San Marino; to both of these institutions I wish to express my appreciation of their magnificent scholarly service.

In the early days of my work I was encouraged and helped by the advice and knowledge of my great teacher, the late John Livingston Lowes, and also by Alfred North Whitehead, Crane Brinton, and Arthur Darby Nock, all of Harvard University. My colleague at Columbia, Charles W. Everett, took time from a holiday to photograph for me at the University of Chicago material relevant to the history of the *Contemporary Review.*

Many teachers, friends, and colleagues at Columbia have been a constant source of knowledge, inspiration, and encouragement. My debt to them is far greater than they know. Without the friendship and patient criticism of Emery Neff, as well as the constant stimulus of his vast knowledge of the Victorian period, the difficulties of my task, undertaken with more confidence than strength during heavy teaching and administrative duties, might on occasion have seemed insuperable. From him, since my first days as a graduate student at Columbia, I have learned the crucial interdependence of all the arts and sciences. Lionel Trilling, who read more drafts of this book than I had the right to expect of any man, gave me many insights into the functions and responsibilities of scholarship. To him and to his wife, Diana, I owe much more—the gift of their unequaled companionship and their deep knowledge of the ways of heart and mind. The critical intelligence and editorial pen of Jacques Barzun were of invaluable assistance in reducing this volume to its present form. Its faults are mine; many of what virtues it may possess are his.

Roger Sherman Loomis and Marjorie Hope Nicolson gave me the benefit of a close reading and a number of helpful suggestions at a critical stage in the preparation of the manuscript. Much of the book elaborates ideas worked out in years of teaching with James Gutmann, whose fine understanding of both literature and philosophy has enriched my own efforts. Horace Friess and Herbert Schneider helped me over several philosophical hurdles; and J. Bartlet Brebner has read the text in the generous light of his knowledge of Victorian history. Finally, Harry Morgan Ayres and Ernest Hunter Wright have each helped me most considerately in various ways with the problems of graduate study over a period of many years.

The Columbia University Press has been very helpful, especially William Bridgwater and Leon E. Seltzer of the editorial department; the latter has labored effectively with many questions of form. Eugenia Porter of the production department has been most coöperative in matters of typography and design.

To my father, Carroll Neide Brown, at his death Professor of Classical Languages at the College of the City of New York, I owe my introduction to the life of the mind and whatever intellectual discipline I have been able to achieve. My mother, Agnes Hutton Brown, a Scottish lady of unusual gifts, led me early to Victorian literature, much of which was almost contemporary in her girlhood. She knows the many senses in which this book is also hers. And without the generous hospitality of my wife's mother, Anita Lawrence Simpson, formerly Dean of New London Junior College, who provided many summers of peace and seclusion at her summer home, "La Casita," on Lake Champlain, the writing would have been a less grateful task.

But the greatest of all debts I owe to my wife, Beatrice, whose patience and enthusiasm supported me at every stage of the work. She was my amanuensis in much of the difficult routine of periodical research, and through months and years typed the entire manuscript in its many forms. When I marvel at the labors of the great Victorians, I remind myself of one who, in the midst of domestic responsibilities and the care of our two daughters, found time from her own active social and intellectual life to devote her best energies and loving care to this book.

Alan Willard Brown

Columbia College
Columbia University
February, 1947

ACKNOWLEDGMENTS

Permission to reprint material from works published by them has been courteously granted by the following: Dodd, Mead & Company, Inc., for excerpts from *The Life and Letters of James Martineau,* by James Drummond and C. B. Upton; Doubleday and Company, Inc., for a passage from *A Modern Symposium,* by G. Lowes Dickinson, to which they now hold the American rights; Harcourt, Brace and Company, Inc., for an excerpt from *Goldsworthy Lowes Dickinson,* by E. M. Forster; Macmillan & Co., Ltd., London, for passages from *William George Ward and the Catholic Revival,* by Wilfrid Ward; The Macmillan Company, New York, for passages from *Henry Sidgwick, a Memoir,* by Arthur and Eleanor Sidgwick; John Murray, London, for an excerpt from *Notes from a Diary, 1873–1881,* by Sir Mountstuart E. Grant Duff; Random House, Inc., for a quotation from *Ulysses,* by James Joyce; Charles Scribner's Sons, for a passage from *The Cambridge "Apostles,"* by Frances M. Brookfield. The Pierpont Morgan Library, New York, has also graciously permitted quotation from the unpublished manuscript correspondence of James Knowles and William Knight, now in that collection.

Introduction

THIS HISTORY of the Metaphysical Society and its influence began more than ten years ago as an examination of the relations of literature, religion, and science in the late-Victorian period. The Metaphysical Society, about which so little has been known, eventually became the center of my study of the intellectual crisis which faced the English mind in the seventies. More than any other institution of the period, it seems to express most vividly and dramatically the fundamental intellectual concerns of that crucial decade. In my opinion it also brings together more of the most distinguished minds and personalities of the age than any similar group in history. Lord Odo Russell used to refer to its members as "the forty of the future Academy."

The social manner of the Metaphysical Society, which goes back at least as far as the "Apostles" at Cambridge in Tennyson's youth, reveals a neglected but important element in the Victorian character. But equally important is the gradual spread through the middle years of the century of the critical, rationalistic, and scientific spirit. The successes, even triumphs, of this spirit are indispensable keys to a proper understanding of the arrogance and pretension of science in the later decades. For the attempts of religious and theological minds to check the spread of this critical spirit were in time qualified by a new spirit of inquiry among religious thinkers themselves. The rich literature of the period, in poetry, the novel, and polemical prose, reflects an age which not only believed in the power of the word, but which perhaps more than any other manifests the power of responsible public discourse to mold and change a society. The growth of the most intelligent tradition in modern journalism must be traced to this fact and this faith; the increased responsiveness of political institutions to public opinion, and even the idea of the political education of the people, are consequences of the firm alliance between journalism and intellect in the Victorian period. The relation of established religions to secular government and public education became one of the major problems of the age and is one not yet solved. Finally, the Metaphysical Society serves, as was its own intention, to bring together these varied and complex questions and attitudes and, through the minds of many of the greatest Victorians, to project them once more into the turbulent intellectual life of the great decade of the seventies.

Throughout, my effort has been to understand the many important senses in which no man is merely "man thinking." Rather, I have tried to show that he is a social being, who belongs to a certain group, inherits a certain tradition, believes in a religion or develops a personal philosophy, and fights for or against certain forms and ideas, not necessarily out of fear or prejudice, but because he thus gives meaning and significance to what he lives by and lives for. I have not denied bias, passion, or hate, but I am convinced that men's irrational fears require as much historical and critical understanding as their noblest achievements.

I have myself tried to be as objective as is compatible with my highly personal interest in the period and its problems, and as disinterested as is possible for one who believes that the history he is writing has considerable relevance to his own day. I believe that every age needs to reconstruct its own significant past, and I find the Victorian period richest in meanings for the present world. I regard so-called "scientific history" as a dangerous myth, however dear to one kind of academic mind; and I am sure that no one will accuse me of attempting to write it. I do, however, believe that some kind of historical truth is attainable and that, however difficult, it is worth striving for. This "truth" I regard as an adequate representation of the spirit of the age studied—justified by the fullest knowledge and the most perceptive emphasis—a representation which will also weigh the contemporary problems which condition the historian's own interests, and reveal honestly, ingenuously, or even artfully, the personal, critical, and intellectual position of the historian himself. If we know the premises of the thought of an age, we know its prejudices and its bias; the same is true of persons. I trust that my own naturalistic position is blind neither to religious values nor to the methods and achievements of science; yet in my effort to characterize and understand the philosophical, social, and moral implications of Victorian thought and feeling, I have also insisted on the prerogatives of criticism.

In the course of my reading and research, I was surprised to discover that a society as important as the Metaphysical had never been the subject of historical or critical study. All the casual references pointed to the distinction of its members and several suggested that it was an impressive symbol of the times. But an eminent contemporary critic of Victorian literature could attribute its founding to *Sheridan* Knowles, the dramatist, and almost no recent writer, however brief his comments upon it, has been wholly accurate. The one notable exception is Houston Peterson, whose description of the Society in his *Huxley, Prophet of Science* is both concise and sound. Even Lytton Strachey, whose essay on "Cardinal Manning" in *Eminent Victorians* devotes a characteristic page to Manning's share in the Society's debates, makes two minor errors and, by implication, a major one when he says that the answers to the questions raised by the Society were not recorded. He may not have known that the Papers had been printed and therefore presumably somewhere preserved, but he could have learned the probability from the Manning papers themselves, as revealed by E. S. Purcell in his *Life* of Manning.

The chief sources of information about the Society are well-known to students of the period. They are Hallam Tennyson's *Memoir* of his father, Leonard Huxley's *Life and Letters of Thomas Henry Huxley,* Wilfrid Ward's *W. G. Ward and the Catholic Revival,* Arthur and Eleanor Sidgwick's *Henry Sidgwick, a Memoir,* and Frederic Harrison's *Autobiographic Memoirs*—all of which have chapters or extensive parts of chapters devoted to the Metaphysical Society. There are innumerable other references, sometimes important, but often unilluminating, in the letters, memoirs, and biographies of the time. I have studied, with varying emphasis and no pretense at complete knowledge, the lives and works of all sixty-two members of the Society, and I hope that no important reference to the Society or its meetings has escaped me. But I should welcome answers to the few unsolved problems which I indicate in the course of the book; the recent war has made impossible a visit to England which might have cleared up some of them.

My greatest good fortune in the course of my research was the generous response I received to inquiries in England about the Society. Grateful thanks for this indispensable assistance have already been given in the Preface. But this volume would indeed have been impossible without the kind coöperation of Miss Diana Russell, daughter of Lord Arthur Russell, who not only made available to me the Papers of the Society, but also sent me a privately printed volume containing her father's Papers and several documents relevant to the history of the Society.

Once these previously inaccessible materials were in my hands, a full history of the Society was at last possible, and I was no longer entirely dependent on following clues which helped to identify this or that periodical article as a Paper read before the Society. In thus finding or in some form identifying *all* the Papers, I have been able to establish a bibliographical canon, as well as to make generally known for the first time the significance of the papers in the intellectual history of the seventies.

But the more narrowly scholarly aspects of my work are not those which I consider most important; in consequence, I have relegated the greater part of the bibliographical analysis to a series of appendixes and have not hesitated, in the course of my critical exposition, to refer the reader to them for answers to many questions. I have tried, however, to treat history, whether of the Society or of the period, with as much attention to detail as seemed necessary to justify the critical generalizations which I consider it my true purpose to make. I do not deny that the facts of the historical picture may be interesting for their own sake; but it is the pattern of the whole to which I invite careful attention.

My true subject is that faith in discourse which was the dominating feature of the intellectual life of the nineteenth century and which filled the minds and hearts of the group of thinkers and men of action who banded themselves together in the Metaphysical Society.

Contents

The debate which ensued was in its scope and progress an epitome of the course of life. Neither place nor council was lacking in dignity. The debaters were the keenest in the land, the theme they were engaged on the loftiest and most vital. The high hall of Horne's house had never beheld an assembly so representative and so varied nor had the old rafters of that establishment ever listened to a language so encyclopaedic. A gallant scene in truth it made.

—JAMES JOYCE, *Ulysses.*

Members

Sir Henry Wentworth Acland
Henry Alford, Dean of Canterbury
The Duke of Argyll
Walter Bagehot
Arthur James Balfour, later 1st Earl of Balfour
Alfred Barratt
Alfred Barry
Matthew P. W. Boulton
Dr. John Charles Bucknill
Dr. William Benjamin Carpenter
Richard William Church, Dean of St. Paul's
Dr. Andrew Clark
Rev. Robert Clarke
William K. Clifford
Rev. J. D. Dalgairns
C. J. Ellicott, Bishop of Gloucester and Bristol
Alexander Campbell Fraser
James Anthony Froude
Francis Aidan Gasquet, later Cardinal
William Ewart Gladstone
Sir Alexander Grant
Sir Mountstuart E. Grant Duff
W. R. Greg
George Grove
Sir William Gull
Frederic Harrison
James Hinton
Shadworth Hodgson
Richard Holt Hutton
Thomas Henry Huxley
James Knowles, Jr.
Robert Lowe, later Viscount Sherbrooke
Sir John Lubbock, later Baron Avebury
Edmund L. Lushington
William Connor Magee, Bishop of Peterborough, later Archbishop of York
Henry Edward Manning, Archbishop of Westminster and later Cardinal
Dr. James Martineau
Frederick Denison Maurice
St. George Mivart
John Morley, later Viscount Morley
J. B. Mozley
Hon. Roden Noel
Roundell Palmer, Lord Selborne
Mark Pattison
Frederick Pollock
Charles Pritchard
George Croom Robertson
John Ruskin
Lord Arthur Russell
J. R. Seeley
Henry Sidgwick
Arthur Penrhyn Stanley, Dean of Westminster
James Fitzjames Stephen
Leslie Stephen
James Sully
J. J. Sylvester
Alfred Tennyson
Connop Thirlwall, Bishop of St. David's
William Thomson, Archbishop of York
John Tyndall
C. B. Upton
Dr. William George Ward

Chapter 1

THE MODEL AND THE SPIRIT: THE CAMBRIDGE "APOSTLES"

In the years of reaction following Waterloo, there was little concern with science in the English universities and only the beginning of that interest in theology which had already been, under the influence of Kant, Schelling, and Schleiermacher, one of the major preoccupations of Continental thought for many years. The Scottish universities, to be sure, had long been the home of an active school of philosophy, which, after the Continental example, had also concerned itself with the problems of science and theology. But although England had lost her scientific preëminence, in literature and the related arts she was beginning a renascence which was to last nearly a century. Between 1815 and 1820 Malthus, Bentham, Ricardo, and James Mill were publishing some of their most significant works in economics and history, and all the great Romantic writers of both generations were writing, some of them at their best, enriching our poetry and our prose, and creating modern English criticism. Perhaps because science was woefully neglected at the universities, it was only to be expected that the new literature should exercise a powerful influence on the minds and imaginations of the undergraduates of this period. At Cambridge, the college studies alone were not invigorating enough for one group of students, and in 1820 a little group of St. John's College men interested in "higher philosophy" founded the "Cambridge Conversazione Society," soon to be better known as the "Apostles."

Formed to bring together men who desired "larger and wider information" on subjects important to them and to their time, "The Society," as it was often familiarly referred to by its members, soon became an influential but almost secret power in Cambridge life. The membership was limited to twelve men in residence, and this, together with the high-minded earnestness imputed to its members, brought upon the society its bantering nickname of the "Apostles." When Frederick Denison Maurice came to Cambridge, Trinity, under the leadership of Sterling, had already become the home of the society. From Trinity Maurice's own influence expanded through the members into the whole of the university; and as the Apostles began to find their careers in religious, intellectual, and political life, this influence spread into the whole fabric of Victorian culture.

To Maurice, entirely deficient in humor, though not without that flexibility of mind and spirit essential to great friendship, the society owed the intensity and moral fervor which characterized it during these early years. His whole life was a progressive development away from the Unitarian doctrine in which he had been brought up. At Cambridge his lack of certainty, his intensely introspective mind, his ability always to see both sides of a question were invaluable influences on the young metaphysicians and political idealists who made up the society. Years after he had left Cambridge in 1827, unable to take a degree because of his refusal to subscribe to the Thirty-nine Articles, his memory was still revered among the Apostles. When in 1829 Maurice went to Exeter College, Oxford (where, under the influence of Coleridge's writings, he changed his religious views and entered the Anglican Church), he was followed by Sterling, who for a brief time after 1827 had edited the *Athenaeum* with him. At Oxford he belonged to Gladstone's Essay Club, a fellowship founded in imitation of the Apostles. Meanwhile he had come under the influence of Coleridge, and in the more theological atmosphere of Oxford he seemed to acquire greater certainty, finally publishing *Subscription No Bondage* (which he had shown to Newman and Pusey) and taking his degree in 1832. But at Cambridge he had left among the Apostles a fruitful tradition: the questioning mind, theological uncertainty, political liberalism, and moral earnestness, all of which were to be characteristic of the best minds of the coming age.

It was Maurice and his influence that certain members of Parliament feared in 1834, when they held up the Apostles as an example of the dangers of admitting dissenters to university degrees; for although Maurice was ordained in the Established Church soon after he was graduated from Oxford, his career continued to be one of inner struggle against the doctrines and formularies of dogmatic Christianity.[1] Although Arthur Hallam had not been at Cambridge while Maurice was there, he was able to say, in a letter to Gladstone: "The effects which he has produced on the minds of many at Cambridge by the single creation of that society of 'Apostles' (for the spirit though not the form was created by him) is far greater than I can dare to calculate, and will be felt, both directly and indirectly, in the age that is upon us."

The most devoted friend of all the early members was W. H. Brookfield, who used to call himself an "*acting* Apostle." Frances M. Brookfield, who married his son Charles, has given us the fullest account of the society in the days of its greatest glory, when Alford, Maurice, Thirlwall, Alfred and Frederick Tennyson, Henry and Edmund Lushington, Hallam, Trench, Sterling, Kemble, Spedding, Buller, Blakesley, Milnes, Venables, Heath, and Merivale were all members. She tells us that "the most stringent of their rules enacted that the absolute freedom of thought and speech they one and all desired should be respected by every member and in all circumstances; and, in order that no one of them in his ideas or convictions should in any way be trammelled or hampered, minutes of their meetings were never published." [2] As regards the meetings themselves, the best account is of the society at a much later date, but there is little reason to believe that there was very much change in the procedure during the years between 1827 and 1857 when Henry Sidgwick became a member:

> The meetings were held every Saturday at 8.30 in the rooms of the "Moderator," that is to say, the man who was to read the essay. The business began with tea, to which anchovy toast was an indispensable, and perhaps symbolic, adjunct; and then the essay was read, the

[1] Maurice was forced to give up his chair in King's College, London, in 1854, in a controversy with the principal, Dr. Jelf, over the views he had expressed on "eternal punishment" in his *Theological Essays* of 1853.

[2] Frances M. Brookfield, *The Cambridge "Apostles,"* New York, Scribner's, 1907, p. 5.

"brethren" sitting round the fire, the reader usually at the table. Next came the discussion. Every one who was there stood up in turn before the fire, facing the circle, and gave his views on the subject, or on the essay, or on the arguments used by previous speakers, or, indeed, on anything which he was pleased to consider relevant to any one of these. The freedom both of subject and of handling was absolute; and not only did no one ever dream of violating this freedom or suggesting any limit to it, but every member would have regarded such an attempt as an attack on the ark of the covenant.

When the discussion was over the moderator replied, usually answering opponents, but in no way bound to do so, since he enjoyed the same absolute freedom of presentment as the rest. The society then proceeded to put the question. But the question as put was by no means necessarily in the same terms, and often not on the same issue, as the subject of the essay; it was always formulated afresh. An attempt was usually made to pick out the deepest, or the widest, or the most interesting of the points raised (by moderator or speakers) during the evening; but the statement of it was often so epigrammatic, cryptic, ironical, or bizarre, that the last state of that question was (to the outward eye) far indeed from the first. When it was at last formulated, presenting some simple alternative issue, every member signed, as on one side or the other, or as refusing to vote, in the page of the society's book where the meeting was recorded. Every member had the right to add a note to his signature, explaining, or further specifying his view, or modifying the apparent meaning of his vote. The notes often contained the most luminous or interesting suggestions, couched usually in humorous or ironic form.

The subjects were chosen as follows:—At the end of each meeting, the man whose turn it was to "moderate" next week was bound to produce four subjects, from which the members chose one. It was usual, possibly in humorous imitation of the Greek drama, to have three serious questions, and the fourth playful. But the choice might as legally fall on the last one as on any of the others. The choice would generally turn on what each voter thought would produce the best discussion, though it was not at all necessary for the essayist to explain what line he would take, or even what the questions meant.[3]

In Tennyson's day the life of an Apostle, as Carlyle tells us in his life of Sterling, was "an ardently speculative and talking one." "On stated evenings was much logic, and other spiritual fencing, and ingenuous collision"; and it is of the Apostles that Sterling writes to Trench, asking to be commended "to the breth-

3 Arthur and Eleanor Sidgwick, *Henry Sidgwick, a Memoir,* London, Macmillan; New York, The Macmillan Co., 1906, pp. 29–31.

ren, who, I trust, are waxing daily in religion and radicalism." Theological and political subjects were most common in their discussions, but "sometimes the theme was purely metaphysical, sometimes scientific or literary." The members "read their Hobbes, Locke, Berkeley, Butler, Hume, Bentham, Descartes and Kant, and discussed such questions as the Origin of Evil, the Derivation of Moral Sentiments, Prayer and the Personality of God." [4]

Tennyson himself, when his turn came, was either too shy to deliver his paper, or too lethargic to finish it. In any case only the prologue of a paper on "Ghosts" survives, in which with clarity but no shyness he looks forward to his own work to come; for he begins, "He who has the power of speaking of the spiritual world, speaks in a simple manner of a high matter," and ends with the conviction of a poet, by claiming that no vision is baseless. At some college discussion, possibly at a meeting of the Apostles, Tennyson seems to have propounded the theory that the "development of the human body might possibly be traced from the radiated, vermicular, molluscous and vertebrate organisms," but usually he sat quietly "in front of the fire, smoking and meditating, and now and then mingling in the conversation." Although by his default in the giving of a paper he should have been forced into the exile of honorary membership, the society seems to have rested "content to receive him, his poetry and wisdom unfettered."

At least in the early days of the society, the Apostles were much concerned in the dramatic and important political events that were becoming part of the battle for liberalism and reform at home and abroad. The fierce hatred felt by James Fitzjames Stephen for the revolutionists of 1848 and the zeal against all popular aspirations which he felt in consequence would scarcely have endeared him, Apostle though he was, to the young liberals who were members of the society in 1830. The reaction which had followed the granting of a constitution to Spain in 1820 had made Ferdinand absolute king once more in 1823. Many Spanish Liberals

[4] Other questions debated before the society were: "Have Shelley's poems an immoral tendency?" "Is an intelligible First Cause deducible from the phenomena of the Universe?" and "Is there any rule of moral action beyond general expediency?" As we might expect, Tennyson voted "No" to the first and "Aye" to the third; but it is interesting in the light of the life-long search recounted in the *Memoir* by his son to find him voting "No" to the second.

fled to England, with General Torrijos, their leader. As they walked about London, "stately tragic figures, in proud threadbare cloaks," they aroused "a fiery sympathy . . . in the hearts of many of the 'Apostles.' "

The story has been often told how a number of these young Cambridge men resolved to help the exiled revolutionaries, not only with money, but with their own persons; how Sterling's cousin Boyd, one or two London democrats, fifty "picked Spaniards," and Torrijos himself set out from England for Gibraltar in the spring of 1830. For most of these, including Boyd, the expedition ended disastrously before a firing squad on the Esplanade at Málaga. The Apostles John Kemble (the Anglo-Saxon scholar and brother of Fanny Kemble, the actress) and R. C. Trench, who had followed the expedition, happily returned alive, but not until after all hope had been given up for their safety. Meanwhile, in July, Tennyson and his beloved friend Arthur Hallam had proceeded through France to the Spanish border, with money for the allies of the bold Torrijos. They held a secret meeting with the heads of the conspiracy and returned via Cauteretz, the French town in the Pyrenees which Tennyson ever afterwards associated not only with the most adventurous episode in his life, but, more important still, with some of his fondest memories of Hallam. Sterling, too, would have been one of this company if his health had not begun to fail him just as the expedition was setting out. Other Apostles also were involved, and the whole adventure is a brilliant translation into action of that high-minded and gallant liberalism combined with youthful ardor and elaborate foolery which characterized the meetings of the society. The adventure ended tragically, but the spirit of its purpose lived on in Sterling, Buller, Thirlwall, and Maurice.

Tennyson's devotion to Hallam and the record of that devotion in "In Memoriam" has become a central part of the Tennyson tradition. However, "In Memoriam" commemorates not only Arthur Hallam but in some measure the whole emotional and intellectual life of which he and Tennyson and the other Apostles were a part. When Tennyson, grief-stricken by Hallam's death, finally returns to Cambridge, he is reminded of Hallam and the Apostles as he visits the room

Where once we held debate, a band
  Of youthful friends, on mind and art,
  And labor, and the changing mart,
And all the framework of the land;

When one would aim an arrow fair,
  But send it slackly from the string;
  And one would pierce an outer ring,
And one an inner, here and there;

And last the master-bowman, he,
  Would cleave the mark. A willing ear
  We lent him. Who but hung to hear
The rapt oration flowing free

From point to point, with power and grace
  And music in the bounds of law,
  To those conclusions when we saw
The God within him light his face . . . ?

Tennyson's lifelong devotion to the Apostles was not unusual; one of the oldest traditions of the society was an annual dinner, always held at the Star and Garter in Richmond, which members young and old, present and past, made a point of attending from time to time.[5] One of the older Apostles, who had since made his name in the world, presided at each of these dinners, which brought the most brilliant men of each university generation into contact with those who had already fulfilled their promise in life. The continuity of tradition and values thus achieved has been largely responsible for the survival of the society, notably unimpaired, into our own day.

Lord Houghton was "as proud of being an 'Apostle' as he was of being an English gentleman," but many members were proud in other ways. Henry Sidgwick, who once wrote a friend that he was "supporting life" on the society and the friendship of J. R. Seeley (the author of *Ecce Homo*), has left an important account

[5] At the dinner held in June, 1880, there were present from the earliest days of the society Lord Houghton (R. M. Milnes: it was his 71st birthday), Venables, Spedding, Trench, and Tennyson.

of its deep influence on himself in the fifties and sixties. He admits that a certain exuberant vitality which the society possessed in Merivale's day was no longer to be found. "But the spirit," he says, "remained the same, and gradually this spirit—at least as I apprehended it—absorbed and dominated me." He goes on:

> I can only describe it as the spirit of the pursuit of truth with absolute devotion and unreserve by a group of intimate friends, who were perfectly frank with each other, and indulged in any amount of humorous sarcasm and playful banter, and yet each respects the other, and when he discourses tries to learn from him and see what he sees. Absolute candour was the only duty that the tradition of the society enforced. No consistency was demanded with opinions previously held —truth as we saw it then and there was what we had to embrace and maintain, and there were no propositions so well established that an Apostle had not the right to deny or question, if he did so sincerely and not from mere love of paradox. The gravest subjects were continually debated, but gravity of treatment, as I have said, was not imposed, though sincerity was. In fact it was rather a point of the apostolic mind to understand how much suggestion and instruction may be derived from what is in form a jest—even in dealing with the gravest matters.
>
> I had at first been reluctant to enter this society when I was asked to join it. I thought that a standing weekly engagement for a whole evening would interfere with my work for my two Triposes. But after I had gradually apprehended the spirit as I have described it, it came to seem to me that no part of my life at Cambridge was so real to me as the Saturday evenings on which the apostolic debates were held; and the tie of attachment to the society is much the strongest corporate bond which I have known in life. I think, then, that my admission into this society and the enthusiastic way in which I came to idealise it really determined or revealed that the deepest bent of my nature was towards the life of thought—thought exercised on the central problems of human life.[6]

Years later, in 1885, after visiting a man for whose convictions he had little sympathy, he wrote to a friend, "We agree in two characteristics, which [are] quite independent of formal creeds —a belief that we *can* learn, and a determination that we *will* learn, from people of the most opposite opinions. *I* acquired these characteristics in the dear old days of the Apostles at Cambridge."

[6] Arthur and Eleanor Sidgwick, *op. cit.*, pp. 34, 35.

The Apostles continued to influence the intellectual life of England throughout the century. When the Metaphysical Society was founded in 1869, Tennyson, Alford, Lushington, Thirlwall, and Sidgwick—all former Apostles—were among the first members; and soon Maurice, Fitzjames Stephen, W. K. Clifford, and other Apostles were asked to join the new society. James Martineau, who although not a Cambridge man had sometimes attended meetings of the Apostles, and J. R. Seeley, who, Sidgwick said, should have been a member, were both among the founders of the Metaphysical Society. The Essay Club, the Apostles' lesser light at Oxford, contributed Gladstone and Henry Acland. Thus more than a sixth of the members of the Metaphysical Society were men who, at one time or another, had been under the influence of the Apostles. The success of the Metaphysical Society, whose aims and procedure were in some ways so similar to those of the older society, was perhaps in no small measure owing to the demanding discipline of mind and manner obtained in the weekly meetings of the Apostles.

Chapter 2

KNOWLES AND TENNYSON

FOR ELEVEN YEARS, from 1869 to 1880, the members of the Metaphysical Society, counting among their number many of the most distinguished men in England, met nine times a year in London to hear papers, written and read by themselves, on the many problems raised anew by the growing antagonism between religion and the critical spirit of science. It was becoming clear that the conflict was between two opposed and seemingly irreconcilable philosophies: the one based on intuition, and often supported by revelation, the other based on experience, supported and tested by experiment, further experience, and the fullest possible use of scientific method. The major accomplishment of the Society, in which it fulfilled many of its original purposes, was the criticism of what was narrow, doctrinaire, or paradoxical in both of these firmly held positions. This was no merely academic achievement, for it is to the fervid intellectual temper of the seventies, of which the Metaphysical Society is a significant and central symbol, that we owe the working compromise which has governed the relations of religion and science ever since. Even more important to any thoughtful solution of our own problems, the history of the society reveals what is essentially inadequate in both philosophies: the danger of putting too much trust in the temptingly irrational appeals of intuition; and the tendency—so often characteristic of the philosophies of experience—to overlook or to oversimplify the variety and complexity of human life.

The great figures of modern philosophy, Nietzsche, Bergson, William James, and Bradley, as well as thinkers and artists like Samuel Butler, Shaw, and Henry James, all came to intellectual maturity in this period and were influenced both by its problems and its attempted solutions. Their successors, Freud, Croce, and Santayana, as well as Dewey, Russell, and Whitehead, have taken much more for granted the questioning and sceptical spirit of the seventies but, often in striking ways, have returned with new insights to the very problems so often raised in the papers of the Metaphysical Society. And indirectly in other ways, our literature, our art, and even our political thinking have felt the reverberations of that profound questioning of basic assumptions which was the principal task of the Society. Here lies the chief interest in a modern examination of the history of this little-known company of brilliant men.

Sir James Knowles was, at his death in 1908, the owner and retired editor of one of the great English journals of opinion, the *Nineteenth Century*.[1] He had long been a friend of the Royal Family; he was known as a connoisseur of the arts; he was famous as a witty conversationalist and as a friend and critic of the great in politics, literature, religion, and journalism. He was a notable host and himself a frequent dinner guest. He had amassed a fortune and knew everyone in every sphere of intellectual life in England and on the Continent, and even in the East and in America. But he was an editor and therefore an even better listener than talker; the letters and memoirs of the period refer to him seldom. Moreover, he was an English editor, who disliked biography and any kind of biographical revelation. The *Nineteenth Century* was his greatest public achievement; he needed no further record of a life well-spent. And he had left far behind him in his younger days an even more important monument, for he was the principal founder and during the greater part of its history the chief impresario of the amazing Metaphysical Society.

Mr. James Knowles, Junior, was a young man of twenty when he visited the Great Exhibition of 1851 at the Crystal Palace. In its machinery, its architecture, its vast promise of future progress, he may have seen symbols of the even greater changes that were to come in the world of thought and feeling. He was the son of a prosperous and successful architect, who had guided and encouraged his artistic and literary tastes. He had been well educated, in the classics, mathematics, and science, at the Rev. Charles

[1] Which had become the *Nineteenth Century and After* in 1900.

Pritchard's admirable Clapham Grammar School and at University College, London. The geological stanzas of "In Memoriam" had moved him profoundly, and he was already wondering, as any of Pritchard's students should, what moral lessons could be learned from the onward march of science and technical progress.

The Pre-Raphaelites, whose religious art he later came to admire, were not yet well-known, but the perpendicular Gothic of the new Houses of Parliament was to him a magnificent reminder of the last age of Christian unity, that late medieval period when Malory had composed his great collection of the legends of King Arthur and the Round Table. The revived architectural marvels of the fifteenth century were indeed in strange contrast to the iron and glass of the nineteenth, so boldly and prophetically presented by the Crystal Palace. But Tennyson had already taken from Malory the matchless story of the *Morte d'Arthur* and, as the new Laureate, deserved even more than before to be called "the divine Alfred," a name which Knowles, in spite of the taunts of his friends, had given to the poet.

When Knowles's essay *Architectural Education* won a prize in 1852, he was serving his apprenticeship in his father's office. The next year, at the age of 22, he became an Associate of the Royal Institute of British Architects. He drew well, but he cared little for the ugly and profitable block-building of mid-Victorian England. He traveled in Italy, studying her great monuments, and returned to design churches like miniature cathedrals and private homes like Palladian palaces or lesser Houses of Parliament. In a professional life of thirty years he built by his own account "many hundreds of houses, besides several churches, hospitals, clubs, warehouses, stores, roads, and bridges"; a busy man, he helped change the face of England. Even after 1870, when he assumed the editorship of the *Contemporary Review*, he continued his architectural practice.

As time went on, Knowles found less and less time for his profession, and after the success of the *Nineteenth Century* he no longer needed commissions. He designed his last building in 1882, a prosaic enlargement of the Sea Bathing Hospital at Margate. His intellectual tastes and systematic curiosity had long needed fuller expression than architecture could afford. The *Nineteenth Century* now took almost all his time and required a vast correspondence. So in 1884 he moved from Clapham to Queen Anne's Lodge, by St. James's Park, "where he constantly entertained a distinguished circle of friends and collected pictures and works of art."

In 1861 he had married Jane Emma, the daughter of the Rev. Abraham Borradaile, but she died soon after.[2] In 1865 he married again, this time Isabel Mary Hewlett, whose brother, Henry Gay Hewlett,[3] had earlier married Knowles's sister Emmeline. Hewlett and he had, several years before, together edited the short-lived *Clapham Magazine,* which had proved a useful encouragement to Knowles's own deep interest in literature and philosophy. And ever since 1862, in minor and apparently anonymous contributions to other magazines and periodicals, he had expressed himself on many critical and intellectual questions. After his second marriage he "grew ambitious of the acquaintance of leaders of public opinion," and through his publisher Strahan and other friends began to be known in London literary society. Unlike his father, who was "a starchy old gentleman," he took greatest pleasure in conversing with more successful men, especially men with keener minds than his own, men who seemed to know better than himself answers to the puzzling questions of faith and knowledge. Wilfrid Ward has testified to what became his own greatest distinction. "In conversation he had a very happy art of finding the subject on which different members of the company could and would talk freely, and of himself putting in the right word, and, as it were, winding up the clock."

He had continued to love Malory. Children liked to hear him recount the adventures of Arthur and his knights, and those who were so privileged marveled at his skill in dramatic narrative. His friends urged him to write down these stories, and little by little he did so. In 1862 he published them in a volume which he dedi-

2 The principal authority for Knowles's life, in addition to fragmentary references in biographies, diaries, and memoirs, is the *Dictionary of National Biography,* Second Supplement, 2 vols. in one, London, Oxford, 1920, II, 407–9. Other biographical materials, chiefly obituaries, are there noted.

3 For a picture of the entire Knowles family and their connections I am indebted to Edward Hewlett's "Introductory Memoir," in *The Letters of Maurice Hewlett,* edited by Laurence Binyon, London, Methuen, 1926, pp. 1–19.

cated to Tennyson, called *The Legends of King Arthur and His Knights of the Round Table,* "compiled and arranged by J.T.K." [4] It is still often reprinted, and many children have had from it their first taste of the Arthurian legends; Knowles's nephew, Maurice Hewlett the novelist, was brought up, not on Malory, but on his uncle's version of the stories. However, far more gratifying than the public success of these simple tales was their private acceptance and approval by the man he revered most in all the world, Tennyson himself, "the divine Alfred."

While vacationing near Freshwater on the Isle of Wight in the summer of 1866, Knowles had one of the great moments of his life: he met the Laureate. Before leaving the island he called on Tennyson at Farringford, but, as was often the case with casual acquaintances of the poet, found him "not at home." Nothing daunted, he returned that evening and was this time shown up to the study, where he was later joined by Tennyson. The enthusiasm, delight, and obvious admiration of the younger man pleased the poet. And Tennyson himself was glad to meet the author of the *Legends of King Arthur,* which had been dedicated to him and which he so much esteemed.

A year later, while waiting for a train at Haslemere station, Knowles again saw Tennyson. Without the least hesitation he reintroduced himself, for he remembered that during his visit to Farringford Tennyson had said, "I am so short-sighted that I shall not know you if I meet you unless you speak to me." He learned with surprise that Tennyson was looking for a site for a cottage, a quiet yet accessible spot which would not only be more convenient to London, but where he could have more privacy, more seclusion, more freedom than was afforded by Farringford, where trippers, the great and near-great, and even friendly neighbors frequently intruded. Mrs. Tennyson reports that the poet said to Knowles, "You had better build me my house"; but Knowles

[4] In the preface to the third edition, Knowles comments upon "the growing popularity of the Arthur story" as "a wholesome sign of the times." And in referring to the role of Arthur in the *Idylls of the King,* he says that Arthur "stands evidently for the Soul, the moral conscience, as the Round Table does for the passions; and everywhere the struggle of the Spirit with the flesh is painted."

insists that he offered to design the new cottage. "The plans for a four-roomed cottage gave way somewhat as I talked the matter over with Mr. and Mrs. Tennyson, the latter giving me certain ideas which she could not express by drawing, but which I understood enough to put into shape; and presently I went to Farringford with designs for a less unimportant dwelling." [5]

The plans grew and grew as Knowles talked them over with Mrs. Tennyson. The poet protested and protested, but all in vain; both wife and architect knew how large were the royalties from *The Idylls of the King;* and, as Knowles hints, the poet began to be secretly pleased at this new vision of himself as a landed proprietor living in a fine house. The foundation stone of "Aldworth," named after a village in Berkshire from which some of Mrs. Tennyson's family had come, was laid on April 23, 1868, the anniversary of Shakespeare's birth. It was a glorious day; Mrs. Knowles and a few friends were present. The poet was in excellent spirits and very pleased with the inscription on the stone: "Prosper thou the work of our hands, O prosper thou our handiwork." When the late-fifteenth-century manor house was completed, the last tile in place, and the coat-of-arms over the door, no one was happier than Tennyson.

Knowles's admiration for the fifteenth century did not extend to its sanitary facilities; he had learned a lot at the Great Exhibition. The new house had all the most modern conveniences; a discreet blending of the old with the new was always one of Knowles's most satisfactory characteristics. "It was delightful to see his [Tennyson's] enjoyment of everything in the new house, from the hot-water bathroom downwards, for at first the hot bath seemed to attract him out of measure. He would take it four or five times a day, and told me he thought it the height of luxury to sit in a hot bath and read about little birds." [6] The bath, however, was not the only delight of the new house. The turf for the lawn

[5] For the relations of Knowles and Tennyson, see Knowles's contribution to *Tennyson and His Friends,* edited by Hallam Tennyson, London, Macmillan, 1911, pp. 245 ff., from which I have quoted freely.

[6] Tennyson writes to Locker (F. Locker-Lampson), August 6, 1869, that "nothing pleases me more than the bath, a perennial stream which falls thro' the house, and where I take three baths a day."

was brought from Farringford Down, where the poet had so often walked; on the blank shield of the mantelpiece were emblazoned devices to represent "the great modern poets, Dante, Chaucer, Shakespeare, Milton, Goethe, Wordsworth"; and in encaustic tiles on the pavement of the entrance-hall was the Welsh motto: *Y Gwir yn erbyn y byd* ("The truth against the world"). Knowles had spared no effort to make "Aldworth" a fitting home for the Laureate.

From this time forth Knowles was a frequent visitor at the Tennysons', not only at "Aldworth," which ironically enough became their "state" residence, but also in the more *gemütlich* family circle of Farringford. Tennyson in his turn was always welcome at Knowles's house in Clapham, where he often stayed when he went to town. The poet found a willing listener to his grievances against publishers [7] and the two had many confidential discussions, punctuated by Tennysonian soliloquies in which he revealed "all his inmost thought and feelings." On one of these occasions when Knowles asked him what was his deepest desire of all, Tennyson replied, "A clearer vision of God." The man who as a youth had been so impressed by the geological stanzas of "In Memoriam" found their author still puzzled by the same problems of faith and knowledge.

Meanwhile the struggle between science and theology had become more acute, Darwin and Huxley were fluttering the dovecotes of the rural vicars, and Tennyson, who tried so desperately and with such difficulty to read the latest scientific books, was more distressed and bewildered than ever. Only in the serenely artificial world of the *Idylls* could his poetic mind find peace, only in a moral projection which escaped the troubling questions of the sixties. But a change in his poetry was imminent, in fact had already begun. He was now considering the publication of the revised "Lover's Tale," a poem he had first written in his early youth, and his "Lucretius" had already appeared.[8] Perhaps there was

[7] Knowles persuaded Tennyson to abandon his former publisher and to go over to Strahan, who had published Knowles's own *Legends of King Arthur*. The agreement with Strahan was apparently completed in November, 1868. Strahan was the publisher of the *Contemporary Review*, of which Knowles became the editor in 1870. See Chap. IX.

[8] In *Macmillan's Magazine*, May, 1868.

a way to obtain "a clearer vision of God"; certainly "In Memoriam" had more of himself and all his deepest aspirations than any of these Idylls which the Queen liked so much, but of whose morality she seemed so uncertain.

Arthur Hallam had long before become the hero, the theme, the glory of "In Memoriam." But had he really? Was not "In Memoriam" really an elegy to something else—to the earnest, hopeful, vigorous life of those Cambridge years, those years of quick energizing companionship, of optimistic adventure, of intellectual discovery, of youthful assurance? Was not Arthur Hallam a symbol of the twelve "Apostles," that little band of chosen spirits who first made the proud, shy, slow-minded, sensitive Tennyson feel his poetic power and the strength of his own nature?

What a distinguished group it was, and how deserving of their name, even if originally given them in derision! In Tennyson's day there was Hallam, of course, the brilliant son of a famous father; Richard Trench, now Archbishop of Dublin; and Henry Alford, now Dean of Canterbury and hard at work on a new translation of the New Testament, and soon to become one of the editors of the Revised Version; he had once been a poet too. There was Charles Merivale, the historian of Rome; James Spedding, the biographer of Bacon; and Edmund Lushington, now Tennyson's brother-in-law [9] and Professor of Greek at Glasgow. But most important of all was Frederick Denison Maurice, one of Tennyson's oldest friends and godfather to his son Hallam, a paradoxical and liberal theologian, one of the bravest and most complex minds of the century; he had given a new spirit to the society and was still remembered with veneration by its members. There were Blakesley and W. H. Thompson and G. S. Venables; and last but not least, Richard Monckton Milnes, now Lord Houghton, once the defender of Keats, lately the patron of young Swinburne, and now famous as the first gentleman of his day. Others came and went: young Sterling, thanks to Carlyle forever young; W. D. Christie; W. H. Brookfield, "Old Brooks"; John Kemble, youthful revolutionary, great Anglo-Saxon scholar; and Charles Buller,

[9] His marriage to Cecilia Tennyson in 1842 is commemorated in the final section of "In Memoriam."

Lord Durham's close associate in the mission to the rebellious Canadas, and in preparing the Report whose formula for colonial self-government was gradually adopted by the British government. What a galaxy now! How young, how gay, how proud, how certain they were then! The Apostles had certainly done a great deal for each other; how much, none of them would ever know, and some would certainly never admit. Was there not something in the free exchanges of independent minds, brought together of their own will, concerned with the same problems, free of pride of birth and position, which brought a sense of clarity, a sense of power, a sense of knowledge that were often lacking in the atomic society of mid-Victorian individualism?

The pattern of Tennyson's life was beginning to change, for his son Hallam had gone away to school and Lionel was soon to go. Living at "Aldworth" proved quite different from Farringford; it seemed somehow closer to many aspects of Victorian life. The poet was in consequence seeking new emotional and intellectual satisfactions. He took up Hebrew with assiduous enthusiasm; he even contemplated making a metrical version of the *Book of Job.* When Jowett, on a visit to Farringford, revealed that he could not read Hebrew, Tennyson was shocked and exclaimed, "What, you the Priest of a religion and can't read your own sacred books!" Everyone was talking about Deutsch's article on the Talmud, and Tennyson was as excited as any scholar. Already he had completed the first version of a psalm-like poem he called "The Higher Pantheism" and was talking much about "all-pervading Spirit being more understandable by him than solid matter." When Longfellow visited him in July, 1868, they discussed spiritualism, although Tennyson insisted that if there were anything in such manifestations, "Pucks, not the spirits of dead men, reveal themselves." In November, while in London, he attended a séance, and tried to "move a table mesmerically." He was thinking once more of the essentially supernatural basis of Christianity; Darwin's visit in August had been reassuring. Tennyson had asked him, "Your theory of Evolution does not make against Christianity?" and the great scientist had answered, "No, certainly not." Materialism still presented grave problems, especially to a poet;

he realized it again in September when he looked through Mr. Pritchard's telescope at the nebula in Hercules. What, after all, is "matter"? Is it not "merely the shadow of a something greater than itself, and which we poor shortsighted creatures cannot see"?

He had long enjoyed conversations with his old friends Maurice and Lushington on the theological and philosophical questions which so concerned him—the existence of the soul, the nature of faith, and the certainty of immortality. Recently the Rev. Charles Pritchard had retired to Freshwater from the headmastership of Clapham Grammar School; his fine telescope had not only revived Tennyson's lifelong interest in the heavens, but it renewed old trains of thought and perplexing speculations. These might bring back memories of his youth—somehow more distant now that the boys were away—but would they invigorate his mind, and his poetry?

His wife thought Mr. Knowles so good for him; "his active nature sometimes spurs A. on to work when he is flagging." Once, Tennyson pointed his finger at Knowles and with a grim smile said, "I was often urged to go on with the 'Idylls,' but I stuck; and then this beast said, 'Do it,' and I did it." Knowles had indeed been good for him; his interests were so wide, his curiosity so exacting.

Chapter 3

THE FOUNDING OF THE SOCIETY

IT WAS in November, 1868, at "The Hollies," his home in Clapham, that Knowles first conceived the plan of what was soon to become the Metaphysical Society. He was entertaining his old headmaster and friendly neighbor, Pritchard, with whom he had spent the previous summer on the Isle of Wight, and who was soon to become Savilian Professor of Astronomy at Oxford. Tennyson, who had recently arrived in town for a stay of several weeks, was also a visitor.[1] Talk drifted, as inevitably it must in the sixties, to the speculative aspects of morality and the theological questions of the day. According to Knowles, Tennyson "joined in so often and so much" that they "made a sort of triangular duel." The idea soon came to Knowles of "a Theological Society, to discuss such questions after the manner and with the freedom of an ordinary scientific society." Knowles volunteered "to bring such a body together if Mr. Tennyson and Mr. Pritchard would promise to belong to it." This they consented to do. Later Knowles wrote that it was the fact of Pritchard, "as a great scientific man, agreeing to join the great poet and 'a man in the streets' " like himself which gave him the courage to get together "the remarkable assemblage" which became the Metaphysical Society.

Knowles, with characteristic energy, proceeded to communicate with all schools of religious thought, beginning with Dean Stanley

1 During this same visit, Tennyson one night read his new poem, "The Holy Grail," to Knowles, Pritchard, and Strahan (his new publisher). The next day he read it again to Knowles and Browning, who found it Tennyson's "best and highest." Browning later returned, bringing with him the Preface to *The Ring and the Book,* which he read in his turn. To Tennyson it was "full of strange vigour and remarkable in many ways; doubtful whether it can ever be popular." The reasons for Browning's failure to join the Metaphysical Society, to which Ward says he was invited, may lie in these conversations.

of Westminster, representing the extreme latitudinarian, Broad Church point of view; Dean Alford of Canterbury, a liberal theologian and sound textual critic; the Catholic Archbishop, Manning; the Rev. James Martineau, leading Unitarian thinker; Ellicott, the Bishop of Gloucester and Bristol, also an eminent textual and exegetical scholar; Dr. W. G. Ward, "Ideal Ward" of the Oxford Movement and editor of the *Dublin Review;* and Mr. R. H. Hutton, editor of the *Spectator,* literary critic and theologian. All of these were willing to join. This plan aimed to bring together all shades of religious and theological opinion, from the Roman Catholic to the Unitarian, in an effort to counteract scientific materialism and unite warring theological factions as much as possible in a common cause. Materialism and the critical spirit had long been troubling some men's minds; but now the scientific spirit was beginning to succeed in an attack on some of the fundamental assumptions of their religion. Wilfrid Ward says that the founders "were men who keenly realized the decline of definite faith in the supernatural among thinking men. They considered, too, that the rising school of scientific agnosticism [although Huxley had not yet coined the word] was assuming an arrogance of tone, and gaining an influence from its self-confidence, which made it all the more dangerous." The opposition between religious and scientific leaders had not sensibly diminished since the famous 1860 meeting of the British Association, and the religious position, especially that based on revelation or authority, seemed to grow steadily less secure.

Dean Stanley was one of Knowles's best friends and as one of the first to be asked was in a position to offer advice. To him and to his wife, Lady Augusta Stanley, the plan for a Theological Society seemed narrow and unwise. All that such a society could do would be to widen the breach between the religious and scientific points of view. *Rapprochement,* Stanley felt, would help more than organized resistance. Martineau, too, refused to join a society of believers to fight unbelievers. Knowles himself, with his own theological uncertainty, his eclecticism of mind, his breadth of social and conversational sympathy, now found himself in hearty sympathy with Stanley's attitude. All finally agreed, with an English love of fair play, that it was only just that their opponents be allowed to state their case. So, apparently at the suggestion of Lady Augusta Stanley, the name of the Society was changed from "Theological" to "Metaphysical," and plans were laid for a tactful ensnaring of the scientific and materialist opposition. With this decision the original plan of a society which would be a rallying point of theists against agnostics was definitely abandoned.

Early in 1869 Archbishop Manning, W. G. Ward, and Tennyson met at Knowles's house and "discussed the claims of the various thinkers of the day to be invited to join." Each undertook to approach certain members of the opposite faction. "Mr. John Stuart Mill was a personage of importance for such an object, both from his unique eminence as a thinker and from his interest in religious metaphysics." Ward undertook to ask him.

Ward wrote to Mill, in a letter of March 24, 1869, that certain theists, fearing his views and those of his disciple Bain, wish direct and personal discussion, feeling that their point of view is unfairly treated by the materialists. They wish to establish a "Metaphysical Society," "in which metaphysical questions shall be discussed in the manner and with the machinery of the learned and scientific societies." Various Catholics have been asked; Ward and the Archbishop have put down their names. Also accepting membership are Browning,[2] Bagehot, and Lubbock. To be asked are either Professor Huxley or Mr. Tyndall [Ward forgets which, but it is to be one *or* the other!], Archbishop Thomson, Dr. W. B. Carpenter, Mr. James Hinton, Dean Mansel, Professor de Morgan, and Mr. Herbert Spencer.[3] All are anxious to have Mr. Bain, but fear that he is a fixture in Scotland. "And they are especially desirous of *you*. . . . Perhaps we can be the better friends from

[2] For Ward's letter and Mill's reply, see Wilfrid Ward, *William George Ward and the Catholic Revival,* London, Macmillan, 1893, pp. 298–9. There is no other evidence that Browning was a member of the Society; Ward was perhaps misinformed or over-hasty. See note on p. 201, below. Wilfrid Ward's whole chapter on the Society is invaluable, and I am here deeply indebted to it.

[3] Dean Mansel, Prof. de Morgan, and Herbert Spencer never joined the Society, although, as we shall see, Spencer was asked several times and always maintained a distant interest in the Society's proceedings through his friendship with Huxley, Lubbock, and Tyndall.

being such *very* pronounced enemies." Here Ward already showed one of the traits most necessary for a member of the new Society, personal if not intellectual tolerance; although the subjects suggested for discussion show that he still regarded the Society as "theological" rather than "metaphysical," if indeed he was ever able to make the distinction in his own mind. He suggested as possible subjects the following, some of which were in fact later discussed:

The immateriality of the soul and its personal identity.
The nature of miracles.
The reasonableness of prayer.
The personality of God.
Conscience—its true character.

He adds that Mr. Knowles, probably unknown to Mill, is the originator of the Society.

Such was the tenor of Ward's invitation, a friendly, straightforward account of the plan, with perhaps too much emphasis on what had been the original plan of a "Theological Society" to appeal to so unreligious a thinker as Mill essentially was. Still, here was no flattery and little to arouse personal or intellectual antagonism. But Mill refused. In a letter of March 29, 1869, he found the purpose laudable but its realization in practice doubtful. He admitted that oral discussion could be more thorough than other means but felt that it must be Socratic, between one and one, and not "shared by a mixed assemblage." He thought it would be useful to the younger members but was himself so busy and so burdened with other duties that he could not undertake it, doubting as he did what benefit he could derive from it. Rising to Ward's use of the word "unfairly" Mill added, "It is very natural that those who are strongly convinced of the truth of their opinions should think that those who differ from them do not duly weigh their arguments. I can only say that I sincerely endeavor to do the amplest justice to any argument which is urged, and to all I can think of even when not urged, in defence of any opinions which I controvert." Two years later, at the meeting of May 16, 1871, the members of the now thriving Society asked Knowles to inquire once more whether Mill would be interested in becoming a member. At the next meeting, June 13, Knowles had to report Mill's continued refusal, this time giving as reason that he was so occupied "that he feared he would be unable to attend the meetings of the Society." Although Mill was now more interested in religious problems, he spent most of the year in France, at Avignon, and, in consequence, at the time of his death in 1873 he was still not a member.

Mr. Herbert Spencer was also clearly one of the leaders of that "opposition" which the founders desired to interest. Sir John Lubbock [4] was chosen to communicate with him, which he did by letter. Spencer, however, refused, declining "for the reason that too much nervous expenditure would have resulted. Every attendance would have entailed a sleepless night; and I did not think that any benefit to be derived would have been worth purchase by this penalty: involving loss of my small working power next day." The members of the new society were disappointed by this refusal, especially R. H. Hutton, who had elected to read the first paper to be given before the new Society, on "Mr. Herbert Spencer's Theory of the Gradual Transformation of Utilitarian into Intuitive Morality by Hereditary Descent." Hutton was so anxious to have Spencer present to defend his own views that he asked Knowles to send Spencer the subject of his paper and again ask him "to reconsider his determination." He offered to put his essay into Spencer's hands two or three days before the meeting so that Spencer "might consider his criticisms at leisure"; but Spencer again claimed that because he "felt the most eager possible interest" in the subject, "such an oral discussion of it as was proposed would excite him very deeply, and that he should perhaps suffer for two or three days afterwards from the results; and, finally, that he must decline once for all to join the Society on the grounds of health alleged." Spencer tells in his *Autobiography* how, several years later, "during an after-dinner conversation in which the proceedings were described as remarkably harmonious, a renewed suggestion was made by Mr. Knowles that I should join. After referring to the statement made that many of the members had

[4] Now more generally known by his later title of Lord Avebury, but here always referred to either as Lubbock or as Sir John Lubbock.

so little thought in common that they slid by one another without grappling, I remarked that Mr. Knowles had better not press me, since most likely were I one of them I should insist on grappling, and that possibly the proceedings would cease to be so harmonious."

Spencer's nervous intransigeance might indeed have proved too wearing, both to himself and to the Society. However, the major failure of the Society's early days was certainly its inability to attract Spencer and Mill, both of whom were, as philosophers and as men, vital to the Society's purpose. John Henry Newman, Wilfrid Ward tells us, also refused to join, but whether Matthew Arnold was asked and, if so, why he did not become a member, I do not know. With other thinkers of the day they were more successful.

A preliminary meeting of the Society was held at Willis' Rooms, the scene of many literary and scientific lectures, on Wednesday, April 21, 1869. This initial meeting was called to establish the society, determine its purpose and functions, and set up the machinery for its proceedings. Present were: Dr. W. B. Carpenter, the leading physiologist of his day, a Unitarian, Registrar of the University of London, and the man who more than any other single person had made its scientific faculties the best in England; James Hinton, doctor, aural surgeon, and philosopher admired by Tennyson; R. H. Hutton, editor of the *Spectator* and influential literary and religious critic; Thomas H. Huxley, physiologist and biological scientist, the principal defender of Darwin's theory of evolution; James Knowles, founder of the Society, soon to become editor of the powerful *Contemporary Review;* Sir John Lubbock, banker, biologist, anthropologist, and psychologist—not yet sanitation expert, free trader, and educational reformer; the Rev. James Martineau, a Unitarian, one of the finest theological and philosophical minds in England; the Hon. Roden Noel, poet, amateur philosopher, and Byronic sympathizer with social reform and past revolutions; the Rev. Charles Pritchard, astronomer and preacher, whose life work (he thought) was "the reconciliation of science with the Bible" but who is most important as a pioneer in stellar photography; J. R. Seeley, the author of

Ecce Homo, about to be appointed Professor of Modern History at Cambridge in succession to Kingsley; Arthur Stanley, liberal Dean of Westminster; Tennyson, Poet Laureate; and Tennyson's friend and neighbor W. G. Ward, Catholic theologian and once a leading figure in the Oxford Movement.

This distinguished and very representative group of men resolved:

That a Society be established in London, under the name of the Metaphysical and Psychological [5] Society, to collect, arrange, and diffuse Knowledge (whether objective or subjective) of mental and moral phenomena.

That the Society may undertake:

I. To collect trustworthy observations upon such subjects as: Remarkable mental and moral phenomena—normal or abnormal,
The relations of brain and mind—and generally of physics and metaphysics,
The faculties of the lower animals, &c., &c., &c., &c.,[6]

II. To receive and to discuss with absolute freedom, at meetings to be held from time to time, oral or written communications made to it on such subjects as:
The comparison of the different theories respecting the ultimate grounds of belief in the objective and moral sciences,
The logic of the sciences whether physical or social,
The immortality and personal identity of the soul,
The existence and personality of God,
The nature of conscience,
The material hypothesis.

III. That meetings of the Society be held once a month during the Session of Parliament, beginning at 8 o'clock—with tea and coffee —and that no visitors, unless foreigners, be introduced at any meeting.

IV. That the annual subscription to the Society be £1.1*s*.
That the following gentlemen become the original members of the Society—with power to add to their number by ballot up to a total of fifty members: [7]

[5] By the first regular meeting, "Psychological" had been dropped from the name of the Society.

[6] These first purposes, so closely related to the growing interest in hypnotism and spiritualism, were most of them never again broached or undertaken as regular concerns of the Society. It was not until the establishment of the periodical *Mind* in 1876, and the foundation of the Society for Psychical Research in 1882, that these subjects were adequately and professionally treated in England. See Chaps. XI and XII.

[7] Of the twenty-six men named as original members in the resolutions of the

A. P. Stanley
J. R. Seeley
Roden Noel
James Martineau
William B. Carpenter
James Hinton
[T. H.] Huxley
C. Pritchard
Richard H. Hutton
W. [G.] Ward
Walter Bagehot
J. A. Froude
A. Tennyson
John Tyndall
Alfred Barry
Arthur Russell
W. E. Gladstone
Henry E. Manning
James T. Knowles, Jun.
John Lubbock
Henry Alford
Edmund Lushington
A. Grant
C. St. Davids [Bishop Thirlwall; actually elected July 14, 1869]
Frederic Harrison [actually elected December 15, 1869]
Argyll [the Duke of Argyll; actually elected July 13, 1870]

The first regular meeting of the Society was held on Wednesday, June 2, 1869, at the Deanery in Westminster, with Sir John Lubbock in the chair. Tennyson's poem "The Higher Pantheism," rewritten for the occasion, was read by Mr. Knowles in the poet's absence, and R. H. Hutton read the first paper—"On Mr. Herbert Spencer's Theory of the Gradual Transformation of Utilitarian into Intuitive Morality by Hereditary Descent"—which was afterwards discussed. All efforts to have Mr. Spencer himself present had, as we know, failed.

Those present resolved that the Society should be limited to forty instead of fifty members, here apparently inviting comparison with the French Academy; that a quorum for the election of a new member be eleven; "that in reckoning a ballot, one vote

preliminary meeting, twenty-two attended one or more of the first five meetings of the Society; one did not attend until the eighth regular meeting; and three did not become members immediately. Thirlwall, Bishop of St. David's, was proposed and elected July 14, 1869, at the second regular meeting, but did not attend until April 25, 1871; Frederic Harrison, the Positivist, was proposed November 17, 1869, elected a month later, and attended faithfully thereafter; the Duke of Argyll was proposed and elected July 13, 1870, attended the next meeting, but later came rarely. However, three others, not among the "founders," were elected at the first regular meeting, June 2, 1869, and began to attend regularly after the second and third meetings. These were Father Dalgairns, Superior of the Brompton Oratory, friend of Newman; George Grove, later famous as editor of a great dictionary of music; and Henry Sidgwick, who had just resigned his fellowship at Cambridge because he felt himself unable to subscribe to the tests, but who was none the less embarking on a successful career as a lecturer and teacher of ethics and a leader in educational reform.

in ten shall exclude"; and that the "meetings of the Society be held on the second Wednesday of every month in the year, excepting the months of August, September, and October." It was decided to hold the next meeting at the Grosvenor Hotel, with dinner at 6:30 "for such members as may wish to dine together (at 5*s.* each)," and that the subject for the evening should be introduced at 8:30. This procedure was followed almost without modification until the meetings came to an end. At the meeting of July 13, 1870, the date of meeting was changed from the second Wednesday to the second Tuesday; and early in 1880, during the last months of the Society's history, the place of meeting was changed from the Grosvenor Hotel to the Grosvenor Gallery Restaurant in New Bond Street.

At the next meeting, July 14, 1869, it was decided "that before any paper be read to the Society, the paper itself, or at least an abridgment of it, shall be printed and distributed to the members of the Society, at least a week before it be read." It was also agreed that papers "be sent to Mr. Hutton, at the office of the *Spectator*, who will undertake the care of the printing." At this meeting Ward was elected treasurer and at the next Sir John Lubbock was elected "chairman of the meetings held during the current session of the Society" (1869–70). Knowles, who was Honorary Secretary [8] through most of the Society's history, was at this meeting elected vice-chairman. The minutes were usually signed by the chairman of the meeting, but from time to time they were kept and signed by other members.

Except for the occasional nomination, election, or nonelection [9] of proposed members, there was henceforth little "business" transacted at any of the meetings. Early enough some difficulty apparently was experienced in arranging the program of papers, for on December 15, 1869, Lubbock, Ward, Hutton, and Knowles were elected a committee "to arrange for the supply of papers

[8] The prefix "Honorary," sometimes abbreviated "Hon.," is a peculiarly English usage intended to remove any public suspicion that the Secretary, Treasurer, or similar dignitary of a society or other organization is a mere hired clerk.

[9] For example, Richard Monckton Milnes, Lord Houghton, proposed by Tennyson and seconded by Lubbock, "was balloted for as a member of the Society, but not elected" at the meeting of December 13, 1870.

for discussion at the meetings of the Society." But the Society's very simple procedure once established and its machinery in working order, the papers were printed, distributed, read, and discussed with notable regularity until the death of the Society on November 16, 1880. The greatest possible tribute to Knowles's energy and effectiveness is that when he resigned the Secretaryship late in 1879 and was succeeded by Frederick Pollock, the Society very rapidly declined; certainly, so long as his spirit and personality supported it with enthusiasm the Society enjoyed vigorous life.

At an early meeting of the Society one of the speakers insisted "on the necessity of avoiding anything like moral disapprobation in the debates." There was a pause. Then W. G. Ward said, "While acquiescing in this condition as a general rule, I think it cannot be expected that Christian thinkers shall give no sign of the horror with which they would view the spread of such extreme opinions as those advocated by Mr. Huxley." Another pause. Then Huxley, thus challenged, replied, "As Dr. Ward has spoken, I must in fairness say that it will be very difficult for me to conceal my feeling as to the intellectual degradation which would come of the general acceptance of such views as Dr. Ward holds." Froude points out that this exchange showed the dangers inherent in this kind of personal innuendo and "from that time onwards, no word of the kind was ever heard."

Wilfrid Ward (son of W. G. Ward), who tells this story, also says "that a good deal of anxiety was felt at first lest some of the most startling subjects of debate might, through the medium of the hotel waiters, find their way to the zealots of Exeter Hall," the stronghold of evangelical orthodoxy. A society at which a Catholic Archbishop met with Anglican Bishops, unbelieving scientists, philosophical materialists, and confessed atheists would have seemed indeed like an invention of the devil to Spurgeon and his fellow-preachers of salvation. However, this fear "was allayed when a member on arriving at the hotel was thus greeted by the porter: 'A member of the *Madrigal* Society, sir, I suppose?' " As early as 1870 the Society was already known among outsiders as the "Atheists," a name given by Lord Odo Russell (the brother of

Lord Arthur Russell), although at the same time the distinction of its members caused him to refer to them as "the forty of the future Academy."

Not all the members, naturally, attended every meeting. At the first eighteen successive meetings, for which we have the incomplete Minute-Book [10] as authority, the attendance averaged fifteen. At the twenty-three scattered later meetings for which we have complete records from other sources,[11] the attendance averaged twelve; but this includes a number of meetings from the Society's declining years. The largest attendance of which we have any record was twenty, at the meeting of February 10, 1874; the smallest was five, at the meeting of November 12, 1878. Complete attendance records are available for only forty out of a total of ninety-six or ninety-seven meetings; at only seven of these did the attendance fall below the Society's quorum of eleven, although this does not include several meetings of which the record is apparently incomplete. Martineau, however, makes an important observation in this connection: "At the larger meetings, the debates, or rather *conversations*, were apt to become desultory, and even to run off into total irrelevance. But now and then, when from six to ten members of congenial culture, raised on the same logical base, were gathered round the table, it became evident as we came to close quarters, how slight and innocent was the incipient divergency which looked so large when measured by its scope in life . . . The smaller meetings, too, instead of being surrendered to a single speaker at a time, succeeded by another and yet another, delivering notes prepared beforehand on the paper read, all waiting for a summary answer at the end, were allowed to slip into easy Socratic dialogue, dealing with each point as it arose." [12] These meetings Mill too, had he lived, might have enjoyed.

Henry Sidgwick observed that "the aim of the Society was, by frank and close debate and unreserved communication of dissent and objection, to attain—not agreement, which was of course beyond hope—but a diminution of mutual misunderstanding." In

[10] See App. B. [11] Biographies, letters, diaries, etc.
[12] Wilfrid Ward, *op. cit.*, p. 312.

spite of this eminently catholic purpose, Newman had been shocked at Manning's consenting to join the Society; he was even more surprised when he heard that Manning had actually listened to Huxley read a paper on the Resurrection (January 11, 1876). "Perhaps it is a ruse of the Cardinal to bring the Professor into the clutches of the Inquisition," he is reported to have said. Apparently, most of the members were delighted, both socially and intellectually, by their somewhat paradoxical relations to one another; certainly the variety of convictions was the most startling as well as philosophically most important aspect of the Society. One of the best accounts of an actual meeting, catching admirably the spirit of the Society, is that given by W. C. Magee, Bishop of Peterborough, in a letter written to his wife soon after attending the meeting of February 11, 1873.[13] It has a special freshness of its own, for this was the first meeting which Magee had been able to attend since his election some time in 1872:

I went to dinner duly at the Grosvenor Hotel. The dinner was certainly a strangely interesting one. Had the dishes been as various we should have had severe dyspepsia, all of us. Archbishop Manning in the chair was flanked by two Protestant bishops right and left—Gloucester and Bristol [C. J. Ellicott] and myself—on my right was Hutton, Editor of the *Spectator*—an Arian; then came Father Dalgairns, a very able Roman Catholic priest; opposite him, Lord A. Russell, a Deist; then two Scotch metaphysical writers—Freethinkers [probably Sir Alexander Grant and Prof. A. C. Fraser]; then Knowles, the *very* broad Editor of the *Contemporary;* then, dressed as a layman and looking like a country squire, was Ward, formerly Rev. Ward, and earliest of the perverts to Rome; then Greg, author of "The Creed of Christendom," a Deist; then Froude the historian, once a deacon in our Church, now a Deist; then Roden Noel, an actual Atheist and red republican, and looking very like one! Lastly Ruskin who read after dinner a paper on miracles! ["The Nature and Authority of Miracle"] which we discussed for an hour and a half! Nothing could be calmer, fairer, or even, on the whole, more reverent than the discussion. Nothing flippant or scoffing or bitter was said on either side, and very great ability, both of speech and thought, was shown by most speakers. In my opinion, we, the Christians, had much the best of it. Dalgairns, the priest, was very masterly; Manning, clever and precise and weighty; Froude, very acute, and so

[13] J. C. MacDonnell, *Life and Correspondence of William Connor Magee,* 2 vols., London, Isbister, 1896, I, 284.

was Greg; while Ruskin declared himself delighted "with the exquisite accuracy and logical power of the Bishop of Peterborough." There is the story of the dinner. Altogether a remarkable and most interesting scene, and a greater gathering of remarkable men than could easily be met elsewhere. We only wanted a Jew and a Mahometan [14] to make our Religious Museum complete.

The papers read before the Society, virtually all of which exist in some form, present a full record of its achievement and reveal the members who took the most active part in furthering its intellectual life and philosophic purpose. Out of a total of ninety-five papers[15] delivered before the Society, R. H. Hutton and James Fitzjames Stephen each read seven papers; Sidgwick, Manning, and Lord Arthur Russell each read six; Frederic Harrison and Dr. W. B. Carpenter each read four. Three papers were read by: Huxley, Ward, Ruskin, Dalgairns, W. K. Clifford, Shadworth Hodgson, and St. George Mivart. Ten members read two papers each: Roden Noel, Martineau, Bagehot, Froude, Pattison, W. R. Greg, G. Croom Robertson, Magee, Ellicott, and Leslie Stephen. Fourteen read only one paper; and twenty-four members of the Society never read a paper at all. Thus two-thirds of the work of the Society, sixty-one out of ninety-five papers, was done by the fourteen who read three or more papers; and of the sixty-two men [16] who at one time or another were members of the Society, only thirty-eight ever read papers. However, among those who never read but who attended as often as their duties would permit, were some of the most interesting figures of the Society—men like J. R. Seeley, M. E. Grant Duff, Tennyson, Gladstone, Thirlwall, Argyll, R. W. Church, and Robert Lowe.

[14] The only visitor of whom I have found any record (visitors, according to the Society's bylaws, must be "foreigners") was Baboo Keshub Chunder Sen, member of the Brahmo, a reformed Hindu theistic church which held beliefs comparable to the rationalistic Christianity of Unitarianism, and in which the late Rabindranath Tagore was brought up. Chunder Sen visited England in 1870, gave more than seventy public lectures and addresses, aroused considerable periodical controversy, and visited the Metaphysical Society on April 27, 1870, when Sidgwick read a paper on "The Verification of Beliefs."

[15] One of these papers was an "oral communication" on "Euthanasia," by Ellicott, and was never printed, the only paper which I have not traced.

[16] Of these sixty-two members, thirty-one were elected during the first year of the Society; of these thirty-one, eleven, including Knowles, never read papers; thus, about a third of the membership was from the start rather "inactive."

The reading of papers before the Society was clearly essential to the most active participation in its discussions. There is a special logic in the order of papers read which reveals naturally enough that a point of view strenuously upheld in the paper presented at one meeting would bring a paper in opposition to it or in its defense at the next or a subsequent meeting.[17] In this sense the history of the Society is a long unfolding of one argument, constantly elaborated, modified, and redirected; an argument which can perhaps be stated as: "What must a man believe? What may or can a man believe?"—not only about God and "reality," but about his own nature. In the presumption of these high themes lie both the accomplishment and the interest of the Society.

[17] See the bibliographical relations made clear in App. C.

Chapter 4

THE FORMS AND THE SUBSTANCE

THE METAPHYSICAL SOCIETY, formed in quiet hope and enthusiasm in Willis' Rooms on April 21, 1869, held its first regular meeting on June 2 of the same year at Dean Stanley's in Westminster. It endured until November 16, 1880, when it was dissolved at a meeting held in Dr. Martineau's house in Gordon Square. The Society which had attracted to its first two meetings nineteen of the most distinguished thinkers in England and soon counted among its sixty-two members many of the leaders in English theology, philosophy, and science, took its own life at a meeting attended by eight members, only three of whom had belonged from the earliest days. Froude had said that if the members hung together for twelve months, it would be one of the most remarkable facts in history; Knowles pointed out that they "hung together" for nearly twelve years, and that the Society came to an end "because, after twelve years of debating, there seemed little to be said which had not already been repeated more than once." Huxley insisted that the Society "died of too much love," by which he apparently meant that mutual misunderstandings had been so removed that "only the fundamentals themselves remained in debate" and in consequence "there was nothing left to be done." According to Leslie Stephen, who, however, had become a member in the Society's declining years, it was this inability to get beyond the fundamentals—which had come to be mere repeated assertions—that led to the decay of the Society. Perhaps we are only now learning the complicated senses in which the effort to "get beyond the fundamentals" is a counsel of perfection, better left to the angels.

Whatever the reasons for its final dissolution, which will later be examined, the Society endured for eleven years and seven months. Of the discussions, which like the papers were completely "private," only a few notes remain; although pen, ink, and paper were set before each member, few, we are told, ever used them. The "Minute-Book" of the Society [1] is now lost in some private collection, although enough is available in the form of a printed proof set up for Mr. James Knowles in 1904 to show that it contained merely a record of the members present, the papers read, and brief accounts of any "business" transacted.

The Three Periods

The *Papers* of the Metaphysical Society survive.[2] An examination of them reveals that the eleven years' history of the Metaphysical Society falls naturally into three periods—1869 to 1873, 1873 to 1878, 1878 to 1880—periods of growth, achievement, and decay. The Society originated at a critical and important time. The year 1869 saw the appearance of Arnold's *Culture and Anarchy,* Clough's posthumous *Poems and Prose Remains,* and Tennyson's *Holy Grail and Other Poems,* which included "The Higher Pantheism." The February issue of the *Fortnightly* had gone into a seventh edition with Huxley's essay on "The Physical Basis of Life," and Darwin's *Origin of Species* had already appeared in a fifth edition. Before the first paper was read, Mill's *On the Subjection of Women,* Lecky's *History of European Morals,* and Galton's *Hereditary Genius* had recently appeared. This period of early development ends with Manning's paper "A Diagnosis and a Prescription" (No. 36 [3]; June 10, 1873), which is a serious effort to appraise and criticize the work of the Society in its first four years, from its birth in 1869 to 1873, the year of Arnold's *Literature and Dogma,* Mill's posthumous *Autobiography,* and James Fitzjames Stephen's *Liberty, Equality, Fraternity.*

In these four years the intellectual and social climate of England and Europe had changed. The Franco-Prussian War, the final unification of Italy, and the rise of Bismarck created political

[1] See App. B.
[2] See complete bibliography of the Papers in App. C.
[3] The number of the paper as listed in App. C.

and economic problems which Europe has not yet solved; and the Vatican Council of 1870 which decreed the dogma of the infallibility of the Pope in matters of faith and morals gave the head of the Roman Catholic church a world-wide spiritual influence and authority such as no Pope had ever dreamed of before the loss of the temporal power. Newman's *Grammar of Assent* (1870) provided the "logic" of the new Catholic position, although Newman himself had been opposed to the ultramontane stand on the promulgation of the doctrine of infallibility. Darwin's *Descent of Man* (1871) showed what scarcely needed showing, the gulf which existed between the Catholic and scientific worlds; and Butler's delightful *Erewhon* (1872) was in its iconoclasm not likely to bridge the gulf. The struggle of science with orthodoxy was now open and unashamed; no wonder that Manning, who was chairman of the Metaphysical Society in 1872–3, should have felt it his duty, both as chairman and as Catholic, to make his "diagnosis" and his "prescription" of June 10, 1873.

The second period of the Society's history begins with the establishment of a Committee on Definitions, early in the autumn of 1873. At the meeting of July 8, 1873, no prepared paper had been available, the "aphonia" of which Manning complained in his previous paper having continued, in spite of his "prescription." This period ends with Mark Pattison's ambiguous but brilliant paper, "Double Truth" (No. 74; February 12, 1878), and a report of the Committee on Definitions, submitted at the meeting of March 12, although never printed. These five years were the time of the Society's greatest success, when its techniques, its subject matter, and its members were not only at their best, but exercising the widest influence on English thought and opinion. These years saw not only the continued adherence of most of the Society's distinguished founders, but also the addition of several new members of equal brilliance, including James Fitzjames Stephen (1873), W. K. Clifford (1874), and St. George Mivart (1874), all of whom proved very active; also, John Morley (1876) and Leslie Stephen (1877), who although not so active, had become members when the Society was beginning to lose some of its vitality.

Disraeli succeeded Gladstone as Prime Minister in 1874. The

new ministry had in the political sphere given facile promise of better things through change; but something happened to the English spirit in the years between 1876, when Disraeli made the Queen Empress of India, and 1878, when he "solved" the Balkan problem by bringing back "peace with honour" from Berlin. In literature it was a period of shifting values, literary and intellectual, during which most of the elder great were still writing, and the "new" writers, with the exception of Swinburne, had scarcely yet made themselves heard. Typical of the period and representative of the very activity which the Metaphysical Society itself enjoyed at this time is W. H. Mallock's clever satire *The New Republic*.[4] In the pages of this book speak several of the most important members of the Society: Ruskin (Mr. Herbert), Huxley (Mr. Storks), Tyndall (Mr. Stockton), and Clifford (Mr. Saunders); as well as Jowett, Pater, Lord Houghton, and Matthew Arnold. Mallock's "dialogues" take place in a country-house, and in his brilliant and damning but essentially frivolous satire there is ironic contempt for the intellectual manner which had brought success to the Society. Mallock was himself a Catholic and scorned the "liberal" and "modernist" approaches to all problems, whether theological or political;[5] but he also very acutely reveals the weaknesses which were to help bring about the gradual failure of the Society and are perhaps consequences of the unresolved paradoxes of the nineteenth-century liberal intellect itself.

As the result of a serious quarrel with the owners of the *Contemporary Review*, the editor, James Knowles, who was still Secretary of the Society, severed his connection with the *Contemporary* and in March, 1877, founded the *Nineteenth Century*.[6] This new review had an immediate success and soon became one of the most

[4] This book, on which the author had worked for several years, was published in 1877 and presents a coincidental parallel to the "Modern Symposium" which ran in Knowles's *Nineteenth Century* from April, 1877, through most of 1878. (See Chap. X, below.) Mallock claims that his models were of course the *Republic* of Plato (even more understandable since he was a student at Balliol, of which Jowett was Master when he first began work on the book), the *Satyricon* of Petronius, and the novels of Peacock; but his uncle, with whom he was very intimate, was J. A. Froude, one of the most active members of the Metaphysical Society, and both Dr. Henry Acland and John Ruskin, whom he knew well at Oxford and afterwards, were also members of the Society.

[5] He later became a fashionable antisocialist.

[6] A full analysis of Knowles's connection with these two periodicals will be found in Chaps. IX and X.

powerful journals of opinion in England. Tennyson contributed a "Prefatory Sonnet" to the first issue, and other members of the Metaphysical Society, many of whom had long been regular contributors to the *Contemporary*, transferred their journalistic allegiance to the *Nineteenth Century*. Knowles had gathered about him a representative group of writers and thinkers which could scarcely be surpassed, even by John Morley's *Fortnightly*. When with the second number he began "A Modern Symposium" on "Morality and Religious Belief," to which the Duke of Argyll, W. K. Clifford, F. Harrison, J. Martineau, Lord Selborne, Sir James Fitzjames Stephen, R. H. Hutton, T. H. Huxley, R. W. Church, and W. G. Ward all contributed, Knowles achieved one of the great journalistic coups of the period and his fortune was made. Few knew that every one of these men was a member of the Metaphysical Society and that the "Symposium" had originated in its papers and discussions. But it was largely owing to Knowles's connection with the Society that he, who seven years before had been relatively unknown and only a moderately successful architect, was now one of the powers in molding the public opinion of his time. He himself admitted that it was from the meetings of the Society that he had derived the idea for this "Symposium."

The success of the first "Modern Symposium" led Knowles to continue his experiment with two more, also based on papers and discussions of the Society, one on "The Soul and Future Life," in the autumn of 1877, with two contributions from men who were not members; and another on "The Popular Judgment in Politics," in the summer of 1878, once more entirely by members of the Society. By this time Knowles's own sure journalistic judgment warned him that the device had done its work.

Knowles himself had now begun to lose interest in the Society, but he continued to serve as Secretary until November, 1879, when he resigned and his place was taken by Frederick Pollock, who served until the Society's final dissolution. Knowles had probably discovered that the clash of ideas and personalities which had been for him the major value and excitement of the Metaphysical Society could be achieved with almost equal success in the pages of his review. Here, by setting man against man, he found a new way to spur the flagging interest of his band of theologians, philosophers, and scientists; here was a substitute for the Society which was beginning to be weakened by the defection of members like Tennyson and W. G. Ward, by the death of others, and by the lack of new members (perhaps a fault of the times) who would equal the great departed.

From the time of Knowles's resignation to the final meeting, the Society is clearly in decline; his organizing ability, his enthusiasm, his personality removed, the Society lost heart and died. The election of a number of new members in 1879 and 1880 failed to halt the inevitable, and the last three members elected probably never attended a meeting. At the final meeting of the Society a resolution was passed, proposed by Martineau, the Chairman, and seconded by Pollock, the Secretary, "That, having regard to the difficulty lately found in keeping up this Society's meetings, and the extent to which this Society's original objects have, since its foundation, been provided for in other ways,[7] it is expedient that this Society be dissolved, and its affairs wound up." Thus closed the third and final period of the Metaphysical Society's history, beginning with Matthew Boulton's question, "Has a Metaphysical Society any *Raison d'être?*" (No. 75; April 9, 1878), and ending with the last paper by C. B. Upton on "The Recent Phase of the Freewill Controversy" (No. 90; May 11, 1880) and the final meeting on November 16, 1880.

It is significant that the Metaphysical Society died with Gladstone's return to the Prime Ministership after his "pilgrimage of passion," the Midlothian campaign of 1880. New political and intellectual compromises lay ahead after the success of Joseph Chamberlain's National Liberal Federation. The decade which had begun with a great war, an atmosphere of moral battle, a struggle between theology and science, and a fresh concern with the problem of authority, ended with an "honorable" peace, a new

[7] Shadworth Hodgson had founded the Aristotelian Society in 1879, was its first president, and continued in that post for fourteen years. He had delivered his first presidential address October 11, 1880, a month before the final meeting of the Metaphysical Society. G. Croom Robertson had founded the influential philosophical and psychological periodical *Mind,* in 1876.

sophistication, a new literature, the seeming abandonment of many old philosophical problems, and a truce between religion and science which still endures. "Compromise" had been in the air ever since the publication in 1874 of John Morley's eloquent formulation of the principle and its dangers in his little volume of that name.[8] It had long been one of the working principles of English political life; but not until Gladstone's return in 1880 did thinking men, faced with the great problems which beset his ministry, come to realize that compromise was not only the *modus vivendi* of English politics but a necessary element in English intellectual life. Surely it is not unimportant that the Metaphysical Society should have taught many of the greatest—and most absolutist—minds in England some, at least, of the arts of compromise. In "compromise" lie the reasons for both the success and failure of the Society; in an examination of its workings the liberal intellect itself can be understood.

The First Meeting

The unequal struggles between religious orthodoxy and science in the sixties brought, as we have seen, searching doubts to the minds of many men not deceived by the easy certainties of an age of material progress. But the men of faith often seemed to be fighting a losing battle, for religious revelation remained static, a given body of truth, while science, as Harold Nicolson has said, evolved a new and startling revelation every few months.[9] Tennyson, long a student of science, had felt many of these doubts much earlier than most, and "In Memoriam," as well as the first "Locksley Hall," had been efforts to reconcile revealed religion with the new science, his own faith with those evolutionary ideas which, years before the publication of Darwin's book, had been spreading in England through Lyell's *Principles* and *Elements of Geology* and through their popularization in Robert Chambers' *Vestiges of the Natural History of Creation*. But it was difficult to reconcile

[8] It is interesting to note that Morley was a constant advocate of Home Rule for Ireland and a consistent enemy of the new British imperialism. In 1914, upon the outbreak of the first World War, he refused to compromise with his pacifist convictions and went into voluntary political retirement.

[9] Harold Nicolson, *Tennyson,* Boston, Houghton Mifflin, 1923, p. 264.

"nature red in tooth and claw" with the idea of purposive progress and even harder to accomplish the integration of what his friend the Duke of Argyll was later to call the "Reign of Law" with the concept of a God of Love. To Tennyson, increasingly dominated by a sense of social and moral responsibility, the foundation of the Metaphysical Society was, therefore, a hopeful attempt to regain some of the certainties of his own earlier solutions, a renewed opportunity to go more deeply into the problems of God, nature, and existence than he had during the lush period of *The Idylls of the King*. Already in a late Idyll, "The Holy Grail," which he considered "one of the most imaginative" of his poems, he had expressed his "strong feeling as to the Reality of the Unseen." [10] But in "Lucretius," a poem of the same period, however masked in a dramatic-monologue form which reminds us of Browning and looks forward to his own later plays, he shows in fantastic imagery of striking sensual and psychological power the nature and quality of his perplexities as to the relation of matter and spirit.

Tennyson had been present at the "organization meeting" of the Metaphysical Society, April 21, 1869, as were Knowles and Pritchard, co-founders with him of the Society. It was only fitting that in order to be represented at the first regular meeting, June 2, 1869, which he was unfortunately unable to attend in person, he should send "The Higher Pantheism," a poem he had been reworking and rewriting for many months. In it he makes what is almost his final, and certainly his clearest, effort to reconcile theism and science. That this pantheistic solution smacks also of mysticism is not strange in one who could, by thinking intently of his own name, throw himself into a state of consciousness in which the spirit was apparently isolated from the body.[11] Swinburne, whose parody of the poem—"The Higher Pantheism in a Nutshell"—is almost more famous than the original, was able to make good fun of a religious state which he himself had probably

[10] *Alfred Lord Tennyson, a Memoir,* by his son, 2 vols., London, Macmillan, 1898, II, 90.

[11] Reported by Tyndall in his reminiscence of Tennyson in *Tennyson, a Memoir,* II, 473. Tyndall points out that this power is later interpreted by Tennyson in "The Ancient Sage" (1885), a poem based on the life and maxims of Lao-Tze.

never experienced, unless perhaps in one of the epileptic fits or alcoholic visions which became for a time his pitiful means of escape from life. But Tennyson's own religious insights are here closer to the visionary power of the greater epileptic, Dostoevsky, than to those of the author of "Hertha." It is possible that the metrical form of Tennyson's poem owes something to Swinburne, but it is more likely that an apparent similarity to Swinburne's style is derived rather from their common study of classical meters, a similarity which Swinburne was quick to exploit in his parody.[12]

The poem itself was indeed appropriate to the opening meeting[13] of the new Society. In effect it appealed to religious philosophers and scientists to see in phenomena the garment of God, a vision of Spirit. Knowles, the Honorary Secretary, who had persuaded Tennyson to send the poem,[14] read it to the assembled members:

The sun, the moon, the stars, the seas, the hills and the plains—
Are not these, O Soul, the Vision of Him who reigns?

Is not the Vision He? tho' He be not that which He seems?
Dreams are true while they last, and do we not live in dreams?

Earth, these solid stars, this weight of body and limb,
Are they not sign and symbol of thy division from Him?

Dark is the world to thee; thyself art the reason why,
For is He not all but thou, that hast power to feel "I am I?"

Glory about thee, without thee; and thou fulfillest thy doom,
Making Him broken gleams, and a stifled splendour and gloom.

12 It is only fair to Swinburne to remind the reader that in his "Nephelidia" he showed himself amusingly able to parody himself.

13 June 2, 1869. Present: Alford, Barry, Carpenter, Hinton, Hutton, Huxley, Knowles, Lushington, Manning, Russell, Stanley, Tyndall, and Ward, thirteen members in all. Although Sir John Lubbock had been at the organization meeting and was later elected President of the Society for the session 1869–70, he was not present at this meeting, according to the Minute-Book. On this point Hallam Tennyson is wrong. For the attendance at all future meetings of the Society, whenever known, see App. C.

14 Knowles had apparently asked Tennyson to contribute the poem and Tennyson did so, writing back: "Your request that you may read the poem at that meeting abashes me. If you are to read it, it ought to be stated surely that I have but ceded to your strongly expressed desire. Hutton [who was to read the first paper] can have a copy of it if he choose; but an I had known that such as he wanted it, I would have looked at it again before I let it go" (*Tennyson, a Memoir,* II, 168).

Speak to Him, thou, for He hears, and Spirit with Spirit can meet—
Closer is He than breathing, and nearer than hands and feet.

God is law, say the wise; O Soul, and let us rejoice,
For if He thunder by law the thunder is yet His voice.

Law is God, say some; no God at all, says the fool,
For all we have power to see is a straight staff bent in a pool;

And the ear of man cannot hear, and the eye of man cannot see;
But if we could see and hear, this Vision—were it not He?

God is law and law is God, says Tennyson, and only "the fool" denies that law is an evidence of deity; however, human senses and the knowledge based on them are inadequate and partial. "For all we have power to see is a straight staff bent in a pool." If we could hear, if we could see, if we had the true visionary power, would we not find that phenomena, all the aspects of so-called reality, are merely the mask of Godhead? Tennyson's faith rests in a unifying theism, God as First Cause, although His rational justification is little stronger than that afforded by Mansel's sceptical imposition of an unknowable Absolute or Unconditioned Cause. Poet and logician are justifying the same "intuition"; both glorify the inscrutability of God, however much we may know of His ways.

Poems, particularly philosophic poems, are always difficult to follow and understand by ear at a first reading; Tennyson's was probably no exception. In any case we are told that there was not a word of comment or criticism from the members of the new society, although, as Martineau says, "Nothing that he ever wrote was more likely to lead to interesting discussion." [15] "The Higher Pantheism" was allowed to remain what in its essence it was, a prologue to the drama of ideas which the Metaphysical Society was about to present.

R. H. Hutton, editor of the *Spectator*, had prepared the first paper to be presented to the new society, "On Mr. Herbert Spencer's Theory of the Gradual Transformation of Utilitarian into Intuitive Morality by Hereditary Descent." [16] Lubbock had

[15] *Tennyson, a Memoir,* II, 171.

[16] As explained in App. C, this paper was apparently never separately printed. It was, however, published in *Macmillan's Magazine,* XX (July, 1869), 266,

earlier tried to persuade Spencer to join the Society and Hutton had also made every effort to get him either to attend the meeting or at least to give the paper the benefit of his criticism, but Spencer had, as we know, refused. Nearly two years later, long after the paper had been published, Spencer made an angry reply, but he did not at that time acknowledge to what lengths Hutton had gone to be fair and just in his criticisms.

Hutton's paper was a clear attack on Spencer's effort to establish an empirical or utilitarian basis for some of those aspects of morality for which the Christian believers in revelation and the sceptical followers of Mansel and Hamilton claimed an intuitive origin. Although Spencer was willing to admit the existence of an Unknowable he was never willing to use the Unknowable as cause and hence subjected all sorts of so-called a priori intuitions to deductive analysis.

Hutton quotes a letter from Spencer to John Stuart Mill [17] which attempts to "connect thought with the other phenomena of the universe," to use the terms which Huxley had made current in his lecture on "The Physical Basis of Life," delivered a few months previously and recently published in the *Fortnightly*. Hutton explains that although Spencer is a utilitarian—testing the rightness or wrongness of an action by the balance of happiness or unhappiness resulting therefrom—he was convinced by the fact that many moral principles now present themselves with an authority not accounted for by the experience of the individual, that the question of the origin of these principles requires a more complex explanation than the purely utilitarian. Spencer has come to the conclusion, quotes Hutton, that "there have been and still are, developing in the race certain fundamental moral intuitions; and that though these moral intuitions are the result of accumulated experiences of utility, gradually organized and inherited, they have come to be quite independent of conscious experience." Not only is each generation better adapted to the universe in which we live, but the process of adaptation is one which transforms

under the less ponderous title, "A Questionable Parentage for Morals," and attracted considerable attention. The *Macmillan's* version is my source.

[17] Reprinted by Bain in his *Handbook of Mental and Moral Science, A Compendium of Psychology and Ethics,* London, Longmans, 1868.

complex into apparently simple ideas and even conceals the secret of their origin. "Necessary" intuitions are thus a conglomeration of our ancestors' best observations and most useful empirical rules.

Hutton refuses to criticize Spencer's suggestion that "what metaphysicians call an intuition or an a priori idea is probably nothing but a special susceptibility in our nerves produced by a vast number of homogeneous ancestral experiences gradually agglutinated into a single intellectual tendency." [18] He also insists that moral intuitions are in a different category from space-intuitions and that Spencer's theory, if it accounts for anything, only accounts for "the drying up of the sense of utility and inutility into mere inherent tendencies—dumb, inarticulate dispositions—to act thus and thus, which would exercise over us not *more* authority but *less* than a rational sense of utilitarian issues."

There is no positive instance of the transformation of a utilitarian rule of right into an intuition; in fact, intuitive rules have generally had to resist the pressure of utilitarian objections to their authority. The particular and special characteristic of intuitions and a priori ideas is in fact sharply opposed to the utilitarian, for these ideas compel us "to deny the possibility that in any other world, however otherwise different, our experience could be otherwise." In other words, Hutton insists that a priori ideas are not only universals but absolutes, and that utilitarian or empirical truths are, by the nature of their origin, relative.

According to Spencer's theory, man must admit the possibility and actual frequency of actions which infringe upon this now intuitive, once utilitarian, moral rule, and must moreover insist that these frequent actions are "wrong," even though the principal test of their wrongness (from the viewpoint of utility, their tendency to destroy happiness) may have largely disappeared. Moreover, this reducing of a moral intuition to the end result of an accumulation of a number of inherited experiences of utility makes of the intuition a dry habit or tendency which it is *uncomfortable* to resist, but which has no rational or sacred ground. Hutton insists that those who act thus are *less* right than those

18 Hutton's words.

of their ancestors who acted according to the greatest-happiness principle. Thus, since "Mr. Spencer's theory of moral intuitions makes them out to be the accretions of once living and now dead individual moral perceptions," moral reverence would decrease instead of increase; which, indeed, although Hutton does not quite admit it, was what most intuitionists thought was happening, blaming materialism and the philosophy of Mill and the experience school. But to Hutton it seemed "even *worse* for one who makes utility the true final criterion of right and wrong to account for the absolute, imperious, and mystic character of our moral perceptions, by the dropping out of the notion of utility, than by the more vivid and intense appreciation of it." Bagehot, his friend Hutton remarks, had shown how gradual has been the growth in the race of political *tameability*—the disposition to submit to government. Surely the growth of a habit, separated from all perception of its natural authority, would account for the drying up of a sense of obligation, but not, in Mill's word, for its *mystical* extension.

The strongest objection, however, Hutton finds in the fact that the "happiness principle" itself has not been consolidated into a moral intuition. Honesty, pity, purity he insists we find good without relation to happy consequences; if Spencer is right there should by now be no controversy over the principle of utilitarianism. Hutton insists that the *intention* to produce happiness is common to both vices and virtues, but that the steady *result* of happiness belongs only to virtue. Moreover, honesty, for example, is often associated with unhappy as well as happy experiences.

Hutton's belief that Spencer's theory of the genesis of duty is disproved "by the mere fact that so many who think about the subject are not utilitarians" is perhaps the weakest point in his argument. However, he asserts that duty itself must be a central moral intuition, compelling to the balance of decision in moral action.

Finally, Hutton asks, what evidence can we point to of the transformation of *moral* species? "The notion of 'honesty being the best policy' is . . . long subsequent to the most imperious enunciation of its sacredness as a duty." Hutton scorns the idea of possible prehistoric origins, something Spencer himself would not have done; to this question Sir John Lubbock was to return in a few months.[19] Moral principles are in advance of their time, are *anticipatory* in character; the prevailing principles of actual action are often opposed to the moral teachings of "intuition." Moral discoveries, unlike the scientific, arouse resistance, even war. There is little evidence of any dramatic moral evolution; new moral principles never weave themselves into "all our thought and actions so effectually as to leave any single society of men with a less serious moral conflict on its hands than that of any previous society, however ancient and primitive." There is always struggle, there is always a moral issue. If Spencer is right, there should be some one moral law or intuition which is as deeply ingrained as the geometrical law that a straight line is the shortest way between two points; and with this final criticism, which was as difficult for the intuitionists to answer as it was for the utilitarians, he asks the members of the Society, "Which of them is it?"

This paper of Hutton's, however unfair to Spencer [20] by the limitation of its argument to the evidence offered by his single letter to Mill, was a sharp criticism of the effort to relate evolutionary concepts to the utilitarian view of man's moral nature. It distinctly opposes the intuitive to the empirical school and, by challenging the leading philosopher of the new science, offers to the Society its most important subjects, the moral nature of man, and the relation between that nature and the world of material phenomena which it is the business of science to understand.

Science, Agnosticism, and Belief

A further effort to examine the relations of religion and science, intuition and experience, characterized Dr. W. B. Carpenter's paper, "The Common Sense Philosophy of Causation,"

[19] "The Moral Condition of Savages" (No. 5; January 12, 1870).

[20] Spencer's reply (published in *Fortnightly Review,* N.S. IX [April 1, 1871], 419, under the title "Morals and Moral Sentiments") attempts to indicate a change of view and to explain that he really meant what he calls the "moral sentiments," *not* the "fundamental moral intuitions" which Hutton had seized upon. It called forth an urbane rebuttal which Hutton soon presented to the Society, "Mr. Herbert Spencer on Moral Intuitions and Moral Sentiments" (No. 18, June 13, 1871), published in the *Contemporary Review,* XVII (July, 1871), 463.

which he read to the second meeting of the Society in July, before the summer recess. Carpenter was a notable physiologist, psychologist, and leader in university reform but had always considered the mutual antagonism of science and religion profoundly injurious to both. As an eminent Unitarian layman he had devoted a good part of his small leisure to efforts at reconciliation. His task was to convince his fellow scientists that theism did not necessarily invoke an arbitrary power to which the order of nature was merely an ornament, while at the same time he tried to persuade churchmen that the concept of scientific "law" did not delimit or eliminate the human will. To Carpenter, the pursuit of science neither explicitly nor implicitly involved an abandonment of Christ and the Christian life. He, on the contrary, believed that a scientific knowledge of the human mind could be legitimately extended "to the notion we form of the mind of the Deity in its relation to [the] Universe."

Carpenter's paradoxical position, suspended, as it were, between the intuitionist and experience schools, peculiarly qualified him to take up the argument which Hutton had left in the form of a question at the end of his first paper. Why indeed is geometrical "law" more self-evident than moral law? Carpenter apparently felt, with many of his more philosophical contemporaries, that this question could not be answered without a further consideration of the nature of "law" and that "law" could not be understood without a theory of causation.

Of Carpenter's paper itself as actually read before the Society no trace remains; it was not published in any periodical and does not appear in the bibliography of Carpenter's writings.[21] Its substance can, however, be determined with considerable accuracy from the final chapter of Carpenter's *Principles of Mental Physiology*, "Of Mind and Will in Nature." [22] Here he concerns himself

[21] In *Nature and Man, Essays Scientific and Philosophical* by W. B. Carpenter, edited by J. Estlin Carpenter, London, K. Paul, Trench, 1888, pp. 467–83. For further bibliographical details and the attendance at this meeting, see App. C. below.

[22] W. B. Carpenter, *Principles of Mental Physiology,* New York, Appleton, 1875, pp. 691–708. A later paper of Carpenter's, "What is Common Sense?" (No. 22; January 17, 1872), was afterwards published in slightly expanded form in the *Contemporary Review,* XIX (February, 1872), 401. This paper finally ap-

not only with the relation of the mind of man to the mind of God, but also with the idea of efficient causation and its relation to the antagonism of science and religion. Relying heavily on the philosophical and religious insights of his teacher and friend Martineau, he insists that the culmination of man's intellectual interpretation of nature is his "recognition of the Unity of the Power, of which her phenomena are the diversified manifestations." The convertibility of physical forces, their correlation with the vital, and "the intimacy of that *nexus* between Mental and Bodily activity, which, explain it as we may, cannot be denied," all seem to Carpenter to lead to one conclusion—"the source of all power in Mind." To have "thought the thoughts of God" was the privilege most highly esteemed by Kepler, and as Martineau had said:

> What, indeed, have we found by moving out along all radii into the Infinite? That the whole is woven together in one sublime tissue of intellectual relations, geometric and physical,—the realized original, of which all our science is but the partial copy. That Science is the crowning product and supreme expression of Human reason. . . . Unless therefore, it takes more mental faculty to construe a Universe than to cause it, to read the Book of Nature than to write it, we must more than ever look upon its sublime face as the living appeal of Thought to Thought.

But Carpenter's "common-sense view of causation" was probably unsatisfactory to both theologians and scientists, to intuitionists and empiricists. In the earnest effort to reconcile scientific and theistic concepts, in which he shows his debt to the Cartesian tradition, he really establishes a dichotomy which he refuses to develop as a dualism. In this he ignores the suggestion often made by Martineau, that religion and science may have different aims and probably occupy different realms of discourse.

However, this effort to find a common ground between scientists

peared, with some small additions, as Chapter XI, "Of Common Sense," in this same volume, *Principles of Mental Physiology*. I think, therefore, that the last chapter of the book can be taken as giving a good idea of the substance of Carpenter's first Metaphysical Society paper. The book itself was the first important English contribution in this growing field and became one of the major starting points for the development of that branch of the new science of psychology, of which G. H. Lewes's *Physical Basis of Mind* (1877) and *A Study of Psychology* (1879), as well as William James's *Principles of Psychology* (1890), are early monuments.

and religionists continued to be the major task of the Society. Carpenter's attempt to make religion scientific and science religious is a step in search of a philosophy which will relate man's knowledge of the phenomenal world to the deepest demands of his own nature, a view of the responsibility of science to which Von Baer and Hartmann had already contributed on the Continent. Such a view leads straight to the kind of philosophical analysis which Bergson and Santayana, in different ways, later undertook. But however devoted Carpenter himself might be to Christ as a "Divine Ideal," professed Christians would look in vain in his "anthropomorphic pantheism" for the Christianity of the New Testament. In a sense Carpenter is thus an example of that kind of scientist who, brought up in sectarian Christianity, adjusts his religion to the basic assumptions of his science but is in the end forced to make of those very assumptions the material of a new "religion." In this, too, he reminds us of Descartes and some of his followers. Carpenter's position, in spite of his own sincerity and good will, becomes, in its implications, not very different from Positivism or the "religion of Humanity," and, like them, is open to the charge that it substitutes science for theology and the "religious feeling" for the life of faith. Carpenter, like Descartes, needs God, in paraphrase of Pascal's words, only to give a fillip to his world of cause and effect.

Not until the first meeting of the autumn, November 17, 1869, was the Society privileged to hear a paper by a true spokesman for the experience school.[23] Huxley was the speaker and delivered a paper entitled, "The Views of Hume, Kant and Whately upon the Logical Basis of the Doctrine of the Immortality of the Soul." His outline of this paper constitutes the first printed Paper of the Society; it was printed privately and sent to the members in advance, in accordance with a decision made at the meeting held July 14, just before the summer recess. But there must have been some dissatisfaction with the brief form of this paper as distributed, and perhaps even with the form in which Huxley delivered it, for all subsequent papers are printed in full and give every indi-

23 For bibliographical note and the attendance at this meeting, see App. C.

cation of being printed in approximately the form in which they were finally read. Parentheses, expansions, and added illustrations may have been frequent; certainly, when many of the papers were later reprinted in periodicals they often appear in a considerably expanded or enriched form. Some of these additions and modifications can be assumed to be the result of the evening's discussion, but many as obviously represent changes by the author himself, either during or after the reading.

Huxley's paper was an attack on the doctrine of the immortality of the soul, using the arguments of Hume and, to a less degree, of Kant and Whately, to prove that the doctrine "is not capable of being demonstrated, or logically deduced, from known facts." Since all three "agree in denying, that a belief in the immortality of the soul can be legitimately arrived at by those processes which lead to certainty in science," Huxley feels justified in asserting that "the Immortality of the Soul cannot be deduced by scientific methods of reasoning from the facts of physical or psychical nature." This simple, doctrinaire, and obvious argument [24] has little interest in itself; its principal importance lies in the fact that Huxley, on the occasion of its delivery, had much to account for and defend beyond the paper itself.

A year earlier, at Edinburgh, he had delivered the famous address on "The Physical Basis of Life," in which he asserts the uniformity of protoplasm as the basis of all life, animal or vegetable, its modification in different organisms, but its understandable and ascertainable physical, material constitution. When the *Fortnightly* printed the essay in its issue of February, 1869, the review went into seven editions, something almost unheard of in the periodical publishing of the day. Morley said that no article that had appeared for a generation excited so profound a sensation. Huxley denied any indestructible or molecular vital force in endless transmutation and asserted that "under whatever disguise it takes refuge, whether fungus or oak, worm or man, the living protoplasm not only ultimately dies and is resolved into its mineral and lifeless constituents, but is always dying, and, strange

[24] Which Huxley later (1878) summarized in his *Hume,* London, Macmillan, 1894, pp. 201 ff.

as the paradox may sound, could not live unless it died." Huxley compares his view of death in life to Balzac's tale of the *Peau de chagrin.* By making the death-drive an inevitable principle of life itself, his apparent paradox anticipates in the physiological sphere the psychic hypothesis which Freud, basing his own argument on physiological discoveries, makes so persuasive in *Beyond the Pleasure Principle.*

Huxley, however, denies he is a materialist, while accepting the "New Philosophy" as a name for "that estimate of the limits of philosophical inquiry which I, in common with many other men of science, hold to be just." He eschews the later Comte, finding in him "a great deal which is as thoroughly antagonistic to the very essence of science as anything in ultramontane Catholicism"—in fact finds his philosophy to be best described in practice as "Catholicism *minus* Christianity." But he asserts his own brand of "positivism," maintaining that the history of modern science had shown that its progress has, in all ages, meant "the extension of the province of what we call matter and causation, and the concomitant gradual banishment from all regions of human thought of what we call spirit and spontaneity." So will "the physiology of the future gradually extend the realm of matter and law until it is co-extensive with knowledge, with feeling, and with action." He is aware how "the consciousness of this great truth weighs like a nightmare" upon many of the best minds of his time; they watch the progress of materialism with the fear and anger of a savage watching an eclipse of the sun. "The advancing tide of matter threatens to drown their souls; the tightening grasp of law impedes their freedom; they are alarmed lest man's moral nature be debased by the increase of his wisdom."

Huxley insists these are gratuitously invented bugbears [25] and that the critical crux lies in the confusion of our human concept of Law, as a generalization from experience, with the notion of Necessity, which implies a knowledge of tendency or purpose beyond experience. In this he is on sure ground but does not quite grasp the implications of his argument. He is formulating the

[25] A contrary view is interestingly expressed by Erich Fromm, *Escape from Freedom,* New York, Viking, 1941.

position to which he later gave the name "agnosticism" at one of the earliest meetings of the Society:[26] "Why trouble ourselves about matters of which, however important they may be, we do know nothing, and can know nothing?" All we know is "that the order of Nature is ascertainable by our faculties to an extent which is practically unlimited" and "that our volition counts for something as a condition of the course of events."

To Huxley, newly read in eighteenth-century philosophy, as to Diderot, who was for a long time one of the most confirmed materialists of the Age of Reason, "matter may be regarded as a form of thought, thought may be regarded as a property of matter —each statement has a certain relative truth." But in science the materialistic terminology is vastly to be preferred to the spiritualistic, which is "utterly barren, and leads to nothing but obscurity and confusion of ideas." In consequence, even in discussion of "spiritual" or religious questions, Huxley insists on using the materialistic terminology.

Huxley's attack, in the name of science, upon the doctrine of the immortality of the soul was of course exactly what the members of the Society had the right to expect from the author of "The Physical Basis of Life." The charge of "gross and brutal materialism" which in that essay Huxley had anticipated from his critics would surely also be leveled at this attack on immortality; and when later (in No. 11; November 8, 1870) he asked "Has the Frog a Soul?" or even, much later (in No. 58; January 11, 1876) criticized "The Evidence of the Miracle of the Resurrection," the theists and Christian thinkers had some pretext for the accusation. However much Huxley was to qualify his position and insist that he was "no materialist," to the Christian party he was the spokesman of the godless even though he did sing hymns at home on Sunday night with his friends. That the degree of Huxley's "atheism" was now determined by a new word "agnostic" only helps to show that his position was sufficiently ambiguous to require an ambiguous label. Huxley, like most of the theologians and philosophers whom he criticized, was troubled by the very

[26] Huxley's own explanation of this position is to be found in the essay, "Agnosticism," reprinted in his *Science and Christian Tradition,* London, Macmillan, 1894. His debt to the Society in formulating the idea is expressed on p. 239.

demon he sought to drive out: he as a scientist is so concerned with causality that he cannot conceive a thorough-going materialism without what he calls "necessarianism"; however, he finds it difficult to reconcile his own conviction of the power of individual volition with what he thinks a materialistic determinism demands. He is sure that every phenomenon has its efficient cause and admits the difficulty of proving any form of spontaneity, yet he is sure of the power of the will at least in part to determine or condition human phenomena. There, on the horns of a great dilemma, he hangs.

That the seeming "spontaneity" of the will is in itself determined not by the history of the individual organism alone but by the genetic history of the individual's ancestors understood in evolutionary terms, was of course accepted by Huxley and in matter of fact by many of his hearers who had not yet accepted Darwin's hypothesis. Superior gifts, superior accomplishments, superior "will" in the superior individual were seen to have a scientific explanation in terms of the "survival of the fittest." At the very time when the tendency toward political equalitarianism was for the second time extending the suffrage,[27] Darwin's theory was making possible a new evolutionary aristocracy in which nobility of blood and action would be manifested either by success in adapting to the environment, or on a "higher" plane (biologically speaking) even more evidently by success in changing and modifying the environment itself. Hence, in part, the great revival of interest in education, public and private, so characteristic of the seventies and in which Huxley played so large a part.

The paper on immortality thus can be seen to have a closer connection than is at first apparent with the Society's first two papers by R. H. Hutton and W. B. Carpenter. Hutton's paper, which was designed to bring Spencer into the Society and in the process clearly oppose the theistic and scientific points of view on man's nature, had tried to point out some of the palpable weaknesses in any theory which hypothesized the biological or psychophysical inheritance of morality, using the word in any large

[27] The new parliament of 1869 was the first elected under household suffrage in accordance with the Reform Bill of 1867.

or significant sense. Hutton and Spencer agreed on the cultural and environmental elements in the formation of a morality, but they differed strongly on the causal explanation of certain tendencies which Spencer would insist were inherited or inheritable and which Hutton would apparently like to attribute to the individual's intuitional nature, to God's providence, or to grace. Froude's recent inaugural address on Calvin, upon accepting the Rectorship of St. Andrews, had raised anew the question whether grace can be earned or deserved, but Hutton probably did not have this in mind when he made his attack on Spencer. The latter insisted that he had been misrepresented and that he had found reason to change his view since writing the letter from which Hutton had quoted, but in any case the opposition between the empiricist-utilitarians and the Christian-intuitionists persisted over this very problem of the causal origin of "moral sentiments," including man's so-called "conviction" of the truth of immortality.

Carpenter's paper had been an effort to introduce to the Society a common-sense view of causation which, coming from a physiologist who was also a theist, would help establish some common ground on which the naturalists and supernaturalists could meet. But Huxley tacitly ignored this earlier effort at reconciliation and with his notorious pugnacity attacked the major assumption of the supernaturalists: that man has a soul and that it is immortal. A denial of the existence of the soul was implicit in his essay on "The Physical Basis of Life" and was to be reasserted with more irony in the later paper "Has the Frog a Soul?" This denial of immortality was a denial of the whole Platonic and Christian tradition of a future state which is known both by intuition and revelation; it was as well an implicit denial that a tradition, however "inherited," can be a guide to truth, for truth, he insists, must be interpreted in the terms and with the vocabulary of science. For to Huxley, as he had already pointed out, the "spiritualistic" vocabulary "is utterly barren and leads to nothing but obscurity and confusion of ideas." We must accept a theory of causality, but no theory of causality will justify the contention that physiological death is or can be the [efficient or sufficient] cause of a so-called "spiritual" immortality or of the continued existence of a soul, the presence of which in the living body it is impossible to demonstrate. This shallow argument, so reminiscent in many ways of Voltaire's optimistic philosopher in *Candide*, represents the kind of reasoning which Huxley thought most important for him to press upon the Society.

It was only just that Huxley's attack on one of the central Christian doctrines should be followed, at the December meeting,[28] by W. G. ("Ideal") Ward's criticism of one of the major assumptions of the scientific school, the trustworthiness of experience in memory. Ward's paper "On Memory as an Intuitive Faculty" (No. 4; December 15, 1869) showed all the logical and dialectical skill for which the editor of the *Dublin Review* was famous; he was not only one of the most eminent of the "renegades to Rome" but was also so accomplished a thinker and so skillful a polemicist that he soon earned the respect of men as various as Tennyson, Mill, Sidgwick, Martineau, and Huxley.

Tennyson's lines on Ward have been often quoted to show the admiration and respect felt toward him even by his theological and philosophical opponents:

> How subtle at tierce and quart of mind with mind,
> How loyal in the following of thy Lord.

Martineau remarked how often, in spite of theological and temperamental disagreement with Ward, he found himself "on the same bench" with him. Whatever his position, he was able to demand for it an intellectual respect which Manning was apparently rarely able to earn for his, even though Ward, too, became one of the most rigorous and unrelenting upholders of extreme ultramontane views. R. H. Hutton tells us that "no man in the Society was more universally liked. The clearness, force, and candour of his argument made his papers welcome to all." Of this very paper on "Memory" Hutton reports that it "fell like a bombshell among the antagonists of intuitive certainty" and was received with "dismay" by the supporters of the experience school.[29] However

28 For bibliographical note and the attendance at this meeting, see App. C.

29 "William George Ward" (1882), in *Criticisms of Contemporary Thought and Thinkers*, 2 vols., London, Macmillan, 1894.

surprising to us the reaction which Hutton noted, it is important as showing how unaccustomed was the scientific school to any questioning of its fundamental assumptions.

Ward had not been present at the previous meeting and had therefore perhaps intentionally missed Huxley's attack on immortality. He had, however, heard Hutton's and Carpenter's papers and had almost certainly heard about Huxley's. In any case he knew the direction which the discussions of the young Society were taking. Ward continues to accept the opposition between the intuitional and experiential, the "spiritualistic" and the materialistic, which was not only dominant in the minds of the founders of the Society, but which had been so clearly drawn in the three previous meetings. He points out that "some philosophical differences are of detail; others of principle; others again of *fundamental* principle: while the most fundamental of *all* philosophical issues is undoubtedly that which is raised so vigorously at the present day, by those whom we may call empirists or phenomenists, against those whom we may call intuitionists."

The former insist that all knowledge is derived from experience, the latter "that phenomenism lays its axe at the root, not only of all philosophy, but of all religion and morality; that it issues legitimately in depriving life of every highest blessing for which life should be valued." It is obvious where Ward's own sympathies lie, especially when he goes on to say: "One cannot be surprised—however one may regret—that a certain asperity of tone is not unfrequently found in this controversy; and I venture to think that phenomenists sometimes do not sufficiently remember, when they are wounded by this asperity, how appalling is the calamity with which we consider them to threaten us." There is a gay arrogance in this reprimand which was a match for Huxley's own.

Ward constructs an ingenious argument, in which he asserts that if a phenomenist were to conclude that even *one* solitary truth was cognizable by the mind alone and was in no sense deducible from experience, this would reconcile him with the intuitionists, since it could no longer be said that he differed from them on a matter of *fundamental* principle. He goes on to establish the opposite contentions of both schools: that the "phenomenists" admit no a priori faculties except what may be called the "experiential," while the intuitionists, admitting these, maintain that man possesses "intuitive" faculties also, "which furnish him with primary premisses of their own."

After an elaborate analysis of intuitive and empirical truths, in which his debt to Hume and the Scottish philosophers is implicit, Ward is content to press a subtle and disturbing paradox: To doubt the trustworthiness of an experiential faculty is a contradiction in terms. It is no contradiction in terms to suppose that man's *memory* may deceive him. Therefore, memory is no experiential faculty and is an intuitive faculty. Since phenomenists are dependent upon the trustworthiness of memory, this argument is a *reductio ad absurdum* of their doctrine. Phenomenists must therefore prove *by present experience*, Ward insists, that man's memory of past experience can be trusted, even though Mill in his *Examination of Sir William Hamilton's Philosophy* (to which Ward refers) admits that no such proof can possibly be given.

The astonishing conclusion to which this argument leads (and which Ward of course entirely ignores) is that the surest test of what to Ward are "intuitive truths" is their fallibility in human experience. That scientists should make errors owing to the inaccuracy of their senses, including what may in a large sense be called the use of their memory, does not seem as damaging or significant an admission as Ward's that we have no way of being sure of the truth of our "intuitive" assumptions except by our "intuitive" conviction of their value. Hume would merely have insisted that the only test of our memory, which to him is itself an experience, is its reinforcement and justification in further experience of sequence and repeated sequence. When Huxley quoted Hume as saying that revelation, not logic, was the only "proof" of immortality, he meant that only revelation could promise man a demonstration of what no man has yet experienced in this world of thought and discourse.

Ward's paper is very persuasive at first glance and of course deals with one of the most perennially difficult aspects of the epistemological problem. He was presumably able to meet criticisms of the argument with better examples, more clearly drawn, but it is questionable whether he had enough knowledge of the scientific method to be an adequate critic of the part played by "memory" in experimental observation or in the formulation of experience. His interest is clearly more in the logical aspects of the argument than in the psychological problem of the nature of memory. We may be sure that men like Huxley, Carpenter, and even the doctor and mystic James Hinton were not slow to point this out. The paper is, however, interesting as a partial reply to Huxley and important to the Society in its contention that one of the principal presuppositions of the scientific school was also subject to criticism and in need of closer examination.

The nature and limitations of the Society's discussions can be clearly seen in these first meetings. Later papers were more important in their influence and, through republication in periodicals, initiated or contributed to wider controversies. A few became minor classics of polemical literature: papers like Bagehot's "On the Emotion of Conviction" and "The Metaphysical Basis of Toleration"; W. K. Clifford's "On the Scientific Basis of Morals" and "The Ethics of Belief"; Ruskin's "The Nature and Authority of Miracle"; and Sidgwick's "Incoherence of Empirical Philosophy." Others, like F. D. Maurice's paper, "On the Words 'Nature,' 'Natural,' and 'Supernatural,'" and Father Dalgairns' "The Personality of God," deserve to be better known than they are. But to single these papers out for particular attention would not show the Society's most characteristic activity, however much they would reveal its literary achievement. For the Society stuck amazingly close to its metaphysical interests and departed very little from its original purposes. The deep seriousness with which this varied group of men of many professions and widely opposed convictions discussed these seemingly abstract questions which they, however, considered central to an understanding of the meaning of human life, constitutes the chief interest of the Society, even to us who are more than willing to leave the examination of such questions to professional theologians, philosophers, or specialists in scientific method. That they, with learning, wit, and passion, could devote themselves to such discussions, is perhaps one explanation of the astonishing moral and intellectual power which we are beginning once more to recognize as the special greatness of the Victorian era.

A Typical Meeting: Hutton's "Reminiscence"

Hutton's first paper had set the tone and temper which were to prevail in all the discussions of the new Society. His own concern with the moral and intellectual implications of religious faith was paralleled by a wide curiosity about the influence of the new discoveries in biology and psychology on the problems of belief and the sanctions of morality. These interests were shared, in large measure, by all the members, whether intuitionists or empiricists. Hutton himself continued throughout the history of the Society to be one of its most faithful and most active members. Five years after its dissolution he contributed to the *Nineteenth Century* a brilliant essay, "The Metaphysical Society: a Reminiscence," [30] in which he reconstructs a typical meeting of the Society, using as the core of his dramatic synthesis the meeting of December 10, 1872, when W. G. Ward read a paper entitled, "Can Experience Prove the Uniformity of Nature?"

By bringing together on this occasion a number of the most eminent members [31] in discussion of one of the most cogent attacks on the presuppositions of the empirical school, Hutton is able to give an engaging and convincing picture of an actual session of the Society in all the variety of its give-and-take among minds. He quotes and paraphrases Ward's paper with notable fidelity, but not until he has drawn a clear picture of the meeting itself, with deft portraits of the personalities present.

"The dinner itself was lively." We read of Huxley "flashing out a sceptical defense of the use of the Bible in Board Schools at

[30] As published in the *Nineteenth Century,* XVIII (August, 1885), 177–96, this reminiscence is preceded by a brief account of the history of the Society, a list of its members, and a selection of titles from the subjects discussed, by the editor, James Knowles. The historical details of this note are used elsewhere in the present volume. Its final words, however, are interesting and relevant: "The subjoined article, kindly volunteered by Mr. Hutton, was suggested by him, not as a portrait of any actual meeting, but as a reminiscence of the sort of debate which used to go on. Its faithfulness is remarkable, except for the omission of his own valuable part in the discussion."

[31] We have no other record of the attendance at this meeting.

one end of the table," while Fitzjames Stephen's [32] "deep bass remarks on the Claimant's adroit use of his committal for perjury" are heard at the other. Ward himself chuckles "with a little malicious satisfaction over the floundering of the orthodox clergy" in their criticism of Dean Stanley's latitudinarianism. We see Father Dalgairns, "a man of singular sweetness and openness of character, with something of a French type of playfulness in his expression," who is discoursing eloquently to Hutton "on the noble ethical character of George Eliot's novels, and the penetrating disbelief in all but human excellence by which they are pervaded." [33] He seemed to convey "that nowhere but in the Roman Church could you find any real breakwater against an incredulity which could survive even the aspirations of so noble a nature as hers." Meanwhile we hear "the sound of Professor Tyndall's eloquent Irish voice descanting on the proposal for a 'prayer-gauge,' which had lately been made in the *Contemporary Review*, by testing the efficacy of prayer on a selected hospital ward." [34]

Hutton himself is very deeply impressed by "the marked difference between the expression of the Roman Catholic members of our Society and all the others."

> No men could be more different amongst themselves than Dr. Ward and Father Dalgairns and Archbishop Manning, all of them converts to the Roman Church. But, nevertheless, all had upon them that curious stamp of definite spiritual authority, which I have never noticed on any faces but those of Roman Catholics, and of Roman Catholics who have passed through a pretty long period of subjection to the authority they acknowledge.[35] In the Metaphysical Society itself there was every type of

[32] Stephen did not actually become a member until 1873.

[33] George Eliot's *Middlemarch* had just been published in book form. F. W. H. Myers records a conversation with George Eliot, as they walked in the Fellows' Garden of Trinity, in which she, taking as text "the three words which have been used so often as the inspiring trumpet-calls of men,—the words *God, Immortality, Duty,*—pronounced with terrible earnestness, how inconceivable was the *first,* how unbelievable the *second,* and yet how peremptory and absolute the *third.* Never, perhaps, had sterner accents affirmed the sovereignty of impersonal and unrecompensing law."—John Morley, "The Life of George Eliot," in *Critical Miscellanies* (*The Works of Lord Morley,* VI), London, Macmillan, 1921, p. 208.

[34] See pp. 177–80 for a fuller commentary on this amazing proposal.

[35] James Martineau, in a letter to a friend who had been converted to Catholicism, speaks in a similar vein of the impression made on him by the Catholic members of the Metaphysical Society, with whom he had "much intimate intercourse, and on whose side [he] almost always found [himself] in the discussions"

spiritual and moral expression. The wistful and sanguine, I had almost said hectic idealism, of James Hinton struck me much more than anything he contrived to convey by his remarks. The noble and steadfast, but somewhat melancholy faith, which seemed to be sculptured on Dr. Martineau's massive brow, shaded off into wistfulness in the glance of his eyes. Professor Huxley, who always had a definite standard for every question which he regarded as discussable at all, yet made you feel that his slender definite creed in no respect represented the cravings of his large nature. Professor Tyndall's eloquent addresses frequently culminated with some pathetic indication of the mystery which to him surrounded the moral life. Mr. Fitzjames Stephen's gigantic force, expended generally in some work of iconoclasm, always gave me the impression that he was revenging himself on what he could not believe, for the disappointment he had felt in not being able to retain the beliefs of his youth. But in the countenances of our Roman Catholic members there was no wistfulness,—rather an expression which I might almost describe as a blending of grateful humility with involuntary satiety—genuine humility, genuine thankfulness for the authority on which they anchored themselves; but something also of a feeling of the redundance of that authority, and of the redundance of those provisions for their spiritual life of which almost all our other members seemed to feel that they had but a bare and scanty pasturage.

W. G. Ward, the speaker of the evening, was one of the earliest of the Oxford converts to Catholicism. A friend and early disciple of Newman, he represented the best in the intellectual tradition of English Catholicism. He had since become one of the strongest supporters of the ultramontane position and one of the most important theological advisers to Manning. His own long exchange of arguments with Mill had many reflections in the meetings of the Society. Hutton says of him:

He was one of the very best and most active members of our Society, as long as his health lasted—most friendly to everybody, though full of amazement at the depth to which scepticism had undermined the creed of many amongst us. A more candid man I never knew. He never ignored a difficulty, and never attempted to express an indistinct idea. His metaphysics were as sharp cut as crystals. He never seemed to see the half-

of the Society. He adds, however, that he has not observed, in the practical effects on character, "any superiority, in force or elevation, in the Catholic type, either of populations in the mass or of individual excellence." (James Drummond and C. B. Upton, *The Life and Letters of James Martineau,* 2 vols., New York, Dodd, Mead, 1902, II, 206–7.)

lights of a question at all. There was no penumbra in his mind; or, at least, what he could not grasp clearly, he treated as if he could not apprehend at all.

Hutton goes on to describe the session:

When dinner was over and the cloth removed a waiter entered with sheets of foolscap and pens for each of the members, of which very little use was made. The ascetic Archbishop of Westminster [Manning], every nerve in his face expressive of some vivid feeling, entered, and was quickly followed by Dr. Martineau. Then came Mr. Hinton, glancing around the room with a modest half-humorous furtiveness, as he seated himself amongst us. Then Dr. Ward began his paper. He asked how mere experience could prove a universal truth without examining in detail every plausibly asserted exception to that truth, and disproving the reality of the exception. He asked whether those who believe most fervently in the uniformity of Nature ever show the slightest anxiety to examine asserted exceptions. He imagined, he said, that what impresses physicists is the fruitfulness of inductive science, with the reasonable inference that inductive science could not be the fruitful field of discovery it is, unless it rested on a legitimate basis, which basis could be no other than a principle of uniformity. Dr. Ward answered that the belief in genuine exceptions to the law of uniform phenomenal antecedents and consequents, does not in the least degree invalidate this assumption of the general uniformity of Nature, if these exceptions are announced, as in the case of miracles they always must be, as demonstrating the interposition of some spiritual power which is not phenomenal, between the antecedent and its natural consequent,—which interposition it is that alone interrupts the order of phenomenal antecedence and consequence. "Suppose," he said, that "every Englishman, in invoking St. Thomas of Canterbury, could put his hand into the fire without injury. Why, the very fact that in order to avoid injury he must invoke the saint's name, would ever keep fresh and firm in his mind the conviction that fire does naturally burn. He would therefore as unquestioningly in all his physical researches assume this to *be* [36] the natural property of fire, as though God had never wrought a miracle at all. In fact, from the very circumstances of the case, it is always one of the most indubitable laws of nature which a miracle [overrides],[37] and those who wish most to magnify the miracle, are led by that very fact to dwell with special urgency on the otherwise universal prevalence of the law." [38]

36 Italicized in the original paper, but not in Hutton's version.

37 The word in the original is "overrules."

38 Ward had also given the following example, interesting in the light of the later discussion: Let us suppose that "when I enter my laboratory to make [a] desired experiment, I find a venerable man seated. He announces himself as com-

After a short pause the discussion is begun by Huxley, "who broke off short in a very graphic sketch he had been making on his sheet of foolscap as he listened." Hutton, in reconstructing the debate, does not hesitate to draw on earlier and later papers by the participating members, as well as his own wide knowledge of their published work. Huxley, in his turn, insisted that:

> Men of science were too busy in their fruitful vocation to hunt up the true explanation of cases of [asserted] miracle, complicated as they generally were with all sorts of violent prepossessions and confusing emotions. He, for his part, did not pretend that the physical uniformity of Nature could be absolutely proved. He was content to know that his "working hypothesis" had been proved to be invaluable by the test of innumerable discoveries, which could never have been made had not that working hypothesis been assumed. . . .

The man of science, however, "who commits himself to even one statement which turns out to be devoid of good foundation, loses somewhat of his reputation among his fellows, and if he is guilty of the same error often he loses not only his intellectual but his moral standing among them; for it is justly felt that errors of this kind have their root rather in the moral than in the intellectual nature." That, I suppose, is the

missioned by God to deliver me some authoritative message. 'And now,' he adds, 'I will give you proof that He sent me. You know, by experiment, that the substance in your hand is naturally combustible; but now place it in the same fire, or in one a thousand times fiercer, and it shall remain unscathed.' If I find the fact to be so, I shall indeed have extremely strong ground for believing my visitor divinely commissioned; but I shall have no ground whatever for doubting that substance is naturally combustible. Nay, my conviction of this fact will be strengthened. For my visitor assumed that it was *naturally* combustible, by the very fact of treating its non-combustion as a *miracle.* And the same answer may be made, however numerous may be the miracles wrought."

Sir Mountstuart Grant Duff, also a member of the Metaphysical Society, records a very interestingly relevant conversation with the scientist Lyon Playfair in 1878. "Apropos of the Algerian conjurors, who apply hot metal to their bodies without suffering, [Playfair] explained to us that, if only the metal is sufficiently hot, this can be done with perfect security; and told an amusing story of how, when the Prince of Wales was studying under him in Edinburgh, he had, after taking the precaution to make him wash his hands in ammonia, to get rid of any grease that might be on them, said, 'Now, sir, if you have faith in science, you will plunge your right hand into that cauldron of boiling lead, and ladle it out into the cold water which is standing by.' 'Are you serious?' asked the pupil. 'Perfectly,' was the reply. 'If you tell me to do it, I will,' said the Prince. 'I do tell you,' rejoined Playfair, and the Prince ladled out the burning liquid with perfect impunity" (Sir Mountstuart E. Grant Duff, *Notes from a Diary, 1873–1881,* 2 vols., London, Murray, 1898, II, 26–7). I have not myself tried the experiment.

reason why men of science are so chary of investigating the trustworthiness of the *soi-disant* miracles to which Dr. Ward is so anxious that we should pay an attention much greater than any which in my opinion they deserve. For the scientific man justly fears that if he investigates them thoroughly, he shall wound many amiable men's hearts, and that if he does not wound amiable men's hearts he shall compromise his own character as a man of science.

Huxley's "rich and resonant voice" is succeeded by Father Dalgairns', who began "in tones of great sweetness." He reproaches Huxley for his "working hypothesis" in the terms of Ward's earlier critique of "the irrefragible trustworthiness of memory": [39]

"When I say 'I believe in God,' I use the word believe just as I use it when I say 'I believe in moral obligation'; and when I say 'I believe in moral obligation,' I use the word believe just as I do when I say 'I believe in the attestations of memory.' 'God is not necessary only to my conception of morality. His existence is necessary to the existence of obligation.' I know God by 'a combination of intuition and experience, which is Kant's condition of knowledge. If there be a God, our imagination would present Him to us as inflicting pain on the violator of His law, and lo! the imagination turns out to be an [experienced] fact. The Unknowable suddenly stabs me to the heart.' I believe in the uniformity of Nature only in the sense in which I believe in every other high probability—for instance, only in the sense in which I believe that the sun will rise tomorrow. I believe in God in the sense in which I believe in pain and pleasure, in space and time, in right and wrong, in myself, in that which curbs me, governs me, besets me behind and before, and lays its hand upon me. The uniformity of Nature, though a very useful working hypothesis, is, as Professor Huxley admits, unproved and unproveable as a final truth of reason. But 'if I do not know God, then I know nothing whatsoever,' for if 'the pillared pavement is rottenness,' then surely also is 'earth's base built on stubble.' " [40]

"There was a certain perceptible reluctance to follow Father Dalgairns," Hutton goes on to say, "which lasted some couple of minutes. Then we heard a deep-toned, musical voice, which dwelt with slow emphasis on the most important words of each sentence,

39 "On Memory as an Intuitive Faculty" (No. 4; December 15, 1869), which was also an attack on Huxley.

40 The quotations are from Father Dalgairns' eloquent paper, "Is God Unknowable?" (No. 27; June 11, 1872). The word "experienced," in this passage, is "experimental" in the original paper.

and which gave a singular force to the irony with which the speaker's expressions of belief were freely mingled. It was Mr. Ruskin."[41]

He insists that, "If a second Joshua tomorrow commanded the sun to stand still, and it obeyed him, and he therefore claimed deference as a miracle-worker, I am afraid I should answer 'What! a miracle that the sun stands still?—not at all. I was always expecting it would. The only wonder to me was its going on.'" He thinks it "the province of some one of our scientific members to lay down for us the true principle by which we may distinguish the miraculous violation of a known law from the natural discovery of an unknown one."

When Ruskin had ceased, "Walter Bagehot, the then editor of the *Economist*, and a favourite amongst us for his literary brilliance, opened his wide black eyes, and, gulping down what seemed to be an inclination to laugh at some recollection of his own," took up the discussion:[42]

> "I believe it will be found that nothing is more difficult than to beat into the majority of minds the belief that there is such a thing as a 'law of nature' at all. So far as I can judge, nine women out of ten have never adequately realised what a law of nature means, nor is the proportion much smaller for men, unless they have been well drilled in some department of physics. Of course, I heartily agree with Dr. Ward that experience cannot *prove* the uniformity of Nature, and for this very good reason, amongst others, that it is impossible to say what the uniformity of Nature means. . . .
>
> "We ought to engage what I have ventured in this Society to call the 'emotion of conviction,' the caprices of which are so extravagant and so dangerous, much more seriously on the side of the uniformity of Nature than we have ever hitherto done. We should all try to distinguish more carefully than we do between possibility, probability, and certainty. . . .
>
> "I certainly cannot agree with Mr. Ruskin that I have always been 'expecting' the sun to stand still. Probably as a child I was always expecting things quite as improbable as that. But if I expected them now I should not have profited as much by the disillusioning character of my experience as I endeavour to hope that I actually have."

41 Ruskin's discussion is based on his paper, "The Nature and Authority of Miracle" (No. 32; February 11, 1873), an avowed continuation of the question discussed by Ward at this December, 1872, meeting.

42 Bagehot's remarks are derived from his paper, "On the Emotion of Conviction" (No. 12; December 13, 1870).

A general smile followed Bagehot's remarks, but this smile disappeared when Fitzjames Stephen began "in the mighty bass that always exerted a sort of physical authority over us." [43] His careful logical analysis of the presumptions in any acceptance of the ordinary evidences of miracle, closes with a sceptical assertion:

"The restoration of a dead body to life might, if it occurred, be proved as conclusively and as notoriously as the death of a living person, or the birth of a child. If such events formed a real class to which new occurrences might be assigned, a large number of instances of those occurrences would be, so to speak, upon record, established beyond all doubt, and the very existence of the controversy shows that nothing of the sort exists."

Archbishop Manning next took up the debate, "looking at Mr. Stephen with a benign smile": [44]

"Mr. Stephen's investigations into the evidence of the interference of unseen agents in human affairs are hardly on a par with some of those undertaken by the Church to which I belong. In canonising, or even beatifying those who are lost to us, the Holy See has long been accustomed to go into the evidence of such events as those to which Mr.

[43] Stephen's discussion as rendered by Hutton is based on and puts together four separate quotations from Fitzjames Stephen's paper, "Remarks on the Proof of Miracles" (No. 56; November 9, 1875). The skill with which Hutton has made a single reply out of these diverse parts of the original paper, and without changing a single word, is a beautiful indication of his editorial ability.

[44] Hutton makes here no direct quotations from any of Manning's six papers read before the Society. I am convinced that Hutton was unwilling to involve the Cardinal in the necessity of defending any quoted statements which might have given a pretext to his enemies for theological and ecclesiastical attack. Many Catholics, including Newman, were shocked that Manning was willing to sit down to a discussion of philosophical and theological questions with the group which Lord Odo Russell (English ambassador to Rome and Lord Arthur Russell's brother) had nicknamed "the Atheists." And Manning himself, owing to his position, may have insisted that Hutton respect the rule of secrecy which it had originally been agreed could be invoked in regard to the Society's debates. Nevertheless, Manning's remarks as here presented are entirely in accord with the tone and temper of the papers which he read, particularly his papers, "That Legitimate Authority is an Evidence of Truth" (No. 26; May 14, 1872) and "The Soul before and after Death" (No. 65; February 13, 1877), the latter of which was delivered the month following one by Frederic Harrison, the positivist, on the same subject. Even the many Latin quotations and the references to St. Thomas Aquinas and the Schoolmen are characteristic of the Archbishop's manner in these two papers. His deference to Ward at the end of his discussion of the question is, I think, Hutton's way of giving expression to the widespread rumor that Ward, although a layman, was often Manning's mentor in theological questions.

Stephen has just referred, and that with a disposition to pick holes in the evidence, which, if he will allow me to say so, could hardly be surpassed even by so able a sifter of evidence as Mr. Stephen himself."

Manning continues with an instance of the well-authenticated miraculous cure of a case of varicose veins, effected in one night by the believing application of Lourdes water to the sufferer. "Here is a case where all Mr. Fitzjames Stephen's conditions are satisfied to the full." But he turns from this example to the original question—"the impossibility of proving the uniformity of Nature from experience alone." Here he falls back on Aquinas and his *Summa*, which he quotes extensively, pronouncing "his Latin in the Continental manner." The burden of his argument is that "the uniformity of Nature is based upon the wisdom of God, and the wisdom of God is manifested in the uniformity of Nature."

Manning is followed by Dr. Martineau, "speaking with a singularly perfect elocution, and giving to all his consonants that distinct sound which is so rare in conversational speech":

"I think that the course of this discussion has as yet hardly done justice to the *a priori* elements in human thought which have contributed to the discovery of the general uniformity of Nature, and to the axiomatic character of the principle which we are discussing. I should not entirely agree with the archbishop or with St. Thomas, if I rightly apprehended the quotations from him, that we ought to ground our belief in the uniformity of Nature *primarily* on our belief in the constancy of the Divine mind. Historically, I doubt whether that could be maintained. For example, the Hebrew Scriptures, which are full of the praise of the moral constancy of the Creator, appear to attach very little importance to the uniformity of Nature's methods, which they often treat as if they were as pliant as language itself to the formative thought behind it. Still less can I agree with Mr. Bagehot's view that everything which rushes into the mind is believed without hesitation till hard experience scourges us into scepticism. I should say rather that the understanding is prepared to accept uniform laws of causation by the very character of human reason itself.[45] . . .

"The uniformity of Nature is the uniformity of force, just as the uniformity of reasoning is the uniformity of thought. But just as the indeterminateness of creative will stands behind the determinateness of

[45] Martineau's discussion is based on two passages from his paper, "The Supposed Conflict between Efficient and Final Causation" (No. 67; April 17, 1877).

the orbit of force, so the indeterminateness of creative purpose stands behind the determinateness of the orbit of thought or inference. I hold that man is not wholly immersed in dynamic laws, that though our physical constitution is subject to them, our mental constitution rises above them into a world where free self-determination is possible. I do not wonder, therefore, that we find it difficult to realise the rigidity of the laws of efficient causation even so far as it would be good for us to realise them. . . .

"But it is one thing to see the evidence of spiritual influence in every page of human history, and quite another to attach importance to such preternatural occurrences as the Archbishop has recently referred to, which are usually so mixed up with superstitions of all kinds, and so great a variety of hysterical emotions, that I for one should despair of any good result from investigating minutely these curious conquests effected by pretentious physical marvels over the gaping intellectual credulity of moral coldness and disbelief."

"Here the general discussion ended," says Hutton, "but Dr. Ward, who had the right of reply, exercised it with alertness and vigour." He cannot see how the fact that Divine interference in the chain of physical causation "is more or less mixed up" with what Dr. Martineau "would regard as superstition and hysterical emotion," justifies us in leaving such matters uninvestigated. Ward argues:

"Surely the whole character of modern civilisation would be altered if we could prove satisfactorily for ordinary minds that the Divine will is a true cause, which manifests itself habitually to those who humbly receive the Divine revelations. Is not Dr. Newman's celebrated assertion that England would be in a far more hopeful condition if it were far more superstitious, more bigoted, more disposed to quail beneath the stings of conscience, and to do penance for its sins, than it is, at least plausible for one who, like Dr. Martineau, believes profoundly that the true worship of a righteous will is the highest end of all human life? . . .

"If God is really ruling you, is it not better to feel His eye upon you, even though you show your sense of that vigilance unreasonably and foolishly, than to live on very much as you would do, if, as Isaiah said, God were on a journey or had gone to sleep? Can any one deny that any awakening, however rude its consequences, to the reality of Divine power, would be infinitely better than the rapidly growing habit of living as if behind Nature there were no God? . . .

"Is it not better to have a vulgar belief in God, than to have a fine susceptibility to scientific methods? Is it not better to have a feverish longing to do His will, than to have a delicate distaste for morbid devotion?"

Ward ends his rebuttal, which Hutton modestly permits to end his "Reminiscence," with the assertion that "The uniformity of Nature is the veil behind which, in these latter days, God is hidden from us." But he believes in that uniformity "far more fervently as the background on which miracle is displayed" than "merely as the fertile instrument of scientific discovery and of physical amelioration."

The skill with which Hutton has reconstructed a typical meeting of the Metaphysical Society manifests the very kind of temperamental restraint and dialectical ingenuity which was cultivated by the Society itself. For Hutton thus dramatized the views of eight representative members in a discussion typical of the whole of the Society's intellectual history. Ward's paper, "Can Experience Prove the Uniformity of Nature?" clearly poses the issue between the intuitionist and experience schools, which Manning later calls "the scholastic and the modern family of metaphysicians"—those "who take their point of departure from the intuitions of the Reason," and "those who take their point of departure from the reports of Sense." Relevant to this discussion are the related questions to which the Society devoted itself steadily: the problem of authority, the grounds of evidence, and the psychology of belief. The eight papers from which Hutton quotes are each concerned with a different aspect of this continuing argument and are chosen from papers read at different times during seven of the eleven years of the Society's history. Here is a selection of opinion from the years of the Society's greatest success; for after 1877 the Society entered upon its decline. Hutton's editorial ability and dramatic skill have given us an account which, whatever liberties it may take with literal history, gives a true picture of the Society in all its freshness and vitality.

Chapter 5

THE CRUCIAL PAPERS

THE THREE PERIODS in the life of the Metaphysical Society have logical and philosophical significance as well as psychological and historical meaning. Twice during the more than eleven years of meetings, papers were read and discussions undertaken whose purpose was to appraise the past accomplishments of the Society and to attempt a redirection of its intellectual activity. The fullest treatment of the Society would require an analysis of all ninety-five papers read before it,[1] but since this is manifestly impossible in a single volume, an effort must be made to characterize its achievement by an extended analysis of the three periods into which its history, in consequence of these moments of appraisal and reconsideration, naturally falls. The papers read on these occasions, as well as their reflections in the later discussions of the Society, have thus every claim to be considered crucial. And although not all of these papers show the Society at its best, they are indeed representative. For they manifest not only the failure of the members to establish or maintain a single universe of discourse, but also the gradual recognition of an inevitable pluralism.

"A Diagnosis and a Prescription"

The first period ends dramatically with Manning's paper, "A Diagnosis and a Prescription" (No. 36; June 10, 1873). This was clearly intended to change the course of the Society's discussions, something which it equally clearly failed to do. But the first act of this metaphysical drama, during which all the Idols of the

[1] This I have already attempted, in a series of paraphrases of *all* the papers, which it is unfortunately impossible to reproduce here. A critical edition of the Papers of the Metaphysical Society is obviously needed, a project which I hope one day to undertake.

Theatre were often worshiped and sometimes examined and criticized, finds its natural climax in Manning's own account of the pretext and spirit of his paper:

It is my painful duty as Chairman to announce that the Metaphysical Society has been visited by symptoms of aphonia. It will make no utterance to-night. Whether or no any symptoms of ataxia have also appeared, whether the members of the body have refused to fulfil their office or not, I have not as yet learned; but for the first time after four years of unintermittent speech, it has suddenly become inarticulate. Had I known the impending danger in time, I for one would have endeavoured to avert that catastrophe; but I learned it too late to apply any stimulants, or to attempt any paper which could be offered to the Society as a thesis for discussion.

Nevertheless, as I am officially bound to announce our disaster, I have laid the fact before you. What I would therefore endeavour to do, is to turn this syncope in our proceedings to some use; and I think it may be made useful if we take a retrospect of the course the Society has thus far pursued, and note any points which need to be amended or supplied.

The Society was avowedly founded with a view to bring together the most various and even opposite schools of metaphysical thought; that is to say, the old and the new, the scholastic and the modern family of metaphysicians, who have multiplied and ramified into endless variations. All, however, may be reduced to two ultimate schools, namely, to those who take their point of departure from the intuitions of the Reason, and to those who take their point of departure from the reports of Sense.

For four years we have met and conversed, sometimes have contended, with great freedom of speech, perfect frankness, unfailing courtesy, and a kindliness which has never been for a moment overcast.

It has been, I think, a good thing that minds so scattered in the search and service of Truth, and moving in paths so incalculable by one another, should have met together and heard each other's speech. If nothing beyond this had resulted from the Metaphysical Society, it would have been alone a result of no light value. But it has done more. The relations of kindness, respect, and friendship, which have sprung up among the Members of the Society, will not be easily dissolved.[2]

2 "But more even than this has been attained," he goes on to say and gives a list of all the Papers so far read before the Society (for the first time establishing the correct numbering). These will, he thinks, "show that the Society has verified its intentions." It is interesting and perhaps important to note that out of the thirty-five titles given, he makes errors in the citation of fifteen, four of the latter seriously changing the meaning both of title and paper. Of all but one of the papers wrongly cited, he must have had (or could have obtained) printed copies. He also makes two errors in referring to authors, calling Sidgwick "Sedg-

With these words Manning paid his tribute to the values of the Society's past and turned his attention to criticism and the problems of its future. As chairman for the year, he felt a special responsibility when he undertook to make this "diagnosis and prescription." For he spoke not only as chairman but inevitably also as a Catholic Archbishop and as one of the most influential figures at the Vatican Council of 1870 which had decreed the dogma of Papal Infallibility. He could have little hope of converting the members of the Society to Catholicism, but he had every motive for desiring to urge upon it a greater Catholicity. Because of the critical as well as historical value of his analysis, it is here reproduced in full:

Three things may be chiefly noted as wanting in our discussions; and it is most desirable, for our better mutual understanding, and I may say, for the progress of metaphysical speculations, so far as we can affect them, that these three wants should be, as far as in us lies, supplied:—

1. The first want of which we must all have been conscious is that of a fixed and accepted Terminology. We have profusely employed the terms substance, matter, cause, law, motive, faith, evidence, authority, life, death, natural, supernatural, freedom, will, agent, personality, soul, right, wrong, morality, conscience, God; but I believe that we should find that the mental equivalents in many of us would have been found widely various, sometimes actually contradictory and exclusive of one another. In the Scholastic Philosophy a terminology ancient and traditional, which underwent a constant refinement and correction, excluded to a great extent equivocation and ambiguity, and fixed to a great extent the positive meaning of terms. So long as the Latin language continued to be the language of science, both Metaphysics and Physics had an universal and ascertained terminology.[3] The breaking-up of this language of the Commonwealth of Science has opened a thousand ways to misconception, and I cannot but believe that a very large part of the Metaphysics of the last centuries has been a logomachy arising from the confusion of tongues. In our last Paper some remarks were made on the tendency of Science to form a terminology apart from common speech. This seems to be an inevitable law. Common speech is at least

wick" and Greg "Gray." It is of course possible that these were printer's errors, owing to difficulty in following his manuscript. But the printing of all the papers is otherwise remarkably free from misprints of any kind.

[3] This seems very questionable. Manning implies a universality in the connotations of the language of scholastic thinking which is clearly not borne out by the history of either early Christian or medieval philosophy.

only approximately definite. Accurate processes of thought record themselves in accurate terms, and purify the terms of ambiguity in the process of appropriation. We have not as yet, it seems to me, if my ears have heard aright, and if I have rightly understood what I have heard, attained to such a mutually intelligible and fixed terminology. But this want springs from one which is deeper.

2. The second want I would note, is that of a Common Method.[4] Where there is no common method, there can hardly be a common terminology. Of the terms enumerated above, many are to certain metaphysical schools idols, non-entities, metaphysical superstitions. It is not surprising if they cease to retain the same mental equivalents in those who believe them to exist, and in those who disbelieve their existence. It is not indeed physically impossible that they should do so, but it is morally certain that in the long run they will not.

Now, we have been conscious throughout our discussions that two opposite methods were face to face: the one which, whether true or false, has been in possession throughout the intellectual history and system of the world,—that, I mean, which takes its starting-point from the Reason and its intuitions, and that which confines the reason within the circle and reports of Sense. In the former method there are truths anterior to those of sense; more certain than the reports of sense; higher, nobler, more human, more divine. I would take as an exhibition of this method the *Summa contra Gentiles* of St. Thomas Aquinas, in which he starts from the intellectual demonstration of the existence and nature of God, and from thence goes on to the nature of the soul, of the human reason, will, and conscience; to the intrinsic contrariety of right and wrong, and the like. This method, I have said, is at least in possession.[5] It pervades the ancient world. It has guided the philosophy of the Christian world; it is the basis of the Scholastic philosophy, and of all mental science derived from it. All science founded upon sense is accessory to it, and interpreted by it. Without it man would be "as trees walking,"—that is,

[4] The purpose of many of the members of the Society, in their papers, seems on the other hand to have been to ascertain the language and the method proper to various branches of human knowledge, in pursuit of the Aristotelian maxim of determining the method and the degree of certainty possible to each. Although "metaphysics" was the subject matter of the Society to many, it is clear from the history of its founding that the name of the Society was arrived at by a kind of compromise, and that its purpose, in bringing together theologians and scientists, was on the whole more what A. N. Whitehead would call "cosmological" than "metaphysical."

[5] The papers read before the Society, as well as much of the history of modern thought since the eighteenth century, would seem to cast considerable doubt on this contention that the scholastic philosophy was "in possession," even in the England of the 1870s. Many readers will note how much the assertions and purposes of our modern Neo-Thomists are in accord with Manning's position.

physical organisations less by a head than the true stature of man. To such as hold this method, the procedure of those who deny it seems to be a mutilation of our nature. To make sense our starting-point, if it be to deny this higher method, is to limit our knowledge to that of which sense is the channel. The axiom *Nihil in intellectu quod non prius in sensu,* if taken as it sounds, denies the whole region of intellectual and intuitional truth as to our rational nature, with all its knowledge anterior to sense and independent of it. I am more certain that there is a God than that any particular report of my senses is accurate. If there be no God, no soul, no will, no conscience, no intrinsic right and wrong, then I must go on to affirm that there is no reason in man; there may be a faculty developed from the instincts of a lower animal, but that is not the human reason, which is the fountain, if it be not the factor, of human speech. This *differentia* of man from all other creatures is ineffaceable in his nature. It is a frontier which cannot be obliterated. It marks him off from all other animals. Man and the lower creatures are indeed one kingdom of God, but man is the king of all the creatures by a right of birth, and nature, and inheritance, which does not ascend from below, but descends from above. Such I understand to be the one method which has been present in our discussions.

The other I will now endeavour as fairly and as justly as I can to describe. It admits that the method I have described is in possession, that it is ancient and wide-spread. But it affirms that it is the theology of human childhood and the superstition of our unscientific manhood. The scientific reason, we are told by Positivists, is that which interprets the reports of sense within the sphere of sense. Facts and phenomena are alone the proper matter of Science. Such metaphysical conceptions as law, cause, and the like, are mental figments. This method seems to be pursued by two kinds of reasoners. The one kind is consequent, thorough-going, and consistent. They deny the existence of all truths which do not reach us through the reports of Sense. We have no report of sense for the existence of the soul, of conscience, or of God. Our physical organisation is all we know. Thought, volition, feeling spring from it, and are its properties. Sense is the channel, the test, the measure of truth in their philosophy; as reason is the source, the test, and the measure of all truth to a rationalist. *De non apparentibus, et de non existentibus, eadem est ratio.* They say they do not and cannot know this no-man's-land of intuitions. The more guarded of this school are content with this *agnosis.*[6] The less guarded deny the existence of that which they cannot prove, that is, they know that what they cannot know does not exist.[7]

[6] Harrison, Huxley, and perhaps Tyndall.

[7] Robertson, J. Stephen, Clifford (but not yet a member), and perhaps Pattison.

The other kind is of more moderate opinions. It admits the facts of our internal consciousness in respect to thought and will, but ascribes them to physical causes.[8] They admit the intrinsic distinction of right and wrong, and the conscience or discernment of moral duty, but appear to deny or to doubt the existence of the independent spiritual soul, in which thought, feeling, and will reside, because the physical organisation gives no evidence of it, and the physical organisation is alone the subject of the Senses.

Now it is clear that they who hold methods so diverse and opposed can hardly find common ground from which to start, and so far as this method exists among us—and I hope that I have not misrepresented it, and I believe that it does exist among us—we have a patent reason why our discussions should often have resembled railroads on different levels. We have seemed to be in contact, but under conditions which rendered it impossible for us to meet.

We have, however, arrived, I think, at one point of approximation. The Psychologists [9] among us have fully admitted the help which may be derived from physiology. I am not so sure that the Physiologists [10] have, in like manner, admitted the need they have of psychology. According to Professor Max Müller, Mr. Herbert Spencer has affirmed that there are in us physical changes parallel to, but not identical with the actions of thought, or that our states of nervous action may be parallel, but never identical with a state of consciousness. (*Fraser's Magazine*, May, 1873, p. 528.) This would satisfy the most ardent psychologist, who would not hesitate to admit any simultaneous modification of the brain, so long as that modification is not affirmed to be identical with thought. The thought is the act of the thinker, and the brain is the thinker's brain, but it is not the thinker himself. This is to beg the whole question. And the tradition of the whole world in its childhood, if you will, and in its metaphysical virility, gives one answer.

It would seem to me, of course, that the true reconciliation of Psychology and Physiology is to be found not in the school of Idealism like that of Berkeley, nor in the school of Sense, like that of Hume, but in the Scholastic Philosophy alone. Nevertheless, as an approximation of this result, and as a cobble-stone in the gulf between us, I would put in Professor Max Müller's account of the philosophy of Kant. I take for granted that he had all the conditions necessary to understand his own countryman. He ought to know the meaning of Kant. Professor Max Müller then says that the world-wide struggle of philosophy may be described as a conflict "for the primacy between mind and matter"; that

[8] Among these "moderates" we can perhaps number Bagehot, Carpenter, Froude, Hinton, Hodgson, Knowles, Noel, and Sidgwick.

[9] Robertson, Bucknill, Noel, and perhaps Sidgwick and Fraser.

[10] Carpenter, Huxley, and in a way Tyndall.

in the middle of the last century, as in the middle of this, the materialistic view had gained the upper hand. "Never, perhaps, in the whole history of Philosophy did the pendulum of Philosophic thought swing so violently as in the middle of the eighteenth century, from one extreme to the other, from Berkeley to Hume." "What secures for Kant his position in the history of Philosophy is that he brought the battle back to that point where alone it could be decided." "He wrote the whole of his Criticism of Pure Reason with constant reference to Berkeley and Hume." "It has been sometimes supposed that the rapid success of Kant's philosophy was due to its being a philosophy of compromise, neither spiritualistic, like Berkeley's, nor materialistic, like Hume's. I look upon Kant's philosophy not as a compromise, but as a reconciliation of spiritualism and materialism, or rather of idealism and realism." "Kant demonstrates that we are not merely passive recipients; that the conception of a purely passive recipient involves, in fact, an absurdity: *that what is given us we accept on our own terms.*" "If anything is to be seen, or heard, or felt, or known by us, such as we are,—and I suppose we are something,—if all is not to end with disturbances of the retina, or vibrations of the tympanum, or ringing of the bells at the receiving-stations of the brain, then what is to be perceived by *us* must submit to the conditions of *our* perceiving, what is to be known by *us* must accept the conditions of *our* knowing." This law Kant draws out into the twelve categories or inevitable forms of thought. "Put in the shortest way, I should say," says Professor Max Müller, "that the result of Kant's analysis of the categories of the understanding is, *Nihil est in sensu quod non fuerit in intellectu.* We cannot perceive any object except by the aid of the intellect. Turning against the one-sided course of Hume's philosophy, Kant shows that there is something in our intellect which could never have been supplied by mere sensations; turning against Berkeley, he shows that there is something in our sensations which could never have been supplied by mere intellect." Professor Max Müller says that all our phenomena become "perceptions of a human self." (*Fraser's Magazine,* May, 1873, pp. 531–9.) It would be more correct to say there is something in our knowledge resting upon sensations which could not have been derived from sense; or, as Leibnitz puts it, *Nihil in intellectu quod non prius in sensu, nisi ipse intellectus.* The receiver is intelligent, or an intelligence who judges, discerns, predicates, and knows. And from this position nothing has yet dislodged the intellectual system of the world: Within this entrenched camp it abides these six thousand years unmoved; covered, perhaps, at times by volumes of smoke, but when the clouds are dispersed it remains in possession. I would put this in the words of Bishop Berkeley. Euphranor says: "By the person Alciphron is meant an individual thinking thing; and not the colour, skin, or visible surface, or any part of the outward form, colour, or shape of Alciphron." Alciphron answers: "This I grant." Euphranor: "And in granting this, you grant that, in a strict sense, I do not see Alciphron, *i.e.*, that invisible thinking thing." This argument he transfers at once to prove the existence of God. (*Berkeley's Works,* Vol. II, p. 145, ed. Fraser.) But perhaps some one may say that the Bishop did not believe in souls except as ideas. If so, I will fall back upon Cicero, who, in the Tusculan Disputations, says: "Nos non sumus corpora nostra; nec hoc dico corpori tuo, sed tibi."

This sound and primeval philosophy has been well laid down by Whewell in the Aphorisms prefixed to his *Philosophy of the Inductive Sciences* [Vol. I, p. xviii] :—

"APHORISMS CONCERNING IDEAS

"I. Man is the interpreter of Nature, Science the right interpretation.

"II. The *Senses* place before us the *Characters* of the Book of Nature; but these convey no knowledge to us, till we have discovered the Alphabet by which they are to be read.

"III. The Alphabet, by means of which we interpret Phenomena, consists of the Ideas existing in our own minds; for these give to the phenomena that coherence and significance which are not objects of sense.

"IV. The antithesis of *Sense* and *Ideas* is the foundation of the Philosophy of Science. No knowledge can exist without the union, no philosophy without the separation, of these two elements.

"V. *Fact* and *Theory* correspond to Sense on the one hand, and to Ideas on the other, so far as we are *conscious* of our Ideas: but all facts involve ideas *unconsciously;* and thus the distinction of Facts and Theories is not tenable, as that of Sense and Ideas is.

"VI. Sensations and Ideas in our knowledge are like Matter and Form in bodies. Matter cannot exist without form, nor form without matter: yet the two are altogether distinct and opposite. There is no possibility either of separating or of confounding them. The same is the case with Sensations and Ideas.

"VII. Ideas are not *trans*formed, but *in*formed Sensations; for without ideas sensations have no form.

"VIII. The Sensations are the *Objective,* the Ideas the *Subjective* part of every act of perception or knowledge."

And this position of Whewell is, after all, only a disinterring of the Scholastic Philosophy, fragrant as fresh earth. It is St. Thomas Aquinas in a Cambridge gown. The proposition that the soul is the form of the body gives ample scope for the two-fold phenomena of Psychology and of Physiology, which I must take leave to say cannot be otherwise accounted for. If the Scholastic Philosophy had never been disintegrated;

if the two elements of reason and of sense, which are the conditions of all knowledge in the human subject, had not been violently sundered,[11] and after their separation falsified by exclusive theories of the opposing schools of intuition and of sense, a great part of our discussions would have been impossible.

We have not yet come to a common theory as to the origin and conditions of human knowledge; it is not wonderful, therefore, that we want both a common method and a common terminology.

3. And this leads to the third want I have to note, namely, the want of definition which has marked our Papers and our discussions. Of the thirty-five Papers which have been read, hardly any bear as their title a definite proposition;[12] almost all bear titles indefinite as to their purport. The definite have either affirmed or denied some predicate. They have been expressed in a definite proposition, and the subject and predicate of that proposition have been more or less defined. The indefinite Papers have, at least, been so far useful that they have raised a general discussion around and about many subjects which have elicited propositions in debate, but have left nothing permanent on record.[13]

The following are the only definitions[14] which our vigilant and diligent Secretary has been able to register:—

FAITH

Archbishop Manning.—"That rational act of the intellect which, after finding sufficient evidence that a thing is revealed—believing it to be true—refuses to doubt it any more."

Duke of Argyll.—"An assured belief or conviction, but with different degrees of assurance."

Professor Huxley.—"The surest and strongest conviction you can have."

Father Dalgairns.—"Reason always makes a reserve—is open to conviction on further evidence. Faith, on the contrary, refuses to make any reserve—no additional evidence can shake it."

WILL

Archbishop Manning.—"A rational appetite."

Professor Huxley.—"The desire of an act of our own."

[11] By Descartes as much as anyone.

[12] This is verbally correct, but at least fifteen of the papers have titles which imply true propositions, and all of these and most of the others make clear their propositional form in the papers themselves.

[13] Manning makes no mention here that one paper often called forth another, as we have seen in the previous chapter. Nor does he take into consideration that seventeen of the first thirty-five papers were published, often in an expanded or revised form, in the *Contemporary Review* and other periodicals.

[14] Most of these "definitions" do not appear in the printed papers and can be assumed to have been offered and recorded during the discussions.

Mr. Hutton.—"The power we have of increasing or diminishing the force of our own motives."

Mr. Sidgwick.—"The *Ego* conscious of itself or acting."

Mr. Hodgson.—"Sense of effort for a purpose."

Professor Robertson.—"Action for feeling."

Dr. Carpenter.—"Purposive determinative effort."

Mr. Knowles.—"The resultant of motives."

Mr. Hinton.—"Necessity."

In reading them over we cannot fail to perceive by what wide intervals of space we are separated.[15] But it is necessary that we should ascertain our distances as the first condition of approach. Unless we know where we are, and in what relation to each other, we can not only never take aim, but we can never shake hands. I would, therefore, propose to the Members of the Society that we should pass a resolution, or an order of the house, which may be called "a self-denying ordinance": namely, that every Paper shall have a definite thesis, in the form of an affirmative or negative proposition; and that, before the writer enter upon his exposition, he shall first define the sense of both subject and predicate, and of any terms he is about to employ. In this way we shall not only save ourselves from much ambiguity and misconception, but we shall greatly enlarge the probability that by our discussions we may at least approximate to a common terminology and to a common method; if not to a common acceptance of the same Philosophical axioms, and to a commonwealth of the same Philosophical Truth.

It is at least doubtful whether Manning's "prescription" was accepted in its entirety by many members of the Society. As Purcell says of Manning, "He had not imagination sufficient to enter into the feelings or position of his Agnostic opponents, nor grasp of mind nor depth of thought to enable him to perceive the subtilties of their argument, nor the ultimate dividing lines which rendered intellectual agreement impossible." [16] This charge could well be leveled against many other members of the Society, even the agnostics themselves in their attitude toward the Christians and

15 The modern reader is unlikely to see between these brief definitions as here stated the "wideness of the intervals" separating them of which Manning speaks. But the papers themselves, in all their variety, do seem to justify Manning's statement in considerable measure.

16 E. S. Purcell, *Life of Cardinal Manning,* 2 vols., London, Macmillan, 1896, II, 514. But Purcell shows elsewhere in passages from Manning's notebooks (II, 772–92), what charity and understanding this rigorous and political mind could feel toward all forms of English Christianity and especially toward the Church of his youth and early manhood.

theists, but Manning did seem to deliver his pronouncement of the lines dividing the Society in a manner so *ex cathedra* that many members may well have taken umbrage not at the fact but the manner of his own certainty. It is clear that of the three "wants" which he found in the proceedings of the Society—want of a fixed and accepted terminology, want of a common method, and want of logical definition and precision—only the last could be expected to arouse recognition and agreement from the entire membership. As we have seen in the preceding chapter, this had in fact been the constant effort of several important members. But it was indeed unlikely that the Society could accept either the scholastic terminology or the scholastic method, and it was even more unlikely that anything less or more would have satisfied Manning. A terminology developed to present the appearance of agreement would only have made more sharp and "disagreeable" the fundamental personal and psychological differences among the members. And the formulation of a common method would have little meaning without an agreement on ends and purposes, something manifestly impossible between, for example, Manning and Huxley.[17] But there is always room for greater precision in thought and language, however much the impulse to a perfect precision inevitably leads either to a technical jargon (the private speech of experts),[18] or to a philosophy of metaphor (the "science" of semantics) often equally private, whether used by poet or metaphysician.

The need for greater precision in logic and definition had, as we have seen, been felt by many. But whether the statement of questions in propositional form is necessarily the way to a greater agreement on what is truth, may be legitimately doubted by any one who has had experience of a college debating society. Certainly Mill, who had had much youthful experience in debate, came himself to feel that whatever truth is, it is more various and yet more ineluctable than the forms of the syllogism. And J. Fitzjames Stephen, one of the great barristers of his day, never used

[17] We have seen modern instances of both these difficulties in the history of Marxist thought and politics since the Russian Revolution (and even earlier).

[18] As G. Croom Robertson clearly admits in his paper, "The Action of So-Called Motives" (No. 35; May 13, 1873).

the strict propositional form in any of his six papers read before the Metaphysical Society. Manning's counsel on this point, had it been followed, would probably have greatly reduced both the interest and the effectiveness of the Society's discussions. Had every paper been presented as an affirmative or negative proposition, with its subject and predicate defined and its terminology reduced to axiom or definition, it is difficult to see how any discussion could have gone far beyond a quibbling over personal presuppositions. Of the latter there were plenty, no doubt, but the temper of the Society showed a firm desire to transcend these limitations. Manning, unlike Newman, was perhaps emotionally unable to understand Pascal's famous aphorism, "Le coeur a ses raisons que la raison ne connaît point"; (it was Manning, after all, who had defined Faith as a "rational act of the intellect"); but his mind was certainly subtle enough to see the complexity of the pun, partly lost in English translation. In this paradox lies the secret of Manning's rigor toward the method of the Society's proceedings. However, what both intuitionists and empiricists, theists and agnostics sensed in common as the burden of Pascal's words is what founded the Society and kept it together for nearly eleven years.[19] And certainly by far the greater part of the Society's efforts was directed toward a fuller understanding of Pascal's "reasons of the heart."

Certain it is that no serious attempt was made to establish either a common terminology or a common method in the future discussions of the Society. Furthermore, only one of the fifty-eight future papers of the Society was presented in strict propositional form,[20] although eight were phrased as questions with their propositional intent more or less clearly implied. Thus far did the members ignore Manning's "prescription." However, his appeal for a greater attention to the problems of definition seems to have borne fruit. For although there was no specially prepared paper [21] at the next meeting in July, the last meeting of the So-

19 Bagehot's paper, "On the Emotion of Conviction" (No. 12; December 13, 1870), is relevant to this question.

20 Ruskin's ironic paper, "Theorem: Social Policy Must be Based on the Scientific Principle of Natural Selection" (No. 53; May 11, 1875).

21 A paper by Hutton, "Euthanasia" (No. 37a), was reprinted from the *Spectator,* and Ellicott read an "Oral Communication on Euthanasia" (No. 37b).

ciety's year, future papers reveal that a "Committee on Definition[s]" was established early in the autumn of the new year. I have been unable to find out who were its members or anything about its workings, except an occasional reference to its existence in the papers and the fact that on March 12, 1878, it submitted a report to the Society which was never printed.

Manning's paper, however, and the committee to which it gave birth influenced the Society for a long time to come. James Hinton, in his first paper of the new year,[22] begins—with what may be an ironic reference to Manning's attitude—by defining as closely as he can several points "on which it is not intended at present to solicit discussion." Sidgwick begins his next paper [23] with the statement, "In writing the present paper, it has been my object to avoid all but incontrovertible propositions." Russell in the next paper [24] begins by saying, "The distinction between the Understanding and Reason has long been recognized among Metaphysicians," and adds, in the second paragraph, "In its pursuit of Truth, the mind can only be guided by its own method (logic), and can acknowledge the authority of no other method." Some or all of these instances may well have been accidents of language, but there is no doubt about Bagehot's meaning when he says in his paper on "The Metaphysical Basis of Toleration," [25] "That I may not be subject to a censure from our Committee on Definition, I should say that, except when it is explained to the contrary, I use the word 'toleration' to mean toleration by law."

How this Committee functioned, and whether it did have the power of censure which Bagehot gaily imputes to it, I do not, as I have said, know. Very significantly, however, Mark Pattison's paper on "Double Truth" [26] was followed by the report of the Committee on Definitions on March 12, 1878, thus dramatizing the end of the second period. At the next meeting Matthew Boulton's paper, "Has a Metaphysical Society any *Raison d'être*," [27] marks the beginning of the final period, for in spite of Boulton's

[22] "On the Relation of the Organic and Inorganic Worlds" (No. 38; November 18, 1873).

[23] "Utilitarianism" (No. 39; December 16, 1873).

[24] "The Speculative Method" (No. 40; January 13, 1874).

[25] No. 41; February 10, 1874.

[26] No. 74; February 12, 1878.

[27] No. 75; April 9, 1878.

affirmative answer to his own question the Society thereafter entered upon its decline. Some of the most distinguished members resigned or ceased active participation, and the Society began to lose its representative quality. The nature of this change remains to be examined, but it is interesting to note that the consistent carrying out of the one element in Manning's "prescription" which the members had adopted seems to have eventually sounded the death-knell of the Society. The Committee may have done its work inadequately, or it may have functioned all too well; the facts remain. The Committee may itself have convinced the members that "only the fundamentals themselves remained in debate" and that in consequence "there was nothing left to be done." [28] If true, this would indeed be an ironic commentary on Manning's "prescription." For even if Manning himself had little hope that the Society would attain to "a commonwealth of the same Philosophical Truth," it is in the sense in which the Society was, at its best, a Philosophical Commonwealth that it still holds interest for us today. And in a Philosophical Commonwealth the "fundamentals" will always be in dispute.

Manning's "prescription" was no doubt a counsel of perfection, for its purpose seems to have been to bring the angels so beloved by the scholastic philosophy to closer grips with the devils of empiricism, materialism, and agnosticism. And since the angels are by definition victorious, in both the legendary and philosophic sense, the struggle was bound to be either unequal or factitious. Shane Leslie has remarked, changing the metaphor, that "the Metaphysical Society was a memorable effort of the Titans to entertain the Olympians to tea, but the Rhadamanthine politeness necessary proved too great a strain, and it died because, as Tennyson said, no one could define the word metaphysics." [29] Leslie does not make clear which were the older and which the younger gods; but of the politeness, so unlike anything the poets have told us of Olympus, there is no question. The necessity of an Homeric courtesy did not prove as great a strain as the effort to define

28 Leonard Huxley's words.

29 Shane Leslie, *Henry Edward Manning*, London, Burns, Oates, and Washbourne, 1921, p. 324.

metaphysics in such a way that its language and realm of discourse could bridge the gulf between Tartarus and Ida, or between the obedient and the fallen angels. Milton, too, was perplexed by this dilemma.

Manning's "diagnosis," however, is precise and cogent, revealing once more what most of the early papers insisted, that the gulf which needed bridging was that between intuitionists and empiricists, a gulf which widened and narrowed under shifting clouds, and sometimes looked very much like what many of us would call the gulf between idealism and naturalism. Manning's use of Kant as a bridge was probably salutary; he has been so used many times, before and since, and in fact so regarded his achievement himself. But the noumena of Kant's philosophy have always seemed too transcendental to most empiricists and other critics of idealism. His critique of time and space and the categories, however, has proved as useful to the naturalists as to the idealists, and Manning was perhaps more right than he knew when he summoned him from the vasty deep to build a bridge through Chaos.

The chaos that Manning saw and felt had its own melody, which swelled in regular diapason through the next five years of the Society's history, in spite of all efforts to bring it into harmony with the music of the spheres. It insisted on being a human, not angelic, chorus, and in the end Gabriel and Raphael were as responsible as the devil and his advocates for driving the Society from Eden. The members continued to savor the fruit which Manning thought forbidden, and in the pluralism of means offered by their varied personalities and professions continued to assert that pluralism of ends which is perhaps the secret of the highest human wisdom.

"Double Truth"

The period which had begun with a Catholic appeal for a return to the scholastic philosophy ended with a sceptical analysis of the morality of discourse based on the pre-scholastic teaching of a Mohammedan Aristotelian, Averroes. On February 12, 1878, Mark Pattison read a notable paper on "Double Truth" (No. 74). Like his first paper, "The Arguments for a Future Life" (No. 25;

April 9, 1872), it is a characteristic reflection of his complexly personal and ambiguously sceptical mind.

In Homer's admonition (Achilles to Odysseus, *Iliad,* ix, 312, 313),

> Who dares think one thing and another tell,
> My soul detests him as the gates of hell,[30]

Pattison sees "one of the earliest generalisations of social obligation, recognised in the dawn of civilisation, and losing none of its validity in the most developed stages." For "on the assumption that (1) we endeavour to see things as they are, and (2) to convey in words exactly what it is we see, all human intercourse rests. A contract to speak the truth is implied in the use of language." But Pattison finds some not inconsiderable limitations to this obligation. The moral law *is* frequently violated in practice, and men *will* lie to each other, but this is not what he means. There are, however, "many cases in which it is not possible to put in practice the intention to be true. If the nature of language implies a contract to be true, the imperfection of language for some purposes makes it impossible to fulfil the contract."

Moral treatises abound in exceptions to the rule of veracity—in social dealings, in promises extorted by fear, in a physician's treatment of his patient, and in others, most of which perhaps come under the head of reticence. "I must not say what I do not think, but I need not say all I think. . . . *Caveat emptor* is the ultimate axiom of market law. . . . You may not state [in a prospectus] that oil-wells in Canada produce 100,000 gallons a day, if they do not do so; but in offering an oil-well for sale to the public, you need not state that a new well has been opened at a lower level than yours, which has drained yours dry."

But passing from business dealings to human intercourse, "we find that *suppressio veri* has a much wider scope. Hardly ever can we find one to whom we can say *all* we think. Life is a search for sympathy, and an unsatisfied search. '*Je mourrai seul!*' Pascal's cry of despair, is echoed by how many of us! And prudent

30 Pattison gives the Greek, and quotes Pope's translation. In Walter Leaf's prose version the lines read: "For hateful to me even as the gates of hell is he that hideth one thing in his heart and uttereth another."

discourse is nothing more than knowing what to keep back from him with whom we talk." This kind of withholding is only "a small part of the deduction we must make from the rule of truth. We say a part of what we mean, and suppress more." Much of this is owing to the inadequacy of language. "Words are the names of things, or of our relations to things. When I name a thing, the thing is there, and the meaning of the word is ascertained by direct reference. But when I try to use these same words as class-names, and when I pass from particular to universal propositions, I have to make the assumption that my hearer will mean by the word exactly what I do myself. Every general proposition involves a hypothesis. . . . When I use a general term, I am tendering a coin of which I can never know at what value it has been taken by receiver."

This is even more true when the terms are attempted generalizations of feelings, "of my relations with things." There is a gulf here between the educated and the uneducated, the cultivated and the uncultivated. "That words may serve the purpose of being the common measure of emotion, the understanding of the words must be reciprocal. Education is a dissociating force, which tends to destroy this reciprocity." Inevitable as this is, "the majority of mankind have always deeply resented the assumption of superiority by the few. Oligarchical power is not so odious as exclusive intellect." No writer today who desired influence would dare to assert the "double truth" in the terms used by Averroes. Pattison himself only ventures "to bring forward this law of language under the protection of a privileged sheet."

"Accommodated speech," or the means of communication between the few and the many, "takes in ordinary conversation the shape called irony, or chaff, or *esprit.* In its simpler forms it is almost as widely used as speech itself. All wit is the conveyance of a thought or emotion in words which literally taken are untrue. . . . How soul-killing is that intercourse in which more is not meant than meets the ear!"

As we ascend to more subtle and spiritual regions of thought and emotion we discover whole spheres of perception in which words, as names of things, become very inadequate means of expression. Two such spheres are Poetry and Religion. But even in poetry the confusion with fact is being made every day; "the greatest statesman of our times persists in reading the 'Iliad' and 'Odyssey,' and I believe, Aeschylus's 'Agamemnon,' as if they were narratives of real events." In religious questions the problem is eternally present. "God" is a general term. To combine the ideal with the historical has been the difficulty of all religions. "In periods in which the religious consciousness has been active, the historic element has tended to vanish in favour of the ideal." In the thirteenth century there was a reaction against the pressure of the hierarchy enforcing dogma, which took the form of asserting the "double truth": true in philosophy, false in theology. "Modern philosophy traces its origin to the thirteenth century, and grew up under the shelter of the doctrine of the double truth"; and Descartes successfully availed himself of "this shield against clerical despotism," although he was accused of a pardonable cowardice.

However, modern philosophy has repudiated the doctrine of the double truth, under the protection of which it "sprang into being." The doctrine may reappear as an *obiter dictum* of Lessing, or in Kant's antithesis of the phenomenal and noumenal worlds, but philosophers of all schools seem now "agreed to maintain that truth is uniform." The "argumentative proof of the being of a God is much in fashion, or, which is the same thing, it is assumed there is none, because reason finds the proof wanting. George Sand indeed knew better,—'Je sentis que la foi s'emparait de moi . . . par le coeur.' Yet though the homogeneity of truth is a postulate of modern philosophy, the modern mind repudiates the surest ground of this homogeneity, viz., the unity of the rational soul, a tenet of the Aristotelian school which was held by Averroes, who, to complete the circle of paradox, was the philosopher who introduced into the West the doctrine of the 'Double Truth.'"

There was a fine irony in Pattison's paper, for in its implications it was as much a commentary on the Society's history as Manning's "Diagnosis and Prescription" of five years before. "True in philosophy, false in theology," the doctrine of the "double truth," however little either theists or agnostics would admit its validity, seems in fact to have been the conclusion forced upon the members by the debates of the Society. Pattison was thus also engaged in diagnosis, and if he was constitutionally unable to render a prescription, the Society itself was not, by this time, much better able to prescribe for itself.

Ever since Manning's effort to persuade the Society to accept the scholastic terminology, or at least to restrict its speculations by the adoption of a stricter system of definitions—an effort which, as we have seen, in large measure failed—the natural politeness of the earlier days had gradually given way to a more formal politeness, the ironic courtesy of friendly antagonists to a colder courtesy, sometimes not far from asperity or sarcasm. And ever since Huxley's paper, "The Evidence of the Miracle of the Resurrection" (No. 58; January 11, 1876), the anguish of the Christian theists at what they conceived to be the arrogance of the scientists and materialists was reflected more than once in the papers and discussions of the Society. Sometimes it is not quite clear which of the parties to the debate is more on the defensive, but it is certain that the Society, during this second period, however vigorous intellectually and polemically, slowly gave up hope of effecting a philosophic reconciliation of theologians and scientists, intuitionists and empiricists. Men like J. Fitzjames Stephen and W. K. Clifford, who became members during this second period, now delighted in argumentative combat with Hutton and the Anglican bishops, with Ward, Dalgairns, and Manning among the Catholics. Carpenter continued in his mediating role, and Huxley, who was chairman for two years from 1875 to 1877, unquestionably kept the discussions of the papers at a high level of discursive analysis and witty repartee, even if not always of disinterested logical and philosophical objectivity.

But these had been vital and exciting years, the debates intense and various, the personal predispositions and presuppositions of the members more and more explicit. In these papers of the second period we are more conscious of men as "thinking reeds" and less of men as thinking machines. However deeply concerned whether men are or are not automata, the members speak and write like creatures of flesh and blood as well as of mind and spirit. The essential pluralism of human ends was brought more and more into the open, and it would be callow as well as ungenerous and pretentious for us of the twentieth century to be harshly critical of these men's increasing inability to accept more willingly a pluralism of means. The greatest "souls" among them, men like Bagehot, Hinton, Hutton, and Sidgwick, achieved more of this kind of wisdom than many moderns; and Harrison, whatever his private delusions about the future of Positivism as a religion for humanity, maintained in the Society, as throughout his life, a spirited balance between thought and feeling. Even Clifford, who died of tuberculosis in 1879 at the age of 33 would, in the opinion of many, have outgrown the rather febrile dogmatism of his psycho-physical materialism to become a worthy supporter of the tradition of his friend and correspondent William James, a tradition to which Shadworth Hodgson had already contributed much. When Mivart asked, more than a little ironically, "What is the good of Truth?" Pattison could reply, in all the fatigue of his learning and from the depths of a heart-felt scepticism which had almost paralyzed his will, that truth was at least double and probably multifarious.

The report of the Committee on Definitions, which was presented at the meeting of March 12, 1878, marks a second turning-point in the history of the Society. It was never printed, but it is clear from references to this meeting in Matthew Boulton's paper, "Has a Metaphysical Society any *Raison d'être?*" (No. 75), which he read at the next meeting, that serious questions were raised, not primarily of definition, but of the nature, scope, and purpose of the Society. The Committee may have attempted to define metaphysics, but we do not know whether their recommendation was to restrict the discussions more narrowly, in a technical philosophical sense, or to continue and perhaps even expand the wider interests which had been implicit in the Society's purposes from the beginning.

Whatever the terms of the report and whatever the action taken by the members upon it, the succeeding nineteen papers of the Society show no marked departure in subject matter from the papers previously read. As we have already seen, from this time on there was a falling off of many of the older and more eminent members, particularly of the scientists and those whose personal interests were not primarily theological or metaphysical; but we do not know whether this was owing to any suggestions made or recommendations accepted at this apparently crucial meeting. It seems likely that some effort was made to rule out certain subjects which had been either exhausted in previous discussions or which had led to passionately irreconcilable differences of opinion, for there are no more papers on belief and evidence, miracles, or Christian theism, while there is perhaps an increase in concern with ethics and psychology and a greater number of technical philosophical papers.

These tendencies, however, may have been the result of the defection of certain members as much as the cause of their loss of interest in the Society. It has already been remarked how the foundation of the *Nineteenth Century* by Knowles, in 1877, seems to have been one of the forces drawing many of the members out of the private forum of the Society into the more public forum of journalistic debate. (This and related influences are examined in more detail in Chapter X.) But it is important to note that men like John Morley, Leslie Stephen, and Frederick Pollock, who became members in these later years, never had a very high opinion of the Society and are in fact the only members who ever spoke of it with anything but enthusiasm or admiration. Morley speaks of its "bad metaphysics"; Leslie Stephen felt that the debaters "did not know what they were talking about," and that "four out of five of its members knew nothing of metaphysics"; and Sir John Pollock has written me that his father, who succeeded Knowles as secretary and officiated at its funeral, was of like opinion.

However, these men all belong to the next generation, and it is a legitimate question whether their attitude toward the Society does not in itself illustrate the change which was coming over the tone and temper of English intellectual life. Leslie Stephen says that the talk of the Society was that of amateurs, not specialists; but the increasing relegation of a serious and impassioned concern with philosophical problems to specialists and professors is surely one of the great differences between the mid-Victorian period and our own. Certainly Stephen's criticisms are all the more remarkable in view of the fact that chief among the older members of the Society who continued an active interest to the very end were the professional philosophers, Sidgwick, Hodgson, Martineau, Croom Robertson, and Upton, as well as the "semi-professionals," Harrison, Hutton, Noel, and Leslie Stephen himself. When the Society finally died, none but these "professionals" were left, and while the older great had already found their field of influence and activity widened by the *Nineteenth Century*, these survivors continued their metaphysical debates in the pages of Croom Robertson's periodical, *Mind*, or in Hodgson's thoroughly technical Aristotelian Society.[31] However, the great majority of the members of the Society never regarded themselves as professional philosophers engaged in professional activity, but rather as thinking men, engaged in discussing the major problems of the human mind and spirit.

As we turn to the years of the Society's decline, we must be conscious of the forces which were breaking up this short-lived philosophical commonwealth, and not the least of these is the growing victory of the new orthodoxy of science over the old orthodoxy of faith. As each dogma, the old and the new, retreated to its own province, it left behind its surviving ambassadors, the professional philosophers, who felt that they held the secret to the best of both worlds: that logic could find in science but one dogma—method, and that philosophy in its various branches could extract from the dogmas of religion and the whole of philosophical tradition all that was truly vital to ethics, the theory of value, and the nature of being. But even the new contributions to these problems became more and more specialized, and "man thinking" turned away from philosophical discourse to the more available public expressions of politics, the novel, and art.

The Metaphysical Society is thus itself a symbol of the last

31 See Chaps. XI and XII.

great effort of the European mind to find a universe of discourse. We, too, have hopes once more that mankind may find a common ground of understanding, and in our search the history of the Society can teach us much. Perhaps we have an even greater need than the Victorians for the kind of heterodoxy which recognizes both the empirical usefulness and intuitive necessity of intellectual and spiritual argument and disagreement among men. Only when men have given up discussion do they take to arms. The sanction for compromise among men lies not only in respect for the individual, but in acceptance of a pluralism of values, whether in religion, philosophy, economics, or politics.

"*Has a Metaphysical Society any* Raison d'être?"

The report of the Committee on Definitions had apparently raised the question of the value and continued usefulness of the Society's debates and discussions. If no common agreement on fundamentals were possible and no system of philosophical definitions acceptable, was the Society doomed to the repeated assertion of individual positions which had become articles of faith? If the primary assumptions of many members were held so strongly by what Bagehot had called "the emotion of conviction" that they were no longer susceptible to criticism, was it profitable or even possible to carry on the purposes for which the Society had been founded? Knowles said that the Society finally came to an end "because, after twelve years of debating, there seemed little to be said which had not already been repeated more than once"; however true this may be of the history of the Society, it is no less true of the whole of human history. Man thinking continues to raise old problems, but in new formulations, colored by new and changing experience, he strives to find new solutions. Nevertheless, men often reach with age personal and intellectual beliefs which are rigorously inexpugnable, and so, too, it seems to be with the history of institutions. The Society had now reached middle age and its social and intellectual arteries were hardening in such a way that the flow and circulation of ideas on which it depended for its vitality were at last seriously impeded. Although a cure is difficult in such circumstances, the wise physician will look for a means of mitigating the condition, and it is to this possibility that the next paper read before the Society was addressed.

Matthew Boulton, in his only paper, invited his fellow-members to consider the question, "Has a Metaphysical Society any *Raison d'être?*" (No. 75; April 9, 1878). At the previous meeting, apparently in the discussion of the report of the Committee on Definitions or perhaps in the report itself, both Huxley and Lord Selborne, the chairman for the year, had denied that the question of the existence of the Deity, or the nature of the Cause of the Universe was, properly speaking, a metaphysical question. In this they impugned the language of Kant, who asserted that the three principal topics of metaphysical inquiry were the existence of God, the immortality of the soul, and the freedom of the will. Huxley had further stated that in his opinion the question of the nature of the Cause of the Universe does not lie outside the limits of experience, here again disagreeing with Kant. To Huxley the questions named by Kant concern φύσις, or Nature, and therefore are physical. Boulton agrees with this, if "physics" be taken in a wide sense to include everything that exists, but adds that by the same token these questions could be termed "physiological." "From such premises it might seem to follow (and the inference has, in fact, been drawn) that a Metaphysical Society has no *raison d'être.* But before coming to this conclusion and breaking up our Society, let us consider the matter a little further."

Grant Duff had propounded another definition of Metaphysics: "Ingenious speculations concerning matters not yet fully cognisable." Boulton is willing also to accept this definition, with the omission of the complimentary word "ingenious." This includes Kant's definition while demanding from Huxley the admission that however empirically the nature of the Cause of the Universe may be examined it is not fully cognizable, and that even if it be phenomenon, that it "has certainly a capacity of hiding itself." In fact, wherever we look, in many fields of both knowledge and experience, we are constantly being faced by "speculations about matters not fully cognisable." The science of Cosmogony, or speculation about the evolution of the universe, is widely cultivated, but it is obvious that our knowledge of this matter is far from full. And the question of the origin of species is not a matter at present fully cognisable, "for we do not know whether the existing species of animals are traceable up to one act of Biogenesis, or to a great number of such acts. Nay, we do not even know whether Biogenesis takes place in the present day, or whether it ceased millions of years ago." Comte denounced such inquiries as unscientific—as lacking positivity—and "unless we are very tolerant of Metaphysics, in Mr. Grant Duff's sense of the word, we should have to do the same," for theories on these subjects fall far short of certainty. Yet Boulton would not agree with Comte in desiring to see them silenced. It seems to him "that conjectures have different degrees of value, and that in some cases the degree is high. If we tolerate only what is absolutely certain, and entirely banish the probable and conjectural, how much of our so-called 'science' will remain?"

A further example is afforded by the relation of the idea of Force to the doctrine of the conservation of Energy, a subject to which Mivart had devoted a paper [32] the previous year. This doctrine claims to be eminently scientific, and yet a teacher of this doctrine can scarcely attempt to define this "Force" except in the most metaphorical terms. Similarly, however positive the science of Dynamics or Mechanics, the concept of Mass, which involves the idea of Force, presents difficulties fully as great as the concept of Force itself. And if the movement of molecules produces thoughts and emotions, we are obliged to assign some mass to these molecules, and here again our powers of understanding fail us. Sometimes we are taught that thoughts and emotions are modes of matter, that nothing exists which is not material, but then matter is merely "our old friend Substance, a noumenon or phenomenon of very unphenomenal kind, a *nescio quid substans.*" If we believe that our material organism is causal or active, but that our thoughts are not so, "that changes in our organism cause thoughts, but thoughts cannot act on our organism," we must ask what is the nature of the causal power or activity which this doctrine

[32] "Matter and Force" (No. 68; May 8, 1877).

ascribes to one sort or class of phenomena, while it denies it to others? "It is needless to insist on the difficulties of this question; it suffices to refer to Hume." The word Law, applied to the movements of apples or comets gives us "no more insight into the nature of things than when we are informed that these movements take place in virtue of the *force* of attraction." Thus, if Grant Duff's definition be correct, "we find that we encounter Metaphysics at every turn,—that we can no more escape from Metaphysics than we can get out of our skins, or jump over our shadows."

But Boulton does not find Grant Duff's definition really sufficient, for many kinds of speculation about matters not fully cognizable—such as where Caesar crossed the Channel, or Hannibal the Alps—are clearly not metaphysical. However, the difficulties he has noted about Force, Activity, Law, Cause, Matter, Substance he considers rightly called Metaphysical. "Such a discussion concerns φύσις, or Nature; but it is carried on by an exercise of the speculative faculty, which is not needed or brought into play in Physics of the more practical and ordinary kind."

Boulton turns to an examination of what Aristotle meant by "metaphysics," and explains the relation of the *Physics*, devoted to a description of phenomena, to the second work, the *Metaphysics*, concerned with knowledge of a more difficult and higher kind—a knowledge which aspires to know causes, principles, and elements. "Naturally, he placed this work *after* the less speculative treatises; he could not in reason have placed it before them." Hence, arose the word "Metaphysical." "It is a waste of time to propound definitions of Metaphysic which do not in the least suit the character of Aristotle's treatise," for his work is clearly physical, and in its scope "more physical than his earlier ones, though doubtless it may be thought that he has not successfully achieved his aim." But Boulton considers it most important to correct the view that μετά means "beyond" and to assert its true meaning of "after." And in this light it is wrong to deny the name Metaphysical to Kant's three questions of God, immortality, and freedom, on the ground that these are about φύσις and therefore "physical."

He concludes "that a Metaphysical Society has good *raison*

d'être, and ample choice of subjects of discussion, these being presented to it by all the Sciences. There is no question, however apparently non-metaphysical, which may not be pursued until we come to the Metaphysical. . . . Whenever we try to *bottom* a question or subject, to use Locke's word (the French word would be 'approfondir') then Metaphysics come[s] in sight . . . Every sentence involves, in some shape or other, the verb 'to be,' and this, if pursued far enough, leads to the heart of Metaphysics. . . . Scientific persons often speak of Metaphysics with scorn, calling them an Asylum Ignorantiae, useful enough to the vulgar, but in no way needed by themselves. They imagine their science to be perfectly luminous, far above the lower regions where Metaphysical mists prevail. But in reality they share the common lot; the ideas of Force, Law, Cause, Substance, Causal or Active Matter, all dwell in the region of metaphysical twilight, not in the luminous ether. . . . The philosopher does not know the intrinsic nature of cause much more than the peasant, the peasant does not know it much more than the philosopher. And as the knowledge which we principally seek and wish for is the knowledge of cause, for a mere knowledge of customary sequence does not content us, our science, owing to such an imperfection, is impaired in a very serious manner."

Boulton's paper was evidently an effort to convince scientists and theologians that there was still ground for further common discussion, that the problems of God, immortality, and freedom were inextricably bound up with the problems of Law, Causality, and Matter. His invocation of Aristotle and Kant is, ironically enough, reminiscent of Manning's "Diagnosis and Prescription" of 1873. But whereas Manning had urged a return to the scholastic reformulation of Aristotle, Boulton reflects the change in the intellectual temper of the decade, both in his concern with the physical aspects of the Aristotelian tradition and in his desire to see scientists concern themselves deeply with a philosophical examination of their basic assumptions. While Manning thought the philosophical terminology sanctioned by the Christian theological tradition sufficient to establish a universe of discourse for the Society, Boulton seems convinced that the Society must forego the conflict of terminologies rooted in the presuppositions of Christian theologians on the one hand, and the physical scientists on the other, in a truly Aristotelian effort to recognize their fundamental problems as identical.

However sound this contention, its consequences both in the history of the Society and in subsequent intellectual history are clear. For the theologians are by profession committed to an unseen world and, further, to a world beyond the grave, while the scientist must keep the phenomenal world, the world as he sees it, constantly before him and as much as possible within his grasp. But here are two universes of discourse, not one; each is interesting to those who think in terms of the other, but principally in the senses in which the terminology and assumptions of one universe help to limit or expand the field of the other. For years, now, the Society had reflected this process of mutual examination and of mutual limitation and definition. The effort to find some kind of truly common ground had not up to this time been notably successful, except in terms of mutual respect and understanding of mutual differences. But now philosophy announces, not for the first but the hundredth time, that in metaphysics itself is to be found this common ground and that neither theologian as theologian, nor scientist as scientist, can cross its asses' bridge without surrender of the basic assumptions of their respective universes of discourse. And it becomes clear, again for the hundredth time, that the surrender must be to philosophy. This was of course implicit in the very idea of a Metaphysical Society, but neither party to the foundation of the Society knew what was now evident after nine years of debate, that the possibility of surrender had never been admitted by either party, but that each had hoped, however politely and courteously, to destroy the other. This having proved impossible, so impregnable being the inner fortresses of each, there was nothing left but honorable truce, with professional philosophy occupying the deserted field of combat, proudly accepting the metaphysical surrender of both science and theology.

Boulton, therefore, invited the Society to devote itself to pure metaphysics, in Aristotle's sense of a concern with the causes, principles, and elements (αἰτίαι, ἀρχαί, στοιχεῖα) of the world of phenomena. This had always been in large measure characteristic of the Society's debates, but much of the activity of the second period had been devoted to an argument over the nature of belief and the grounds of evidence, which was often not "metaphysical" in any strict sense. The papers of the final period are more uniformly and technically metaphysical, but in them, even as in Boulton's own attempt at definition, it is obvious that the interests of the members transcended any formal or abstract limitations. There is, therefore, an element of constraint in these final papers, as if the members were trying desperately to prove themselves metaphysicians, and in this effort a great deal of the vitality of earlier papers is often lost. If the Society had already begun to be tired of strong personalities maintaining seemingly inflexible positions, before the final meeting they must have been very weary of the attempt to become a perpetual committee on metaphysical definition. In this sense the Society can be said to have died of its own virtues.

The Final Paper

There is perhaps a special fitness in the fact that the last paper read before the Metaphysical Society was a technical critique by a professional philosopher. C. Barnes Upton, of Manchester New College, pupil, disciple, and colleague of the venerable Titan, Martineau, was one of the last men elected to the Society, in an unsuccessful effort to restore its waning vitality. This final paper was his only contribution. On May 11, 1880, he read "The Recent Phase of the Free-Will Controversy" (No. 90).

Upton finds that "the Libertarian view of man's moral nature and moral responsibility is now being hard pressed by each of the two schools of philosophical thought which at present divide between them the greater part of the little interest which the British mind can spare for discussions concerning fundamental truths." The Sensational Idealists see that "if the Ego possesses any faculty of free self-determination, their account of the Ego, as an aggregate of states of consciousness, becomes unintelligible"; while the "Agnostic Evolutionists find that their theory cannot be harmonised with the doctrine that Man, whom they regard as a part and product of Nature, should in any portion of his activity violate that principle of uniform sequence which is elsewhere observed to obtain." Hence, a vigorous revival of the debate over "Free-Will."

Upton is unable to see the force of Sidgwick's contention that in respect to Ethics, the side taken in this question is of little practical importance, and "that it would be quite possible to compose a treatise on Ethics which should completely ignore the Free-will controversy." And yet Sidgwick had admitted that on the Determinist theory, words like "ought," "responsibility," "desert," and similar terms have to be used in new significations. Certainly the sentiments we are justified in feeling toward sinners[33] and criminals are different, according as we accept the Libertarian or Determinist position. From a Determinist point of view, would a criminal judge be justified, "for the sake of moral effect, in addressing wrong-doers as though they had been free in the commission of the offence, while he himself believes that the action has been the necessary outcome of their motives and their character [?] . . . Surely this is a practical question, and will become of no small importance when the first principles of scientific morality are taught in elementary schools."

The Determinist may intensely dislike the "motives" which, with Dr. Priestley, he may consider the most important causal element in the determination of his moral choice; or, if he follows Shadworth Hodgson in regarding "the previously formed 'character' as playing the chief part in producing the evil act," he may be disgusted with those features of his character and past volitions which have fashioned his moral nature. But in neither case can he regard his own motives and character, or those of others, with the "sentiment of moral approval or disapproval which implies the reality of personal merit or demerit." Similarly, the motive of a potentially troublesome Conscience would be removed if a man could be persuaded that "personal merit and demerit" answer to no facts, and that he is not in the ordinary sense of the word responsible "for any moral deformity which his character may then present."

33 This is, I am almost sure, the only reference to "sin" or "sinners" in the Papers of the Society.

The Determinist argues that "the unbroken uniformity of sequence observed in all physical and in a large section of mental phenomena, affords a very strong presumption in favour of the doctrine that all mental phenomena succeed each other in a like uniform way." This is urged both by the followers of Hume and by those who refer phenomena and their relations to a permanent power in Nature. But "the Libertarian Theist, who regards no phenomenon as the cause of another phenomenon, but looks upon all natural phenomena as owing their existence and their mutual relations to the action of one eternal spiritual Cause," accepts the uniformity of Nature "as a fact of observation, which seems to him to be in complete harmony with his idea of the nature and character of the Eternal." He feels, moreover, that in his own moral nature he is in some measure a free cause, "and therefore essentially differenced from the phenomena of Nature," and that Libertarian Theism furnishes "the simplest and most satisfactory *rationale* of the facts given in perception and in self-consciousness."

Far more formidable, in Upton's opinion, is another argument adduced by the Determinists, that free self-determination violates the principle of Sufficient Reason, by implying that the Ego is free to take either of the two alternatives, regardless of "the force of the motives which appeal to it," or "the intrinsic drift of its previously formed character." But Upton feels that in "the great bulk of our actions, the Libertarian may well admit that our self-determinations are in accordance with our motives and with our character" and are therefore in large measure predictable; but he insists that "in acts where *a change of moral character*, for good or ill, is taking place," that the Ego feels itself the seat of a free causality, and by the exercise of what Ward calls "an anti-impulsive effort" represses "the importunity of violent, but degrading impulses" and preserves or elevates its moral character. The Determinist asks, says Upton, "Why, then, does the Ego decide this way, rather than that?" Upton's answer is that to ask why a cause acts in a certain way is to forget that it is a cause and to treat it as a "vehicle of causation." For to him, a *cause* which is wholly *caused* is a contradiction in terms. The

Ego cannot act in the absence of motive; but only when there is more than one motive, and these motives are of "different ethical rank," are the conditions present "for the exercise of its causality in the way of free choice."

Upton assumes "that the Ego is a substance, and not a mere aggregate of properties with no proprietor." He is "as intuitively certain that there is a Self which thinks and chooses, as that there are states of consciousness called thinking and choice." And although "there are many changes in our inner life which we attribute to influences which do not emerge into consciousness," he thinks these "totally unlike the cases in which the Ego recognises in itself a true first cause, and approves or disapproves itself on the ground of this felt free causation." However, he does, in conclusion, admit that he regards "but a comparatively small portion of human actions as wholly beyond the range of calculation and prevision," and insists that "the statement of the late Professor Clifford and others that Free-will renders morality impossible, implies a misapprehension of the true character and limitations of the Libertarian doctrine."

Upton concludes that a study of the freewill controversy reveals "that recent physical and mental science has furnished no universally recognised facts of a character to render untenable the Libertarian position; and that the Determinists' arguments now, as heretofore, finally turn upon readings of consciousness and assumed philosophical theories which do not necessarily approve themselves to all equally competent thinkers, and for which the Libertarian feels that he is justified in substituting other readings of consciousness and other theories. The discoveries of Science and the evidence of statistics do not seem to him to be incompatible with the view that our nature is so constituted as to afford rational ground for the ascription of personal merit and demerit, and that at the same time our actions are sufficiently correlated to character and open to prediction to furnish a solid basis for moral discipline and ethical science."

With this earnest elaboration of the ancient and complex question of freewill, the Metaphysical Society closed its discussions of the problems of the human mind and spirit. The Society had heard no truly distinguished paper since January 14, 1879, when Sidgwick read his paper on the "Incoherence of Empirical Philosophy" (No. 80). Harrison's paper, "The Social Factor in Psychology" (No. 84b), and Sidgwick's, "The Scope of Metaphysics" (No. 87), presented problems of exposition and definition which would perhaps have been of less interest in the earlier periods of the Society, but which may have filled a real need in these latter days when new and younger members who had not participated in the whole of the great argument, were trying to find their own place in the discussions. Hutton's paper, "Is Causation or Power in Nature a Reality or a Mere Anthropomorphic Fancy" (No. 85), had shown his critical power of striking at the root of a difficulty; and Pollock's, "Generic and Symbolic Images" (No. 88), had opened a new field of discussion which would be elaborated by others for many years, but which did not reflect in large measure the central interests of the aging Society. Many of the older members were still faithful in attendance, but four out of the five final papers were by new members, who knew little of the earlier history of the Society, and who lacked the experience of discussion and debate which was so indispensable to the fullest participation in the give-and-take of ideas and personalities.

There is a final irony in the fact that Upton's paper presented the position of a theological philosopher, a Unitarian Theist, who was convinced that his rational intuitions of God and Freedom were not incompatible with "the discoveries of Science and the evidence of statistics." For in spite of the polemical efforts of Huxley, Fitzjames Stephen, and Clifford, and the subtler philosophical analysis of Shadworth Hodgson, the members of the Society continued to accept, as the world has always in large measure accepted, the fundamental position here asserted by Upton. Voltaire's epigram that if God did not exist, it would be necessary to invent him, is paralleled by the profoundly human conviction that even if freewill does not exist, we must and do act as if it did. In this sense the intuitionists, who were not all theologians, can be said to have carried off the final victory over the empiricists, who were not all scientists. This seems clearly true in the history of the Society, and is true, perhaps, only because it is so true of all mankind. But even if the empiricists and scientists had done no more than qualify and limit the field of operation of intuition, and the intuitionists and theologians nothing but criticize the assumptions and presumption of science, the Society would still have made a notable contribution to the intellectual and religious compromises of the seventies. But the Society did more, for as a center for the assertion and questioning of fundamental opinion, it became a germinal influence, through many periodicals, upon that popular journalism of ideas which before and since has been one of the special glories of the English cultural tradition.

Dissolution

The final meeting was held November 16, 1880, when, at the home of the chairman, Dr. Martineau, 35 Gordon Square, it was determined to dissolve the Society: [34] "The following resolution, of which notice had been given by special circular to all who were Members at the date of the last meeting, was proposed by the Chairman, and seconded by the Secretary:—'That, having regard to the difficulty lately found in keeping up this Society's meetings and the extent to which this Society's original objects have, since its foundation, been provided for in other ways, it is expedient that this Society be dissolved, and its affairs wound up.' "

There had been no meetings in June and July, probably because no adequate papers were available; and during the recess it had become clear to all that the Society had now outlived its usefulness. Voluntary euthanasia was preferable to a lingering decrepitude, and in this spirit the Society took its own life. Eight members were present at this final meeting—Bucknill, Gasquet, Hodgson, Martineau, Noel, Pollock, Robertson, and Upton—but of these, only three, Hodgson, Martineau, and Noel, had been members from the beginning; while three others, Gasquet, Pollock, and Upton, had been members only for about a year. The most distinguished members, with the exception of the chairman, Mar-

[34] See App. D for the full documentation of the notice of dissolution and the minutes of the final meeting.

tineau, were conspicuously absent; and James Knowles, who was not only the principal begetter of the Society but had been its skillful pilot for so many years, was not present, nor did he send any written opinion on the resolution. Perhaps these men, like Dr. Bucknill and Roden Noel, who attended the meeting but did not vote on the question of dissolution, were unwilling for purely sentimental reasons to be party to the break-up of what had meant so much to so many of them for so long. Lord Arthur Russell, Bishop Ellicott, and R. H. Hutton, who had been among the most interested and most faithful members, also did not attend the meeting but sent letters concurring in the resolution. This must indeed have been a difficult thing for Hutton to do, for he, with the assistance of Harrison, Manning, and Sidgwick, had done all in his power to keep the Society alive. "Dean Church used to tell how a fillip was often give to the discussion, by Mr. Hutton rising, when interest flagged, and carrying the subject along new and deeper channels." [35] And Hutton's critical essays, as well as his "Reminiscence," show how deep was his interest in and debt to the Society.

Further resolutions were carried in regard to the printing of a list of the Papers read, "with dates, and the names of the writers," to be distributed to the members, past and present; and the disposition of the ultimate surplus of the Society's assets, which was to be turned over "to the Publishers of *Mind*, for the use of the Proprietors." The final resolution, also carried, was, "That the Chairman be requested to accept the Minute-book, with the documents thereto belonging, as a token of the Society's thanks during the past year.[36] . . . The Minute-book was accordingly delivered to Dr. Martineau, and the meeting broke up."

The Metaphysical Society was dead, but its influence endured, often in unusual ways. Its members continued their discussions and debates in many periodicals, in the specialized form of technical philosophy, in the pages of Croom Robertson's *Mind*, and,

[35] John Hogben, *Richard Holt Hutton of "The Spectator,"* Edinburgh, Oliver and Boyd, 1900, p. 27.

[36] See App. B.

on a more popular but still serious and intellectual level, in Knowles's highly successful *Nineteenth Century.* Hodgson's Aristotelian Society had been founded a year before the dissolution of the Metaphysical, and although it was designed to attract those primarily interested in the problems of professional philosophy, its constitution, bylaws, and method were modeled directly upon those of the older society. Harrison in 1889 tried to persuade Manning to form a Theological Society on the pattern of the Metaphysical as originally planned; and in 1896 the Synthetic Society was founded, in the hope of carrying on a part of the unfinished work of the Metaphysical Society by seeking a philosophical basis for religious belief. Several of its most distinguished members were men who had been active in the Metaphysical. These successors to the Society, which are discussed in a later chapter, show how the tradition and influence of the Society survived its dissolution.

Apart from occasional dining clubs like the *X*, to which Huxley, Lubbock, Spencer, and Tyndall belonged, and enormous organizations like the British Association, there was no general scientific discussion club to parallel the Metaphysical Society. Science was moving out of the universe of verbal discourse into the universe of mathematics, and the biological sciences themselves, which had long been the most verbal and polemical of all, withdrew once more from the public platform to the laboratory. Huxley would continue in his educational and iconoclastic aims, but after his death we should have to wait for figures like his grandson Julian Huxley and J. Arthur Thomson, or for learned journalists like H. G. Wells, before again hearing scientific authority speak in popular voice.

Gladstone was still able to say in 1881, with the whole history of the Metaphysical Society behind him, and in conversation with Tennyson, Froude, and Tyndall, who had all been members of the Society: "Let the scientific men stick to their science, and leave philosophy and religion to poets, philosophers, and theologians." And Manning, while objecting, strangely enough, to "the prominence of Popery" in Harrison's proposed Theological Society, adds that "the ostracism of judges and physicists is as wise as it is personal."[37] Harrison has told us elsewhere[38] that "the Society lost something of its urbanity, and more of its cohesion when Fitzjames Stephen introduced into metaphysics the style of the *Saturday Review* or a court of law." Doubtless, Stephen's attack on Mivart in his paper, "On the Utility of Truth" (No. 81), was an instance of what Harrison meant.

But Fitzjames Stephen, whose "mighty bass," according to Hutton, exercised a kind of physical authority over the members, was in many ways the dominating figure of the latter half of the Society's history. There is a symbolic anecdote involving him, appropriate in conclusion of this examination of the crucial papers. At the meeting of November 9, 1875, after Stephen had concluded his paper, "Remarks on the Proof of Miracles" (No. 56), there was a long silence. Gladstone, who was in the chair, scribbled something on a slip of paper and passed it to Lord Arthur Russell; he had written two lines from the *Iliad*, in Greek: "Then did the whole assembly fall into deep silence, marvelling at the words of Diomede, tamer of horses."[39]

[37] Shane Leslie, *Henry Edward Manning,* London, Burns, Oates, and Washbourne, 1921, p. 324.

[38] *Autobiographic Memoirs,* 2 vols., London, Macmillan, 1911, II, 87.

[39] This slip of paper, with explanation attached, was recently found by Miss Diana Russell among her father's papers.

Chapter 6

THEISTS AND CHURCHMEN

WILFRID WARD quotes an account by a European traveler of a visit to one of the meetings of the *Motekallemin,* or Mohammedan rationalists of Bagdad, in the time of Charlemagne.[1] This society of "teachers of the Word" bore, as Grant Duff observed, a striking resemblance to the Metaphysical Society, not only in its composition and procedure, but also in the intellectual atmosphere of the times which gave it birth:

> There were present not only Mussulmans of every kind, orthodox and heterodox, but also misbelievers, materialists, atheists, Jews, Christians; in short there were unbelievers of every kind. Each sect had its chief, charged with the defence of the opinions it professed, and every time one of the chiefs entered the room all arose as a mark of respect, and no one sat down again until the chief was seated. The hall was soon filled, and when it was seen to be full, one of the unbelievers spoke. "We have met together to reason," he said. "You know all the conditions. Mussulmans, you will not bring forward reasons taken from your book or founded on the authority of your prophet, for we do not believe in the one or the other. Each must limit himself to arguments taken from reason." [2]

Although more than half the members of the Metaphysical Society were practicing believers in various forms of Christianity, an examination of the papers of the Society reveals how rare, and in fact almost nonexistent, are the references even by the most Christian thinkers to the word or authority of the Bible or of Christ. We have also seen how Martineau's refusal to join a Theological

1 Wilfrid Ward, *William George Ward and the Catholic Revival,* London, Macmillan, 1893, pp. 277–8. Ward quotes this from a French writer (unnamed), but, from a reference elsewhere in the book, it seems to have been communicated to Ward by Grant Duff. The quotation is obviously a modern paraphrase of the original account.

2 Ward adds: "Such were the conditions accepted by the Christian disputants in the city of Haroun al Raschid. And they were accepted by Mr. Ward in his intercourse with Mill and Martineau, Bain and Huxley."

Society to combat atheists and materialists led to the foundation of a modern *Motekallemin* in which all kinds of views on ultimate philosophical, religious, and psychological questions would have equal opportunity for expression. In this form the Society came to deserve the name of a Victorian "Academy," and an account of its members and their principal positions and beliefs should throw further light not only on the papers and discussions of the Society, but also on the intellectual and moral climate of England in the seventies.

The original idea of a Theological Society to determine in discussion the bases of morality—"after the manner and with the freedom of an ordinary scientific society," in Knowles's words—presupposed the initial adherence of a number of Christian theists and philosophically minded churchmen. The founders, Tennyson, Pritchard, and Knowles, were Christian believers who had long been concerned with the impact of new scientific and philosophical ideas upon the traditional Christian culture of their day. Tennyson, as a poet, had written his finest poetry upon this theme; Pritchard, an astronomer who helped open the most distant parts of the heavens to our understanding, had felt anew the wonder of that supernal universe and saw in it fresh evidence of God's power and divine contrivance; Knowles had acquired from his friend Stanley and his own reading in Continental thinkers a confidence that the new philosophical insights and the liberating method of science could still be reconciled with the Christian faith and Christian revelation. But all three were seekers who turned naturally, even if somewhat diffidently, to the leading Christian thinkers of the time for answers to their own questions.

Dean Stanley of Westminster had the honor of becoming the first-named member of the new Society. His toleration, liberalism, hatred of religious factions and devotion to church unity made him not only the acknowledged leader of the Broad Church tendency in the Anglican communion, but a symbol of the spirit and the aims of the Society's founders. He who had begun his intellectual life under the influence of Dr. Arnold of Rugby and had become his biographer, had been ordained in the established church in spite of his deep antagonism to the damnatory clauses in the Athanasian Creed. With his friend Jowett, he had in 1844 traveled and studied in Germany and, under the influence of the Hegelian tradition, had undertaken the historical works which were his contribution to the liberal Victorian attack on creeds and dogmas. His only paper before the Society, "Do we Form our Opinions on External Authority?" (No. 21; December 19, 1871), is typical of his religious and intellectual position, as well as marking the degree to which a churchman could take issue with ecclesiastical dogmatism. Stanley's private and ecclesiastical independence was enormously enhanced by his marriage in 1863 to Lady Augusta Bruce, one of Queen Victoria's ladies-in-waiting, but the strength of his personality and the operative firmness of his liberal convictions were the true secret of his influence in English religious history.

James Martineau, to whose own profoundly dialectical nature the Society owed its final form, was, like Stanley, one of the men who applied the methods of German philosophy to his own religious and philosophic beliefs. Although a Unitarian in church affiliation throughout his life and for most of it a professor in Manchester New College, a Unitarian stronghold, his early scientific training combined with a philosophical learning unsurpassed among English thinkers of the nineteenth century to make him resist increasingly all narrowing dogmatisms and even to fear the systematic organization of a Unitarian communion. Like W. G. Ward, he was a critic of the deterministic tendencies of empirical philosophy, and his profound discursive works, *Types of Ethical Theory*, which he published in 1885 at the age of 80, and *The Seat of Authority in Religion*, which appeared in 1890 when he was 85, assert with overwhelming force and a most moving faith his convictions of God, freedom, and immortality. His two papers before the Metaphysical Society, "Is there any Axiom of Causality?" (No. 9; June 15, 1870), and "The Supposed Conflict between Efficient and Final Causation" (No. 67; April 17, 1877), are able analyses of the theistic postulate in its application to the problems of human freedom and causation in nature. His excellent *Study of Spinoza* (1882) reflects his continued concern with this problem.

R. H. Hutton must be mentioned among the theists, because, although he was most influential as co-editor of the powerful weekly *Spectator*, he himself regarded his religious studies as the most important activity of his intellectual life. He became a more convinced believer than his teacher Martineau in the efficacy of Christian Church institutions as interpreters of religious truth, and, as we have already noted, felt at home himself in many different churches. His seven papers before the Society [3] include two criticisms of Spencer's views on the utilitarian origin of morality, a paper on euthanasia, two critiques of the mind viewed as a machine, one on the relation of evidence to conviction, and another on the problem of causation, which he views from a position not very different from that of Martineau. As one of the most active contributors to the Society's debates and one of those most constant in attendance, he bore more of the burden of defending the theistic postulate than many of the churchmen and did so with dialectical skill and ironic wit.

The Roman Catholic members were effective defenders of the philosophical bases of their faith. W. G. Ward's three papers attack what he considered the untenable presuppositions of the empirical school: "On Memory as an Intuitive Faculty" (No. 4; December 15, 1869), "Can Experience Prove the Uniformity of Nature?" (No. 30; December 10, 1872), and "A Reply on Necessary Truth" (No. 46; July 14, 1874). Ward was the most skillful logician of the English ultramontane Catholics and the most unrelenting antagonist of the empiricists and scientists in the Society. Huxley called him "a philosophical and theological Quixote," but Sidgwick, comparing Ward and Huxley as the best debaters in the Society, said that Ward's dialectic interested him more, "apart of course from any question of agreement with principles or conclusions, not only from its subtlety, but from the strong and unexpected impression it made on me of complete sincerity and self-abandonment to the train of thought that was being pursued at the time." But Ward was not only an uncompromising theist, he was dogmatically certain of his own position on Catholic doc-

[3] See App. C. His papers are: No. 1, June 2, 1869; No. 18, June 13, 1871; No. 37a, July 8, 1873; No. 43, April 14, 1874; No. 71, November 13, 1877; No. 79, December 17, 1878; and No. 85, December 9, 1879.

trine. Sidgwick once asked him for the Catholic teaching on some point of conduct, and Ward answered, "Opinions are divided; there are two views, of which I, as usual, take the more bigoted." [4] The members seem agreed that candor was one of Ward's most engaging qualities.

Father J. D. Dalgairns of the Brompton Oratory was one of the many noble personalities among Newman's original followers, and he was also one of the few English Catholics of his time who was well-grounded both in German philosophy and the literature of the higher criticism. His scholarly work was little known outside his own church, but, like Newman, he was often sought out by Protestants seeking admission to the Catholic fold. The warmth of his nature and the fervor of his faith can be detected even in his anonymous writings for the *Dublin Review*. Although he died in 1876, and for the last year of his life suffered from a serious brain ailment, he was one of the most faithful and respected members of the Society in its early years. His three papers, "The Theory of a Soul" (No. 7; March 16, 1870), "Is God Unknowable?" (No. 27; June 11, 1872), and "The Personality of God" (No. 44; May 12, 1874), are the most poignant and, from the literary as well as philosophical point of view, among the most accomplished and moving papers ever presented to the Society. His faith is close to that of Pascal, and even his prose recalls the rhetorical power of that great French religious thinker. One of the finest passages in all the papers, already quoted by Hutton, appears in "Is God Unknowable?": "If there be a God, our imagination would present him to us as inflicting pain on the violator of His law, and lo! the imagination turns out to be an experimental fact. The Unknowable suddenly stabs me to the heart."

Henry Edward Manning, Catholic Archbishop of Westminster and later Cardinal, enjoyed a position in the Society which was partly owing to the prestige and authority of his high office and partly to that political skill which made it possible for him to meet, on a social and discursive level, men with whose opinions he had no official sympathy. The Society itself recognized this gift in electing him chairman for 1873. His personal and ecclesiastical suc-

[4] Wilfrid Ward, *op. cit.*, p. 314.

cess at the Vatican Council of 1870–1 had not endeared him to the English public, still strongly anti-Roman. And in the Society itself Froude, for one, was a constant personal antagonist. The latter's study of St. Thomas à Becket in its turn aroused Manning's fire and led Manning to friendship with Froude's opponent, Freeman. Manning's own deep concern with social and trade-union problems did not begin until the eighties and was perhaps the consequence of a complex personal sense of guilt not wholly incompatible with the more properly Christian professions of his faith. But in the days of the Society his chief interest was the assertion of the principles and authority of the scholastic philosophy, in refutation of agnosticism and materialism. Manning's scholasticism reflected his ignorance of recent Continental thought and theological criticism, but it was also to him a bulwark against what he regarded as the dissolving liberalism of all nineteenth-century speculation. This insistence on an unqualified scholasticism is the more remarkable in view of the tradition that Dalgairns was one of his most respected theological mentors; for Dalgairns, like Ward, had grappled with the contemporary philosophical tradition. Many modern critics, including Lytton Strachey, have found in all of Manning's personal relations, notably his relations with Newman and his old friend Gladstone, evidence of a constitutional duplicity. But such a view ignores much of the mass of evidence presented by his letters and journals. The "secret" of his personality has not yet been resolved,[5] although it seems to me to lie in a troubled feeling of isolation from the religious and cultural tradition of an England he dearly loved—a feeling which we also find in Newman and other sensitive Catholic converts of the time. Manning fled to an extreme ultramontane position, thus castigating many of his own deepest emotions; in this he made a very great sacrifice for his faith—but this also made him unwilling to mitigate Newman's even greater sacrifice, and in consequence he refused to permit Newman's return to Oxford. Manning lacked the subtle ingenuity of Ward and shared only superficially the latter's power

[5] Especially not by Shane Leslie, whose *Henry Edward Manning,* London, Burns, Oates, and Washbourne, 1921, attempts unsuccessfully to "correct" the full portrait of Manning presented in E. S. Purcell's massive *Life of Cardinal Manning,* 2 vols., London, Macmillan, 1895.

of seeing the differences between philosophical and religious systems in terms of basic premises. To him assertion took the place of analysis, and in his every assertion can be seen a temperamental longing for its contrary. The great churchman never forgot that his father's financial failure had led him away from politics and into the church; every success he achieved thereafter became a symbol of sacrifice. This can be interpreted as intellectual or moral weakness and thus be labeled duplicity; but is it not rather a reflection of the inescapable dualism of man's fate—to be ever suspended, in some sense, between earth and heaven?

Manning's six Metaphysical Society papers [6] all apply the principle of authority and the method of scholastic thought to the problems of the will, the laws of evidence, the use of definition, the nature of the soul, the existence of a spiritual world, and the ultimate relation between philosophy and the order of nature. But Purcell wisely points out that Manning "in his attendance at these discussions in the Metaphysical Society was not so effective a witness to the Truth as he was edifying as a moral martyr." [7]

F. N. Gasquet, who as Dom Aidan became prior of the Benedictine monastery at Downside in 1878, was a young Catholic scholar who was elected to the Society a year later, not long before its dissolution. He achieved distinction as one of the leading historians of his Church and one of the most learned medievalists of our time. After twenty years' research in the manuscript rooms of the British Museum, working on his exhaustive study, *Henry VIII and the English Monasteries,* he became librarian of the Vatican Archives, where he continued to serve the scholarly world. At his death in 1929 he was the only English Cardinal *in curia.* He became a member of the Society too late to take a very active part in its discussions, but his only paper, "The Relation of Metaphysics to the Rest of Philosophy" (No. 89; April 13, 1880), repeats his older friend Manning's contention that the abandonment of scholasticism has been disastrous to the philosophic integration of religion and science; but he expresses

6 See App. C. His papers are: No. 13, January 11, 1871; No. 26, May 14, 1872; No. 36, June 10, 1873; No. 65, February 13, 1877; No. 84a, May 27, 1879; and No. 84c, November 25, 1879.

7 Purcell, *op. cit.,* II, 514.

the hope that a new metaphysics may bring them together once more under the moral sovereignty of a higher Being.

Four Anglican bishops were members of the Society: Ellicott of Gloucester and Bristol, Magee of Peterborough, Thomson of York, and Thirlwall of St. David's. Only the first three were truly active members.

C. J. Ellicott, biblical critic, served his double see of Gloucester and Bristol for 42 years and at his death in 1905 was called the "Nestor of the Bishops." He had earlier been Professor of New Testament Exegesis at King's College, London, and Hulsean Professor of Divinity at Cambridge. One of the most competent and most active critics of the authors of *Essays and Reviews,* he later became chairman of the New Testament Revision Committee and presided at 405 of its 407 sittings. He was a leader in Convocation and an enthusiastic Pan-Anglican, although always a firm opponent of the Ritualists. Disraeli once seriously considered him for the Archbishopric of Canterbury. His only prepared paper read before the Society was "What is Death?" (No. 19; July 11, 1871), in which he maintains the curious thesis that to "personal beings" such as man there is perhaps something *alien* in death. His second contribution, an "Oral Communication on Euthanasia" (No. 37b; July 8, 1873), I have been unable to trace, but it is reasonably certain that one who was so confident that God meant death to be a release of the immaterial ego would not have countenanced any human hastening of this mysterious process.

W. C. Magee, Bishop of Peterborough,[8] was the wittiest and most effective dialectician among the bishops in the Society. He was a devoted churchman, whose annual charges to his diocese were famous. Disraeli was responsible for his being named to the see of Peterborough in 1868, although Magee always regarded himself as a moderate Liberal. He supported Gladstone's program for the disestablishment of the Irish Church on political grounds, an extraordinary position, since Magee was, in his own words, "the first Irishman since the Reformation to hold an English see." But he was suspicious of Gladstone's overtures to the Radicals and feared the rising democratic temper of England. The voter of an

[8] For the last year of his life he was Archbishop of York.

older time he found boorish, dull, impassive. "But your modern, half-taught, newspaper-reading, platform-haunting, discussion-club frequenter, conceited, excitable, nervous product of modern town artisan life, is a most dangerous animal. He loves rant and cant and fustian, and loves too the power for the masses that all this rant and cant is aiming at, and he seems to be rapidly becoming the great ruling power in England." [9] Magee had signed the Oxford Declaration against *Essays and Reviews*, although he did not entirely approve of such manifestoes, and at the 1868 meeting of the British Association at Norwich preached a sermon in which he claimed for the facts of Christian experience their place in the domain of experiment and fact. He spoke constantly, however, against what he called "the pet doctrine of the modern materialist, 'the scientific basis of ethics,'" a thing which seemed to him "about as intelligible and practical an idea as that of the olfactory judgment of pictures." [10] In a letter of 1866 he had said: "Science loves hypotheses and theories, and theology abhors them. . . . Science regards knowledge as progressive only by the revelation of new facts or dogmas. The dogmas of science are conclusions; the dogmas of theology are premises." [11]

Magee's wit and gift for irony are seen in his first paper for the Society, "Hospitals for Incurables Considered from a Moral Point of View" (No. 52; April 13, 1875), one of the most paradoxical and entertaining of the Society's papers. His statesmanship and wise tolerance are convincingly revealed in his second paper, "The Ethics of Persecution" (No. 76; June 11, 1878), in which he invokes a higher Power as a sanction for the sacred and inalienable rights of the individual. Magee was one of the most respected members of the Society, where his extraordinary gift for extempore speech made him as effective a debater as he was in Convocation or the House of Lords.

William Thomson, Archbishop of York, was, like Magee, a moderate political liberal and a theological conservative. Although originally a sympathizer with the Broad Church movement, he had

[9] J. C. MacDonnell, *The Life and Correspondence of William Connor Magee*, 2 vols., London, Isbister, 1896, II, 92.

[10] *Ibid.*, II, 148.

[11] *Ibid.*, I, 145.

in 1861 edited *Aids to Faith*, a High Church rejoinder to *Essays and Reviews*. His philosophical and theological achievement was not great, but his *Outline of the Necessary Laws of Thought*, published in 1842 when he was only 23, earned the admiration of philosophers and gives him a place in the history of modern logic. Kept from the meetings of the Society by the arduous duties of his large diocese, he read only one paper, "Will and Responsibility" (No. 50; February 9, 1875), in which he insists that "social laws are mental laws written large."

F. D. Maurice became a member of the Society in 1871, just a year before his death. Born a Unitarian, he was ordained in the Established Church, after falling under the influence of the theological teachings of Coleridge. One of the founders, with Kingsley and Ludlow, of Christian Socialism, he was dismissed from his professorship at King's College, London, because of his too liberal views on the question of eternal punishment. Maurice, like Martineau, deplored all sectarianism and especially disliked the Broad Church label which was so often given him. He called Stanley a "bigot for toleration," and in 1868 broke with him over the latter's Erastianism. He had been elected in 1866 to the Knightsbridge Professorship of Casuistry, Moral Theology, and Moral Philosophy at Cambridge, but by that time his complex influence had begun to wane. Men as different as Mill, Carlyle, and Huxley failed to appreciate his genius, and even his friend Ruskin found him "puzzle-headed, and, though in a beautiful manner, wrong-headed." M. E. Grant Duff never carried away from Maurice "one clear idea, or even the impression that he had more than the faintest conception of what he himself meant." But his brother-in-law, Julius Hare, said that "no such mind had been given to the world since Plato's," and an anonymous contemporary is reported as saying that "there have been only three great theologians since the time of the Apostles" and that Maurice was one of them. His insistence on his direct knowledge of the presence of the Infinite within him and the felt guidance of the everlasting Will, marks him as a mystical interpreter of a tradition which is common to both Catholic and Protestant theology, although Maurice, like many other modern theologians, also made full use of the insights of German philosophy. But he proposed to begin his Cambridge lectures with Locke, as the starting point in modern English philosophy, "and as being so characteristically English in his faults and virtues, so unintelligible in his looseness and contempt of system to Frenchmen and Germans." [12] The paradoxes, both of Maurice's influence and of his philosophy, remain to be satisfactorily explained, but of the fact of that influence there can be no question. The burst of national feeling at his death is said to have been greater than anything that had shown itself in England since the death of the Duke of Wellington.

He read only one paper before the Society, "On the Words 'Nature,' 'Natural,' and 'Supernatural,'" (No. 20; November 21, 1871), a subtle, penetrating, indeed beautiful paper, in which it is hard to see the mistiness so often complained of by his contemporaries. Maurice never seems to have attended more than this once, but the desire he expresses in this paper to discover the connection between the Law that is over man and the Law that is over nature, is the chief concern of the Society throughout its history.

Dr. Henry Wentworth Acland, Regius Professor of Medicine at Oxford, friend of Ruskin, Dr. Oliver Wendell Holmes, and Jenny Lind, belongs among the theists because his activity in the Metaphysical Society was restricted to a defense of the Christian faith against what his friend Manning called "the semi-materialism of Huxley." Acland had known all the leaders in the Oxford Movement, both those who went over to Rome and those who remained Anglicans, and, as Pusey's personal physician, had the reputation of helping to prolong his life. Pusey's last sermon, "Unscience, not Science, Averse to Faith," was dedicated to Acland. When Newman made his triumphant and pathetic return to Oxford in 1880, the only private visit he made outside of Trinity was to Acland. Although he was Professor of Medicine at Oxford, his life work at the university was the development of the Radcliffe Museum, and he seems never to have taught medicine, properly speaking, at all. For involved reasons, he opposed the establishment of a true

12 Frederick Maurice, *The Life of Frederick Denison Maurice,* 2 vols., New York, Scribner, 1884, II, 598.

medical school at Oxford, although he was an important figure in the reform of medical education and the improvement of hospitals. In 1879 he visited America to inspect the new Johns Hopkins Medical School and Hospital. His one paper before the Society, "Faith and Knowledge" (No. 33; March 11, 1873), is an eloquent plea that modern scientific knowledge not close the minds of men to the power of faith, for which Maurice and others had found secure sanction in the human heart.

A number of other eminent theists and churchmen were members of the Society, although most of them attended rarely and none ever read a paper. HENRY ALFORD, Dean of Canterbury, who died early in 1871, and GEORGE GROVE, editor of *Macmillan's Magazine*, attended only the first few meetings. The DUKE OF ARGYLL was too social, too busy, and too thinly spread in his interests to give the Society more than his occasional presence. ALFRED BARRY, Canon of Windsor, Principal of King's College, and later Primate of Australia, attended more often; his Bampton Lectures of 1892, *Some Lights of Science on Faith*, delivered after his final return from Australia, and which reflect interests appropriate to his Broad Church position, perhaps also owe something to the meetings of the Society.

R. W. CHURCH, Dean of St. Paul's, literary and historical critic and historian of the Oxford Movement, was a High Churchman but not a ritualist. He was a scholar at heart, who loved seclusion, and although he at first found the Deanship of St. Paul's a wearisome task, he restored the cathedral to its former and rightful place in the national life by the force of his warm personality and passionate piety.

CONNOP THIRLWALL, Bishop of St. David's, great historian and theologian, was the oldest member of the Society, the only one born in the eighteenth century, three years before its close. His enormous learning and ironic gifts were still impressive on the few occasions when he attended the Society's meetings, in spite of his age and the fact that his scholarly days were by this time long past.[13]

[13] See John Connop Thirlwall, Jr., *Connop Thirlwall: Historian and Theologian,* London, Society for Promoting Christian Knowledge, 1936.

J. B. Mozley, who, like R. W. Church, was in his youth an ardent Tractarian, and who almost followed Newman into the Catholic fold, became a Gladstonian in church politics and in 1871 was appointed Regius Professor of Divinity at Oxford. He was a solid theological scholar who turned against the ritualistic excesses of the High Church party. As a member of the Society, he is most important for his Bampton Lectures of 1865, *On Miracles*, in which he tries to prove their credibility, but in an a priori manner which the later discussions of the Society would fail to accept.

W. E. Gladstone, whose long political career came to full fruition in his first ministry of 1869 to 1874, regarded himself also as a lay leader in both the political and religious life of the Establishment. Although his own sympathies were vaguely High Church, he was paradoxically liberal on many theological questions. In spite of his own early friendship with many of the Tractarians, both with those who stayed in the Anglican communion and those who went over to Rome, he was a firm opponent of what he called "Vaticanism" wherever it appeared. Although he never read a paper before the Society, he was elected chairman in 1875.

Roundell Palmer, Lord Selborne, politician, jurist, and theologian, is best remembered for his settlement of the Alabama Claims with the United States after the Civil War. He was a Gladstonian Liberal and High Churchman who served as Lord Chancellor from 1872 to 1874 and again from 1880 to 1885. He broke with Gladstone the next year on Home Rule. He did not become a member of the Society until 1876 but was elected chairman in 1878. The later meetings of the Society were often enlivened by passages at arms between him and J. Fitzjames Stephen.

All the theists and churchmen were inevitably and perhaps naturally drawn into the intuitionist camp in the debates and discussions of the Society. Even those most influenced by the rationalistic tendencies of the higher criticism—men like Martineau, Thirlwall, Stanley, and even, to a certain extent, Ellicott—however much they might be forced to modify accepted doctrines of Revelation, could never abandon that inner voice of the heart by which man communed with God through Christ, and which was the voice of Faith. Argument there might be whether this inner voice were an a priori intuition in a philosophical sense; but if it were not, then it must be either a direct revelation to some other receptive and intuitive faculty or an oft-repeated miracle. Thirlwall's preface to his translation in 1825 of Schleiermacher's *Introduction to St. Luke* had impugned the historical accuracy of the scriptures, thus bringing the spirit of biblical criticism to England; but very few historical critics of the Bible were ever led by the results of their researches to a complete abandonment of their intuitive certainty of Christian truth. Thirlwall, for example, became a bishop and served his diocese faithfully for thirty-four years, and Temple, one of the authors of *Essays and Reviews,* ended as Archbishop of Canterbury. The intuitionists in the Society were usually able to maintain with at least partial success that however necessary and inevitable was the application of human reason to theological dogmas, equally necessary is the recognition of the inadequacy of that reason to a complete understanding of its own basic assumptions. Kant had not given a final answer to the problem, but he had shown that criticism itself is not incompatible with the kind of knowledge of God that is proper to the human mind. And although most of the theists in the Society had some acquaintance with Hegel's Absolute, they were more unwilling than their intuitionist brethren among the scientists to identify that Absolute with Spencer's God, the Unknowable.

Chapter 7

RATIONALISTS AND SCIENTISTS

ALTHOUGH ALL the founders of the Society realized keenly the decline of a faith in the supernatural among thinking men, the theologians among them were irrevocably committed to a God who, however deprived by human reason of those earthly manifestations commonly called "supernatural" in the colloquial sense, remained by definition as well as intuition a power above and beyond Nature. But although individual theists would grant the rational impossibility of this or that supernatural occurrence or revelation, they could never wholly agree on what human reason could accept and what that reason, fortified by the scientific spirit, must or should reject. Between Catholic and Anglican, Broad Churchman and Unitarian, mystic and believer in the argument from design, there was inevitable disagreement on issues which the opponents of supernaturalism in all its forms were not slow to criticize. Thus the rationalists and scientists in the Society, whose function was so often destructive of what they regarded as conventionalized superstitions, presented an appearance of solidarity which they did not truly possess; and, conversely, the Christian theists, who, whatever their differences, all accepted the teaching of Christ as the principal foundation of the moral law, were deprived of the support of this unanimous agreement by the necessity of defending their separate positions from critical attacks which each feared would undermine his own particular theological structure.

The personal disagreements among the opponents of theism were even greater than among the churchmen, for the latter grouped themselves largely according to churches, creeds, and systems, while the rationalists and scientists were often more surely convinced of what they did *not* believe acceptable to the human reason than of what were in truth their own basic assumptions. But so strong was the rationalistic agreement in criticism, and so powerfully did it dominate the meetings, that Odo Russell, Lord Arthur Russell's brother, gave to the Society the nickname of the "Atheists," and by that name it was pretty generally known. Actually, this second group of rationalists and scientists turns out, upon analysis, to be no larger than that of the theists, also numbering twenty-one members, and included—in addition to professional scientists—Huxleyan "agnostics," modified materialists, antireligious sceptics, compromising dualists, Comtean positivists, and converted utilitarians. It seems best to consider first the rationalists, those whose attack on traditional Christianity was undertaken in an effort to establish a new philosophical view of man's moral, spiritual, and intellectual nature which would be able to make use of the dissolving criticism of reason and scientific method.

James Hinton, philosopher and aural surgeon, became one of the earliest members of the Metaphysical Society at the suggestion of Tennyson, who had been much impressed by his *Life in Nature* (1862) and *The Mystery of Pain* (1866). Although he read only one paper before the Society, "On the Relation of the Organic and Inorganic Worlds" (No. 38; November 18, 1873), he attended regularly until his premature death in 1875. One of the most perplexing minds in the Society, so "advanced" in his social and moral ideas that he earned public misunderstanding and undeserved opprobrium in his own day, he nevertheless made a noble impression on his friends and colleagues in the Society. His *Life in Nature* exerted a great influence on Havelock Ellis, who at one time contemplated an elaborate study of Hinton's work—a plan later carried out by Mrs. Ellis.[1] Hinton's philosophical

[1] Edith M. O. Ellis (Mrs. Havelock Ellis), *James Hinton, a Sketch* (with a preface by Havelock Ellis), London, S. Paul, 1918. This is thus far the best study of Hinton. Ellice Hopkins, *Life and Letters of James Hinton,* London, Kegan Paul, 1878 (with an introduction by his friend Sir William Gull, later a member of the Metaphysical Society), is a dignified and pious work which attempts a justification of Hinton's essential spirituality, but at the expense of a true and full picture. Havelock Ellis himself wrote a valuable essay on Hinton in *Mind,* IX (July, 1884), 384 ff.

achievement was an almost mystical effort to bring science to bear upon the great moral problems both of everyday life and the religious emotions. Although he borrowed the words "altruism" and "altruistic" from G. H. Lewes's translation of Comte, he is credited with their naturalization in English. He who believed that "passion is power" can be properly considered one of the first of that long line of modern thinkers and psychologists who have asserted the centrality of the sexual impulse in human life. Although sex, except among savages, was never mentioned in the Metaphysical Society, at least not in the prepared papers, it is incredible that Hinton should not have used the discussions of the Society for the statement of his own strongly held views on the morality of marriage. He not only believed polygamy and a form of free love morally justifiable, but he was convinced that the world of the senses and the world of intellect can only be brought together by the moral reason, experimentally used, with close attention to the spiritual lessons of bodily health and pain. He could say, "Is it not evident that our life is a joke, a kindly joke, a very expression of sportive fun, though so serious too, and loving, and with a work achieving so great an end, purifying all the pain, but still most visibly a joke? For instance, this union of man and woman made to be so much to us. Is it not absolutely embodied fun?" But he could also say,[2] "What is the world that science reveals to us as the reality of the world we see? A world dark as the grave, silent as a stone, and shaking like a jelly. That the ultimate fact of this glorious world? Why you might as well say that the ultimate fact of one of Beethoven's violin quartettes is the scraping of the tails of horses on the intestines of cats." And in declaring that "the happy Christian homes are the dark places of the world" he is commenting on all the subtle family aggressions which modern psychology has done so much to lay bare and so little to cure. He further remarks, "Nowhere have I seen a person deliberately tortured to death except in connection with the home, nor a life deliberately gambled with except in connection with the Church. I have seen many places, and lived in some, but nowhere seen these things except in the English home and the English

[2] In a letter to Mrs. Hopkins, *op. cit.*, p. 139, note.

Church." Havelock Ellis has recorded that Hinton's view of the natural world "as at once scientifically explicable mechanism and a satisfyingly beautiful vision" greatly aided him in "obtaining a harmonious conception of life and the universe." When Hinton once published "a paper on Force," possibly his Metaphysical Society paper, Tyndall remarked to him, "You have the physical mind"; and Havelock Ellis finds it natural that, on turning to morals, Hinton treated the great questions "as a problem in the redistribution of force." [3] In his philosophy and aesthetics Hinton was a good deal of a Kantian, but he dreamed of a new philosophical method which would identify Conscious Being with Nature. This almost Spinozistic pantheism would make spirit and matter one by denying any distinction between the organic and the inorganic, and would find in the joy and freedom of life itself and all its impulses, including the moral impulses and the dictates of conscience, the highest understanding.[4] His altruism, by which he placed great store, would require having "a true response to every claim, whether of self or others"—not Spencer's "myself and others"—but the moral unity, "myself in and for others."

Frederic Harrison, also an early member, was the only representative, in the Society, of official Positivism, that "religion of humanity" which virtually made scripture of Comte's *Positive Philosophy*. English Positivism, under its leader, Richard Congreve, even acquired many of the paraphernalia of a religious sect, with appropriate services to take the place of the sacraments of baptism, marriage, and the like, together with an apparatus of "heroes of humanity" in place of saints and saints' days. Harrison continued an ardent and "practicing" Positivist to the end of his days, but the amazing fact of his brilliant influence by his own confession owes little to his adherence to the fantasies of Positivism. However, Comte's philosophical creed undoubtedly

[3] For these references see E. M. O. Ellis, *op. cit.*, Preface, and pp. 37, 224, and 228.

[4] Compare Freud's equally paradoxical but subtle and ingenious materialism in *Beyond the Pleasure Principle.* Hinton once wrote: "How will people persuade girls not to be prostitutes and make them value so highly a bodily purity, while the very women who urge them to it let their souls sink into a defilement of greedy isolation, a whoredom of the soul in which to keep the body pure? It is cause for laughter, seeing one woman swallowing a camel and begging the other not to swallow a gnat." E. M. O. Ellis, *op. cit.*, p. 118.

gave a unity and consistency to his thought and his criticism not always to be found among his fellow rationalists. The Positivists were never a large sect, and it is more than likely that Harrison's wealthy wife, herself an early "convert," was one of the principal financial supporters of their enterprises. But Harrison had been a member of Mill's circle, along with Morley and Leslie Stephen, and although the latter were never converted to doctrinaire Positivism, together the three friends exercised a great influence on liberal and rationalist thought and action. Harrison was a successful teacher of the law and one of the early contributors to modern English labor and trades-union legislation. He was also one of the few Englishmen of stature who was not seduced by the rise of German power after the Franco-Prussian War; and again in 1914, in extreme old age, he warned England against "the German Peril." He regarded himself as a republican but later in life insisted that he had always been conservative; he regarded all religions as false but insisted on the human necessity of worship. Of his position in the Metaphysical Society he remarked, "Of course, I was a Positivist; and much as I sympathised with the social and spiritual aims of the theologians, I could not but agree intellectually with the Agnostics—as far as they went. But this was not enough for me. When it came to religion the Agnostics had nothing to say. And perhaps a hypothetical religion is better than none at all." [5]

One of Harrison's earliest literary efforts was his article on *Essays and Reviews* in the *Westminster* for October, 1860. The book had been in danger of being quietly ignored and forgotten until Harrison's attack on what he called its "Neo-Christianity." He was on personally friendly terms with three of the *septem contra Christum,* Pattison, Wilson, and Goodwin, but was at that time looking for a regeneration of religion which he felt could never come out of the spirit of *Essays and Reviews.* Harrison's article attracted wide public attention to the book, and he could wittily misapply to himself the well-known *après moi, le déluge.*

His own four papers before the Metaphysical Society, all of

5 Frederic Harrison, *Autobiographic Memoirs,* 2 vols., London, Macmillan, 1911, II, 91–2.

which were sooner or later published or reprinted, together offer a consistent critique in positivist terms of the Society's chief interests. They are: "The Relativity of Knowledge" (No. 10; July 13, 1870), "On the Supposed Necessity of Certain Metaphysical Problems" (No. 28; July 9, 1872), "The Soul before and after Death" (No. 64; January 9, 1877), and "The Social Factor in Psychology" (No. 84b; June 10, 1879). In a forceful if somewhat too facile and disarming style he attacks absolutes, metaphysics, and Christian views of immortality, while with priestly unction he calls mankind to a new sociology and a new faith.

Henry Sidgwick, ethical and political philosopher, had just resigned his fellowship at Trinity College, Cambridge, when, at the age of 31, he became an early member of the Society. Although he was to continue to lecture at Trinity, he had gradually come to feel that the change in his religious views, which he shared with his close friend, J. R. Seeley, the author of *Ecce Homo,* compromised his conscience under the tests then required of fellows. His resignation was one of the strongest influences in the final abolition of university religious tests in 1871. He soon became not only a leader in university reform, but one of the founders of the higher education of women in England, helping in 1871 to establish at Cambridge Newnham Hall, later Newnham College. Sidgwick's other great interest, outside his professional philosophical activity, was the Society for Psychical Research, which will be discussed in a later chapter.[6] His *Methods of Ethics,* which appeared in 1874 when he was only 36, is still an important work. In 1876 he married Eleanor Balfour, sister of Arthur Balfour, who himself became a member of the Metaphysical Society in its last days.

Sidgwick was one of the most faithful members of the Society and came down from Cambridge fairly often for its meetings. He read six papers, which reflect his deep and earnest effort to regard all philosophical problems not only in the dry light of reason, but with a due respect for the promptings of the heart. His first paper, "The Verification of Beliefs" (No. 8; April 27, 1870), reflects the state of mind which led to the resignation of his fellowship. The second, "Utilitarianism" (No. 39; December 16, 1873),

[6] Chap. XII.

marks his turning away from the earlier influence of Mill and the beginning of his insight into the limitations of pure empiricism revealed in his fifth paper, the "Incoherence of Empirical Philosophy" (No. 80; January 14, 1879). His interest in the philosophical implications of evolution is seen both in "The Theory of Evolution in its Application to Practice" (No. 55; July 13, 1875) and in "The Relation of Psychogony [7] to Metaphysics and Ethics" (No. 73; January 15, 1878). His final paper, "The Scope of Metaphysics" (No. 87; February 10, 1880), is his contribution to the salvaging of the fatigued Society by a further effort to define and limit its subject matter. He tries to show that the popular distinction between physics and metaphysics is inaccurate and commits himself to the belief that the fundamental premises of empirical science are themselves the concern of metaphysics. Sidgwick's ability to see both sides of every question infuriated some members of the Society, one of whom attributed this to the constitutional lack of passion in a Cambridge professor! But he was one with Knowles, Hutton, Ward, and Fitzjames Stephen in his active interest in and continued support of the Society's purposes.

Mark Pattison, Rector of Lincoln College, Oxford, became a member of the Society in December, 1869. Brought up, like Newman, in the Evangelical tradition, he fell under the influence of the Tractarians while at Oriel; under the guidance of Newman, with whom he lived for a time, he assisted in the translation of Aquinas' *Catena Aurea*. For a time he was a fervid High Churchman; but gradually, and possibly as a consequence of repeated academic disappointments, a curious change came over both his mind and his personality. He became increasingly sceptical, not only in questions of religion, but in many of the ordinary concerns of daily life, frequently giving way to moods of suspicion and melancholy which only the keenness of his mind and his own gifts of analytic introspection kept from becoming truly pathological. His *Memoirs*, so frank in their criticism of himself as well as of others, appeared after his death and both troubled and confused his friends and contemporaries. But there is perhaps no other

7 G. H. Lewes's term for "the history of the origin and primitive condition of the mind."

work of the Victorian period which it is more illuminating to read side-by-side with Newman's *Apologia;* in many ways it is an accident of will that their roles in English life were not reversed. Pattison himself became a sceptical deist and remained at Oxford, where in spite of the complexities of his mind and personality he developed into a successful teacher and exerted a considerable influence, especially in university reform. Morley, who studied under him at Lincoln, did not recognize the power found in him by some of his less positive-minded students, and has testified to what he calls Pattison's "profound weakness of will and character," adding, "Nobody knows what deliberate impotence means who has not chanced to sit upon a committee with Pattison. Whatever the business in hand might be, you might be sure that he started with the firm conviction that you could not possibly arrive at the journey's end." [8] But Pattison's scepticism about men and means did not extend to his view of the dignity and power of scholarship. His study in German universities and his survey of Continental education gave him the ideal of a university as a center of mature research, a view new to the Oxford and Cambridge of his day. His own scholarly work is small but of the highest quality. His contribution to *Essays and Reviews* has survived as one of the most penetrating historical monographs of the time, and Leslie Stephen paid tribute to its influence on his own *History of English Thought in the Eighteenth Century.* Morley, who calls the popular identification of Pattison with the Casaubon of George Eliot's *Middlemarch* [9] an "impertinent blunder," considered him in spite of all his weaknesses "the shrewdest and most widely competent critic of his day." [10]

Pattison's two papers before the Society are typical of the man and of his thought. The first, "The Arguments for a Future Life" (No. 25; April 9, 1872), weighs the changes in opinion on this subject in the past two hundred years and points out that science has not yet directly denied that the universe is a moral

[8] Morley, "On Pattison's *Memoirs*," *Critical Miscellanies* (*The Works of Lord Morley,* VI), London, Macmillan, 1921, pp. 240–1.

[9] *Middlemarch* appeared in 1871–2; Pattison's own great study of *Casaubon* was not published until 1875.

[10] Morley, *op. cit.,* p. 261.

system, and that more recently in Germany new proofs of immortality are being sought in empirical psychology and psychic phenomena. Pattison's own scepticism is here implicit, but it is seen even more clearly in his second paper, "Double Truth" (No. 74; February 12, 1878). Few men so profoundly sceptical and self-critical have made their nature serve more admirably the obligations of criticism and scholarship.

W. R. Greg, who became a member of the Society in 1871, was the brother-in-law and close friend of Walter Bagehot. He was educated at Edinburgh, where he was trained in philosophy by Sir William Hamilton and learned classical economics in the tradition of Adam Smith. For a number of years he was associated with the Board of Customs and, later, with the Stationery Office, but his chief importance is as a learned and uncompromising political writer who loved controversy and who, like Fitzjames Stephen, never hesitated to express with the utmost rigor his gloomy view of the future. Born of an eminent nonconformist family, he became a Unitarian and represents the extreme rationalism of one wing of that sect. For three years he labored on an analysis of scriptural Christianity in which all the arguments of English and Continental scholarship were carefully weighed. He came to the conclusion that the dogmatic interpretation of the inspiration of the scriptures is baseless and untenable and that the Apostles "only partially comprehended and imperfectly transmitted the teaching of their Great Master." This work, which was apparently first undertaken for his own use and satisfaction, was finally published in 1851 as *The Creed of Christendom* and attracted less attention than it deserved. But after the publication in 1872 of his major philosophical work, *The Enigmas of Life*, the earlier book was republished and in the more critical atmosphere of the seventies was widely read. Although Greg always considered himself a Christian, he was Christian only in that Unitarian sense which sees Christ as the noblest of men and institutional Christianity as an organized perversion of Christ's teaching. His family were mill-owners with a deep interest in their workers; Greg himself for a time went into cotton manufacturing but failed in the crash of 1850. His own economic views were vigorously paternalistic; he believed in the duties and prerogatives of the privileged classes, in an aristocracy of intellect and virtue, and deplored the indifference in the public mind to anything like general views and abstract principles of society. He was, significantly enough, a close friend of Tocqueville, and among English politicians admired most Sir George Cornewall Lewis. The chapters on "Malthus" and "The Non-Survival of the Fittest" in his *Enigmas of Life* impress a modern reader, as they did Morley, with their insight into yet unsolved social and moral problems.[11]

Greg's two Metaphysical Society papers are subtle and ingenious essays which make paradoxical commentary on the chief interests of the members. The first, "Wherein Consists the Special Beauty of Imperfection and Decay?" (No. 23; February 13, 1872), is ironically inconclusive but impressed Grant Duff as the finest paper he ever heard at the Society. The second, "Can Truths be Apprehended Which Could not be Discovered?" (No. 48; December 8, 1874), insists that what the theists would call "intuition" is merely an anticipation by the mind of its own later processes.

James Fitzjames Stephen joined the Society in 1873 and thereafter was a very active member. A friend of Carlyle's and Froude's, and a constant early contributor to the *Saturday Review*, he had a successful legal and judicial career in India and England and became both a historian and a codifier of the criminal law. But the publication of his *Liberty, Equality, Fraternity* in 1872 marks his appearance in England as the most impressive defender of political conservatism since the later Burke. His brother Leslie, who disagreed with him on most issues as completely as Morley did with Greg, wrote an eloquently objective life of Fitzjames which is a valuable source of information and opinion about the later years of the Society. Their father, also an eminent lawyer and historian, was a confirmed Sabbatarian; it is reported that the only time he ever broke the Sabbath was to draw up the bill for the abolition of slavery. But the son Fitzjames was destined to

[11] Morley's essay on W. R. Greg in his *Critical Miscellanies* seems to me a model of the biographical essay. Morley disagreed with Greg on almost every social, political, and even religious question, but presents a brilliant, balanced, and completely objective portrait.

become one of the most confirmed anti-Christians of his day, whose attacks on miracles, supernatural sanctions, and the logical bases of belief were understandably enough the terror of Christian theists both in and out of the Metaphysical Society.

Stephen's controversies with Manning and Ward were initiated in the Society and grew out of an earlier debate with Newman over the logical integrity of the latter's *Grammar of Assent.* Although Stephen had ceased to believe in the historical truth of Christianity and had stopped attending church in 1869, he would have admitted that he believed in God on the grounds of probability and might even have called himself a kind of Christian. He believed all religions equally effective in maintaining the vital distinction between man and beast, but felt that all creeds must be justified by their beauty or their utility, not by the canons of demonstration. If truth be claimed for historical creeds, they become "the most corrupt and poisonous objects in the world, eating away all force, and truth, and honour so far as their influence extends." And in this respect he always reserved his special wrath for the Catholic Church. But he never ceased believing that religion was necessary for the mass of men as a sanction for morality, and that without the hope of a future life and the fear of eternal punishment—a conviction held over from his early evangelical training—mankind would return to the jungle. Influenced considerably by Mill, he insisted on being a utilitarian in a perverse sense, justifying authority rather than freedom on anti-anarchic principles which would have appealed to Machiavelli and perhaps to Burke. Toward the intelligence and worth of the common man he showed a Calvinist suspicion and scorn not unlike that of Greg. He felt the hollowness of mere agnosticism in religion and in this respect was closer to Harrison than to any other member of the Society. He is really a "secularist," but without the negative compulsions that characterized Holyoake and Bradlaugh. He was indifferent to the moral and political implications of Darwinism; in Leslie Stephen's words, "Darwin was to his mind an ingenious person spending immense labour upon the habits of worms, or in speculating upon what may have happened millions of years ago. What does it matter? Here we are—face to face with the same facts." [12]

His seven papers written for the Society are the most coherent, consistent, and closely reasoned body of opinion contributed by a single member. "Some Thoughts on Necessary Truth" (No. 42; March 10, 1874) initiates a controversy with Ward which is continued in "On a Theory of Dr. Newman's as to Believing in Mysteries" (No. 49; January 12, 1875) and returned to in "Remarks on the Proof of Miracles" (No. 56; November 9, 1875). In "What is a Lie?" (No. 63; July 11, 1876), he comments on an earlier paper by another Catholic, the physiologist Mivart. "The Effect of a Decline of Religious Belief on Morality" (No. 63y; December 12, 1876) became the lead article in Knowles's first "Modern Symposium" in the new *Nineteenth Century*.[13] He undertook a debate with Gladstone in "Authority in Matters of Opinion" (No. 66; March 13, 1877), which had repercussions in Knowles's third "Modern Symposium" on "The Popular Judgment in Politics." And in his last paper, "The Utility of Truth" (No. 81; February 11, 1879), he attacks theism once more in a relentless reply to another earlier paper of Mivart's. Stephen was thus the most prolific as well as the most ardent contributor to the Society's debates; for his seven papers in five years are equaled only in number by Hutton's seven in ten years. And although his manner and pugnacity eventually became a disrupting influence, there is no question that his intellectual passion did much for the Society in its fruitful middle years.

W. K. Clifford became in 1874, at the age of 29, the youngest member ever elected to the Society. His premature death in 1879 deprived both the Society and English science and philosophy of a most promising mind.[14] At Trinity College, Cambridge, he was a member of the Apostles and for a time an ardent High Churchman, but he had completely abandoned all Christian affiliations under the influence of his scientific and philosophical readings. He

[12] Leslie Stephen, *Life of Sir James Fitzjames Stephen,* London, Smith, Elder, 1895, p. 375.

[13] See Chap. X.

[14] One of Clifford's most important books, *The Common Sense of the Exact Sciences,* which originally appeared posthumously in 1885, has just been republished (New York, Knopf, 1946).

became Professor of Applied Mathematics at University College, London, in 1871, at the recommendation of Clerk Maxwell, and a member of the Royal Society in 1874, having refused nomination earlier. But he was not only a distinguished mathematician and philosopher of science; he was a person of great charm and considerable literary ability. His friend Frederick Pollock records that "When he came home from the meetings of the Metaphysical Society (attending which was one of his greatest pleasures, and most reluctantly given up when going abroad after sunset was forbidden him), he would repeat the discussion almost at length, giving not only the matter but the manner of what had been said by every speaker, and now and then making his report extremely comic by a touch of plausible fiction." [15] He once said of an acquaintance, "He is writing a book on metaphysics, and is really cut out for it; the clearness with which he thinks he understands things and his total inability to express what little he knows will make his fortune as a philosopher." But although he had "utterly dismissed from his thoughts, as being unprofitable or worse, all speculations on a future or unseen world," he never gave up interest in the construction of a metaphysical system on mathematical and scientific principles—in this anticipating the effort of several modern schools of philosophy, and at the same time reflecting his own great debt to Spinoza.

His three papers before the Society, published in an expanded form in the *Contemporary* and *Mind*, did much to create the public image of Clifford as an atheist and revolutionist, no friend to God or man. But they also bulk large in his small published work and reveal him as a "materialist" who refuses to be pinned down to matter and whose philosophical position is not far from the psychophysical parallelism of Hinton, who also owes much to Spinoza's twin attributes of "thought" and "extension." But some critics have insisted that he was an idealist, because, like Hinton and in a sense Berkeley, he makes consciousness the central fact in his metaphysics. This doctrine is subtly argued in his first paper, "On the Nature of Things in Themselves" (No. 45; June 9, 1874).

15 See Pollock's biographical introduction to Clifford's *Lectures and Essays*, 2 vols., London, Macmillan, 1901 (1st ed., 1879), edited by Pollock and Leslie Stephen, both members of the Society.

He came to agree even more with Berkeley that mind was the ultimate reality, but soon evolved his famous hypothesis, controverted by William James, that consciousness as presented to us is made up of simple elements or atoms of "mind-stuff." This, again, was perhaps an effort to translate Spinoza's "substance" into modern terms. In "The Scientific Basis of Morals" (No. 51; March 9, 1875), he asserts that ethical maxims are hypothetical, that they are derived from experience, and that they assume the uniformity of nature. But this is only true of the generalized maxims of the tribe. Clifford somewhat paradoxically insists that the individual moral sense is intuitive, and that "the conscience gives no reasons." His final paper, "The Ethics of Belief" (No. 60; April 11, 1876), is a moving defense of the scientist's moral imperatives, and attracted wide attention when it was published as part of a longer article with the same title in the *Contemporary.*

Clifford's position on belief and evidence in these papers is closest to that of Fitzjames Stephen, with whose political opinions, however, he was in considerable disagreement, being an ardent libertarian and a convinced republican. But toward the end of his brief life he wrote: "On the whole I feel confirmed that the English distrust of general principles in a very complex affair like politics is a sound scientific instinct, and that for some time we must go blundering on, finding out by experience what things are to be let alone and what not."

John Morley and Leslie Stephen will be later discussed as editors and journalists. Morley became a member of the Society in 1876 and read only one paper, "Various Definitions of Materialism" (No. 72; December 11, 1877). Here he asserts his own materialism and relates it not only to what he calls "the great system" of Holbach, but to the whole history of the theory since the time of the Greeks. Here Morley (who, like so many admirers of J. S. Mill, at the time and since, was gravely disturbed by Mill's posthumous *Three Essays on Religion*) in the conclusion to this paper somewhat incoherently insists that materialism is not "logically incompatible with a theistic hypothesis of the universe."

Leslie Stephen became a member in 1877 and read two papers, "Belief and Evidence" (No. 69; June 12, 1877) and "The Uniformity of Nature" (No. 82; March 11, 1879). In the first he goes over some of the ground already covered by his brother Fitzjames before he himself became a member of the Society, and concludes that whatever the utilitarian "verification" which creeds have undergone, "false beliefs satisfy those who act on them as well as true," and that candor requires that assent must not outrun evidence. In the second paper he analyzes the philosophical difficulties in proving the uniformity of nature but insists that he must assume it, because he is "quite unable to conceive of any alternative, or any alternative except a negation of all thought."

It is characteristic of the mood of the seventies that all of the nine members who can properly be called "rationalists" contributed papers to the Society. Their intellectual aggressiveness, combined with unquestionable honesty and profound conviction, did much to persuade the theists that the days of theological and ecclesiastical influence over the minds of "free spirits" had already drawn to a close. They, even more than the scientists, helped effect a truce in the battle between science and theology.

The scientists in the Society restricted themselves in their papers to subjects bearing essentially on the problems of philosophy, metaphysics, or logic. The most distinctively "scientific" contributions were in psychology, thus furthering one of the Society's declared purposes. However disappointing to a modern critic that men like Huxley, Mivart, and Carpenter did not discuss problems of method derived from and illustrated by their own researches, this silence parallels the convention by which the Christians did not invoke the authority of scriptural revelation. The purposes of the Society being metaphysical and psychological, in the sense of seeking light on the problems of the human mind, the scientists forswore to a greater extent than have modern philosophical critics the evidence of their specialized researches. Equally puzzling is the failure of the scientists to make more use of the evolutionary hypothesis in their arguments. It is true that the periodical literature of the seventies is somewhat surprisingly free from discussions of evolution; the sixties had seen the great debates. But although the scientists and philosophers of the school of Spencer had apparently accepted the general hypothesis, controversies (such as that between Mivart and Huxley) which turn on scientific issues not yet wholly resolved are seldom reflected in the discussions of the Society. The members who did raise questions about the social and philosophical implications of evolution were not the scientists, thus revealing that among many of the leading minds of England the philosophical worth of these implications was still being criticized in terms not unlike those used by modern critics of evolutionary optimism. But the questioning and often iconoclastic spirit of the scientists reflected the fundamental premises of their method and brought to the debates of the Society a vigorous insistence on the value of empirical evidence.

Dr. W. B. Carpenter, the eldest of the scientists in the Society and an original member, belonged to the notable group of Bristol Unitarians among whom Bagehot was also brought up. He attended his father's excellent school and had intended to be an engineer but turned to medicine under the influence of Dr. Estlin, another important member of the Bristol circle. A trip to the West Indies with Estlin opened his eyes to social injustice, and he was ever thereafter a moderate reformer in political matters. He studied medicine in London and physiology at Edinburgh, and in 1839 published his *Principles of General and Comparative Physiology,* the first English work to treat biology adequately as a separate science. He found ordinary medical practice both too demanding and too limiting and in 1844 became Fullerian Professor of Physiology at the Royal Institution; in the same year he was elected to the Royal Society. In 1856 he resigned his professorship to become registrar of the University of London, thereafter playing an important part in building up the greater university. He became much interested in marine zoölogy and made several voyages to study undersea life in its relation to the circulation of ocean currents. He accepted the Darwinian hypothesis with reservations, for the psychology which he based on his own physiological researches insisted on the reality of an independent will. He was elected president of the British Association in 1872. Throughout his life he remained a believing and practicing Unitarian, deeply concerned with the reconciliation of science and his religious convictions.

His four papers before the Metaphysical Society reveal his debt to the common-sense school of Scotch metaphysics which he had absorbed not only at Edinburgh but also among the Bristol Unitarians. The first, "The Common Sense Philosophy of Causation" (No. 2; July 14, 1869), has already been discussed in detail. The second, "What is Common Sense?" (No. 22; January 17, 1872), is an attempt to reconcile Reid's metaphysics with recent psychological and physiological experiments, and to identify Common Sense with that "immediate insight" which is manifested in the physiological realm by the reflex action of the brain. He returns to a related theme in "On the Doctrine of Human Automatism" (No. 47; November 17, 1874), in which he criticizes the views of Huxley and Clifford on this subject as laying too great stress on the positiveness of the data without sufficient emphasis on verification by the "High Court of Consciousness." Carpenter had himself propounded the doctrine of the automatic nature of many of our bodily activities, but he cannot agree that the Will is "merely the last line in a chain of antecedents." In his final paper, "On the Fallacies of Testimony in Relation to the Supernatural" (No. 57; December 14, 1875), he shows the essential rationalism of his Unitarian convictions, anticipating one aspect of the religious position of William James and insisting that the value of testimony depends on our knowledge of the prepossessions of the individual.

Thomas Henry Huxley has been the subject of so many books and so many competent critical studies [16] that little attempt will be made here to characterize the whole of his complex and varied achievement. Huxley had a casual education and had intended to be an engineer before he turned to the study of medicine. He became assistant surgeon on the *Rattlesnake*, sent to explore the

[16] I have found one of the best of these to be Houston Peterson's *Huxley, Prophet of Science,* London and New York, Longmans, 1932. Peterson's account of Huxley's relation to the Metaphysical Society (pp. 166–75) is easily the best modern treatment of the Society's importance and achievements. I find that on several points of opinion and emphasis Dr. Peterson has anticipated my own conclusions.

Great Barrier Reef off Australia, and thus laid the foundations for all his subsequent scientific and intellectual achievements. Perhaps the extent to which he was himself self-taught is responsible for the great interest he always took in education, both in its extension to all classes of the population and through his own continuous and burdensome teaching, lecturing, and writing. In 1851 he was elected a member of the Royal Society and in 1852 began to teach at the Royal Institution, forming close and lifelong friendships with Tyndall, Hooker, and Darwin. After the publication of *The Origin of Species* in 1859, Huxley became the most famous defender of Darwin's theories. Distinguished scientific professorships now came his way, but in that pursuit of knowledge which characterized his entire career, he devoted a part of his busy life to a study of modern philosophy and wrote clearly and often discriminatingly on Descartes, Berkeley, and Hume. Later he turned to biblical criticism and the problems of ethics, casting the light of his agnostic and rationalist convictions on both Hebrew and Christian tradition. His humor and wit, as well as the warmth and sincerity of his personality, often concealed a deep melancholy which sometimes took the form of prolonged fits of depression and which some of his critics have attributed to the psychological paradoxes of his agnostic position. Certain it is that no man ever manifested more of the moral presuppositions of a Puritan evangelicalism; but no man was ever more convinced of the necessity of a physical and empirically rationalistic basis both for human knowledge and human morality. He was always a conservative Liberal and hardly deserved the social and moral anathemas hurled at him by his defensive opponents.

The Metaphysical Society, of which he was twice chairman and over which he often presided as temporary chairman, played an important part in his philosophical and polemical education. He read three papers, "The Views of Hume, Kant, and Whately upon the Logical Basis of the Doctrine of the Immortality of the Soul" (No. 3; November 17, 1869); "Has the Frog a Soul?" (No. 11; November 8, 1870), in which he somewhat ironically and in an almost Goethean spirit tests the doctrine of the existence of a soul against physiological evidence; and "The Evidence of the Miracle of the Resurrection" (No. 58; January 11, 1876), the most notorious paper ever presented to the Society and the only one to which an additional evening was devoted for further discussion. Apropos of this last paper Newman wrote to his old friend Dean Church: "I hear that you and the Archbishop of York (to say nothing of Cardinal Manning, etc.) are going to let Professor Huxley read in your presence an argument in refutation of our Lord's Resurrection. How can this possibly come under the scope of a Metaphysical Society? I thank my stars that, when asked to accept the honour of belonging to it, I declined." [17] But any reader of Huxley's paper can see his logical reasons for selecting this greatest of all miracles for an examination in the light of the laws of scientific evidence. It would be naïve to suppose that Huxley had no further intention of startling his theistic opponents, but the choice reveals the essential strength of his polemical method, which is always to carry the battle squarely into the enemy's camp. However, Huxley's papers before the Society do not represent him at his best; they are brief and concise, resembling scientific abstracts rather than his own more rhetorically polished published essays or the even more distinguished papers prepared by other members. It is certain from countless references that he reserved his polemical power and rhetorical brilliance for the discussions, in which he conducted himself, as Harrison observes, "in the manner of a great criminal lawyer." It must be admitted, however, that the Huxley of the Metaphysical Society is only in part the Huxley of "The Physical Basis of Life."

Sir John Lubbock, friend of Huxley, Tyndall, and Spencer, and with them a member of the famous *X* Club, was one of the original members of the Metaphysical Society and in 1869 its first elected chairman. Lubbock came of a wealthy banking family; his father shared the boy's interests in science and was himself treasurer of the Royal Society. Lubbock went to Eton but left at the age of 15 to enter his father's bank. His family were neighbors of Darwin, and the boy was thus from earliest youth encouraged

17 Wilfrid Ward, *The Life of John Henry, Cardinal Newman,* 2 vols., London, Longmans, 1912, II, 333, note. The letter continues with the words already quoted earlier: "Perhaps it is a ruse of the Cardinal to bring the Professor into the clutches of the Inquisition."

in his scientific researches. He was not only an entomologist and anthropologist of reputation, but from 1870 to 1900, when he became Baron Avebury, he was an active member of the House of Commons, a successful banker, and a hard-working public official. His choice of the "hundred best books," although not the first such effort—Comte and his later English disciple Harrison had attempted a similar selection in their "Positivist Library"—is important not only because it is still astonishingly "canonical," but because of the subsequent educational influence of its central idea.[18] Lubbock was a fine example of the English amateur scientist whose interests so often extend beyond science into literature and philosophy. He delivered only one paper before the Metaphysical Society, "The Moral Condition of Savages" (No. 5; January 12, 1870).

G. Croom Robertson, who will later be considered at length [19] in connection with the philosophical journal *Mind*, became a member of the Society in 1872 and is here included among the scientists because his two papers are primarily psychological in emphasis and point of view. The first, "The Action of So-Called Motives" (No. 35; May 13, 1873), is a cogent criticism of the difficulties encountered in the use of language to characterize psychological states. The second, "How Do We Come by our Knowledge?" (No. 63x; November 14, 1876), is an exposition of Robertson's own effort to bring the psychological formulae of the English empirical tradition into line with more recent experimental evidence.

St. George Mivart, physiologist and evolutionist, friend, disciple, and eventually antagonist of Huxley, became a member of the Society in 1874. He attended Charles Pritchard's school at Clapham, as well as Chiswick and Harrow, and continued his

18 See Sir John Lubbock, *The Pleasures of Life, Part I,* London, Macmillan, 1896 (107th thousand!), "The Choice of Books," pp. 70–93. Lubbock's share in the history of this educational idea has been often overlooked. His list is closer in nature to that developed at Columbia College by John Erskine (compare *Classics of the Western World,* 3d edition, edited by the present writer, Chicago, American Library Association, 1943) than to that used at St. John's College, Annapolis, and at the University of Chicago. The latter list bears striking resemblances to that proposed by Comte.

19 In Chap. XI.

education at King's College, London, but left when he was converted to Catholicism in 1844. He was admitted to the bar but never practiced, devoting himself entirely to scientific studies and research. He taught comparative anatomy at St. Mary's Hospital from 1862, lectured at the London Institution, and received a Ph.D. from the Pope in 1878, later becoming, with little pleasure or success, professor at Louvain from 1890 to 1893. His *Genesis of Species*, published in 1872, brought him into conflict with Huxley not only over the processes of "natural selection," which he could not reconcile with his own teleological convictions, but over the evolutionary origin of man, which his Catholic beliefs would not permit him to find among the higher apes. He insisted continually and emphatically that evolution is owing to some internal force directed toward definite ends, and that it is the result of processes which are sudden and distinct, not gradual, in this latter respect anticipating modern mutation theory. He was, however, a Modernist in theology and Church politics and this eventually brought him into conflict with Cardinal Vaughan, who "anathematized where he was unable to refute, and brought about [his] excommunication" [20] not long before his death—poor thanks, indeed, for a lifetime devoted to the defense of Catholic science. He was a brilliant and witty conversationalist, widely read in history, although he disliked poetry, and throughout his life devoted much of his attention to religious and metaphysical problems.

His three papers before the Society are all ironic justifications of his Catholic position, fencing so dexterously with self-contradiction and paradox that they invite criticism on logical as well as metaphysical grounds. It is easy to see how they would infuriate as plain-speaking a defender of verbal honesty and positive reason as Fitzjames Stephen. But they are imaginative and subtle, appealing to several levels of the mind. He asks his fellow-scientists to be more clear in their terms in "What is the Good of Truth?" (No. 62; June 13, 1876). In "Matter and Force" (No. 68; May 8, 1877) he asks men "better informed" than himself what they mean by such abstract terms. And in "The Religion

[20] *Proceedings of the Royal Society of London,* London, 1905, LXXV ("Obituaries"), 99.

of Emotion" (No. 83; April 8, 1879), he attacks the positivist and agnostic belief that the religion of emotion or emotion of religion can exist independently of religious conviction, a view which he regards as "an inane nervous tremor,—the religion of folly."

Dr. J. C. Bucknill, physician, psychiatrist, and alienist, was elected a member of the Society in 1873. He had studied at Rugby under Dr. Arnold and attended University College, London, before becoming a doctor. He specialized in mental diseases and was head of the Devon County Asylum from 1844 to 1862, when he became the Lord Chancellor's "medical visitor of lunatics." In 1876 he returned to private practice, having established himself as one of the most respected and successful psychiatrists in England. He was co-author with D. H. Tuke of *A Manual of Psychological Medicine*, published in 1858, one of the earliest English scientific contributions to the treatment of insanity, and long a standard work. He was also an impressive student of the relation of mental illness to criminal acts. In 1878 he helped to found *Brain: A Journal of Neurology*. He is perhaps best remembered today as the author of a curious but ingenious critical volume, *The Psychology of Shakespeare* (1859), successfully republished in 1867 as *The Mad Folk of Shakespeare*. His one paper before the Society, "The Limits of Philanthropy" (No. 77; July 9, 1878), is a rhetorical and Harley Street effort to make a distinction between disinterested philanthropy, which observes the Christian ethic, and benevolent policy, which keeps a weather eye open to the dictates of Malthus and classical economics. In conclusion, of course, lip-service is paid to Christian philanthropy: "Love is Creation's final Law."

Sir William Gull, also a successful physician and a Fellow of the Royal Society, was elected to the Metaphysical Society in 1879. He became Ruskin's doctor about the same time and did much to relieve Ruskin's attacks of brain-fever. He was a defender of vivisection and a leading figure in the school of medicine attached to Guy's Hospital, as well as a convinced opponent of homeopathic medicine, which acquired a considerable fashionable vogue in the last decades of the century. Grant Duff quotes a story to the effect that Disraeli once called in a homeopathic doctor, causing someone to ask Gull, "Why on earth should the Premier trust himself in the hands of that quack?" Gull replied, "Similia similibus curantur" ("Like is cured by like"), the central doctrine of homeopathy. Gull read only one paper before the Society, "What are the Elements of a Sensation?" (No. 86; January 13, 1880), in which he examines the relation between the two aspects of sensation—the physical and the mental, the peripheral and the central, the material organism and the mental sensation—concluding that mind precedes organization. Gull was a believing layman who, like Carpenter, was concerned with the differences between man and other animals as reflected not only in man's more highly organized consciousness but also in his exercise of will.

Several other scientists and doctors belonged to the Society, but never read papers. CHARLES PRITCHARD, with Tennyson and Knowles one of the founders of the Society, was also the founder and headmaster from 1844 to 1862 of the famous Clapham Grammar School, where many distinguished men received their early education. Dean Bradley, George Grove, Mivart, Knowles, and the sons of Herschel, Airy, and Darwin all were trained at Clapham, where Pritchard himself taught both classics and mathematics; he allowed no modern history, although one day a week was devoted to science and mechanics. Pritchard had studied medicine and had also, in 1834, been ordained in the established church. In 1870 he became Savilian Professor of Astronomy at Oxford, where he contributed to the development of the new science of stellar photography and completed in 1875 a new observatory. Knowles has remarked that Pritchard seldom attended meetings of the Society which he had helped to found, being "rather hermit-like in his relations with the world" and preferring the quiet of Oxford where he could also pursue his hobby, an elaborate exegetical effort to reconcile science with the Bible.[21]

JOHN TYNDALL, physicist and geologist, began his career as an engineer, for which his early aptitude for mathematics and drawing fitted him in the early days of the development of railways. But he was determined to be a scientist and to gain this

21 See Ada Pritchard, *The Life and Work of Charles Pritchard,* London, Seeley, 1897.

end took a position as mathematics instructor in a small school. Finally, in 1848, at the age of 28 he went to Marburg in Germany, where in 1850 he received a Ph.D. degree, continuing his studies at Berlin. In 1853 he became Professor of Physics at the Royal Institution, where he assisted Faraday, later succeeding him as Director. Tyndall's treatise on *Heat Considered as a Mode of Motion,* which appeared in 1863, is considered to have done more than any other work to establish in both the scientific and philosophical mind the kinetic view of matter and the mechanistic explanation of all natural phenomena.[22] He became one of the most successful scientific lecturers of his day and, with his old friend Huxley, was largely responsible for the high level of popular scientific education in the mid-Victorian period. A lecture tour to America in 1872 netted $13,000, which he left behind to endow graduate fellowships at Columbia, Harvard, and the University of Pennsylvania. Like Leslie Stephen he was an ardent mountaineer, and some of his best writing is devoted to the Alps and their glaciers. Although he never read a paper before the Metaphysical Society, he attended fairly often, and his famous address to the meeting of the British Association at Belfast in 1874 attracted more public attention than any other public pronouncement of the seventies and had its repercussions in the debates of the Society. It will be considered in more detail in a later chapter. He was a member of the *X* Club and was often regarded as one of the atheists and agnostics who were reputed to be in conspiracy to destroy the religious faith of England. But he loved to sing hymns with Huxley and was far more tender than the latter toward religious-minded men, insisting always on the value of religious experience to those who truly believed. His German education and an admiration, amounting to worship, of Carlyle gave him more sympathy with what must be called the Romantic element in the Victorian tradition than many of his more positivistic-minded scientific brethren.

J. J. Sylvester, great mathematician, was a professor at Cambridge when he was elected to the Society in 1873. He attended

[22] J. T. Merz, *A History of European Thought in the Nineteenth Century,* 4 vols., Edinburgh and London, Blackwood, 1907–14, II, 57.

rarely and never read a paper. In 1876 he came to America to become for a time Professor of Mathematics at the new Johns Hopkins University. He is credited with developing the theories of George Boole, who had analyzed the logical as well as the arithmetical value of the language of symbols. He thus did much to encourage a study of Boole's *Laws of Thought* (1854), one of the most influential works in the history both of modern logic and of modern mathematics. Sylvester himself conceived the "sole proper business of mathematics to be the development of the three germinal ideas—of which continuity is one, and order and number the other two." He was a charming and versatile person, with considerable interest in poetry and a critical interest in verse forms and metrics.

Dr. Andrew Clark, the most successful and fashionable physician of his day, doctor to the royal family and to most of the great and near-great in England, was elected to the Society in 1874 but never read a paper. He was reputed by his friends to have great scientific abilities and was elected to the Royal Society; but his published work is slight. He seems to have been a "lion hunter" and belonged to almost every organization in London, apparently for social as well as professional prestige. He was, however, the only member of the Metaphysical Society for whose election there seems to have been no good reason, unless it was felt that in the elderly and fragile state of the members it would be well to "have a doctor in the house." He was certainly a brilliant practicing physician and probably attended the last illnesses or was present at the deathbed of more distinguished men [23] than any doctor who ever lived. At the time of his own death he was President of the Royal College of Surgeons.

Robert Clarke, Catholic priest and professor, friend and assistant of St. George Mivart, was elected to the Society in 1879, but perhaps never attended more than one meeting. He had received a medical education in Scotland, but was converted to Catholicism, and ordained priest in 1868. First known as a physiologist and comparative anatomist, whose chief interest was in

23 Including many of the most important members of the Metaphysical Society.

vertebrate structure, he became an eminent textual scholar, and was eventually appointed to the Biblical Commission by Leo XIII. But it was his private reputation as a metaphysician and much admired friend of the Wards which must have been responsible for his election to the Society in its final months. He therefore, perhaps, could be numbered more properly among the theists. When he died, in 1906, the London *Times* called him "one of the most learned men among the Roman Catholic clergy."

With the exception of Tyndall, and possibly Sylvester, each of the scientists who could be expected to have something to say to the Society read at least one paper and attended often enough to take some part in the discussions. But only Carpenter, who gave four papers, and Huxley and Mivart, who each gave three, can be said to have made real and active contributions to the Society's success. This diffidence on the part of the scientists was perhaps a sign of the rapidly increasing specialization of scientific effort and may mark the beginning of that growing separation of the scientific mind from the main currents of social and philosophical thinking which has become so marked in our own century and is now so widely deplored by scientists and nonscientists alike. It is the recognition of the dangers in this tendency which has led many modern thinkers to hope that the reëstablished interdependence of mathematics, logic, and the physical sciences may contribute to a new philosophical synthesis. Such a synthesis may not, to be sure, bring the scientists back into the humanistic realm of discourse, but it should make more available to all thinking men the methods, procedures, and philosophical implications of scientific achievement.

Chapter 8

CRITICS AND PHILOSOPHERS

CATEGORIES are often infuriating, especially when they involve men, in all the variety of their personalities and convictions. There is no sure criterion for identifying a critic, at least when he is to be distinguished from a churchman or a scientist. The same can be said for philosophers. Thus, in a sense, this final group can be characterized only loosely. It even includes some men who might with some justice be severally considered either among the theists or the rationalists. But the larger number are philosophers, amateur or professional, and in so far as their positions in the Society's debates do not represent polemical commitment to any faction, they are treated separately here. Several poets, critics, statesmen, and professors, as well as a lawyer and a historian, belong in this group because their function in the Society was either that of aloof observation of the disagreements of others, actively attempted mediation, or critical reconciliation. As might be expected of men essentially removed from a concern with the battle between reason and revelation, ten of the twenty members here discussed never read papers and of these ten, at least five attended never or very rarely. Of the ten who read papers, one, Lord Arthur Russell, read six; two read three; three read two; and four read one. This entire group, representing a third of the membership, thus contributed a little more than a fourth of the papers read before the Society.

LORD ARTHUR RUSSELL, an original member of the Society, was the brother of the 9th Duke of Bedford and of Odo Russell, who was English diplomatic representative at the Vatican Council of 1870–1, then English ambassador to Berlin, and later, in 1881, Baron Ampthill. Arthur Russell was brought up almost entirely on the Continent, for his father, Lord George William Russell, who had been an important general in the Peninsular War, was himself in the diplomatic corps and served as minister to both Lisbon and Berlin. Arthur never had very much formal education at school or university, but he became one of the most widely cultivated minds of his day, with a background in European literature and philosophy matched by only a few other members of the Society. His mother, Lady William Russell, after her husband's death established a salon in London, which until her own death in 1874 was, in the best tradition of the old Whig aristocracy, frequented by many of the most brilliant and conversational minds in Europe. Her son Arthur, shy, diffident, observing, loved the great world, however, and was not only "clubbable" in Dr. Johnson's sense but also possessed a rare gift for friendship. He had lived in Austria in the family circle of the great Count Széchenyi, and was an intimate friend of the ill-fated young Archduke Maximilian. He was deeply interested in Germany, whose philosophical tradition he much admired, but was one of those who hoped for ultimate German unity through freedom rather than absolutism; these hopes were finally frustrated by the death of his friend the Emperor Frederick III in 1888 after a reign of only a few months. In 1865 he had married the eldest daughter of the Vicomte de Peyronnet, and thereafter his contacts with France were numerous. Among his French friends were Tocqueville, Montalembert, Jules Simon, Rémusat, Guizot, Taine, and, most devoted of all, Renan. He was one of the founders, in 1866, of the Breakfast Club and was a constant frequenter of both the Athenaeum and Brooks's.

But Lord Arthur Russell was not merely a fortunate member of distinguished European society. He was a hard-working politician, who had acquired much practical experience as private secretary to his uncle, Lord John Russell, from 1849 to 1854. From 1857 to his retirement in 1885 he served as member of Parliament from Tavistock, attending regularly, making few speeches, but observing and criticizing, manifesting what his close friend Grant Duff has called "the final outcome of the highest wisdom, the power to say 'yes' and 'no' in the right place." [1] Meanwhile, he was travel-

[1] M. E. Grant Duff, *Out of the Past,* 2 vols., London, Murray, 1903, II, 127.

ing widely, interesting himself in the work of the Royal Geographical Society, the Linnaean Society, and the Anthropological Institute. He shared his friend Matthew Arnold's views on religion and on the relations between Church and State, although he was perhaps more of a deist than Arnold. Also like Arnold, he was always deeply concerned with the problems of education and its reform. In politics he was a Liberal of the center, resisting the Radicals on the one hand and the old Whigs on the other; on Irish and Empire questions he became a Liberal Unionist. Moderation was one of his clearest characteristics, although, as his papers before the Metaphysical Society show, he was no friend to compromise in matters of intellectual principle. When he died, in 1892, his friend Renan passed upon him a judgment which seems to have been shared by all who knew him: "C'était un des hommes les meilleurs qui aient existé."

From the beginning Lord Arthur Russell was one of the most faithful and active members of the Metaphysical Society. He served as chairman for a year and from time to time as temporary chairman. He read six papers, notable for their conciseness and brevity as well as their firm defense of Hegelian doctrine. The first, "On the Absolute" (No. 15; March 14, 1871), concludes that since the Absolute is a necessary logical idea, "speculative theology is a legitimate branch of metaphysical science." The second, "Darwinians and Idealists" (No. 31; January 14, 1873), remarks on the idealistic implications of Darwin's comment on the preference for beauty among female animals, and concludes that "the phenomena of physics are practically interpretable only by the methods and formulae of mind." In "The Speculative Method" (No. 40; January 13, 1874) he defends the saying of Aristotle that reason can only have reason for its object and points out that even Huxley had admitted that if he were compelled to choose between absolute materialism and absolute idealism he would choose the latter. In "The Right of Man over the Lower Animals" (No. 54; June 8, 1875) he defends vivisection as "the birth-right of man in his struggle for existence." In "The Persistence of the Re-

This volume contains the best account of Lord Arthur Russell. My great debt to Lord Arthur's daughter, Miss Diana Russell, has already been expressed.

ligious Feeling" (No. 61; May 9, 1876) he identifies God with the Absolute and, while admitting the decline of faith among "the wealthier classes," believes that both the clergy and the mass of men will continue to find ways of reconciling religion with modern science, in spite of the aggressive, intolerant, and sometimes repulsive attitudes of many scientists and atheists. In his last paper, "On Ideas as a Force" (No. 70; July 10, 1877), he asks how the doctrine of the Conservation of Energy can be reconciled with consciousness, and invites the Society to further discussion of this difficulty.

Shadworth Hodgson, a philosopher who delighted in being called a metaphysician, was educated at Rugby and Oxford. He devoted his entire life to philosophy, and founded the Aristotelian Society in 1879–80.[2] He was also one of the active supporters and frequent early contributors to G. Croom Robertson's *Mind.* Like his friend James Hinton, he was influenced in his early years by the philosophical writings of Kant and Coleridge. But the major effort of his thought was the continuation and expansion of the work of Hume and Kant in relation to more modern analyses of experience. William James, whose own pragmatism Hodgson later criticized, gave the name of Radical Empiricism to Hodgson's philosophy and found much in it useful to his own doctrine. In spite of Hodgson's wide friendships and constant philosophical writing, he had few followers, although his emphasis on a resolute and thoroughgoing psychological analysis is one of the most attractive features of his empiricism and one of the respects in which he anticipated Bergson, especially in his *Time and Space* (1865).

Hodgson became a member of the Metaphysical Society soon after its founding and read three papers. The first, "Five Idols of the Theatre" (No. 29; November 12, 1872), is a Baconian analysis of the "impositive idols" of metaphysics which he sees as now giving way to the positive and true philosophical concerns which they counterfeit. This paper presents a concise but complex statement of his own central philosophical position. In "The Presuppositions of Miracles" (No. 59; March 14, 1876) he criticizes

[2] See Chap. XII.

somewhat over-elaborately the idea that the morally good effects of a belief in miracles offer a predisposing probability in favor of their occurrence. He concludes that only a philosophical theory of the unseen world and its connection with the seen can justify a belief in the miraculous. His final paper, "Is Monism Tenable?" (No. 78; November 12, 1878), criticizes all monisms as too systematic and too hypothetical and asserts that although these monistic hypotheses were once very useful, the time for such hypotheses is past. "The universe is larger and more various than we thought." However, because action, emotion, and thought cannot be justly harmonized in a monistic system does not mean that they cannot be harmonized at all. Their true harmony is the business of philosophy.

John Ruskin's life is so well-known, and the many aspects of his genius as art critic, social pamphleteer, and reformer have been so fully studied by many competent critics that little further exposition is here required. As a friend and in many ways a disciple of Carlyle, he kept alive in the late-Victorian period that immediate sense of the dignity of man and that concern with the importance and necessity of moral and social judgments upon all man's works which is in the end the great lesson of Carlyle's teaching. This is the constant burden of his attacks on the doctrines of classical economics, as well as the central motive of his criticism of the vulgar materialism of so much of Victorian life. If he always regarded science as essentially descriptive, and thus no more than one form of artistic vision, he also believed that mechanical progress, like architecture, must be criticized in the light of moral origins and moral consequences. Hobson has pointed out that Ruskin's judgments were based on a static conception of value and attributes this to the formulation of his creed before the general acceptance of evolutionary principles.[3] But Ruskin's criticism of the social and moral applications of evolution was undertaken with a clear perception of where such applications might lead, and modern critics would perhaps consider him in this respect considerably in advance of his time. Although he always considered himself a Tory, he had little sympathy with government as it was—by any party. His own ardent espousal of Chris-

[3] J. A. Hobson, *John Ruskin, Social Reformer,* London, Nisbet, 1898, p. 101.

tian Socialism, his foundation of the fantastic St. George's Guild, and the brilliant series of letters "to the workmen and labourers of Great Britain" written between 1871 and 1884 and published as *Fors Clavigera,* testify not so much to the radicalism of which many people suspected him, as they do to his wish to see men take their social world and their moral lives in their hands and fashion them into a work of art with the order, beauty, and varied yet persistent meaning of Nature herself.

Ruskin was elected to the Metaphysical Society early in 1870 and attended fairly often, whenever his health and his duties as Slade Professor at Oxford permitted. His responses to the debates of the Society were always a little ironic and sometimes tinged with sarcasm, as is seen in his own papers. Writing to Charles Eliot Norton of the meeting at which Huxley had read his paper "Has a Frog a Soul?" (No. 11; November 8, 1870), he said: "I wanted to change the frog for a toad—and to tell the company something about eyes—but Huxley wouldn't let himself be taken beyond legs, for that time. I came back impressed more than ever with the frivolous pugnacity of the world,—the campaign in France not more tragic in reality of significance, than the vain dispute over that table." [4] But not long after, Ruskin read his own first paper, "The Range of Intellectual Conception is Proportioned to the Rank in Animated Life" (No. 16; April 25, 1871), in which he claims that "no quantity of the sternest training in the school of Hegel" would ever enable a painter to think the Absolute, and after several brilliant illustrations expresses the hope that metaphysicians will one day show that it is appointed for us "to live in the midst of a universe the nature of which is as much better than we can believe, as it is greater than we can understand." His second paper, "The Nature and Authority of Miracle" (No. 32; February 11, 1873), is one of his most brilliant short pieces and was quoted and paraphrased by Hutton in his "Reminiscence." [5] His last paper, "Social Policy Must be Based on the Scientific Principle of Natural Selection" (No. 53; May 11, 1875),

[4] *Letters of John Ruskin to Charles Eliot Norton,* 2 vols., Boston, Houghton Mifflin, 1905, II, 30.

[5] See Chap. IV. A reprint of this paper is one of the suspected forgeries examined by Carter and Pollard in their *Enquiry into the Nature of Certain Nineteenth Century Pamphlets,* London, Constable, 1934.

is a witty attack on the presumptions of social and religious reformers and an assertion of his own evangelically Christian faith that "the laws of Christ and satisfaction in His Love" require more than merely oral submission.

RODEN NOEL, poet, philosopher, critic, and humanitarian, was one of the earliest and ablest members of the Society. Through his mother, the Countess of Gainsborough, who was lady-in-waiting to Queen Victoria, he was appointed Groom of the Privy Chamber to the Queen in 1867 but in 1871 resigned the post as incompatible with his increasingly republican and democratic sympathies. He had been educated at Harrow and Trinity College, Cambridge, and traveled a good deal in Europe and the Near East. Although he was originally intended for the Church, his own religious and philosophical convictions were so influenced by German philosophy and his Eastern experiences that he abandoned this plan and for a brief time entered business. "Ludicrously incapable" at this, he turned to literature, and in poetry, criticism, and periodical journalism devoted the rest of his life to the cause of social justice and the formulation of a mystically Spinozistic philosophy. He was a warm admirer of Whitman, whom he considered not only a great poet but a great seer. As a firm critic of "art for art's sake," he is in his own verse one of the earliest modern interpreters of what we today call "social significance" in literature. Little of his poetry has survived the years, but many of his critical and philosophical essays are still worth reading, for he was a thoughtful critic and wrote vigorous prose. He read two papers before the Metaphysical Society. In "What is Matter?" (No. 6; February 9, 1870), he agrees with Reid in asserting "the validity of our sense-intuitions against the refinements of idealism" and claims that it is perception, not sensation, which must be explained. "Personality," he says, "cannot come out of protoplasm," and "God as Cause must remain utterly unknowable, not only by our intellect, but by any conceivable intellect." In his second paper, "On Will" (No. 34; April 8, 1873), he presents his conviction that the problem of the will is destined to remain the major problem of moral philosophy. Human freedom is dependent on the relations of reason, conscience, and desire; pain is at the root of all higher life; but will is not a separate faculty at all. "To desire one movement in preference to another is to will it. Afterwards we recollect, we judge, we reason, we invent." The individual, like the universe itself, first does unconsciously what later in consciousness and self-knowledge becomes the work of freedom under law.

WALTER BAGEHOT, literary and political critic, will be discussed later as editor of the *Economist*. He was one of the earliest members of the Society and attended often until his death in 1877. He read two papers; the first, "The Emotion of Conviction" (No. 12; December 13, 1870), has become one of his best-known short pieces. It is a brilliant attempt to underline the emotional rather than the intellectual and evidential elements in assent. Bagehot's early admiration for Newman is here manifest once more. But he warns us to be careful of this intense emotion and to utilize it rather than be used by it. A "provisional enthusiasm" should never blind us to the importance of true evidence in the weighing of probabilities and certainties. His second paper, "The Metaphysical Basis of Toleration" (No. 41; February 10, 1874), is an effort to establish on pluralistic philosophical grounds the value of toleration in a society. He concludes with the Miltonic view that "the human mind, when of a certain maturity, prefers good arguments to bad, and so selects from discussion truth rather than falsehood."

JAMES ANTHONY FROUDE, historian and critic, was also for many years editor of *Fraser's Magazine*. He became one of the first members of the Society and read two papers. The first, "Evidence" (No. 17; May 16, 1871), is, in spite of later animadversions on Froude's own historical accuracy and biographical integrity, a precise and classic statement of the historian's attitude toward evidence. He maintains that an implicit belief in an alleged historical event such as the raising of a dead person to life, when the witnesses cannot be examined and the circumstances not inquired into, "is illegitimate, and so far as it is allowed to influence our conduct, immoral." His second paper, "Are Numbers and Geometrical Figures Real Things?" (No. 24; March 12, 1872), reveals his debt to Spinoza but criticizes the latter's geometrical method in philosophy. His own view of mathematics is Berkeleyan, colored by what he must have read or heard of the critical spirit of the new geometries of Gauss, Riemann, and Lobachevsky. He insists that when we say "five" or "three," we mean only five or three somethings; but that however conclusive the solution of a mathematical problem, "we are dealing with phantoms in a world of our own creation,—in a sphere which has no point of intersection with the objective system of things."

Sir Alexander Grant, the only member of the Metaphysical Society of American origin, was born in New York, spent his first years in the West Indies, and was then taken back by his parents to England, where he was educated at Harrow and Balliol. As a young Oxford tutor he produced his most important work, a scholarly text of the *Ethics* of Aristotle. After a number of years as a leading figure in Indian education, he returned to Britain to become principal of Edinburgh University, a post he filled with dictinction from 1868 until his death in 1884. His *Story of the University of Edinburgh* (1884), was long considered a model of institutional history. He often deplored the fact that his administrative duties had curtailed his philosophical activity, but it seems clear that the human and practical aspects of philosophy always interested him more than the abstract and metaphysical. He believed, for example, in metaphysics as an answer to materialism, rather than as a "quest for the absolute." He was one of the original members of the Metaphysical Society but attended rarely because of his Edinburgh duties. He read only one paper, "On the Nature and Origin of the Moral Ideas" (No. 14; February 8, 1871), in which he compares Spencer's view with those earlier expressed before the Society by Hutton and Lubbock, contrasts the views of Bishop Butler and Paley, and proposes that the Aristotelian emphasis on self-approval is the real explanation of Kant's "categorical imperative." But he denies the intuitive origin of the moral sense and insists that "morality is essentially, beyond anything else, the relation of soul to soul."

Matthew Boulton, classical scholar, amateur philosopher, physicist, and authority on the history of photography, is one of the most elusive members of the Society, since critical and biographical information about him is almost nonexistent. He was educated at Trinity College, Cambridge, and later served as a Justice of the Peace and, in 1848, as a High Sheriff. His verse translations of books from the *Iliad* and the *Eneid* were well received, but his principal works seem to have been essays on photography and solar and stellar heat. He was elected to the Metaphysical Society in 1874 and read only one paper, "Has a Metaphysical Society any *Raison d'être?*" (No. 75; April 9, 1878), a brilliant paper which we have already seen to mark the beginning of the final period of the Society's history.

Frederick Pollock, later Sir Frederick Pollock, Professor of Jurisprudence at Oxford from 1883 to 1903 and one of the great jurists of the last half-century, friend of Clifford, Leslie Stephen, and Justice Holmes, was the last survivor of the Metaphysical Society, dying in 1937 at the age of 91. He was elected to the Society in 1879, at the age of 34. His book on Spinoza is still valuable, and the great *History of English Law,* which he helped F. W. Maitland to plan and to which he himself contributed, is one of the monuments of late-Victorian scholarship. At the time of his death, the London *Times* called him "perhaps the last representative of the old 'broad culture.' " In addition to being a competent philosopher and excellent mathematician, he "easily and habitually" wrote verse in Latin, Greek, French, German, and Italian, as well as parodies of the great English poets from Chaucer down to his friend Swinburne. He was also fairly well acquainted with Persian and Sanskrit. He was an ardent fencer and one of Leslie Stephen's most faithful Sunday Tramps. He had a biting wit and was perhaps a good deal of an intellectual snob. "It is said that on one occasion he thought it unnecessary to reply to a speech by an opponent before the Judicial Committee of the Privy Council as it was so full of obvious fallacies!" [6] The most attractive side of his personality is best seen in his correspondence with Holmes. He does not seem to have thought very highly of the Metaphysical Society,[7] but in the few months of his membership he succeeded Knowles as secretary and read one

6 London *Times,* January 19, 1937.

7 Sir Frederick Pollock, *For My Grandson,* London, Murray, 1933, pp. 93–5.

paper, "Generic and Symbolic Images" (No. 88; March 9, 1880). This paper is a commentary on recent experimental work by Francis Galton. Pollock himself believes that every sensible image is generic because of the multiplicity of sensations which contribute to the formulation of an image. A particular image which is consciously taken as representative he calls "symbolic." He asks, in conclusion, what is the relation of the "generic image" of the psychologist to the "concept" of the logician.

C. Barnes Upton, philosopher and theologian, student, colleague, and critical expositor of James Martineau, in 1875 became Professor of Philosophy in Manchester New College, later Manchester College, Oxford. Upton was elected to the Society in 1879 and can only have attended a few meetings. But he records: "Not only were the debates often of high interest, but the mere spectacle of several highly gifted thinkers, of very different types of faculty and genius, and with such a variety of facial expression, was itself a treat of no mean order. Towards the close of the evening the debate often passed into a conversation, and the genial affability with which the most eminent among them freely interchanged ideas with the humbler members suggested the fancy that we in modern times were enjoying a feast of reason in somewhat of the old Athenian style." [8] Upton read only one paper, the last ever presented to the Society, "The Recent Phase of the Free-Will Controversy" (No. 90; May 11, 1880), an earnest and full account of contemporary attitudes toward the problem. He himself maintains the libertarian position, feeling that recent discoveries in physical and mental science have done nothing to strengthen the determinists' argument.

The ten members of this final group who never read papers before the Society must be headed by the indefatigable secretary, James Knowles, whose name, personality, and accomplishments have sounded through this study with the elusive persistence of a minor theme. Even if he never manifested the authority of a conductor—to keep the musical analogy—he was certainly an admirable concertmaster and was personally responsible for the

[8] C. B. Upton in his survey of Martineau's philosophical work, a section of his and James Drummond's *Life and Letters of James Martineau,* 2 vols., New York, Dodd, Mead, 1902, II, 370–1.

contrapuntal harmony of the great fugue which echoed through the Society's debates. Until his retirement from the secretaryship in 1879, he seems to have attended virtually every meeting, and although he never read a paper, he took an active part in the committees without whose constant efforts the Society could not have endured.

Tennyson's sole contribution to the Society which he helped to found was the poem "The Higher Pantheism," which was read at the first regular meeting by Knowles in the poet's absence. Including the organization meeting, Tennyson attended only eleven times,[9] and although Grant Duff claims that he never took any part in the discussions, he remarks that "his mere presence added dignity to a dignified assemblage." His last appearance was at the meeting of February 12, 1878, when Mark Pattison read his paper "Double Truth" (No. 74). On one occasion, when Martineau read his first paper, "Is There Any 'Axiom of Causality'?" (No. 9; June 15, 1870), Tennyson presided. He showed considerable discrimination in choosing which meetings to honor with his presence, for the papers he heard discussed are among the best ever written for the Society in its early years. All his visits but the last were during the first four years of the Society's history. He resigned December 9, 1879.

Sir Mountstuart Elphinstone Grant Duff was educated at Edinburgh and Balliol and trained for the bar. He was one of the early writers for the *Saturday Review* and was elected to Parliament from the Elgin boroughs in 1857, the same year as his close friend Lord Arthur Russell. He became a leading Liberal politician and served from 1868 to 1874 as Under-Secretary of State for India and in 1880 as Under-Secretary of State for the Colonies. From 1881 to 1886 he was Governor of Madras. He retired from active political life in 1887 after breaking with Gladstone over Home Rule and devoted the rest of his life to study, travel, and the editing of his voluminous *Notes from a Diary*

[9] The dates of these meetings, along with the authors of the papers read, are: Organization meeting, June 2, 1869; No. 2, July 14, 1869, Carpenter; No. 9, June 15, 1870, Martineau; No. 10, July 13, 1870, Harrison; No. 12, December 13, 1870, Bagehot; No. 19, July 11, 1871, Ellicott; No. 20, November 21, 1871, Maurice; No. 28, July 9, 1872, Harrison; No. 29, November 12, 1872, Hodgson; No. 39, December 16, 1873, Sidgwick; and No. 74, February 12, 1878, Pattison.

which are so valuable a source of anecdote and comment upon the social and intellectual life of the late-Victorian period. Although he had a delicate constitution and very weak eyes, he was a voluminous reader, and in spite of a high-pitched voice was always in great demand as an after-dinner speaker. He was one of the most famous clubmen of his day and wrote interesting brief histories of several of the clubs to which he belonged. Like Lord Arthur Russell, he was a close friend of Renan's and published an interesting memoir of the latter after his death. From 1892 to 1899 he was President of the Royal Historical Society. Although he never read a paper before the Metaphysical Society, he attended fairly often and has left us several epigrammatic personal accounts of some of the meetings. He was in many respects the last of the great *dilettanti.*

Robert Lowe, later Viscount Sherbrooke, was one of the major Liberal leaders of the period and, although he often manifested a conservative distrust of democracy, was deeply interested in public education. Himself one of the finest classical scholars of the age, and a former tutor at Oxford, where he numbered Charles Reade, Clough, and Dalgairns among his pupils, he was defeated by Lushington in 1835 in an election to the Professorship of Greek at Glasgow. He was an almost complete albino, and in consequence could never read by artificial light. He once remarked that he was astonished "how persons who have all their winter evenings to themselves contrive to know so little." In youth an admirer of Mill and Bentham, he became for a while a religious liberal of the school of Dr. Arnold. He was opposed to Tractarianism, root and branch, and played an active part in the controversy over *Tract XC.* He became a student of German philosophy, especially Hegel, and must have been one of Hegel's earliest English followers. In 1840 he left Oxford to study for the bar, to which he was admitted in 1842. At that time he was told he would be blind in seven years and was advised to go to the South Seas. He took the advice, bad though it doubtless was, and went to Australia, where he made a brilliant name for himself as a lawyer in Sidney. Just when he was becoming one of the most important men in the colony, he returned to England and an active political career as a leader-writer for the *Times*. He retired from the *Times* in 1868 and in the same year was elected to Parliament from the University of London, after Bagehot and his own friend Sir John Lubbock had withdrawn from the race. Within a month he was Chancellor of the Exchequer. His famous characterization of the consequences of the Reform Bill of 1867, "We must educate our masters," [10] was often quoted. But he devoted himself to implementing his epigram and became one of the warmest supporters of Forster's Education Bill. His attack on classical education carried unusual weight for many years because of his own great love for and competence in the ancient languages.[11] But he believed more attention should be paid to English and French and that the greatest stress should be put on the teaching of the physical sciences.

Although he never read a paper before the Society, his relations with several of the members, notably Lubbock, Gladstone, and Lord Selborne, were very close. Ward, with whom Lowe had engaged in controversy at Oxford and who had been senior prefect when he was prefect at Winchester, continued in the Society to cross swords with him in the manner of their earlier encounters. He had been a great friend and admirer of Sir George Cornewall Lewis and thus met Greg and Bagehot. Archbishop Tait had belonged to his Oxford circle, and Darwin he came to know through Lubbock. He was regarded as a somewhat cold and inflexible opponent, but in spite of his physical handicap was considered by his contemporaries one of the best debaters in the House of Commons. Manning once said of him, "Whatever comes from Lord Sherbrooke, by speech or writing, is sure to be sharper than a two-edged sword."

J. R. SEELEY, who succeeded Charles Kingsley as Professor of Modern History at Cambridge in 1869, is as famous for his youthful and anonymous study of Christ, *Ecce Homo* (1865), as for his major historical works, *The Expansion of England in the*

[10] Lowe actually said, "I believe it will be absolutely necessary to compel our future masters to learn their letters." See A. Patchett Martin, *Life and Letters of the Right Honorable Robert Lowe, Viscount Sherbrooke,* 2 vols., London, Longmans, 1893, II, 323.

[11] During his years as Chancellor of the Exchequer, when he was most vigorously attacking traditional education, he studied Hebrew and read twice through the Hebrew scriptures.

Eighteenth Century (1883) and *The Growth of British Policy* (1895), both landmarks in the political and imperial view of British history. The rationalistic deism of *Ecce Homo,* which attempted to show the social roots and moral power of Christianity, free from all supernatural sanctions, had a great influence on the intellectual temper of the later sixties, especially on Seeley's close friend Sidgwick. Seeley had been educated at Christ's College, Cambridge, and, before returning to Cambridge, served as Professor of Latin at University College, London. In 1882 he published an essay called *Natural Religion,* in which he attempted, in the spirit of Balfour, to deny the conflict between science and religion by relegating them to entirely different spheres. But his chief interest was always political history, and he said of Cambridge, "Our University must be a great seminary of politicians." He seems to have attended the Metaphysical Society rarely, for he was not a very talkative person and no great lover of polite companionship. But in private conversation he was reported to be "infallibly brilliant and epigrammatic." [12]

Edmund Lushington, whose marriage to Tennyson's sister is commemorated in the final lines of "In Memoriam," was a fellow-Apostle of Tennyson and Hallam at Cambridge. He remained on terms of close intimacy with the Tennyson circle throughout his life, even during the long period of his professorship of Greek at Glasgow, to which he was elected in 1835 in preference to Robert Lowe and A. C. Tait. His literary and critical writing is sparse and unimpressive, but he seems to have been a fine teacher, and in 1884 the students of Glasgow University elected him Lord Rector. Although he was an original member of the Society, he almost never attended, even after his retirement to Maidstone from Glasgow in 1875.

Alexander Campbell Fraser, a pupil of Sir William Hamilton, and Professor of Philosophy at Edinburgh, is best known as the editor of Berkeley and as a critic of English empiricism. He was educated at Glasgow and Edinburgh and ordained in the

12 G. W. Prothero, Memoir prefixed to Seeley's *Growth of British Policy,* 2 vols., Cambridge, Cambridge University Press, 1895, I, xxi.

Free Church. But he turned gradually away from both Scottish theology and the older forms of the Scottish philosophical tradition, finding in a modified Hegelianism the most workable reconciliation of a healthy scepticism with a deep moral faith. He remained a theist, insisting in his Gifford Lectures on *The Philosophy of Theism* (1895 and 1896) on the necessary quality of faith at the basis of all philosophical premises. From 1850 to 1857 he edited the *North British Review.* His *Biographia Philosophica* is a satisfying self-portrait of a devoted teacher and of a profoundly questioning mind that never achieved any fixed philosophical position. He was elected to the Metaphysical Society early in 1871 but attended only during his infrequent visits to London.

Three members of the Society were elected in 1880 and may have never attended a meeting. ARTHUR BALFOUR, later first Earl of Balfour, began his philosophic career with *A Defence of Philosophic Doubt,* one installment of which appeared in *Mind* in 1878 and another in the *Fortnightly;* it was finally published entire in 1879. Morley, then a close friend, confided to Balfour that he could not understand a word of it; [13] but the book has continued to be read and admired. In spite of its title, it is an attack on those who presume to speak philosophically in the name of science. Balfour doubts the dogma that everything which cannot be proved by scientific means is incapable of proof, and attempts to establish the basis on which belief in science and belief in religion should rest, concluding that their foundations are distinct and that neither is built solely upon rational proof. This latter position he elaborated further in *The Foundations of Belief,* published in 1895. The task of relating his own ideas to those of Bergson was later undertaken by Balfour himself.[14] Like his old teacher and brother-in-law, Henry Sidgwick, he was much interested in psychic phenomena and became an active member of the Society for Psychical Research and later its president, as well as a member of

[13] A. J. Balfour, *Retrospect, an Unfinished Autobiography, 1848–1886,* edited by Blanche E. C. Dugdale, Boston, Houghton Mifflin, 1930, p. 67.

[14] See Wilfrid M. Short, *The Mind of Arthur James Balfour,* New York, Doran, 1918, pp. 50–62, 103–5.

those stepsons of the Metaphysical Society, the Synthetic Society [15] and the British Academy. The political career to which the greater part of his life was devoted, culminating in his position as Conservative Prime Minister and later as Chief of the British Mission to the United States in 1917, began with his election to Parliament in 1874 and his post as private secretary to his grandfather, Lord Salisbury, at the Berlin Conference of 1878.

JAMES SULLY, psychologist and philosophical critic, was educated in small nonconformist colleges and at Göttingen and Berlin. He had intended to become a minister but turned instead to science as a consequence of his German training and his interest in evolutionary ideas. In psychology he was an associationist, strongly influenced by Bain. He wrote a number of very readable popular essays on aesthetics and the psychology of genius for the *Contemporary* and the *Nineteenth Century*, but the works which contributed most to his reputation in the seventies were *Sensation and Intuition*, studies in psychology and aesthetics, published in 1874, and *Pessimism*, which appeared in 1877. He was Grote Professor of the Philosophy of Mind in University College, London, from 1892 to 1903. He contributed the article on "Evolution" to the ninth and eleventh editions of the *Encyclopedia Britannica* and was one of the first to point out the many foreshadowings of modern ideas, especially the evolutionary, in Herder, although later critics have insisted that Herder anticipates Von Baer rather than Darwin.

ALFRED BARRATT, linguistic and philosophical prodigy, died in 1881 at the age of 37, just after he had been appointed Secretary to the Oxford University Commission, whose report on the state of the university he had drafted. He could read Hebrew and some Arabic and Persian by the age of 14 and was an accomplished classical scholar. He also read easily in German, French, Italian, and Spanish. He was educated at Rugby and Balliol, where he had a career of "unexampled brilliancy," achieving at the age of 22 the unprecedented distinction of five firsts in four years and two months, a double first in "mods," and firsts in classics, mathematics, law, and modern history. In 1869 he published his *Physical*

[15] See Chap. XII.

Ethics, or Science of Action, with which he "had amused himself" at Oxford. In 1872 he was called to the bar and practiced, but his absorption after 1876 in philosophical studies connected with his *Preface to Physical Metempiric* interfered with his success in the law. The pressure of burdensome legal, philosophical, and university activities proved too much for his health, and he was attacked by some form of paralysis not long before his death. In ethics he was an opponent of Sidgwick's altruism, and in an article called "The Suppression of Egoism," which he published in *Mind,* he defends himself as an "egoist" against Sidgwick. His friend Leslie Stephen has remarked on his strong love of art and a "character of singular charm." [16]

Eminent theists, churchmen, critical rationalists, productive scientists, philosophers, politicians, and literary men of varying degrees of distinction, do not, in these somewhat abstract and conventional categories, necessarily compose an academy. Not every one of the forty "Immortals" of the French Academy has deserved this form of immortality, however much the apparent method of their election and presentation may symbolize cultural continuity. A true academy should be representative of the best in the thought of many different professions and the intellectual traditions of the most varied types of human activity. The Metaphysical Society, in so far as it realized this idea in the decade of the seventies, deserves the name. And the great theme of its debates—the nature of man and his most fundamental beliefs—is surely more worthy of a true academy than is a Dictionary.

There is little question that the Metaphysical Society attracted the most distinguished and representative Englishmen of the seventies, with the exception of Matthew Arnold, G. H. Lewes, and the aged Carlyle,[17] besides Browning, Mill, Newman, Spencer, and Bain, who were asked but refused to join. There were statesmen:

[16] In *Mind,* VI (July, 1881), 448–9. Barratt himself was a frequent contributor to the early numbers of *Mind.*

[17] "Carlyle would never join the Metaphysical Society, which had just been founded, but laughed at its deliberations."—Lady St. Helier (Mary Jeune) *Memories of Fifty Years,* London, Arnold, 1910, p. 154. The same authority tells us that Sir James Knowles "deferred to many of Carlyle's prejudices and predilections."

Gladstone, Robert Lowe, Lord Selborne, and the Duke of Argyll; powerful ecclesiastical figures: Archbishop Manning, Thomson, Archbishop of York, and Magee, Bishop of Peterborough; politicians and men of the world: Grant Duff and Lord Arthur Russell; lawyers: Fitzjames Stephen and Frederick Pollock. There were others whose primary concern was with the life of the heart and the intellect; theologians: Martineau, Maurice, Mozley, Ward, and Dalgairns; scholars: Bishop Ellicott and F. Gasquet; professional philosophers: Sidgwick, A. C. Fraser, Hodgson, and C. B. Upton; amateur philosophers and philosophical critics: James Hinton, Roden Noel, Matthew Boulton, Balfour, and Barratt. There were historians: Thirlwall, Froude, Seeley, Stanley, Church, Grove, and Pattison; important editors and critics; R. H. Hutton, Alford, Leslie Stephen, Morley, Knowles, Bagehot, W. R. Greg, Frederic Harrison, and Ruskin. There were great physiologists: W. B. Carpenter, Huxley, and Mivart, as well as the latter's friend Robert Clarke; an astronomer, Pritchard; a physicist, Tyndall; an anthropologist, Lubbock. There were the psychologists G. Croom Robertson and James Sully; a famous mathematician, Sylvester; and a philosophical mathematician, Clifford. There were academic leaders from great universities: Alfred Barry, E. Lushington, Sir Alexander Grant. And there were the distinguished representatives of the profession of medicine: Dr. Henry Acland, Dr. J. C. Bucknill, Sir William Gull, and Dr. Andrew Clark. And aloof from them all, symbolizing the virtues as well as the weaknesses of that brilliant and tortured age, Tennyson, the Poet Laureate.

Chapter 9

VICTORIAN JOURNALISM AND THE "CONTEMPORARY REVIEW"

No development since the invention of printing itself has had a more important influence on public opinion and cultural history than the astonishing growth of periodical journalism in the nineteenth century. Between 1800 and 1900 more than one thousand new magazines of various kinds were started in London alone, catering to every kind of person, every kind of mind, and every pocketbook. This development was of course made possible by the application of steam power to the printing press—an event which bore its first fruit in the rapid expansion of daily newspaper journalism. The cheap and rapid production of schoolbooks which also resulted, in its turn encouraged an increase of literacy and an extension of the habit of reading which provided an audience for all kinds of periodical literature. Many, indeed most, of these new publishing ventures were short-lived, appealing briefly to small groups or to temporary interests and enthusiasms. But the great reviews, like the *Edinburgh* and the *Quarterly*, were established early in the century, found a cultivated and educated audience ready at hand, and have continued until our own day as powerful mediums for the expression of thought and opinion. However, it is to the growing popularity of the serialized novel in the middle of the century, in the period between 1830 and 1880, that most of these newly founded magazines owed their success. Dickens' *Household Words* and dozens of similar weekly journals not only prepared the way for an extension of the practice of issuing novels in parts—itself a profitable method of spreading the reading habit among masses of admirers of particular authors —but also encouraged the establishment of monthly magazines which resembled in some ways the eighteenth-century miscellanies and which offered in addition to serial installments of one or more novels, articles of general interest in politics, literature, art, and science. It is to the successful example of this later type of periodical, magazines like *Macmillan's* and the *Cornhill*, as well as the older *Fraser's*, that the new reviews such as the *Fortnightly*, the *Contemporary*, and the *Nineteenth Century* owe their origin. These reviews soon became even more influential than the anonymous roar of the mighty *Edinburgh* and *Quarterly*.

Macmillan's Magazine was founded in November, 1859, a year in which 115 new periodicals of all types were begun in various parts of the British Isles.[1] The decade between 1860 and 1870 saw the establishment of the greatest number of new magazines; in London alone in this period there were 170 new publications, about one every three weeks.[2] Most of these did not last very long; they are, however, symptomatic not only of the hopeful vitality of journalistic enterprise, but also of the increased number of readers and the mental ferment of the times. In the seventies there were 140 new publications in London; but after 1880 there is a marked decline—70 in the eighties and only 30 in the nineties, a decade which most people think of as a period of great journalistic activity. Actually, the number of new magazines issued between 1891 and 1900 is "less than the number issued a hundred years earlier, between 1791 and 1800." [3] The reasons for this decline are probably complex and various, but it can be pointed out that this parallels a vast increase in the publication of cheap books of all kinds, an increase in the scope, power, and cost of advertising, and a corresponding increase in the circulation of the prosperous and well-established periodicals. Publishers and printers, then, as now, came to prefer taking a chance with a book which, if it failed, could be replaced by one hopefully more successful, than

1 Walter Graham, *English Literary Periodicals*, New York, Nelson, 1930. I am, like all historians, deeply indebted to Professor Graham's survey of English periodical literature. In addition, many individual magazines have been already thoroughly analyzed by other scholars; and in time we shall have studies of most of the important periodicals of nineteenth-century England. See subsequent notes to this chapter for references to many already published.

2 For these facts and figures I am indebted to a fine article by G. F. Barwick, "The Magazines of the Nineteenth Century," *Transactions of the Bibliographical Society*, Vol. XI, Oct., 1909–March, 1911.

3 Barwick, *op. cit.*

risking a new periodical which, however brilliant its opening numbers, must continue month after month to compete for its writers with rich and influential reviews paying handsomely for contributions and reaching large audiences. Interestingly enough, the Darwinian theory of natural selection, however controversial in the field of biology or in its many loosely conceived cultural applications, is nowhere better illustrated in all its startling paradoxes than in the history of modern periodical journalism. Thus, the history of the English mind and of English public opinion cannot be written without careful attention to the influence and history of periodical literature. Those who waited eagerly for the morning post or the afternoon train to bring them their *Spectator* or their *Saturday Review* were equally anxious to see the next month's issue of the *Fortnightly* or the *Nineteenth Century*. Each of these periodicals brought its readers into a particular kind of confraternity which had some, if not all, of the characteristics of a society of peers. Arthur Waugh, writing in 1902, is able to say that "what an Academy has done for France, the Quarterly and Monthly reviews have to no small extent done for England." [4] It is thus, perhaps, not strange that there should have existed so close a connection between the Metaphysical Society and the reviews of the seventies.

Of the sixty-two members of the Society, ten were editors of widely read reviews, magazines, and weeklies. Alford was the first editor of the *Contemporary*, succeeded in 1870 by Knowles, later the lifelong editor of the *Nineteenth Century*, which he founded. G. Croom Robertson was founder and editor of the important philosophical review *Mind*. R. H. Hutton was co-editor of the weekly *Spectator*. W. G. Ward edited the *Dublin Review*. Walter Bagehot, who had been co-editor of the old *National Review*, had become in 1860 editor of the influential *Economist*, founded by his father-in-law, James Wilson. J. A. Froude edited *Fraser's;* George Grove, *Macmillan's;* and Leslie Stephen, the *Cornhill*. John Morley was for fifteen years after 1867 the great editor of the *Fortnightly* and later, for brief periods, editor of the *Pall*

[4] Arthur Waugh, "The English Reviews: a Sketch of their History and Principles," *The Critic,* New York, XL (Jan., 1902), 26. Waugh was from 1902 to 1930 managing director of the publishing house of Chapman and Hall.

Mall Gazette and *Macmillan's*. All except Grove and Morley were among the most active members of the Metaphysical Society. Many of the other members were introduced to the Society by one of these men, and many owed to the friendships formed in the Society, and the intellectual and polemical impression made in its discussions, their introduction to the more public world of periodical journalism. The Metaphysical Society thus became a focal point for the dissemination of ideas and the cultivation of a tone, a manner, and a temper destined to put its mark on the whole subsequent history of English journalism. The spirit of the old *Edinburgh* and *Quarterly* is henceforth on the wane, and even the attitudes of the fearsome *Saturday Review* were influenced by the new urbanity and a new respect for responsible opinion.

Mr. James Knowles was not only the founder of the Metaphysical Society, but, as we have seen, he was also the editor, in succession, of the *Contemporary Review* and the *Nineteenth Century*, each in its turn one of the most powerful reviews of the late-Victorian period. Early in the sixties he had had a brief taste of editorial responsibility in the conduct of the *Clapham Magazine*, one of the short-lived experiments in periodical journalism noted above. But it was not until his successful organization of the Society that he succeeded Dean Alford as the editor of the *Contemporary*. This review had been established by Alexander Strahan, in 1866, to be an organ of liberal religious thought with a strong evangelical coloring. Henry Alford, Dean of Canterbury, became, at the age of 55, its first editor and gave it the tone of solid learning and quiet fervor which long characterized its religious articles. Alford, whose youthful poetry Wordsworth had admired, was one of the earliest disciples in England of the German school of biblical criticism and had himself spent the year 1847 in Germany mastering the language and studying the German critical method. He became one of the leading textual scholars in England and was an important member of the New Testament revision committee, helping thus to complete a work which he had begun privately years before.[5] He was a voluminous writer and, among his

[5] His own revised translation of the New Testament was published in 1869.

many literary recreations, translated the *Odyssey* into blank verse. But apart from a few hymns and his textual criticism he will be longest remembered for his courageous editing of a liberal religious review in the years when freedom of religious thought and the discussion of religious questions in the light of the new movements in science and philosophy were still suspect in England.

The *Contemporary* was designed to make the same kind of appeal to liberal opinion within the Church that the newly founded *Fortnightly* made to a more secular audience. The *Fortnightly*, established in 1865, had resolutely set its face against anonymous journalism and was already meeting a considerable popular response when the *Contemporary* was begun on similar principles. The liberal clergy, in both the Church of England and the leading nonconformist communions, provided a large and responsive audience for this new monthly review. But from the beginning the *Contemporary* was no Church organ or merely theological journal. Its first issue, in February, 1866, contained the first of Mansel's (anonymous) attacks on Mill's *Examination of Sir William Hamilton's Philosophy*, a splendid article by Edward Dowden on "French Aesthetics" (Cousin, Jouffroy, Lammenais, Lévèque, and Taine), and an essay by Lowes Dickinson, the elder, on "Modern Portrait Painting." The intellectual balance of this first number was maintained in large measure by Alford throughout his editorship; and the *Contemporary* was one of the first journals of the period to give wide and extensive treatment to art (R. St. John Tyrwhitt), music (H. R. Haweis), criticism (Dowden), and science (J. Hannah, C. Pritchard, J. Young). It continued the battle in defense of Colenso, gave considerable space to French literature and thought, interested itself early in the problems of education, especially that of women, and even dared to discuss with amazing frankness the causes and cure of prostitution. Among its regular contributors in this period were Plumptre, Fremantle, Merivale, Westcott, J. Gairdner, Philip Schaff, Tulloch, Lightfoot, Maurice, J. M. Ludlow, Edward Zeller, W. C. Magee, J. B. Mozley, G. Rawlinson, and Bonamy Price, all men who left their mark on nineteenth-century thought.[6]

[6] It is perhaps interesting to note a brief anonymous review of the first part

The *Contemporary* became one of the most important organs of the Broad Church position, but its interests were never primarily ecclesiastical or political, in this reflecting the wide interests of its editor, Alford himself, who was not only a churchman and a textual scholar, but a poet, a painter, a musician, and a warm sympathizer with the poor and the unhappy. An important attack by J. Boyd Kinnear on "Anonymous Journalism," in the July, 1867 issue, not only established the rationale of the *Contemporary's* own editorial policy but was itself influential in helping to break down a long English tradition. And perhaps because under Alford's editorship the *Contemporary* remained a truly Christian journal, its warm interest in the reunion of Christendom at a time when the Roman Catholic Church was making this less and less possible, mark it as a liberating and unifying force far in advance of its time. Its attitude toward the higher criticism and the effects of science and historical scholarship on Christian doctrine and belief show an astonishing willingness to accept even the most advanced religious ideas, and a firm conviction that Christianity, and particularly the English Church, cannot afford to gamble with deceptions and reactionary sophistries in the name of Christ. Its reviews of books like Seeley's *Ecce Homo* and Renan's *Les Apôtres* accept the conclusions of the new historical method

---

of Karl Marx's *Das Kapital,* which appeared in the *Contemporary,* VIII (June, 1868), 317:

"We have here the first part of what bids fair to be an elaborate treatise on Political Economy. The author spares us none of the abstractions or subtilties of the science—such, for instance, as the discussions which have arisen on the definition of value,—but he is very far from forgetting in such abstractions the human interest—the 'hunger and thirst interest,' which underlies the science—if science it can be called—of Political Economy. An accusation often foolishly levelled against the student of this branch or phase of our social system, cannot be applied to Herr Marx; he cannot be called a 'cold-blooded Economist.' In treating of capital he has ever before him the human beings whom the capital employs and feeds. What direction his sympathies take may be gathered from the dedication of his book to his friend, 'the bold, true, noble champion of the workman,' Wilhelm Wolff, who died in exile in Manchester.

"There are many subjects on which we learn from the Germans,—some in which we are confessedly their pupils—but in Political Economy, we here in Great Britain, have taken the initiative, and still keep the lead. We do not suspect that Karl Marx has much to teach us, whether he discourses abstrusely on those relations which the use of money has brought into society, or in a more animated manner on those social amendments which he thinks our advanced knowledge ought to enable us to make."

while continuing to assert the power and usefulness of the Christian ideal. During this period the *Contemporary* is rarely exciting and not so open to public controversy in its own pages as it later became, but it is solid, distinguished, and sometimes eloquent in a great cause.

Alford was one of the earliest members of the Metaphysical Society and an admirer of Tennyson. Alexander Strahan, the publisher of the *Contemporary,* had (partly through the good offices of Knowles) become Tennyson's publisher, in 1869, with the appearance of the *Idylls of the King.* Tennyson later claimed that a review of the *Idylls* by Alford in the *Contemporary* for January, 1870, and an anonymous review in the form of a letter to the *Spectator* by Knowles, were the best criticisms he had received. When Alford's labors on the revision of the New Testament became more arduous, this and his failing health required, early in 1870, that he give up the editorship of the *Contemporary.* In these circumstances, it was perhaps natural that Strahan should choose Knowles, Tennyson's friend and his own, to succeed Alford as editor. Alford had met Knowles through the Metaphysical Society, and Knowles himself had perhaps already seen how useful the Society could be to an enterprising editorial mind. But before the founding of the Society, Alford had published in the February, 1869, issue of the *Contemporary* an article by Knowles (signed J.T.K.) on "The Alternation of Science and Art in History," a neo-Hegelian piece which must have impressed both Alford and Strahan as showing a full consciousness of the cultural conflicts and dramatic tensions of the time.

This article is important primarily for its prophetic conclusion, so right in many ways, and so extraordinary as coming at the dawn of an age of science:

> There is again in these days that forerunner of an age of art and synthesis—the revival of *à priori* philosophies, doctrines of intuitions, and innate ideas (the school of Coleridge in this country), and their consequence—Authority—a counterpart of the neo-Platonism which succeeded the science period of Rome. There is in all directions an increase of speculation and theory, a love for broad though hasty generalizations, and extensive though superficial knowledge, rather than deep, close, mathematic thought. There is a want of power of concentrated attention.

There are Mormonisms and spirit-rappings and ghostologies without end. There is an ever-increasing host of minor minstrels, a growing love for poetry, music, painting, and architecture. There is an exhaustless appetite for new inventions, and for abstract science made straightway tangible. All which things seem the beginnings of change, and to herald the advent of an imaginative cycle once more. . . . In spite of the fashionable materialism of the hour, he [our Cartophilus, who is but the human mind] may be about to open the golden gates of the twentieth century to Art and Poetry and Faith.

Through the greatness of the decade yet to come, Knowles here sees hopefully what was to characterize the even more hopeful and optimistic convictions of the end of the century and the beginning of our own. He characterizes, with a sure touch, what was to be not only his own editorial policy but also the public temper of a later age. And his final vision he shares, in his own fashion, with many of the greatest spirits of the twentieth century, who, for good or evil, have tried to justify his dream.

The last issue edited by Alford was that of March, 1870, which carried a postscript, probably by Strahan, announcing Alford's retirement and stating the reasons. There is no mention of Knowles, although he began his editorial duties with the April issue. Some ambiguity continued to characterize Knowles's connection with the review throughout his editorship, for, as became clear seven years later when Knowles abandoned the *Contemporary* and founded the *Nineteenth Century*, Alexander Strahan exercised a proprietary control and even, on occasion, insisted on an editorial power which ultimately led to Knowles's break with him under unpleasant circumstances. However, in this postscript Strahan says, "The Review will be conducted on the same principles which have hitherto guided it; and will continue to express the views of those 'who,' in the words of its late Editor at its commencement, 'holding loyally to belief in the articles of the Christian faith, are not afraid of collision with modern thought in its varied aspects and demands, and scorn to defend their faith by mere reticence, or by the artifices too commonly acquiesced in.' "

Even under Alford, the *Contemporary* had begun to be in some sense an organ of the members of the Metaphysical Society, carrying, in August, 1869, an important article by Charles Pritchard on the new science of spectrum analysis and, in November, one by Alfred Barry on "The Battle of the Philosophies—Physical and Metaphysical." But it is with Knowles's editorship that the review takes on the complexion of the Society itself. Maurice, later a member of the Society, contributed an article on Newman's *Grammar of Assent* to Knowles's second (May) number; and in the ten succeeding issues of Knowles's first year as editor, five numbers contain one article by a member of the Society, four contain two, and one (December, 1870), three. Of these sixteen articles, only three were papers read before the Society; but Knowles had obviously no intention of making the *Contemporary* a metaphysical journal, nor was he ever blind to the journalistic value of authoritative articles by specialists in their own fields, however skillful he became in eliciting from these same specialists articles of general interest on the important questions of the day, social and political as well as philosophical. The three Metaphysical Society papers he published during this first year were by Martineau, Dalgairns, and Manning [7]—the first, the leading nonconformist theologian of the age, and the two latter, influential Catholic thinkers. The publication of these papers in an avowedly Broad Church review was the first of Knowles's many journalistic experiments. But the issues of this first year also contained two articles by Hutton, one on Arnold and one on Bismarck and Louis Napoleon; three by Huxley, on British ethnology, "On the Formation of Coal," and on the School Boards; two by Dean Stanley on the Athanasian Creed; three by that vigorous polemicist W. R. Greg on social and political questions; and one by W. B. Carpenter on his researches into ocean currents. Already the tone of the *Contemporary* had begun to change, and already it was one of the most interesting reviews of the seventies. The choice of Knowles as editor proved momentous; the *Contemporary* was never again what it had set out to be.

It would be tempting but inappropriate to examine in detail the many controversies begun and continued in the pages of the *Contemporary* and the large share taken in these debates by the mem-

[7] See App. C.

bers of the Metaphysical Society.[8] Still, it is important to note that during the seven years of Knowles's editorship of the *Contemporary,* thirty-six of the members of the Society contributed to his review, ten of them only once, but all the others at least twice, and one, Gladstone, seventeen times. W. R. Greg contributed fifteen articles; W. B. Carpenter, thirteen; Grant Duff, eleven; A. P. Stanley and St. George Mivart, each nine; Huxley, eight; J. Fitzjames Stephen and the Duke of Argyll, each six; and Hutton, Manning, and Tyndall, each five.[9] During the early years of Knowles's new *Nineteenth Century,* from March, 1877, through November, 1880, the month of the dissolution of the Society, some of these writers continued their relations with the *Contemporary,* but the most important transferred their allegiance to Knowles's new review and, as we shall see, some of them contributed even more frequently to a journal which was not under the watchful eye of Alexander Strahan. In fact, seven Metaphysical Society members who had never published in the *Contemporary* hastened to contribute to the *Nineteenth Century* in its first years. It is perhaps interesting to observe that of the nineteen members of the Society who never contributed to either review during the seventies, only seven had contributed papers to the Society and taken any truly active part in its discussions (Boulton, Hinton, Hodgson, Morley, Leslie Stephen, Thomson, and Upton); and all of these had full access to other reviews, notably the *Fortnightly,* the *Cornhill,* and *Mind.*

We would have a false impression of the *Contemporary* and of Knowles's editorial catholicity, however, if we imagined it during the seventies as primarily or dominantly a mouthpiece of the Metaphysical Society. Knowles continued Alford's policy of giving con-

8 The periodical or book publication of papers read before the Society is fully noted in App. C; wherever possible or convenient the relation to current controversies of each paper so published is also there indicated.

9 Other members who contributed (with the number of their contributions) were: Acland (2), Alford (2), Bagehot (2), Bucknill (1), Clifford (4), Dalgairns (3), Ellicott (1), Grant (1), Harrison (3), Knowles (1), Lowe (1), Lubbock (2), Martineau (4), Maurice (2), Mozley (1), Noel (3), Pattison (1), Ruskin (3), Russell (2), Sidgwick (2), Sully (2), Tennyson (1), Thirlwall (1), W. G. Ward (1). During Knowles's editorship of the *Contemporary,* Metaphysical Society members thus contributed a total of 156 articles or other papers to the review.

siderable space to literature, music, art, and politics, although he abandoned many of his more clerical and academic writers, many of whom did not again contribute to the *Contemporary* until his editorship had ceased. Among the well-known writers of the seventies who appear more or less often during Knowles's editorship, the most important is Matthew Arnold, who contributed to ten issues. Herbert Spencer is represented in eighteen issues, here publishing the whole of *The Study of Sociology.* Robert Buchanan writes often; in the October, 1871, issue appeared his famous attack on the Pre-Raphaelites, "The Fleshly School of Poetry," first published over the name of "Thomas Maitland." Among other literary contributors were Edward Dowden, Julian Hawthorne, H. G. Hewlett, David Masson, James Spedding, and J. A. Symonds. Historians and writers on politics included J. Gairdner, S. R. Gardiner, G. J. Holyoake, J. M. Ludlow, Mazzini, Bonamy Price, and F. Seebohm, as well as the Metaphysical Society members mentioned above. Among philosophers and theologians, not "Metaphysicians," were E. Caird, Colenso, W. S. Jevons, J. Tulloch, and A. R. Wallace. And there were Frances Power Cobbe and Max Müller, who could write on almost anything.

Not all the debates in the *Contemporary* can interest a modern reader, even one concerned to understand the seventies. But one of the most amazing deserves some mention here, if only because of its relation to the long-continuing discussion of miracles and evidence before the Society. This was the controversy begun in the July, 1872, number with a letter—"communicated" by Tyndall from an anonymous member of the Athenaeum Club—published as "The 'Prayer for the Sick': Hints towards a Serious Attempt to Estimate its Value." The author is concerned to know whether it may not be possible to study the workings of God's Providence by estimating the value of prayer scientifically. Not all forms of prayer, it is reverently assumed, are susceptible of this kind of study, but the "Prayer for the Sick" offers certain opportunities which should not be ignored, since we are assured that here we are "in contact with a source of power available for human ends." The author proposes that the occupants of a particular hospital ward receive for two or three years the special prayers of all the clergy and all the faithful in England, and that the results be compared with established health and mortality statistics. The most scientific way of conducting the experiment would be to have one ward receive the benefit of prayer and another to be denied it, but the author realizes that this would be impossible since, human nature being what it is, the deprived group would receive as many secret and private prayers as the other.[10] But if prayers for the sick are truly effective, we cannot avoid the obligation to study their workings.

It is almost impossible to judge at this distance how completely serious was this proposal. It was obviously made in a sceptical spirit but put forward both by the author and Tyndall with the utmost respect and truly reverent consideration not only for the feelings of believers, but also for the high seriousness of any proposal to examine the power of God. It was perhaps ultimately ironic in the way that all serious things turn to irony in the light of the highest intelligence; but this may have been the very quality in the letter which loosed the floodgates of controversy. It was taken seriously. R. F. Littledale, in the August number, wrote in reply "The Rationale of Prayer," a long attack on both sceptics and weak believers among the clergy, as well as a defense of prayer as too holy and sacred for human examination. In October Tyndall and the author of the original letter replied to Littledale, while President McCosh of Princeton wrote from across the Atlantic a harshly impassioned analysis of prayer as a means of grace denied to sceptics.

But what had been a pious periodical debate became a national issue after the publication in the January, 1873, issue of William Knight's article, "The Function of Prayer in the Economy of the Universe," in which he, a Scottish Presbyterian clergyman, critic, and philosopher, insisted that prayer cannot change the physical order or the immutable laws of nature, and that all it can do is to affect the spiritual world: that it can so influence men's souls as to enable them to use their freedom and their knowledge more wisely.

10 This proposal for a "prayer-gauge" is referred to by Hutton in his "Reminiscence"; see Chap. IV. Francis Galton published his "Statistical Inquiries into the Efficacy of Prayer" in the *Fortnightly,* N.S. XII (August, 1872), 125, an early contribution to the controversy.

This seemed dangerous heresy to many true believers, and Knight was prosecuted in a Scottish court, being accused among other things of having preached in Martineau's Unitarian Chapel, which he had done in a conscious effort to promote church unity in Britain. The case dragged on for many months, producing hundreds of pages of newspaper reports, and although in the end the prosecution failed, it led to Knight's voluntary abandonment of the church of his fathers.

Knight meanwhile was answered by the Duke of Argyll, in the February, 1873, issue, in an arrogant article called "Prayer: The Two Spheres—Are They Two?" Knowles was making full use of the controversy during the time when public interest was at its height. On March 12 he writes to Knight expressing the hope that Knight is feeling enough better to go on with his reply to the Duke and that the article will be in Knowles's hands by the 20th, since he is saving a place for it in the April *Contemporary*. On April 17 he writes again, not having yet obtained the article, now insisting that there is only "a difference of detail after all between the Duke and yourself," and "that what will appear unreasonable to one man may not do so to another," adding, "You will be the 'Dean Stanley' of Scotland soon." But Knight is still in the midst of his defense and has not yet written his reply to the Duke when Knowles again, on April 27, tries to get it from him for the June issue. Knight has wished to put it off until his case is settled, but Knowles feels that it should be published before the decision, so that "it would not then be said to be influenced or colored by that result." "Moreover I venture to think—that in a sort of a way—and if taken at intervals in more harassing matters of business—such an article would act upon you like a larger and purer air— To breathe atmosphere of patient scientific thought and enquiry—about a subject—is much so elevating a change from the stifling air of theological squabbling over it—that it would make rather for health and strength than against them." [11]

Knight's reply, which finally put an end to what had already ceased to be a question of wide public concern, appeared in the

[11] Knowles's unpublished letters to Knight are now in the Pierpont Morgan Library, to which I am indebted for the permission to quote from them here,

December, 1873, issue. "Prayer: 'The Two Spheres'—They *Are* Two," proved an able and philosophically convincing resolution of the problem. We hear no more proposals for gauging the physical efficacy of prayer, but neither do we find in England modern miracle-working like that of Lourdes and Ste. Anne de Beaupré. The whole controversy is important, not only as showing how high religious feelings could run in the seventies and how still unresolved were the problems of free expression of religious opinion, but also as an indication of Knowles's ability to make use of any kind of controversy in the interests of both a successful and an enlightened journalism. The persistency and enthusiasm which were so useful to the Metaphysical Society are also seen in his correspondence with Knight, in which he spared no effort to get what he wanted for his review.

However, Knowles's essential openmindedness in religious matters, combined with his increasing involvement in the spirit of the new science,[12] eventually brought him into conflict with Alexander Strahan, his pious publisher and "editorial director," who early in 1877 sold his periodicals to a group of sectarian nonconformists.[13] I have failed, after the most diligent search, to discover all the details of how and why Strahan and his new publishers broke with Knowles. The new publishers must have feared Knowles's liberalism and his willingness to make the *Contemporary* a free platform for the expression of even the most irreligious opinion. Moreover, new owners often like new policies. The publication, in the January, 1877, issue, of W. K. Clifford's "The Ethics of Belief," a part of which Clifford had delivered as a Metaphysical Society paper,[14] had created a storm of controversy among religious-minded men. Strahan and the new publishers seem to

[12] Huxley was soon to collaborate with him (and a group of anonymous compilers) in the writing of an extensive section of the *Nineteenth Century* called "Recent Science," which appeared several times a year.

[13] Samuel Morley, Francis Peek, and the Rev. Mr. Paton of the Independent College at Nottingham, who formed Strahan and Co., Ltd., to publish Strahan's successful magazines—not only the *Contemporary,* but also the popular religious journals *The Day of Rest* and *Good Things for the Young,* as well as one called *Peepshow.* Strahan was to be retained as editorial director, under the control of the new publishers.

[14] "The Ethics of Belief" (No. 60; April 11, 1876).

have felt that Knowles was guilty of allying both himself and the review with the forces of atheism and materialism, for Clifford had insisted that "No simplicity of mind, no obscurity of station, can escape the universal duty of questioning all that we believe." Strahan may have earlier tried to dissuade Knowles from publishing it; in any case, we know from a letter to William Knight, February 13, 1877, that soon after its publication the break between Knowles and Strahan was complete and that Knowles was already beginning the establishment of his own review, the *Nineteenth Century*. Strahan had meanwhile circulated, presumably among contributors and friends of the *Contemporary*, a document marked "Private" presenting his account of the crisis. This document Knowles thought libelous and threatened to make the true facts known by a paper which his lawyers said they would permit him to send to anyone who had received Strahan's version of the story. These two documents, which I have been unable to trace,[15] would probably, between them, tell the whole story. Knowles says to Knight that Huxley had seen Strahan's document and found it something that "it never entered his imagination a man could have done."

The parting between publisher and editor must have been indeed acrimonious. Knowles let it be known publicly that he was retiring as a consequence of the change in ownership of Strahan and Co. The *Bookseller*, a trade journal, carried a note to this effect in its issue of February 2, 1877, which also announced the foundation and forthcoming appearance of the *Nineteenth Century*.[16] This note adds that "Mr. Alexander Strahan, who originated the work [the *Contemporary*], and who has all along been the actual, if not the nominal, conductor," has issued an explana-

15 Strahan's statement may be the notice quoted from the *Bookseller*, below.

16 An advertisement and prospectus of the new *Nineteenth Century* appeared in the *Spectator* L (February 10, 1877), 191. This also reviewed the facts in the change of ownership of Strahan and Co. and asserted anew the policy—which Knowles claims had guided him in the conduct of the *Contemporary*—of maintaining an open platform for the expression of all responsible opinion. Knowles appends a list of 104 distinguished names of men who have consented to help him in the new *Nineteenth Century*, including *all* the then members of the Metaphysical Society, as well as men like Arnold, Newman, and G. H. Lewes. The contents of the first number and other future contributors are also given.

tory notice. Strahan hopes that in its twelve-year history his review has justified its title. "But certain gratuitous statements and rumours, founded upon inaccurate information—these being followed by criticisms made even more in the dark—call, perhaps, for a word of comment." It is not true that the change of Strahan and Co., into Strahan and Co., Ltd., will have the effect of "altering the policy or narrowing the basis of the *Contemporary Review*. On the contrary, the change will have the effect of preventing the *Review* from becoming the organ of any sect or party, or otherwise ceasing to be the open platform which it was intended to be from the beginning. The *Contemporary Review* will continue to be edited by me; and I leave it, with cheerful hope, to speak for itself and its conductor."

It is possible that London gossip was establishing some kind of sinister connection between the now jealously regarded Metaphysical Society and the *Contemporary*. The publication of Clifford's article may have been all that was necessary to bring these curious suspicions to a head. Or perhaps Knowles was by this time anxious to have a review of his own, and himself precipitated a situation with Strahan. We must observe, however, that from this time on some of the more conservative members of the Metaphysical Society began to attend less regularly and that the years of the Society's decline lie not far ahead. Some of the club gossip may have taken effect, and the popular idea of the Society as a force undermining the faith and the principles of old England become too widespread for social comfort. The privacy, even secrecy, of the Society's meetings and discussions would naturally do much to encourage this view in the public mind. And of course one of the great dangers, from a public point of view, of any such regular meetings of such distinguished men, lies in the conspiratorial implications which the outsider seems to see in their proceedings. In any case, after the triumphant success of the *Nineteenth Century* in its first year of publication, Knowles himself began to lose interest in the Society and began to turn to younger contributors whose views and tempers were more in accord with those of the coming age. It is, therefore, the *Contemporary* which best reflects the impact of the Metaphysical Society upon the intellectual history of the seventies; but it is the *Nineteenth Century* which translates the spirit and method of the Society into a popular journalism which would continue to affect the thought and attitudes of England long after the Society had ceased. And for both, James Knowles was in the largest measure responsible.

Chapter 10

KNOWLES AND THE TRIUMPH OF THE "NINETEENTH CENTURY"

The *Nineteenth Century* first appeared in March, 1877, and created a sensation. Few periodicals have begun with so brilliant and so distinguished a list of contributors and few have maintained for so long their initial character. Wilfrid Ward says that it was "one of the most signal immediate successes . . . in the history of reviews." Knowles had obtained from his father a £2,000 guarantee, but he was never obliged to touch the money, and in fact made many thousands of pounds a year from the review.[1] The wide friendships he had formed in the Metaphysical Society and the experience he had obtained as editor of the *Contemporary* stood him in good stead; few founders of new reviews have ever been so fortunate.

The first number opened with a prefatory sonnet by Tennyson which, in its graceful but allusive references to both the *Contemporary* and the Metaphysical Society, was probably designed to heal any major rifts caused by the difficulties with Strahan:

> Those that of late had fleeted far and fast
> To touch all shores, now leaving to the skill
> Of others their old craft seaworthy still,
> Have chartered this; where, mindful of the past,
> Our true co-mates regather round the mast;
> Of diverse tongue, but with a common will
> Here, in this roaring moon of daffodil
> And crocus, to put forth and brave the blast;
> For some, descending from the peak
> Of hoar high-templed Faith, have leagued again
> Their lot with ours to rove the world about;
> And some are wilder comrades, sworn to seek

1 Wilfrid Ward, *Ten Personal Studies*, London, Longmans, 1908, p. 72.

If any golden harbour be for men
In seas of Death and sunless gulfs of Doubt.

This tribute is addressed both to Knowles's editorial energy and to the spirit of the Society itself.

The lead article was a controversial review by Gladstone of Sir George Cornewall Lewis' *An Essay on the Influence of Authority in Matters of Opinion,*[2] followed in its turn by James Fitzjames Stephen's Metaphysical Society paper "Authority in Matters of Opinion" (No. 66; March 13, 1877), published in the second number of the new review. W. R. S. Ralston, an authority on Russia and the Near East, contributed an essay on "Turkish Story-Books"; Sir John Lubbock wrote "On the Imperial Policy of Great Britain"; and C. J. Ellicott discussed "The Church of England, Present and Future." M. E. Grant Duff contributed the first of two important articles on Russia; J. Baldwin Brown asked "Is the Pulpit losing its Power?"; and G. Croom Robertson told "How We Come by our Knowledge," which is almost certainly a version of his unprinted Metaphysical Society paper, No. 63x, November 14, 1876. Cardinal Manning offered the first of five very interesting articles on "The True Story of the Vatican Council," in this returning to a theme on which he had earlier crossed swords with his old friend Gladstone, whose own contribution to this very number was on a subject close to Manning's heart. Matthew Arnold is represented by "Falkland," an essay in defense of political disinterestedness. Finally, Knowles, in collaboration with Huxley, himself offered the first of a series of surveys of "Recent Science," which became one of the most important features of the new review.

This first number is notable for its concern with political questions, which was always to characterize the *Nineteenth Century* and which led to Knowles's extraordinary influence in the formulation of public opinion. Knowles continued his early preoccupation with religious and philosophical questions, but his sure sense of the temper of the age was already turning him toward that interest in the political implications of the new tendencies in thought which

[2] Originally published in 1849, but republished in 1875 by Sir Gilbert Lewis, Sir George's brother.

was to characterize the intellectual life of the eighties as surely as the impact of science on religion had characterized the seventies. Wilfrid Ward later said that "for those who had a wish and right to claim a hearing from the public no rostrum commanded so wide an audience, except a letter to 'The Times,' as 'The Nineteenth Century,'" and that although Knowles systematized the total absence of all editorial views whatever, the Queen of Holland once called him "le quatrième pouvoir de l'État Britannique." [3] A French contributor has quoted Frederic Harrison as saying to Knowles, "Except for Bismarck and the Pope, you have had as collaborators all the eminent men of the world": [4] and however exaggerated this statement, it probably does represent Knowles's constant effort and intention.

Tennyson himself once said to Wilfrid Ward, "No man ever had his brain in his hand as Knowles had. He could learn in half an hour enough of a subject which was quite new to him to talk about it, and never talk nonsense. When we first planned the Metaphysical Society Knowles did not know a 'concept' from a hippopotamus. Before we had talked of it for a month he could chatter metaphysics with the best of us." Ward points out that "it was this quickness and alertness which also made his editorship so singularly successful in the days of his prime. He applied at the right moment to the right man to address the public on the right topic." [5] Knowles was, as Tennyson said, no metaphysician, and with this Ward agrees. "The philosophy of religious belief had no special interest for him. But accident led him to discover that the subject had at that moment very special interest for a large number of exceedingly eminent and representative men." [6] It is perhaps the function of a great editor to let men and their times speak for themselves; an editor must always be a midwife to the human spirit; and whatever may be the limitations of intellectual midwifery,[7] it is difficult to see how the human intellect can come

[3] Wilfrid Ward, *Ten Personal Studies,* London, Longmans, 1908, pp. 69, 74.

[4] Yves-Guyot, "Ma Connexion avec la 'Nineteenth Century,'" *Nineteenth Century,* CI (March, 1927), 305.

[5] Wilfrid Ward, *op. cit.,* pp. 70, 71.

[6] *Ibid.,* p. 70.

[7] Limitations which were clearly recognized, even in Knowles's London *Times* obituary.

to full fruition without it. But to some, at least, the example of a man like Morley, who was in many ways an even greater editor than Knowles, stands as a warning that the greatest minds can be forced to abdicate their highest functions by the continued pressures of editorial responsibility. Only, perhaps, because there were not enough Knowleses to go 'round, did men like Morley and Hutton fail, in the last analysis, to exert the critical and creative influence of a man like Matthew Arnold.

The first number of the *Nineteenth Century* was, as we have seen, very largely the work of members of the Metaphysical Society. Of its eleven contributions, only three were not by members; in the five numbers of Volume I, 29 out of 55 articles, or more than half, are by members of the Society. In succeeding volumes this proportion is decreased, reflecting not only Knowles's gradual loss of interest in the Society, but also his care for the future of his review and the development of his political interests and influence. Some of his old collaborators were dead or dying; some were old and verging on retirement. But until the dissolution of the Society at the end of 1880 its members are still heavily represented in his review. In the first four volumes, 78 out of 238 contributions are by members of the Society, and in the next four, 48 out of about 240. Thus, out of about 480 contributions in the less than four years between the founding of the *Nineteenth Century* and the end of the Society, 126, or more than a fourth of the total, are by members. However, only twenty-six members, of whom seven had never contributed to the *Contemporary* under Knowles's editorship, produced this notable mass of journalism. Gladstone furnished the chief exhibit; he contributed 23 articles in less than four years, on subjects about evenly divided between politics and Homer. Huxley was next, with 13, including his share in "Recent Science." Ruskin appears 10 times, and Froude 9, arousing the ire of Freeman who in the now rival *Contemporary* attacked Froude mercilessly and unfairly as a man incapable of telling the truth. Tennyson contributed 8 poems, 3 of them sonnets, and including "The Revenge" and "The Defence of Lucknow." M. E. Grant Duff is represented by 7 admirable political essays, and Cardinal Manning by 6 articles, including the five parts of his "True Story of the Vatican Council." Robert Lowe, who had been Chancellor of the Exchequer in Gladstone's first ministry, and W. R. Greg, an old writer for the *Contemporary*, each contributed 5 political articles. W. K. Clifford, who died in 1878, appears 4 times, as do also Frederic Harrison, Dean Stanley, James Fitzjames Stephen, and Tyndall. Altogether, it is fair to say that the most important and the most active members of the Metaphysical Society continued to give strong support to Knowles in his new enterprise.[8]

With the *Nineteenth Century*, however, as with the *Contemporary*, Knowles did not rely entirely on his galaxy of Metaphysicians. Many of his occasional writers are today almost forgotten, but among the contributors of the first four years who were not members of the Society are many who had earlier been writers for the *Contemporary* and others who later made their mark in many fields. Among historians and political writers were Dicey, Holyoake, Maine, Seebohm, and Lecky, as well as Lord Stratford de Redcliffe, Justin McCarthy, and H. D. Traill. In literary and social criticism were Matthew Arnold, F. W. H. Myers, and Henry Irving, in addition to James Spedding, Henry Morley, W. H. Mallock, Sidney Colvin, H. G. Hewlett, Anthony Trollope, and Lionel Tennyson. Knowles's lifelong interest in art was given wide expression in his new review; there are intelligent articles by some of the principal painters of the day—Holman Hunt, Watts, and Leighton, as well as art criticism by R. St. J. Tyrwhitt, Sir Robert Collier, and others. Fewer of the religious writers have been long remembered, perhaps a sign of the times; but Bishop Charles Wordsworth and Lord Blachford deserve mention, as well as W. H. Mallock, that witty and often irresponsible genius, who was publishing at this time—in both the *Nineteenth Century* and the *Contemporary*—in the name of his own Catholic faith, devastating attacks upon atheism, socialism, positivism, science, and even civilization. Knowles continued his emphasis on science as the breath of the new day and, in addition to the contributions

8 Other members who contributed during the remaining years of the Society were: Barry (1), Bucknill (1), Ellicott (3), Gasquet (1), Gull (2), Lubbock (2), Magee (2), Mivart (3), Pollock (1), Croom Robertson (1), Sidgwick (1), and W. G. Ward (1).

by its Metaphysical Society representatives, published articles by A. R. Wallace, G. J. Romanes, Francis Galton, and W. Crookes.

All these writers appeared before the end of 1880; after that date their number was notably increased by the younger lights of the end of the century, and at least until 1900, when its name was changed to *The Nineteenth Century and After*,[9] the review continued to be both a splendidly representative and powerfully influential journal of opinion. Knowles continued the editorial direction of the review until his death on February 13, 1908, after which date it was continued by his son-in-law, and, later, by other editors; but until relatively recent times it remained in considerable part a property of the Knowles family and maintained as much as possible Knowles's policies. It is still published, in the original format.

During the first year and a half of the new review Knowles tried one of his most successful journalistic experiments, itself based, by his own admission, upon his experience with the Metaphysical Society. This was "A Modern Symposium," which began in the second number of the *Nineteenth Century*, April, 1877. In an editorial note Knowles says: "A certain number of gentlemen have consented to discuss from time to time, under this title, questions of interest and importance. Each writer will have seen all that has been written before his own remarks, but (except the first writer) nothing that follows them. The first writer, as proposer of the subject, will have the right of reply or summing-up at the end. The present discussion will be continued and concluded in the May number of the *Review*." The first Symposium began with a paper on "The Influence upon Morality of a Decline in Religious Belief," by James Fitzjames Stephen, which is almost certainly the paper, or a rewritten version of the paper, read by Stephen before the Metaphysical Society, "The Effect of a Decline of Religious Belief on Morality" (No. 63y; December 12, 1876).[10]

[9] I have encountered the rumor that some enterprising creature had copyrighted the name *The Twentieth Century* and tried to persuade Knowles to purchase the right to use it. But it is more likely that Knowles was unwilling to sacrifice a name which had brought him such success. The review still bears the title *The Nineteenth Century and After*, "Founded by James Knowles."

[10] This paper was not printed; see App. C.

Many of the contributors to the Symposium may have heard Stephen's paper at that time, and from the discussion which it raised Knowles may have formed the idea of the usefulness of such a Symposium in the launching of his new review. Other contributors to this first experiment in the April number were, in order, Lord Selborne, Martineau, Harrison, Dean Church, the Duke of Argyll, and Clifford. It was continued in the next number by W. G. Ward, Huxley, and Hutton, with a brief rebuttal by Stephen. All these contributors were members of the Society. Here was expressed every kind of judgment, by the leaders of almost every school of religious and moral thought. The differences of conviction and opinion, expressed publicly by members of the Society in this and the two succeeding Symposia, must have done much to convince all concerned that not only had the Society failed in its original purpose of discovering some common ground on which theists, agnostics, and scientists could meet, epistemologically and cosmologically, but also that this kind of public airing of their still unreconcilable positions was all that was now left for them to do. In this sense Knowles's "Modern Symposium" is both a successor to the Society and one of the forces bringing about its decline.

The second "Modern Symposium" was initiated in a slightly different way with Frederic Harrison's two articles on "The Soul and Future Life," published in June and July, 1877. These are an expansion of Harrison's Metaphysical Society paper "The Soul before and after Death" (No. 64; January 9, 1877), which had been replied to by Manning in his paper (No. 65), on the same subject, of February 13.[11] These two articles became the text for a new Symposium on "The Soul and Future Life," which Knowles started in the September number in discussion of Harrison's positivist thesis. Criticism was begun by R. H. Hutton and carried on by Huxley, Lord Blachford, and Roden Noel. In October the battle continued, having become by this time in the eyes of later participants a conflict between Harrison's positivism and Huxley's agnosticism. The polemical positions of these skilled antagonists were further analyzed and criticized by Lord Sel-

[11] See App. C.

borne, Alfred Barry, W. R. Greg, Rev. Baldwin Brown, and W. G. Ward. Harrison summed up in a very long reply, which in itself shows to what degree the public debates of the seventies and the discussions of the Metaphysical Society had humanized and even "naturalized" the theological bases of any public discussion of the soul and immortality.

Knowles's third and last "Modern Symposium" began in the May, 1878, number, with a discussion by Lord Arthur Russell of the question, "Is the Popular Judgment in Politics more Just than that of the Higher Orders?" While two contributors to the second Symposium, Lord Blachford and Baldwin Brown, did not belong to the Metaphysical Society, this final debate is once more carried on entirely by members of the Society. Russell's question reflected a contention of Gladstone's in a recent controversy with Robert Lowe, who, as a moderate and even conservative anti-democratic Liberal, had taken issue with his former chief. Russell himself does not approve of flattering the sovereign people by depreciating the value of knowledge and education. The demagogue has always preferred an uneducated audience. To Russell it seems "obvious that the uneducated masses are only in the right when led by right-minded leaders." R. H. Hutton continued the discussion in the same issue, insisting that Russell had misunderstood Gladstone's meaning. The masses *are* teachable. Throughout the half-century since the first Reform Bill, this has manifested itself in the increasing political intelligence of the members of Parliament themselves. The doubly reformed Parliament of 1867 was by far the most intellectually distinguished and politically responsible of all English parliaments to date. In a brilliant analysis of recent political history, Hutton shows in what senses Gladstone was fundamentally right. M. E. Grant Duff carries on, pointing out that there is less difference between Gladstone and Lowe than their words would indicate. He repeats Bagehot's quotation of Newman, who had said, "When we have stated our terms and cleared our ground, all argument is generally either superfluous or fruitless." The minority of the minority must always teach the masses. It is for this reason that Grant Duff prides himself on being, like Russell, a Liberal politician. Frederic Harrison concludes this first part of the Symposium, remarking with his customary force that of course right judgment is due to education, and that of course politics requires leadership. But political education and literary or cultural education are different. Many a workman, union leader, or tradesman has not only more political education than most members of the "higher orders," but he often has, in issues which affect the interest of all, better political judgment.

The second part of this Symposium appeared in July, 1878. W. R. Greg, a lifelong critic of liberal political doctrine, takes the position that the masses and the uneducated generally are more guided by impulse than by those above them. Where the problem is one of heart or equity, and the issues at stake in these terms are clear, the people is wise. Robert Lowe, with wit and irony, points out that Gladstone agrees with Aristotle on the popular judgment, but he goes on to defend his own moderate position and to insist that the history of English liberalism is the history of benefits granted to the people by the intelligence of those above them. He regards himself as a Liberal politician who neither wants nor needs the aid of the working classes in the improvement of the political state of the country. Gladstone himself comments on the whole debate and says that he naturally prefers the positions taken by Hutton and Harrison. But he believes that the superiority of popular judgment is "due mainly to moral causes, to a greater mental integrity, which, again, is greatly owing to the comparative absence of the more subtle agencies of temptation" which afflict the propertied and cultured classes. He, too, feels that political education and judgment—not the same as qualified and expert political experience—is different from cultural education. Lord Arthur Russell recapitulates and sums up the argument, and himself in the end agrees in large measure with Hutton and Grant Duff. The whole argument shows clearly the extent to which the fall of Gladstone's first ministry and the rebirth of Toryism under Disraeli had made inevitable a further debate on suffrage and the ultimate extension of the franchise. But it also shows even more clearly how inadequate to the changed political situation was the political and economic liberalism of the mid-century.

This turn from a discussion of moral and religious subjects to politics marks not only a shift in Knowles's intellectual and journalistic interests, but also a change in popular opinion and the climate of thought. The battle between science and religion was almost over, but, perhaps more important, the era of Radical hopes, so splendidly exemplified by the success of Morley's *Fortnightly Review* and the dialectical liberalism symbolized in the political sphere by Gladstone's first ministry, was now past; and in its place we see the growing imperialism of Disraeli's England and a concomitant relegation of the Church and all ultimate moral and philosophic issues to the service of a militant nationalism. The next twenty years were to see the gradual decay of the spirit of high questioning, the fervent criticism of morals and methods, the noble tension between scepticism and affirmation which mark the true greatness of the Victorian Age. Knowles knew, as well as Morley and Harrison, that England was passing through a period of cultural transition, but he also realized that a fresh interest in mass politics would become one of the inevitable consequences of Disraeli's imperial and international policies. It would be unfair to his flexible intelligence to call him merely a journalistic opportunist. He had long savored the implications of Lowe's observation on the Reform Bill of 1867, "We must educate our masters." And although the *Nineteenth Century* was never a journal for the populace, it gradually attracted to itself not only many of the most important writers of Morley's *Fortnightly*, but also those readers of the *Fortnightly* who had begun to lose faith in a compromisingly critical Radicalism and who looked to Gladstone as the remaining symbol of a liberal faith which might stem the demagogic power of the new political irrationalism.

Politics is one of the most important aspects of the intellectual history of any period, but it is impossible here to analyze in detail the change which came over English political life between 1870 and 1880. A third of the members of the Metaphysical Society were either active political leaders or important critics of politics. Their concern with philosophical issues was not merely a major characteristic of the intellectual life of the seventies; it was a normal consequence of the concentration of political power in the hands of a social and intellectual elite. Politicians have rarely been philosophers, but many have recognized that political practice inevitably raises philosophical issues. The political history of our own century has clearly demonstrated this fact; and ever since the time of Plato, the notion of a philosopher-king or of a philosophically justified sovereign has dominated Western political thought. But when politics ceases to be the prerogative of a cultural elite, the wisdom of this elite is no longer a powerful element in politics. The major problem of democratic political life is how to make the best use of the knowledge and wisdom of the few, while at the same time serving the many and raising the level of their political intelligence. England, more than any country in the modern world—with the possible exception of the Scandinavian countries—seems to have faced and met this problem with considerable success. The discussions of the Metaphysical Society were rarely political in any exact sense, but the discussions of evidence, belief, and authority which dominate its meetings are the indispensable groundwork, both in method and conclusion, to any resolution of the political problem. When the Society had talked itself out on these questions, its members transferred their intellectual activity to other fields, and both in the great reviews and in more specialized philosophical activity continued to evolve answers to this vital question: how to make the propagandist power of word and deed best serve the public interest without serving either an oligarchical or a popular tyranny. England is still ruled by an elite, but an elite which has developed a wider and wider popular base; in this development the reviews have exercised a considerable influence, and, through Knowles's *Nineteenth Century*, the Metaphysical Society itself shared in the process.

The greatest days of the *Nineteenth Century* came in the eighties and nineties and thus fall outside the scope of the present study. But the continued success of Knowles's editorship is borne out by a professional observation from Arthur Waugh, certainly an unprejudiced critic, for his firm of Chapman and Hall was until almost our own day the publisher of the *Nineteenth Century's* predecessor and competitor, the *Fortnightly*. Writing in 1902,

Waugh says that since its founding, the *Nineteenth Century* has held its own "as the most widely read of the monthly reviews. Mr. Knowles has an enviable faculty for being first upon the scent of novelty; and rival editors will confess how often they have been disappointed in finding him before them in securing the promise of the right man's view upon the new political or social complication." And further, "The *Nineteenth Century* is now certainly the most popular of the monthly reviews, and probably enjoys the most weight." [12] He admits the force of a contemporary criticism that Knowles depends more on the distinction of his authors than on the contents of his review, and finds it "indeed true that the long array of names upon the front cover is sometimes more imposing, from an official or social standpoint, than are the views or the style of the articles themselves." [13] But even if this tendency marked the growing failure of a once notable editorial policy, it continued to be remunerative and Knowles never abandoned his search not only for experts, but also for the best-acknowledged experts in every field. The success of the *Nineteenth Century* was not only a just reward for Knowles's skill and enthusiasm in organizing and maintaining the Metaphysical Society, and a tribute which the surviving members of the Society continued to pay him in friendship and journalistic devotion throughout their lives; but in terms of the wide public which they reached through his pages and the handsome remuneration which Knowles was able to offer them for their articles, it was also a reward for the mutual loyalty to a method and a spirit which they themselves had demonstrated in the Society.

[12] Arthur Waugh, "The English Reviews: a Sketch of their History and Principles," *The Critic*, New York, XL (Jan., 1902), 36.

[13] This certainly began to be true about the turn of the century, but Knowles was 70 in 1901 and can perhaps be excused for a failure to keep in complete touch with the men and movements of the day. Even so, he continued with only slowly diminishing success until his death in 1908.

Chapter 11

THE THREADS OF DISCOURSE

THE INTELLECTUAL BATTLES of the seventies represent a struggle not merely between popular faith and popular science, but also between at least two major English philosophical positions, the intuitional or a priori and the empirical or experience schools. However, slowly, through the mid-century, the prestige and influence of Continental and especially German thought had been growing in England. The final abolition of religious tests in the universities and the opening of almost all university positions to all men, whether or not they were ordained in the established Church, made possible intellectual careers in the universities for those who had been trained in the school of Hegel's rationalist followers and who had breathed the bracing air of the new scientific spirit. University reform was both cause and consequence of this new academic atmosphere, a development which had had a long and often exciting history. But it was not until the seventies that the temper of the educated popular mind found itself in essential agreement with the prevailing moods of the universities, instead of in disagreement or contradiction.

Men like Henry Sidgwick, who had earlier resigned his fellowship at Cambridge because he could not with a clear conscience adhere to the tests, now found large portions of the educated public sympathetic with their views. And as part of the same process, fewer and fewer of the most distinguished minds went into the Church and more and more chose the professional academic life, in science, in mathematics, in philosophy, and in the "social sciences," not yet so infelicitously named. What was the Church's loss became the universities' gain; but it is even yet not clear whether the national culture gained similarly. For while the universities in the eighteenth century and a good part of the nineteenth were peaceful refuges for clerical gentlemen of intellectual tastes, the new dispensation made them equally sheltered havens for the professional academic mind; and even in England, which has happily been freer than America from the fascination of the Germanic ideal of "scholarship," great and powerful minds have been "cabin'd, cribbed, confined" within the walls of miniature worlds which are often tragically remote from the world of feeling and action. The universities had always sent many of their most active-minded young men into politics; this they continued to do in large measure; but even politics has suffered by the skimming-off of many talented minds into academic life. So long as the Church was a highly promising career for intelligent and capable young men, the universities were the center from which the influence of a philosophical concern with social and moral problems of a high order was disseminated not only to a few youthful undergraduates but to dioceses and parish communities all over England. The Church may never again recover this influence; it is possible that the universities are now in other ways regaining this long-lost power.

G. Croom Robertson and "Mind"

Late in 1875, George Croom Robertson, a brilliant young Scot who was Professor of Mental Philosophy and Logic at University College, London, and a member of the Metaphysical Society, issued a prospectus for a new quarterly review which was to be called *Mind.* Robertson had been elected to the London chair in 1866 at the age of 24, being chosen in preference to James Martineau, whom George Grote had opposed on the ground that the position was incompatible with any clerical profession. Robertson had studied at Heidelberg, Göttingen, and Paris and had later been for several years an assistant and collaborator of Alexander Bain's at Aberdeen. Bain not only must have helped him get the London chair, for Grote was one of Bain's oldest friends, but also became, in 1874, the originator and financial backer of *Mind,* on the one condition that Robertson be the sole editor. Thus was founded a review which was in itself one of the major signs of the growing secular and professional influence in the universities.

There is even a special fitness in the fact that *Mind* was begun and edited by a man who was a professor in University College, London, an institution which had been founded long before, in 1827, as a home for teaching free from all religious tests. But it is also thus true that what we mean by the "academic mind" had there been in longer possession. The importance of this complex situation lay in the growing fear among professional academics that the popular journalism of the period and the tremendous public urge to self-education and the spread of popularized knowledge and discussion would in some sense debase the aims and functions of the higher learning. This attitude on the part of an academic aristocracy, together with the growing influence of Continental example, led not only to the founding of a host of specialized scholarly journals, but also to the elaborate extension of the principle of rigorous examinations which has for so long characterized English education *below* the university level, and which figures so largely in the periodical debates of the eighties. It is probably fair to say that the inadequacy of truly public education in England in modern times can also be traced, not only to the opposition of the Church to wholly secular education,[1] but also, at least in part, to this prejudice against the popular mind, although I must admit that our own efforts in a somewhat different tradition have not been notably more successful.

If we are to take at their face value some of the sceptical comments on the usefulness of the Metaphysical Society already remarked, this prejudice on the part of the professional intellectual was not restricted to a suspicion of popular thinking, but was extended to the philosophical activities of the leaders in English opinion themselves. Men like Huxley, however, not only never ceased their activities in behalf of public education, but devoted a good part of their busy lives to popular teaching and popular writing, often earning in the process only the opprobrium of their more highly professionalized colleagues. Huxley's reputation has indeed suffered under this criticism in our own day. Not all men

[1] Seen in the compromises of Forster's Education Act of 1870. Compare Edwin M. Everett, *The Party of Humanity: the "Fortnightly Review" and its Contributors,* Chapel Hill, University of North Carolina Press, 1939, pp. 153–61.

feel Huxley's double vocation, but Milton might well have been critical of the "fugitive and cloistered virtue" of the professional academic mind.

G. Croom Robertson's new review was from the very beginning one of the most distinguished of professional academic journals, and perhaps because of the inveterately amateur nature of English intellectual activity, which has continued to give English learning a vigor and charm sometimes lacking elsewhere, it has always been open to nonacademic writers. But in the idea of its inception was implied much of the academic attitude I have tried to characterize here. And it is true that at the very time when the great popular reviews were beginning to exclude the more profound philosophical and scientific papers and turn to more popularly based articles, *Mind* appeared in answer to a need. As the Metaphysical Society declined, its most philosophically minded members turned increasingly to *Mind* rather than to the *Nineteenth Century;* and this, too, was a sign of the times.

The first number of *Mind,* a "quarterly review of psychology and philosophy," appeared in January, 1876. The editor, G. Croom Robertson, opened it with a good many "Prefatory Words," which themselves illustrate both the new situation and the new academic attitude:

> The first English journal devoted to Psychology and Philosophy,[2] MIND appears in circumstances that call for some remark.
>
> That no such journal should hitherto have existed is hardly surprising. [English inquiry into the things of the mind has been until now unprofessional and in this respect is distinguished from all other countries, Scotland excepted.] Bacon, Hobbes, Locke, Berkeley, Hume, Hartley, the Mills did their philosophical work at the beginning or at the end or in the pauses of lives otherwise active, and addressed for the most part the common intelligence of their time. It may not have been

[2] *The Zooist,* "A Journal of Cerebral Physiology and Mesmerism and Their applications to Human Welfare," was published in London from 1843 through January, 1852. It published a good deal of useful psychometric and psychophysical material of real value and was one of the first journals in any language to publish psychopathic case histories. *The Journal of Speculative Philosophy,* edited by William T. Harris, had been published in America (St. Louis and, later, New York) since 1867. Eighty-eight numbers appeared, with many English and Continental contributions, before it came to an end in 1893.

ill for their fame; but their work itself is not what it otherwise might have been,[3] and their manner of thinking has affected the whole character and standing [4] of philosophical inquiry in England. If their work had been academic, it would probably have been much more sustained—better carried out when it did not lack comprehension, more comprehensive when it was well and carefully begun. The informality of their thought has undoubtedly prevented philosophy from obtaining the scientific consideration which it holds elsewhere.[5] There has not been wanting in England a generally diffused interest in the subject, such as is fed by discussions, more or less philosophical, mixed up with lighter literature in the pages of miscellaneous magazines, but of special interest, like that felt in mathematics or physics or chemistry by a multitude of active workers and a multitude of trained and continuous learners, there has hitherto been little.[6] Even now the notion of a journal being founded to be taken up wholly with metaphysical subjects, as they are called, will little commend itself either to those who are in the habit of declaring with great confidence that there can be no science in such matters, or to those who would only play with them now and again.[7]

[There is, however, a new interest in mental science and philosophy in England, and physical inquirers are calling for a wider and deeper comprehension of nature.] The unity that belonged to human knowledge under the name of Philosophy, before the special sciences were, is now, when the sciences stand fast, again sought for under no other name than Philosophy.

[The founders of the Review are] not prepared to be responsible for a publication that would display only or chiefly the speculative differences of individual thinkers. [Psychology has always been important to English philosophy, and, more significantly, ought to yield] a continuous harvest of results. [MIND intends] to procure a decision of this question as to the scientific standing of psychology.

[The prospectus has shown the breadth of the fields to be covered in both philosophy and psychology, including the problems of education. And it is the hope of the new review to uncover in psychology a common ground for philosophers and metaphysicians. If this psychological base can be found, it will be useful to all scientific inquiry.]

3 This is unquestionably true; but what is the drift of this observation? Robertson could hardly have meant that they did not construct great systems on the German model, for he himself was not that kind of thinker, being himself a Millite in the manner of his master, Bain.

4 This comment seems to be a defensive recognition of a common Continental criticism of the "shallowness" of English philosphy.

5 The ghosts of the German professors walk through these two sentences.

6 How long have the humanistic subjects yearned for the method and prestige of the sciences! Observe the German curse in the field of literature alone.

7 A reference to the Metaphysical Society?

This final observation puts *Mind* back squarely in the main tradition of English philosophical thought, and in spite of the degree of rivalry with and imitation of German tradition explicit in the earlier parts of these "Prefatory Words," *Mind* has largely continued the English tradition of a primary concern with empiricism, epistemology, and the psychological implications of metaphysics and moral philosophy.

The opening number contained the first of Shadworth Hodgson's three articles on "Philosophy and Science," in which he resumed the purpose of his papers before the Metaphysical Society —an effort to make distinctions, not definitions, the business of philosophy. Also published in this first number was Henry Sidgwick's Metaphysical Society paper "The Theory of Evolution in its Application to Practice" (No. 55; July 13, 1875). Pollock replied to this article in the July number; and Sidgwick began his long and often unequal battle with Bradley in a review of the latter's *Ethical Studies* in the October issue. W. K. Clifford published in the January, 1878, number his first Metaphysical Society paper, "On the Nature of Things in Themselves" (No. 45; June 9, 1874). Hodgson and Sidgwick each appear several times before 1880, and among other members of the Society represented in the early years are G. Croom Robertson himself and Leslie Stephen, as well as the young Alfred Barratt and A. J. Balfour, who, although both elected in 1880, probably never attended a meeting of the Society. J. F. Payne contributed a memorial notice of James Hinton to the April, 1876, number, not, however, doing full justice to his philosophy or his influence. William James began to contribute in 1879, publishing in the January number his paper "Are We Automata?" and in July the important essay on "The Sentiment of Rationality." [8] Robertson's own concern with the academic pursuit of philosophy is reflected in the early numbers in three interesting essays on the state of philosophy in the English universities. Mark Pattison contributed the first, on "Philosophy at Oxford"; Henry Sidgwick writes later on "Philosophy at Cambridge"; and Robertson himself then discusses "Philosophy in London."

[8] Only the first part of this essay as reprinted in *The Will to Believe, and Other Essays,* appeared in *Mind.*

One of the most interesting aspects of the new review was its elaborate "departmentalization." Each issue began with original philosophical articles, followed by "Critical Notices" of important philosophical books by authorities who volunteered thorough and careful examination in the form of essays or reviews. This section was followed from time to time by reports of important psychological or philosophical researches, accomplished or under way. Next, was one of the most important departments, "Notes and Discussions," in which comment on and criticism of the various contents of the review were undertaken by a large number of contributors and other philosophers. This feature is often reminiscent in tone and manner of both the Metaphysical Society and Knowles's "Modern Symposium." In fact Knowles may have developed the idea of the symposia in part from his perusal of these early numbers of *Mind*. The section devoted to "New Books" made no effort to be critical but merely gave a concise idea of the contents of each, much in the manner of modern scientific abstracts. Last of all, there was from time to time a brief section devoted to "News," containing notices of the meetings of learned societies and conferences, personal notes about philosophers, English and foreign, and brief obituaries.

G. Croom Robertson himself gave every promise of being a productive scholar in both philosophy and psychology. It is therefore especially unfortunate that he who was so much concerned with the lack of professional philosophy in England should have made no major contribution beyond the founding and editing of *Mind*. To this task he gave himself freely and unstintingly in addition to heavy teaching obligations in University College and elsewhere. But his youthful precocity had left him fragile and sickly, and in consequence he never dared to overtax his strength. His health finally broke down almost completely; and he was tended like a brother in his last illness by his devoted friend Leslie Stephen. As with W. K. Clifford, his friends and admirers, who were many, were sure that if his health had been better he would have done great things. But men like Hutton and Leslie Stephen, who luckily overcame the illness and incapacity of their youth, manifest an unconscious pride in their excuses for others less fortunate. And perhaps *Mind,* which is still published and still enjoys the highest prestige among philosophers, is a sufficient monument to Robertson's gifts.

Hutton of the "Spectator"

Among the editors in the Metaphysical Society, none was more actively interested in its debates than R. H. Hutton, co-editor of the *Spectator,* and none made a greater impression on thoughtful readers of the literature of the age. In a lifetime of writing critical and philosophic "middles" for the weekly *Spectator,* Hutton probably read, pondered, compared, and criticized more of the important and serious books of his time than any other man in any period. Such a continued diet of words and writing cannot in the abstract be good for the soul of any man, but Hogben, his admirer and only biographer, admits that in spite of what he calls Hutton's bad art, it is "his generous purpose and real but orderly enthusiasm, that one loves to dwell on." [9] This enthusiasm, generosity, and balance of wit and sympathy, combined with a depth of historical and philosophical learning almost unmatched in his own day, is what makes Hutton one of the greatest, even though today most neglected, critics of the late-Victorian period. Morley considered him "a fine English critic" and Gladstone, whose literary opinions, to be sure, are negligible and who was undoubtedly prejudiced by his long friendship, called him "the first critic of the nineteenth century."

Hutton's style, however, has been much more harshly dealt with than it deserves. In spite of a predilection for overlong sentences, often broken up by a too frequent use of the dash—that indispensable and carelessly used mark of punctuation without which many modern writers who lack his skill in the handling of complex ideas would be helpless—Hutton's prose remains the flexible instrument of his thought at every step in an elaborate argument. One writer has called Hutton's style "from the aesthetic point of view, deplorable," [10] and Virginia Woolf, in *The Common Reader,* has

[9] John Hogben, *Richard Holt Hutton of "The Spectator,"* Edinburgh, Oliver and Boyd, 1900.

[10] William Beach Thomas, *The Story of the "Spectator," 1828–1928,* London, Methuen, 1928, p. 70. This book, a centenary volume, is also our best authority

described it as a "voice which is as a plague of locusts—the voice of a man stumbling drowsily among loose words, clutching aimlessly at vague ideas." But such critics can have read very little of Hutton or, what is more likely, have not known the literature he was criticizing. For Hutton's style is a vehicle which can be used with equal ease and, be it remembered, equal pretended anonymity, in literary, philosophical, religious, and scientific criticism. And yet his warm, passionate, and noble personality shines forth from almost every page, as any reader of "The Metaphysical Society: a Reminiscence," can see. I suspect that Hutton's literary style, in the earlier years of the present century, bore the brunt of a criticism which was really addressed to the personality and "style" of the man himself, a "style" which seemed to a more blasé and irresponsible generation outmoded and "Victorian."

The *Spectator* had only four editors during almost a hundred years of its history, and two of these, Hutton and Meredith Townsend, served the greater part of their lives as co-proprietors and co-editors. Robert Stephen Rintoul, who founded the weekly paper in 1828, was its editor until shortly before his death in 1858, by which time it had begun to lose circulation to the successful new *Saturday Review*, begun in 1855.[11] An unknown Mr. Scott purchased it from the aged Rintoul and conducted it blunderingly during a brief interregnum which ended in 1861 with the sale of the paper to Meredith Townsend, a young journalist recently returned from India, where he had edited *The Friend of India*.[12] Soon after, Walter Bagehot, with whom Hutton edited the *National Review* from 1855 to 1864,[13] introduced Hutton to Townsend, and at this first meeting Townsend proposed to Hutton

for the history of the *Spectator*. It is a chatty and discursive book, but full of interesting material.

11 For the early history of this weekly rival to the *Spectator*, see Merle M. Bevington, *"The Saturday Review," 1855–1868*, New York, Columbia, 1941. For the early history of the *Spectator's* only other important weekly rival, see Leslie M. Marchand, *"The Athenaeum," A Mirror of Victorian Culture*, Chapel Hill, University of North Carolina Press, 1941.

12 See W. B. Thomas, *op. cit.*

13 Hutton also assisted Bagehot in the editorship of the *Economist* from 1858 to 1860, an experience that was later of considerable use on the *Spectator*.

that they become co-editors and co-proprietors of the *Spectator*. The alliance thus formed lasted until 1886, when Hutton retired from active editorship, although he continued his part-proprietorship and continued to write for the *Spectator* until a few months before his death in 1897. After Hutton's death, Townsend himself retired, and J. St. Loe Strachey, who had become assistant editor some years before, became sole editor and sole proprietor, continuing in both capacities until his retirement from active conduct of the paper in 1925.

The *Spectator* has thus had a more unified history than any other modern periodical. From 1861 to 1897 the partnership of Hutton and Townsend imposed upon it a character which has since influenced every liberal weekly in the English-speaking world. No two men could have been more different than Hutton and Townsend in interests, personality, or temperament, but the history of great partnerships in almost every field bears witness that this difference is perhaps an indispensable attribute of their success. From the beginning Townsend was the political editor and Hutton the literary and philosophical editor, but each occasionally trespassed into the other's province. Disagreements on policy were few, but when they did occur Hutton always deferred to Townsend as "first proprietor." Early in their joint history they earned public wrath by their strong support of the North in the American Civil War, but the postwar public approval of Northern victory vindicated their policy and began the period of their great success. The paper continued its strong support of the Liberal party until both editors broke with Gladstone over Home Rule and became Liberal Unionists, although Hutton never permitted any personal attack on his old friend Gladstone, whom he still deeply admired.

The most important friendship in Hutton's life, however, was that with Bagehot, whom he had known since the age of 17, when they were both students at University College, London. Hutton edited Bagehot's literary, biographical, and historical *Studies* after his death, and also wrote the biographical memoir accompanying his collected works. The relation between the two men was unusually close; each has paid tribute to the personal and intellectual influence of the other. There is no question that Hutton's wide interests and even wider reading did much to keep Bagehot's task as editor of the *Economist* from absorbing all his varied energies and helped to liberate Bagehot's mind for the literary and political writing for which he will be longest remembered. Bagehot's death, by removing a rationalistic and even somewhat sceptical influence, may have been in part responsible for the increasing orthodoxy of Hutton's religious position in later years and may have contributed indirectly and in complicated intellectual and emotional ways to his growing admiration for Cardinal Newman.

Hutton's praise of Newman is the more interesting as coming from one who had not felt his personal and intellectual charm in youth, but who had come, as he says, to admire the spiritual character of a life standing in strange contrast "to the eager and agitated turmoil of confused passions, hesitating ideals, tentative virtues, and grasping philanthropies amid which it has been lived." There is special interest in the fact that Hutton, who had begun his intellectual life as a Unitarian and a pupil of James Martineau, and who had studied in Germany at Heidelberg, Berlin, and Bonn,[14] turned in the end to a highly personal theism which embraced the paradoxical tension between mind and spirit so typical of Newman. We have earlier seen that throughout the debates of the Metaphysical Society Hutton was on the side of the intuitionists and, even more specifically, on the side of Ward, Newman's younger friend and early apostle, whose own conversion to Rome did so much to spur Newman's. But Hutton never became a Catholic, in fact never pledged himself completely to any Church. His intelligence, like his heart, remained his own. But at his death, we are told, "round his grave were grouped Anglicans, Roman Catholics and Unitarians, in about equal numbers and in equal grief."

The *Spectator* continued its tradition of anonymity until almost the end of Strachey's reign. But its columns were always

[14] Mommsen, under whom Hutton sat at Bonn, said of him afterwards, "That young man took away from my lectures not only all the knowledge I could give him, but much mental nutriment, for which he was indebted to his own genius" (W. B. Thomas, *op. cit.*, pp. 62–3).

open to signed letters. Among members of the Metaphysical who conducted controversial correspondence in its pages were Huxley, Tyndall, the Duke of Argyll, Harrison, Church, and Lubbock; while among its more or less regular anonymous writers and reviewers were of course Hutton himself, who wrote at least a "middle" every week, Bagehot, Pollock, Martineau, Lubbock, Stanley, Knowles, and Morley, as well as a host of figures who were not members of the Society. Here, as in the other periodicals we have examined, the influence of the members of the Society spread widely through late-Victorian life. And although the nature of the *Spectator* did not allow it to become one of the means by which the papers of the Society were brought to public notice,[15] Hutton himself in his devotion to the Society shows how much it meant to his own intellectual life. If the Society had no other significance, its role as a meeting place of editors with each other and with the leading minds of the time would still make it unique.

Ward of the "Dublin Review"

W. G. Ward, Catholic philosopher and theologian, was one of the most active members of the Metaphysical Society, its second chairman, in 1870, and often occasional chairman in succeeding years. His ability to see the burden of opposing arguments and to direct attention both to their weaknesses and their strengths was a quality notable in a chairman, as well as being unusual in one who held his own views so rigorously and inexpugnably. These gifts, which he shared with Mill, whom he regarded both as a friend and as his major philosophical opponent, contributed largely to his success as editor of the *Dublin Review* from 1863 to 1878.

The *Dublin Review* had been founded in London in 1836 to be a journal of educated Catholic opinion not only in theology but also in the social, political, and literary questions which were agitating Catholics as well as non-Catholics during the heyday of the Oxford Movement. After the defection to Rome of Ward, Newman,

15 A "middle" by Hutton on "Euthanasia" was reprinted for the Society in an emergency (No. 37a, July 8, 1873; see App. C). In this connection it is interesting to note that Hutton was also a firm opponent of vivisection, and his propaganda in the *Spectator* was credited with being largely responsible for the act of Parliament in 1876 limiting and restricting experimentation on living animals.

and a host of others, a journal called the *Rambler* was founded in 1848, first as a weekly but soon as a monthly, to be the organ of those liberalizing Catholics who feared the spread of Italianate ultramontane influence in England. By 1858 Cardinal Wiseman, Manning, and Ward (who had meanwhile become professor of theology at the diocesan seminary of St. Edmunds)—all of whom were strongly ultramontane in sympathy—felt a growing fear of this journal and its policies as an influence which might lead to heresy or at least to a break in that solidarity in the faith which they felt to be so important to the spread of Catholicism in England. With this in mind they persuaded Newman to become editor of the *Rambler* in 1858, with the expectation that he would bring it more into line with what they considered central Catholic teaching. Ward was offered the editorship of the *Dublin Review* at the same time, in the hope that if Newman refused the *Rambler*, a strong policy in the now sleepy *Dublin* would counteract the *Rambler's* nefarious influence. Ward, feeling no vocation for editorship, refused the *Dublin* when his old friend Newman accepted the *Rambler*. Newman, however, edited only two numbers of the *Rambler* and retired. He had come to believe that he was not made for theological controversy and had the suspicion, which became an increasingly morbid conviction in all his dealings with the Church, that he would be used as the tool of ecclesiastical politicians. The *Rambler*, turned into a bimonthly with Newman's first number in May, 1859, then passed into the hands of a new group of liberalizing Catholics of whom Sir John Acton, the historian, later Lord Acton, was the chief, and became a quarterly under the new name of the *Home and Foreign Review*. This review continued to offend the hierarchy, and in 1863 it was censured by the English Catholic bishops.

Wiseman, the editor in possession, and Manning had meanwhile in October, 1862, again persuaded Ward to take over the *Dublin Review* and to make it a bulwark of the faith. With all his customary pugnacity and all the determination of his indomitable will, Ward set about the task. He wrote to Newman saying, "It is certainly a new phenomenon to have the editor of a quarterly profoundly ignorant of history, politics, and literature." Some of these wants in himself he hoped Newman would help fill; but Newman replied that if he wrote for the *Dublin* he would also have to write for the *Home and Foreign* (which had not yet been censured), "and I mean to keep myself, if I can, from these public collisions, not that in that way I can escape the evil tongues of men, great and small, but reports die away and acts remain." [16] Ward continued to depreciate his own abilities as an editor, telling Newman, "Now in all such matters as literature proper, etc., etc., I am like a man deprived of some sense. I literally can no more get on with it than I can read Hebrew without having learned." Newman's refusal to write for the *Dublin* is one with his refusal to join the Metaphysical Society; English Catholic thought suffered from both, and the influence he could have earned through the *Dublin*, even under the eye of a watchful ecclesiastical censorship, might have done much to make his life in his adopted Church happier and more meaningful. His very aversion to controversy made him the butt of many petty squabbles within the Church, although his long silences made more effective his greatest utterances and perhaps help to explain both the power and the prestige of his *Apologia*.

Ward's first number of the *Dublin Review* appeared in July, 1863. From the start he had the assistance of Manning and the frequent help of Father Dalgairns, a friend of Newman's and, like him, a master of English prose. During the first ten years of his editorship the *Dublin* carried Ward's own vigorous and polemically successful attacks on empiricism—attacks which had grown out of his book *Nature and Grace* (1860), where he had first assailed empiricism on the ground of its failure to grapple with the problem of memory.[17] Latterly, the attack was addressed principally to Mill, and it is a notable tribute to both men that Ward always sent proofs of his articles to Mill before publication and that Mill never failed to admit the value and force of Ward's arguments.[18] Although all the articles in the *Dublin* were published

[16] Wilfrid Ward, *William George Ward and the Catholic Revival,* London, Macmillan, 1893, p. 155. See this book not only for the whole history of the above conflicts, but also for the best single treatment of the relation of an individual member to the Metaphysical Society (pp. 296–319).

[17] See Chap. IV, above, for Ward's first Metaphysical Society paper, "On Memory as an Intuitive Faculty" (No. 4; December 15, 1869).

[18] Ward spoke of Mill's death, probably humorously, as a "severe controversial disappointment" (Wilfrid Ward, *op. cit.,* p. 295).

anonymously, there never seems to have been much secrecy about their authorship; the Catholic intellectual world was small and self-contained. The review always remained a purely Catholic publication and never opened its pages to outsiders, except to offer in its correspondence columns opportunity for refutation of errors and inaccuracies. Thus, men like Church, Stanley, and Hutton occasionally appear as commentators on Catholic thought, and the review itself comments on arguments and debates in the pages of the *Contemporary, Spectator,* and *Fraser's.* The long-continued evolutionary controversy between the agnostic Huxley and the Catholic Mivart in the *Contemporary* in the early seventies is thus fully discussed in the *Dublin.* But a journalistic liberalism like that of Knowles was never to be found in Ward's review. Such freedom Ward reserved for the Metaphysical Society and for his frequent conversations with the dangerous infidels whose acquaintance he had made at its meetings. Knowles tells the story of going with Huxley to Ward's house for dinner. "The first thing he [Huxley] did was to go and peer out the window. Dr. Ward asked him what he was doing, on which he said, 'I was looking in your garden for the *stake,* Dr. Ward, which I suppose you have got ready for us after dinner.' "[19]

Ward had been president of the Oxford Union in 1832, and there, in company with Robert Lowe and Roundell Palmer, had learned well all the arts of debate and polemical discussion. He had also, during his days as a tutor at Balliol, imbibed a good share of English empirical and Scottish intuitional philosophy. His principal common-room antagonist in this period was Archibald Campbell Tait, later Archbishop of Canterbury, and he had gathered about him at Oxford a host of young admirers, including Jowett, Mark Pattison, Stanley, and Clough. Tait remained a lifelong friend, in a spirit which I fear has almost entirely disappeared from modern life; but Clough, greatly to Ward's distress, escaped with relief in 1839 from "the vortex of philosophism and discussion of which Ward is the center." Ward has been compared to Pascal as a man who fled to ecclesiastical authority as a refuge from limitless rationalism, but Ward himself never ad-

[19] *Ibid.,* p. 316.

mired Pascal, and it is doubtful whether the "reasons of the heart" ever spoke to him with any power. Certainly, the young men whom he most influenced at Oxford turned not to Catholicism but to various kinds of rationalism or scepticism, and in this fact may lie an explanation for Ward's own opposition to the plan so ignominiously defeated to establish a Catholic Hall at Oxford with Newman at its head. But on the other hand, Ward, in spite of his ultramontane sympathies, did not share Manning's somewhat pedestrian admiration of Aquinas and the scholastics and even had only a partial sympathy with the neo-scholastics of his own day. He disliked their tendency to treat the words of the schoolmen as authoritative texts,[20] and felt that just as St. Thomas had brought to bear on Christian doctrine all the philosophical insights of the pagan and Mohammedan worlds, so the Catholic philosophy of his own day should grapple with modern philosophical tradition in the preparation of a new *Summa,* an effort to which he devoted what time his failing health would allow in his final years. His own attitude toward the scholastics was much closer to that of Dalgairns, who himself, like Newman, is so much more sympathetic to Pascal. Dalgairns wrote: "I am perfectly convinced that you may as well address the House of Commons in Chaldee as attempt to reach the intellect of the world with scholastic philosophy. . . . You may define your terms if you will, but your definitions will fall cold upon the hearts of men whose minds have been cast in another mould, and to whose whole mode of thought the very ideas are grotesquely strange. For fighting purposes the schoolmen are as wooden ships to iron-clads. . . . Our very first condition of obtaining a hearing is being intelligible." [21] But the Ward who believed that Catholic thought must meet and defeat in a fair field the claims of the new philosophy and the new science is none the less the same Ward who gravely

[20] *Ibid.,* p. 275. Wilfrid Ward himself, who fell under the influence of Newman and became his biographer, was in sympathy with this point of view. He was editor of the *Dublin Review* himself at a later date (1906–16).

[21] From the expanded version of Dalgairns' Metaphysical Society paper, "On the Theory of a Soul" (No. 7; March 16, 1870), published as "The Theory of the Human Soul," *Contemporary Review,* XVI (December, 1870), 21. Interestingly enough, this was quoted in the *Dublin Review,* XVI (January, 1871), 225–6, in a brief review.

suggested that the progress of science would probably be accelerated by the submission of all scientific hypotheses to papal censorship. Ward would fight liberalism, rationalism, and scepticism to his dying day; and until illness forced his retirement from active editorship in 1878, the year of his resignation also from the Metaphysical Society, he conducted the *Dublin Review* on these principles.

Cardinal Manning, in a letter to Ward published in the *Dublin Review* for October, 1878, gives ample praise to Ward for his success in pursuing these aims: "The principle and spirit which has governed the *Dublin Review* in all these years, has been to represent fully and faithfully the guidance of the Supreme Pontiff in his authoritative acts, by teaching neither less nor more, and, so far as possible, by reproducing his own words." Manning himself, however, had been so much influenced by Ward and by the success of the Church in asserting the dogma of infallibility in 1870, that he was himself able to write in 1877, "It is necessary for Catholics to prepare themselves on the relation of society and science. . . . They cannot meet without being forced into the time-spirit. We do not live in an exhausted receiver. The Middle Ages are past. There is no zone of calms for us. We are in the modern world,—in the trade-winds of the nineteenth century,—and we must brace ourselves to lay hold of the world as it grapples with us, and to meet it, intellect to intellect, culture to culture, science to science." [22] Whatever the modern political implications of such a statement, it reflects the degree to which Manning and Ward had both entered into the spirit and achievements of the Metaphysical Society. And Ward, shortly before his death, could say to his son, "If ever I recover I shall take one lesson to heart which I have learned in thinking over my past life and during my illness, and that is to make more allowance than I ever did for the inevitable differences between one mind and another." [23]

Bagehot of the "Economist"

Walter Bagehot is most important to the Metaphysical Society as a critic of belief, evidence, and authority, an aspect of his genius

22 H. E. Manning, *Miscellanies,* 2 vols., London, Burns and Oates, 1877, I, 94.
23 Wilfrid Ward, *op. cit.,* p. 415.

which received fullest popular expression in the social interpretation of Darwinian principles seen in his *Physics and Politics* of 1872. But as a public figure in mid-Victorian life his major influence was exerted through his editorship of the *Economist*, a weekly journal which then, as now, was the indispensable critical voice of English banking, shipping, and industry. In this role he was not only an authority consulted by the leaders in business and finance but also the adviser and often the friend of many successive Chancellors of the Exchequer. The *Economist* had been founded during the corn-law agitation of 1843 by James Wilson to represent the application of free-trade principles to English commerce. Bagehot had in 1858 married Wilson's daughter; and in 1860 he became editor and manager of the *Economist*, enjoying during his first two years the editorial assistance of R. H. Hutton, with whom he also edited the *National Review* from 1855 to 1864.

Bagehot had been brought up in the rich intellectual atmosphere of the Bristol Unitarians, and his mother's brother-in-law, Dr. Prichard of Bristol, one of the founders of English anthropology and the author of an early study of the races of man, had a great influence in forming his mind and intellectual tastes. Unable to enter Oxford because of the religious tests, he went to University College, London, where he formed his lifelong friendship with Hutton. He read for the law and was admitted to the bar in 1852, but never practiced, going instead into his father's shipping business. A little later he entered the London office of Stuckey's Banking Company, an important West of England house of which his father was managing director and vice-chairman. All his earlier life and experiences were not only preparation for his professional career as editor of the *Economist* but also the most valuable kind of introduction to the social and political studies which throughout his life competed for attention with his literary and philosophical interests.

In Hutton Bagehot found a friend who was always willing to discuss with him not only "the immensities and eternities" but also "the problems that perplexed the land," the newly raised problems of "political economy." [24] Although in his youth more impressed than Hutton both by Newman's teaching and the historical and

[24] M. E. Grant Duff, *Out of the Past,* 2 vols, London, Murray, 1903, II, 2.

social authority of the Catholic Church, he also fell under the influence of A. H. Clough, who was at that time Principal of University Hall. He was in Paris at the time of the coup d'état of 1851, and, however surprising in the light of his later attitudes, approved the actions of the prince-president, Napoleon. He tried several times, always unsuccessfully, to enter Parliament, but he was, as he himself put it, too much "between sizes in politics" and could appeal neither to the ordinary Conservative nor to the ordinary Liberal mind.[25]

The *Economist*, to which he devoted the major part of his short life and which he edited until his death in 1877, was, like the *Spectator*, strictly anonymous, and could never by its very nature become one of the journals through which the Metaphysical Society exerted its influence on English thought. Bagehot himself often editorially comments in the pages of the *Economist* upon the public careers of men like Lowe, Selborne, and Gladstone, but his own literary and philosophical articles were published chiefly in the *Contemporary* and the *Fortnightly*. However, that the editor of a journal like the *Economist* should meet men like Fitzjames Stephen and Gladstone in discussion, for example, of the problem of authority, is one of the aspects of the Metaphysical Society which had its indirect consequences in the political activity of the crucial years of Disraeli's second ministry, from 1874 to 1880. Bagehot is always at his best as a critic and as an unveiler of other men's mysteries, and in this capacity he served the Society well; in return, the Society must have given him much to ponder and understand. Bagehot considered the meetings of the Society "extremely interesting" and, according to his biographer, found that "the discussions revived trains of thought which he and Mr. Hutton had shared together, lines of argument which they had threshed out in conversation or correspondence in earlier days." [26] The Society reawakened in him "thought and speculation more in harmony with the trend of his feelings in those early days when Shelley and Keats were first delicious to him, and when Wordsworth and John Henry Newman were his daily food." [27]

[25] *Ibid.*, II, 7.

[26] Mrs. Russell Barrington, *Life of Walter Bagehot*, London, Longmans, 1915, p. 422.

[27] *Ibid.*, p. 8.

Bagehot will perhaps be remembered longest as a literary critic and political observer, not as editor of the *Economist*. But the Metaphysical Society surely contributed to both the depth and breadth of his interests, and especially to his long concern with the correlation of the social and the metaphysical.

Froude of "Fraser's"; Grove of "Macmillan's"; and Leslie Stephen of the "Cornhill"

Three of the editors who were members of the Society, James Anthony Froude, George Grove, and Leslie Stephen, deserve only brief mention in this chapter, for the magazines which they edited do not figure largely in the history of thought in the seventies and rarely published articles by members of the Society. Furthermore, all three were editors in the midst of busy lives devoted largely to other pursuits and, for this reason, were known in their own day and are remembered in ours for reasons other than their editorial or journalistic abilities. All three magazines were "miscellanies" rather than reviews and published only fiction, poetry, literary criticism, and articles of the most general interest. All three are significant as illustrating the concerns of their editors and the literary taste of the educated middle class. But an extended examination of these aspects of the seventies lies outside the scope of the present study.

James Anthony Froude became the editor of *Fraser's Magazine for Town and Country* [28] in December, 1860, and edited it with occasional assistance from Charles Kingsley and Sir Theodore Martin until July, 1874, when he was succeeded by William Allingham. *Fraser's* had fallen somewhat from the high place it enjoyed in the days of Maginn, Thackeray, and Carlyle,[29] but it remained the most widely read of the older magazines which stuck to the principle of anonymity. Its avowed interests were literature,

[28] It became simply *Fraser's Magazine*, "edited by James Anthony Froude," in 1870. After 1874 it carried no editor's name. Until July, 1879, it was printed in an unpleasant double-column page. It continued in this form until October, 1882; with the issue of November, 1882, its publishers changed its name and nature and established the new *Longman's Magazine*, which lasted until October, 1905.

[29] See Miriam M. H. Thrall's study of these early years, *Rebellious "Fraser's,"* New York, Columbia University Press, 1934.

politics, art, and science, but under Froude's editorship it devoted more space to travel, geography, archaeology, and history than any other popular journal of the period. It carried penetrating articles on the art of war, always one of Froude's specialties, and took seriously the new concern with spiritualism and mesmerism. In deference to its country readers it also presented competent studies, well documented with statistics, of the present state and future expectations of English agriculture. It can thus be seen that *Fraser's* was a true miscellany, catering on a relatively high level to that growing desire for information as well as entertainment so characteristic of the mid-Victorian period. But its truly miscellaneous nature is perhaps best symbolized by the final article in the last issue of October, 1882, Edwin De Leon's "How I Introduced the Telephone into Egypt."

The principle of anonymity was not always strictly observed, for in almost every number there was at least one signed article, and others were occasionally signed with initials. Among the regular contributors who signed we find Bonamy Price, J. G. Fitch, Leslie Stephen,[30] and F. W. Newman; while others include Florence Nightingale, Frances Power Cobbe, Henry Fawcett, Max Müller, J. W. Cross, Edmund Gosse, Moncure Conway, William Allingham, and S. R. Gardiner, as well as R. A. Proctor, John Tyndall, and Richard Owen in the field of science. John Stuart Blackie wrote an interesting article in the August, 1873, number on "The Relation of Metaphysics to Science and Literature,"[31] in which he insisted that "metaphysics is the supreme seeing science, and the eye of all the rest"; but such subjects are notably rare in *Fraser's*. Froude himself, as editor, contributed a number of his most important political and historical studies. At least one novel, and usually two, ran anonymously in serial form in each number. Whatever the value of the principle of anonymity in some kinds of journalism, it is puzzling to understand its continued application to the magazine serialization of novels, especially since most of

30 Leslie Stephen was a constant contributor even after he had become editor of the *Cornhill,* where he published his "Hours in a Library," and even while he was contributing political and philosophical articles to the *Fortnightly.*

31 A lecture delivered before the Philosophical Society of Edinburgh, March 26, 1873.

them carried the author's name when finally published in book form.[32] Perhaps the excitement of gossip and attempted identification maintained public interest and curiosity and possibly even aided the sale of the book when it appeared. Certainly, by the end of the seventies the principle was breaking down in all except the weekly journals of opinion, and by 1880 even *Fraser's* had almost entirely succumbed.

Although Froude was a successful editor, the chief interest of his career lies elsewhere. At Oxford he had early fallen under the influence of the Tractarian movement, but unlike his brother, Richard Hurrell Froude, one of Newman's most devoted friends and followers, he gradually turned toward a profound religious relativism and even scepticism rather than toward a deeper and more Catholic faith. His brother had died young in 1836, before the great exodus to Rome, leaving nothing but some fervid and very upsetting memorials of his religious experiences. J. A. Froude himself was thus, perhaps, emotionally drawn into Newman's circle and subsequently contributed a life of St. Neot to Newman's *Lives of the English Saints;* but even in this work his scepticism toward miraculous or supernatural occurrences shows itself. His partly autobiographical "novels," *Shadows of the Clouds* (1847) and *The Nemesis of Faith* (1849), mark his final separation from the Oxford Movement. The latter book was publicly burned at Oxford, and Froude resigned his Exeter College fellowship. Whately and Hampden found *The Nemesis of Faith* a symptom of the evils of Tractarianism, but Froude himself later called it "heterodoxy flavoured with sentimentalism." In London he now became a warm admirer of Carlyle, with important consequences not only for his own views of history and politics but also for the reputation of Carlyle, whose chief literary executor he became.[33] He shared Carlyle's view of the importance of the great man in history, but although, like Carlyle, he was anti-Negro and favored the abandonment of representative government in the West Indies, he was one of the warmest advocates of a reform in English policy

[32] Notable exceptions include many of the novels of Trollope and Bulwer-Lytton.

[33] This is not the place to examine the Froude-Carlyle controversy which has been ably, even if not entirely conclusively, discussed in many books.

toward Ireland. In his long controversy with Freeman, already referred to, he conducted himself with the most admirable restraint; in fact, few men have borne themselves better in such circumstances. His own *History of England from the Fall of Wolsey to the Spanish Armada* began to appear in 1856 and was completed in 1870, but he continued his historical writing until almost the end of his life. In spite of an occasional carelessness in the use of historical materials—a failing which has been reproved out of all proportion to its importance—he is one of the great masters of English style and one of the most evocative of all historical writers. Although he was a pioneer in the use of unpublished sources, he denied the claim of history to be a science and quoted with approval Talleyrand's remark, "Il n'y a rien qui s'arrange aussi facilement que les faits." The final triumph of his life was his return to Oxford in 1892 as Regius Professor of History in succession to his archenemy Freeman.

In November, 1879, he published in *Fraser's* a delightful fantasy, "Siding at a Railway Station," in which, at the end, he imagines an examination of his own lifework before the bar of the Last Judgment. A magic fluid with the power of testing literary and historical truth is applied to the pages of his books. Page after page disappears, leaving only those which his enemies had most attacked and those on which he himself had expended least time and care. This is not merely an obscurantist parable; it has, in spite of its autobiographical nature, a Dostoevskian irony and objectivity; it sums up the virtues and weaknesses of the man himself.

His lifelong interest in Spinoza and the relation between philosophy and mathematics, as well as the history of his own religious convictions, made him a useful member of the Metaphysical Society, where his quiet diffidence and ironic humor often justified themselves in discussions of miracles, authority, and evidence. Froude knew what many "scientific" historians did not yet know, that history is the discovery and interpretation of significant facts, but that since the meaning and significance of particular collocations of facts change from generation to generation, history must be rewritten in every age. For the Victorian view of history we go to Macaulay, Carlyle, Froude, and Green, not to Freeman and Gardiner. Froude can never be rewritten; Freeman and Gardiner have already been in large measure supplanted. If Froude was not a philosophical historian, he was a philosopher about the art of history. In words which reflect his admiration for Spinoza, he says, "Perfection is not easy; it is of all things most difficult; difficult to know and difficult to practise." [34]

George Grove, editor of *Macmillan's Magazine* from 1868 to 1883, began his professional career in 1839 as an engineer. He built a lighthouse in Jamaica in 1842 and later helped to build the railway station at Chester. But in 1849 he became Secretary to the Society of Arts, which was in large measure responsible for the planning and execution of the Great Exhibition of 1851 in the Crystal Palace. When the Crystal Palace was reërected at Sydenham in 1854, Grove became Secretary to the new corporation and, although entirely self-taught in music, devoted himself to developing, with the assistance of the musician August Manns, the musical concerts which continued until our own day as one of the popular glories of London life. Grove's first analytical program notes were written in January, 1856, for a series of concerts to celebrate the centenary of Mozart's birth, an important step in the musical career which was to lead to Grove's famous and still indispensable *Dictionary of Music and Musicians*, the foundation of the Royal College of Music in 1883, and his own role as its first director. Meanwhile, through his brother-in-law Granville Bradley and Charles Pritchard, at whose school in Clapham he had studied as a boy, he met Tennyson and Stanley. Stanley became his closest friend and encouraged him in the biblical studies which his early evangelical training made one of the constant concerns of his life. Stanley also helped him with the study of Hebrew, and together they visited the Holy Land in 1858. Owing to his friendship with Tennyson, Pritchard, and Stanley, and his interest in religious problems, he became one of the earliest members of the Metaphysical Society, although he attended seldom and, according to Knowles, after December, 1871, never. Grove himself said that it did not suit him at all. He apparently

[34] Froude's review (1850) of Emerson's *Representative Men*.

was one of the few members who could not brook the Roman Catholic mind. He says, apropos of W. G. Ward's relation to the Society, "No doubt the Church of Rome has wonderfully improved in vigour like the Church of England. I am always looking for the time when the modern scientific spirit shall invade it. It must come sooner or later." [35]

Macmillan's Magazine was founded by Alexander Macmillan in 1859 and continued publication until 1907. David Masson was its first editor, being succeeded by Grove in 1868. Grove's acceptance of the onerous task of editing the *Dictionary of Music and Musicians* for Macmillan necessitated his resignation from the Crystal Palace Company in 1873; the foundation of the Royal College of Music and his duties as director led to his giving up the editorship of *Macmillan's* in 1883. He was succeeded as editor for two years by John Morley, who had recently surrendered the *Fortnightly*.[36]

Macmillan's was one of the first magazines to use signed articles only. It was not primarily a literary periodical but dealt with travel, history, politics, manners, and other subjects of general interest, as well as publishing novels in serial form. The first paper read before the Metaphysical Society, R. H. Hutton's (No. 1; June 2, 1869), was published in *Macmillan's* under the title "A Questionable Parentage for Morals." The first six numbers contained Thomas Hughes's *Tom Brown at Oxford*, and in its most successful years it published contributions from W. E. Forster, the Lushingtons, Masson, F. D. Maurice, R. M. Milnes, Alexander Smith, and F. T. Palgrave.[37] Its coloring was always clearly Broad Church. Grove published Tennyson's "Lucretius" in 1868, and other later contributors included F. Marion Crawford, Bret Harte, Ernest Rhys, and Gilbert Parker. The magazine maintained its miscellaneous nature and its appeal to a largely proper and evangelical audience by never engaging in controversy. Except for the notable literary works which were first published in

35 Charles L. Graves, *The Life and Letters of Sir George Grove, C.B.*, London, Macmillan, 1903, p. 401.

36 Mowbray Morris then edited *Macmillan's* until its end in 1907.

37 Walter Graham, *English Literary Periodicals*, New York, Nelson, 1930.

its pages,[38] it therefore has only an incidental interest to the historian of thought. And although George Grove was in many ways one of the most unusual men of his day, after 1874 his musical interests gradually weaned him away from his editorial responsibilities, and Alexander Macmillan himself exercised the major control. And it is for his work in the cause of music, not for his magazine or his metaphysics, that Grove is important in Victorian cultural history.

Leslie Stephen, younger brother of James Fitzjames Stephen, became editor of the *Cornhill Magazine* in October, 1871. He served until November, 1882, when he resigned the editorship to his friend James Payn to devote his entire time to the *Dictionary of National Biography.* During these years he continued to write for the *Saturday Review,* the *Fortnightly,* and *Fraser's.* From 1866 to 1873 he had contributed a fortnightly political article to the New York *Nation.* His *History of English Thought in the Eighteenth Century,* a book which most scholars would regard as a lifework, was published in 1876, and in the same year, the year following the death of his first wife, he wrote fourteen articles for the *Cornhill* and four for the *Fortnightly.* Few Victorian journalists wrote so much, and none left so strong a reputation, not only as journalist and critic, but as scholar and historian.

The *Cornhill,* which Stephen took over after it had begun to lose circulation,[39] was founded in 1860 by George Smith of Smith, Elder and Co., just two months after *Macmillan's.* Thackeray was its first editor, and he and Trollope were early contributors to its immediate and overwhelming success. After the first number, 100,000 copies were printed monthly for several years. Its purpose was to combine a critical review with an illustrated serial novel, the major contents being displayed anonymously. Since 1860 the *Cornhill* has offered a representative history of British fic-

[38] The magazine, like *Fraser's,* was unfortunately printed in narrow double column, making it one of the hardest of all Victorian magazines to read.

[39] When Stephen became editor its circulation had dropped to 25,000, and by the end of Stephen's regime it had dropped further to 12,000. James Payn attributed this to the growing failure of the "classical essay," but it seems more likely that a drop in the popularity of the serialized novel is the true explanation.

tion, publishing in its first thirty years novels by Thackeray, Trollope, the Brontës, Lever, George Eliot, Mrs. Gaskell, Charles Reade, Willkie Collins, H. S. Merriman, Thomas Hardy, Mrs. Humphrey Ward, and E. F. Benson. Poetry was always signed, and poets represented include Tennyson, Browning, E. B. Browning, Arnold, Meredith, Swinburne, Palgrave, and Alfred Austin. Articles were contributed, sometimes signed, by J. A. Symonds, G. H. Lewes, R. M. Milnes, Ruskin, Edward Dowden, Edmund Gosse, and Sidney Colvin.[40] The list of identified contributors could be expanded almost indefinitely; few literary figures of importance have failed to appear sooner or later in the *Cornhill.* It is important to note that Matthew Arnold's *Celtic Literature, Culture and Anarchy, St. Paul and Protestantism,* and *Literature and Dogma* all appeared in the *Cornhill,* as well as Leslie Stephen's own editorial contribution, the series of "Hours in a Library," which began in 1871. Arnold became such a fixture in the *Cornhill* that he had a bed made up for him in the Smith, Elder office when he was kept in town too late to get home to Harrow or Cobham.[41]

Thackeray had edited the magazine for only two and a half years, and for the next several years it was edited by various individuals and committees of the Smith, Elder firm. But in 1871 Leslie Stephen, who had married Thackeray's daughter in 1867, was persuaded to become the editor, and in this post was enabled to give more time to his historical and philosophic studies than in his earlier days of free-lance journalism. Stephen had been educated at Eton, King's College, London, and Trinity Hall, Cambridge. He had taken deacon's orders in the Church in 1855 to retain his fellowship, and for ten years he taught mathematics to undergraduates and even preached in the college chapel. But he found teaching and the atmosphere of the university troubling both to his mind and to his conscience and left in 1865 for London. He did not, however, surrender his fellowship until his marriage and strangely enough did not abandon his deacon's orders under the act of 1870 until 1875, by which time he was already known

40 Walter Graham, *op. cit.*

41 Leonard Huxley, *The House of Smith, Elder,* London (privately printed), 1923. Leonard Huxley himself became editor of the *Cornhill* in 1916.

as one of the most convinced leaders of the agnostic school. Stephen, in fact, is given the credit for popularizing the word "agnostic," which Huxley, as we have seen, had invented to describe his own position in the Metaphysical Society.

Stephen himself did not become a member of the Metaphysical Society until 1877, when the Society had begun to decline, and, as he tells us in his admirable life of his brother Fitzjames, he was never very much impressed by the Society's debates. He became an increasingly convinced rationalist and, according to Frederic Harrison,[42] shrank more and more from all modes of spiritual exaltation. But he was, with Tyndall, one of the great mountain climbers of his day and did more perhaps than any other man to popularize that incredible, fantastic, and utterly irrational passion which offers physical and spiritual exaltation alike to saint and sinner, sceptic and believer.[43] In one of his articles in the *Cornhill*, Stephen humorously proposed the establishment of a Society for the Suppression of Useless Knowledge (S.S.U.K.); but he himself devoted the last twenty years of his life to the gigantic and in many ways supererogatory task of compiling the *Dictionary of National Biography.* Although he retired from active editorship of the *Dictionary* in 1891, he continued to write for it and before his death had himself completed a total of 378 articles, almost any one of which might have earned an American a Ph.D. degree. Leslie Stephen remains a not inglorious example of the enormous capacity of the Victorian mind for hard work. But it is perhaps well to remember that Stephen's *History of English Thought in the Eighteenth Century* was planned as a background to what was to have been the principal task of his life, a history of English thought in the nineteenth century, and that of this projected undertaking only *The English Utilitarians,* which does not live up to the promise of the earlier work, was completed. Thus, Leslie Stephen, like his friend Morley, was a victim not only of the new journalistic opportunities of the age, but of his own restless versatility. His friend Meredith's portrait of

[42] *Realities and Ideals,* New York, Macmillan, 1908, p. 366.

[43] The late Pope Pius XI was also an ardent mountain climber and wrote very well about his experiences.

him as Vernon Whitford in the *Egoist* has an essential truth. He remained a promising young man with a brilliant future until the day when he became an old man with a worthy past.

Morley of the "Fortnightly"

The *Fortnightly Review* had been founded early in 1865 by Anthony Trollope, George Henry Lewes, Cotter Morison, Edward Chapman, and others, in imitation of the long-successful French *Revue des Deux Mondes,* which also appeared twice a month. From the beginning, also like the *Revue,* its policy was to admit only signed articles. Anthony Trollope, earlier, as we have seen, one of the principal supporters of the *Cornhill,* claimed that its purpose was to be not only "good in its literature, but strictly impartial and absolutely honest." Its original backers, however, soon lost the £8,000 they had invested, and in spite of the brilliant editing of G. H. Lewes, who resigned under the pressure of the task, were forced to sell the review to its publishers, the firm of Chapman and Hall. Under Lewes the review had become a monthly, with no change in name or policy. Trollope and the new owners, late in 1866, under the influence of Cotter Morison chose as new editor the young John Morley, who, since leaving Oxford in 1859, had made a precarious living as a hack journalist in London. In 1861 he had edited the short-lived *Literary Gazette,* but he admitted later that his first real success was owing to anonymous "middles" he contributed to the *Saturday Review.* Meanwhile, through Cotter Morison, he had met John Stuart Mill and had begun to express that rationalistic liberalism which not only dominated the *Fortnightly* during his editorship and led to the parliamentary and administrative statesmanship of his later years, but which also made him the chief interpreter of Mill's political opinions after the latter's death.

During the fifteen years of Morley's editorship, from 1867 to 1882, the *Fortnightly* was the principal organ of mid-Victorian rationalism in literature, politics, and philosophy. It is unnecessary here to examine in detail the history and contents of this great review, which became, at least during the period of Morley's editorship, the most talked about journal in England. This has been done in Morley's own *Recollections* and in a series of able recent studies presenting a mass of material which it would be gratuitous to recapitulate here.[44] But several aspects of its relation to the journalistic and political history of the period require comment. It is certainly appropriate that Trollope, who made his own literary fame from novels satirizing county society and the life of parish rectory and cathedral close, should become one of the founders of a review which would attack unceasingly the privileges and pretensions of that society and both the spiritual and material prerogatives of the Established Church.

The *Contemporary Review* itself had been set up soon after the *Fortnightly* to establish a forum, which, although to begin with not so free as the *Fortnightly*, never in its best years made a dogmatic virtue of its unquestionable liberal tendency. The greatest philosophical weakness of the *Fortnightly*, which was of course also its polemical strength, was its often jejune insistence on being critically rationalistic at all costs. That this spirit was one of the dominant influences on English thought in the sixties and seventies is well known; the *Fortnightly* became its major instrument. But from our present vantage point this spirit is seen to have corrupted even as it revitalized the liberal spirit. For after Mill's death that spirit became increasingly political and doctrinaire on all major religious and philosophical questions. In politics it combined devastating criticism of individual personalities and group programs, even when they were Liberal in origin or tendency, with a principled Radicalism which was often irresponsibly remote from practical solutions. Here can be seen the influence of Positivism and its English high priests, Beesly, Bridges, Congreve, Morison, and Frederic Harrison. The emphasis on history and a historical view of po-

44 F. W. Hirst, *Early Life and Letters of John Morley,* 2 vols., London, Macmillan, 1927, is indispensable. Edwin M. Everett, *The Party of Humanity: the "Fortnightly Review" and its Contributors, 1865–1874,* Chapel Hill, University of North Carolina Press, 1939, is an admirable study of the relation of the review to positivism, science, and rationalism. Warren Staebler, *The Liberal Mind of John Morley,* Princeton, Princeton University Press (for the University of Cincinnati), 1943, is a well-written critical study of Morley. And Frances Wentworth Knickerbocker, *Free Minds: John Morley and his Friends,* Cambridge, Harvard University Press, 1943, is a warm and convincing as well as fully documented study of the Morley circle, with special reference to Morley's relations with Frederic Harrison and Leslie Stephen.

litical theory, which is one of the best aspects of Positivist teaching, influenced Morley in his own studies of Voltaire, Rousseau, Diderot, and Burke; but the historical way of regarding political principle makes for a long-range view of what in practical politics are immediate issues. The Positivists lost their influence by a too firmly held historical optimism, while Morley and his Radical followers, anxious to hold on to the present in the name of a more glorious future, were eventually forced into the arms of politicians like Chamberlain and other middle-class opportunists.

Gladstone's resigning as leader of the Liberal party in 1873, to be succeeded by Bright, marks the end of the *Fortnightly's* power of integrating liberal policies through disinterestedness and tolerance. Gladstone's own unifying influence was gradually to give way before the rising power of Morley's new friend Chamberlain, in whose cause Morley prepared a part of the "Radical Programme" of 1885. Morley himself did not return wholeheartedly to Gladstone's camp until his own split with Chamberlain on the Irish question later in 1885. Certainly, during the years 1874 to 1880, when the Liberals and Radicals were in opposition, they failed completely, as opposition parties so often fail, to develop a coherent liberal theory and an organized political mechanism for the attainment of their hopes in the changing times to come. And in the years between 1880 and 1885 the major Radical maneuver was to get rid of the Whigs and attempt to take over the Liberal party. But Chamberlain's National Liberal Federation was opposed to Home Rule for Ireland and, under the banner of Unionism, became, in opposition to all of Morley's principles, the paradoxical defender of British Imperialism. Not until the foundation of the Fabian Society, from which has developed the modern Labour party, did England begin to see the terms on which Liberal political theory and practice were to be reconciled in the new century.

Morley's four articles "On Compromise" in the *Fortnightly* in 1874 were published in book form in the same year, with a new introduction and an appendix on liberty. Morley attempted to understand the nature, use, and social justification of compromise, but, as was remarked by several contemporaries, compromise appears only in the title of the book. Morley's own later political career, as we see in the *Recollections,* taught him many of the political arts which would have made the *Fortnightly* even more effective in the seventies; but Morley never entirely overcame his early conviction that the right principles of an intelligent and right-reasoning minority should and would prevail were it not for the ignorance and irrationality of other minorities in positions of power.[45] Practical Liberal politicians like Grant Duff and Robert Lowe might fear political democracy and the demagoguery they suspected in both Disraeli and Gladstone, but they were experienced parliamentarians who knew that the arts of legislation and public policy require the most careful weighing of alternatives and the most judicious balancing of opposed forces. This was the kind of political realism that Morley did not learn until his own days in Parliament. It is hard for the idealist to admit that the political victories obtained by the triumphant popular acceptance of a great cause or a seemingly noble faith are often, when seen through the eye of history, steps in the enslavement of a people. This Morley believed in his *Fortnightly* days and never entirely forgot, just as he was later to learn that the most permanent and successful political reforms are always those that are hammered out on the anvil of popular and parliamentary debate by realistic politicians who are responsive to the needs and desires of the people at the same time as they themselves resist appeals to class and group interest. Morley's essay *On Compromise* shows a theoretical knowledge of these truths, but perhaps he was too much the philosophical critic to be at this time a wholly successful political leader. In many ways he deserves in this period to inherit Mill's title of the "saint of rationalism."

After 1874 the *Fortnightly* began to share its most important writers with Knowles's increasingly successful *Contemporary,* and after the establishment of the *Nineteenth Century* in 1877, many more of them began to shift their allegiance to Knowles's new review, which became known as Gladstonian in politics, although

45 Morley boasted in 1873 that the *Fortnightly,* with its circulation of 2,500 and upwards, reached the minds of at least 30,000. But even this was small compared with the more than 100,000 circulation reached by magazines like *Macmillan's* and the *Cornhill* in their most successful years.

virtually all opinions could obtain a hearing in its pages. It is a curious fact that Gladstone, who wrote so freely for the *Contemporary* and the *Nineteenth Century*, never appears under his own name in the *Fortnightly*, although he did finally contribute an anonymous article in 1880. The *Fortnightly*, of course, had frequently attacked Gladstone in the name of more Radical policies, and throughout the seventies not only actively supported the idea of the disestablishment of the English Church, but also took constantly an antitheistic and antireligious attitude. Morley, for example, was supposed to have always spelled God with a small *g*. These opinions would never have attracted Gladstone to the review. But Morley in the eighties became one of Gladstone's strongest supporters, and in the end wrote the official life of the Grand Old Man, a massive political biography. However, by 1880 the *Fortnightly* had begun to lose both its appeal and its audience. The battle between reason and revelation was over, and the frustrated political Radicals of the seventies were destined to divide into three increasingly opposed groups: those who continued to follow Gladstone, those who were willing to play with the dangers of Chamberlain's National Liberal Federation, and those few who looked to a new political alignment in which radicalism could play its own role in a third party.

Morley's own editorial days were drawing to a close. In May, 1880, he had accepted the editorship of George Smith's evening newspaper, the *Pall Mall Gazette*, and although his editorial temperament was better fitted for monthy than daily journalism, he began to lose interest in the *Fortnightly*. In the autumn of 1882 he quarreled with Chapman and Hall, the publishers of the review, and in October resigned the editorship. For a time he talked with Leslie Stephen and other friends of starting a new review of his own, but nothing came of the plan. In 1878 he had undertaken the general editorship of the "English Men of Letters Series" for Macmillan, and through this relationship he was persuaded in May, 1883, to become editor of *Macmillan's*, in succession to George Grove. In the same year he gave up the *Pall Mall Gazette* to his assistant W. T. Stead, who was to become the *enfant terrible* of modern English journalism. The new period of his active political life had begun in 1882 with his election to Parliament as Liberal member for Newcastle, and when Gladstone returned to his brief third ministry in 1885, Morley became chief secretary for Ireland, after having resigned the editorship of *Macmillan's* during the summer months preceding the general election.

Morley's own harsh comment on the editorial life applies not only to himself but in some measure to most of the editors we have discussed in this chapter. "Writing year after year upon instructions . . . can hardly be good for mental health, and I have in my mind's eye more than one contemporary of mine with first-rate literary talent, whom this check upon initiative reduced to rather second-rate work and name." But he adds that "though journalism may kill a man, it quickens his life while it lasts." [46]

Morley himself did not become a member of the Metaphysical Society until 1876, and read only one paper, "Various Definitions of Materialism" (No. 72; December 11, 1877). Like his friend Leslie Stephen, he did not think much of the Society in its later years, although he was pleased at the honor of election. At the time he said, "I hardly feel worthy; for I care less for these abstract things than I used to do." After reading his only paper, he wrote to his sister mentioning the fact and referring to the Society as "an illustrious little club which first confuses itself with a bad dinner, and then makes confusion worse confounded by bad metaphysics." [47] But Morley's mind, however broadly cultivated in literature, was in his *Fortnightly* days so committed to a critical and philosophical rationalism that he could hardly have been more than entertained by the opinions and points of view of his theistic and intuitionist opponents. Few of the Society's papers were published in the *Fortnightly;* I have identified only two of Harrison's and one by Sir Alexander Grant.[48] Morley's own unquestioned personal charm and social tolerance should have made him an agreeable member of the Society, but like that of many Liberals his intellectual tolerance spread only just beyond his own party, somewhat loosely delimited. And the dogmatic apostle of a new

[46] Morley, *Recollections,* 2 vols., New York, Macmillan, 1917, I, 33.

[47] Hirst, *op. cit.,* II, 8, 56.

[48] Harrison's, No. 10, July 13, 1870, and No. 28, July 9, 1872; Grant's, No. 14, February 8, 1871. See App. C.

political attitude is as watchful for heresy as any religious believer.

The *Fortnightly* had exhausted Morley's intellectual passion against religion and the men who exalted faith and intuition. By the time he joined the Society, he considered as won the battle in which his own forces had been so effective. It was his old friend George Meredith who was to become, in a critical and rationalist but also affirmative sense, the most eloquent voice, in this period, of the "reasons of the heart." The *Recollections* reveal a warmer Morley, with more of what Stead called, in reminiscence of Carlyle's Ram Dass, "the fire he has got in his belly." But the emotional life, except when dignified by intellectual friendship or social conviction, was something he seems always to have feared. His later friendship with Matthew Arnold was a liberating force, but there remains an unresolved paradox in the life of this man of thought who longed to become a man of action. This is perhaps a common paradox, and yet one cannot read Hirst's closing words without regret: "The air of Olympus agreed with him. He enjoyed it, and he enjoyed also the pomps and ceremonies and privileges of high office." The last great English republican kissing the Queen's hands at Osborne in 1886 is a symbol both of the greatness and the pettiness of modern English political history.

Chapter 12

MATTER, SPIRIT, TRUTH, AND GOD: "CHAOS, COSMOS"

We are accustomed to find the thinking men of every age divided on great issues. It is only when the age is our own that we are inclined to deplore disagreement and long for unity. Each of us sees his opponents' views leading toward chaos; and each is convinced that his own world-view will justify itself as a true cosmos, a significant order. The Metaphysical Society was an attempt to criticize this human tendency, but its failure to discover a common philosophical realm is perhaps an illustration that the distinctive quality of any age lies in the nature of the conflicts between its major cosmologies. When the issues are deeply felt and social, moral, and political choices of no mean consequence are involved, the fullest powers of men are called upon, and not only leaders and thinkers but whole nations or classes of men show their true greatness. Such an age the nineteenth century assuredly was, and such a period was the Victorian, in the sixties and seventies. "Resolution" of these conflicts may bring peace; but fundamental issues are seldom entirely resolved by compromise; they are even rarely eliminated by defeat. Fundamental issues are by definition those that recur.

Tyndall's Belfast Address

Nothing that was ever said in the Metaphysical Society brought this problem so clearly into the open, and none of the Society's papers reprinted in any periodical attracted as much public attention or caused as widespread public debate as two papers read before the annual meeting of the British Association at Belfast in 1874. Both were by members of the Metaphysical Society: the first and most important by John Tyndall, president of the Association for the year, then and now known simply as "The Belfast Address"; the second, more specialized in its emphasis, by T. H. Huxley, delivered before one of the sections, "On the Hypothesis that Animals are Automata, and its History." Tyndall's address must be analyzed in detail, but Huxley's is essentially an historical elaboration of the evidence presented in his second Metaphysical Society paper, "Has the Frog a Soul?" (No. 11; November 8, 1870). Both clearly proposed a physical and naturalistic cosmology; and however explicitly each disclaimed "materialism," each left only materialism as a residual philosophy after attacking all other interpretations of the origin of life. The efficacy of natural causes still in operation to explain not only the world of material phenomena but the appearance of life itself, was thus asserted as an axiom of scientific cosmology. But such an axiom is inexorably opposed to both theistic hypotheses of special creation and any attempt to establish the dependence of the human soul, as a preeminent vital principle, on a personal God.

The British Association had become the largest and most representative organization of British scientists, and its meetings had often heard the announcement and discussion of important, even epoch-making, scientific discoveries. But its presidential addresses had been for the most part dignified and "respectable" eulogies of science and the scientific spirit. Tyndall's address at Belfast proved to be an unanticipated exception. He had written his paper carefully, during a holiday in the seclusion of the Alps. But after its delivery he was accused of having said things no man would have uttered in cool detachment or with confirmed intention. This, we know, was not the case; Tyndall meant what he said and followed his prepared text. He expected it to arouse controversy; he did not know that it would prove a bombshell. Eighteen-hundred members of the Association were present, representing every field of science and every shade of religious, philosophical, and scientific opinion. Tyndall could nowhere else in Britain have found so large or so distinguished an audience.

The address, delivered on the evening of August 19, 1874, began with a careful history of man's efforts to understand "the sources of natural phenomena" and the relation between human experience and the origin of things. He examined the characteristics of Greek science and compared the place of Socrates and Plato as scientific thinkers with the imaginative hypotheses of Democritus, Epicurus, and Lucretius. He propounded the atomic philosophy as a key to any understanding of the behavior of material phenomena and asked what had so long ago stopped "the victorious advance" of the scientific intellect. One reason he found in the obscurantism of the Church and the inadequacy of the scriptural revelation. The spirit of the Middle Ages he characterized as "a menial spirit." The influence of Aristotle he described as pernicious, for although, like Goethe, Aristotle possessed extraordinary powers of observation and great skill in the detection of remote analogies and in the classification and organization of facts, he could not formulate distinct mechanical conceptions and did not understand the nature of Force as Cause. "He put words in the place of things, subject in the place of object. He preached Induction without practising it, inverting the true order of Inquiry, by passing from the general to the particular, instead of from the particular to the general." His ideas lacked the "one essential quality in physical conceptions," the "capability of being placed as coherent pictures before the mind," what the Germans express by *vorstellen* and *Vorstellung*. The Arab physicists, especially Alhazen, were far more advanced and, in many respects, anticipated our own discoveries.

To illustrate the attitude of the Church toward physical science, Tyndall turns to the careers of Copernicus, Giordano Bruno, and Galileo. He traces the attitudes of Kepler, Bacon, Descartes, and Gassendi. He remarks that Gassendi's observation, "I eat, therefore I am" or "I love, therefore I am" is as convincing a demonstration of personal existence as Descartes' "I think, therefore I am." Although "through fear or love, Descartes was a good churchman," he finds him to have been "the first to reduce, in a manner eminently capable of bearing the test of mental presentation, vital phenomena to purely mechanical principles." Tyndall insists that "were a capricious God at the circumference of every wheel and at the end of every lever, the action of the machine would be incalculable by the methods of science. But the actions of all its parts being rigidly determined by their connections and relations, and these being brought into play by a single motive power, then though this last prime mover may elude me, I am still able to comprehend the machinery which it sets in motion." This notion is acceptable to some minds, like Newton and Boyle; it is utterly repugnant to others, like Goethe and Carlyle. "The analytic and synthetic tendencies of the human mind are traceable throughout history"; one tends to adopt some form of pantheism, while "a detached Creator, working more or less after the manner of men" is often assumed by the other. Gassendi is hardly to be ranked with either, for he believed that God created in the first place a definite number of atoms, which constituted the seed of all things, and concluded that "the principle of every change resides in matter." This is the view of Clerk Maxwell, with whose logic, however, Tyndall does not wholly agree. He is, nevertheless, convinced that, without the atomic conception, no "theory of the material universe is capable of scientific statement."

Tyndall now passes to an imaginary conversation between Bishop Butler and a modern follower of Lucretius. In this dialogue, Tyndall admits the difficulty of establishing "logical continuity between molecular processes and the phenomena of consciousness." This he believes to be the "rock on which Materialism must inevitably split whenever it pretends to be a complete philosophy of life." But he implies that he here prefers an expression of honest ignorance to any dogmatic hypothesis. This unanswered question leads him to a brilliant exposition of the theory of evolution, as propounded by Lamarck, Robert Chambers (the author of the *Vestiges of Creation*), Darwin, and Huxley. He insists that it is the mind "stored with the choicest materials of the teleologist that rejects teleology, seeking to refer these wonders to natural causes." From evolution he turns to physics and to the doctrine of the conservation of energy, "the ultimate philosophical issues of which are as yet but dimly seen." But besides physical life and the phenomena of physics, there is a psychical world, "presenting similar gradations, and asking equally for a solution." Tyndall analyzes some of these stages and expresses the conviction that "the evolution of intellect and the evolution of tactual appendages go hand in hand. . . . Man crowns the edifice here, not only in virtue of his own manipulatory power, but through the enormous extension of his range of experience, by the invention of instruments of precision, which serve as supplemental senses and supplemental limbs." Herbert Spencer has shown that experience cannot be restricted to the individual but is an accumulation of the race, either in the form of instinct or in potentially organized capability. In all these great questions Tyndall himself insists that, "By a necessity engendered and justified by science I cross the boundary of the experimental evidence,[1] and discern in that Matter which we, in our ignorance of its latent powers, and notwithstanding our professed reverence for its Creator, have hitherto covered with opprobrium, the promise and potency of all terrestrial life."

But is there the least evidence that any form of life can be developed out of matter? "Spontaneous generation" has perhaps indeed been disproved, but he reminds his hearers that chemists now produce from inorganic materials "a vast array of substances, which were some time ago regarded as the sole products of vitality." However, true scientists will "frankly admit their inability to point to any satisfactory experimental proof that life can be developed, save from demonstrable antecedent life." And Tyndall himself asserts that "the whole process of evolution is the manifestation of a Power absolutely inscrutable to the intellect of man. As little in our day as in the days of Job can man by searching find this Power out. . . . Man the *object* is separated by an impassible gulf from man the *subject*. There is no motor energy in the human intellect to carry it, without logical rupture, from one to the other."

Awe, reverence, wonder, love of the beautiful, physical and moral, in nature, poetry, and art, are mighty facts of consciousness, themselves, like man, evolved "from the interaction of organism and environment through countless ages past." And there is "that deep-set feeling" which has incorporated itself in the religions of the world. Tyndall goes on to observe:

[1] Tyndall observes in a footnote: "This mode of procedure was not invented in Belfast."

You, who have escaped from these religions into the high-and-dry light of the intellect, may deride them; but in so doing you deride accidents of form merely, and fail to touch the immovable basis of the religious sentiment in the nature of man. To yield this sentiment reasonable satisfaction is the problem of problems at the present hour. And grotesque in relation to scientific culture as many of the religions of the world have been and are—dangerous, nay, destructive, to the dearest privileges of freemen as some of them undoubtedly have been, and would if they could, be again—it will be wise to recognize them as the forms of a force, mischievous if permitted to intrude on the region of objective *knowledge,* over which it holds no command, but capable of adding, in the region of *poetry* and *emotion,* inward completeness and dignity to man. . . .

Science has already to some extent leavened the world; it will leaven it more and more. I should look upon the mild light of science breaking in upon the minds of the youth of Ireland,[2] and strengthening gradually to the perfect day, as a surer check to any intellectual or spiritual tyranny which may threaten this island, than the laws of princes or the swords of emperors. We fought and won our battle even in the Middle Ages: should we doubt the issue of another conflict with our broken foe?

The impregnable position of science may be described in a few words. We claim, and we shall wrest from theology, the entire domain of cosmological theory. All schemes and systems which thus infringe upon the domain of science must, in so far as they do this, submit to its control and relinquish all thought of controlling it. Acting otherwise proved always disastrous in the past, and it is simply fatuous today. Every system which would escape the fate of an organism too rigid to adjust itself to its environment, must be plastic to the extent that the growth of knowledge demands. [Science, to be sure,] not infrequently derives motive power from an ultra-scientific source. [And] the world embraces not only a Newton, but a Shakespeare—not only a Boyle, but a Raphael—not only a Kant, but a Beethoven—not only a Darwin, but a Carlyle. Not in each of these, but in all, is human nature whole. They are not opposed, but supplementary—not mutually exclusive, but reconcilable.

In thus making a contrast between the *knowing* and the *creative* faculties of man, Tyndall says in conclusion: "Here, however, I touch a theme too great for me to handle, but which will assuredly be handled by the loftiest minds, when you and I, like streaks of

[2] Seventy students and ex-students at the new Catholic University in Dublin had protested in November, 1873, that the lecture list for the faculty of science, published a month previously, did not contain the name of a single professor of the physical or natural sciences. How far indeed from Newman's "Idea of a University"!

morning cloud, shall have melted into the infinite azure of the past." [3]

It is easy to see from this abstract what offended so many Christian believers, whether scientists or not. An occasional arrogance of phrase was not so damning as the fundamental thesis, that science not merely may ignore theology, but must replace her in any sphere in which the two may come in conflict. This had been said many times before, notably by the Encyclopedists, but rarely had it been presented with such confidence and such seeming authority to the entire intellectual world of a nation. Space does not permit full treatment of the subsequent controversy. The Catholic hierarchy in Ireland issued a denunciatory manifesto, to which Tyndall replied in a well-documented and highly polemical "Apology for the Belfast Address." [4] In England James Martineau, among many lesser critics, attacked Tyndall, at the opening of the 1874 session of Manchester New College, in an address entitled "Religion as Affected by Modern Materialism." Martineau and Tyndall had previously been in considerable agreement on many points of biblical cosmogony, but Martineau took vigorous exception to the spirit of the Belfast Address as denying the validity of the "sources of religious faith" in "the scrutiny of nature" and "the interpretation of sacred books." Tyndall replied with "The Rev. James Martineau and the Belfast Address," which appeared in the *Fortnightly Review*, [5] and in which he, too, insists that "the world will have religion of some kind, even though it should fly for it to the intellectual whoredom of 'spiritualism.' "

[3] I have used throughout the version of the original address reprinted by Tyndall in *Fragments of Science,* 6th ed., London, Longmans, 1879, II, 137–203. A separate pamphlet version, also published by Longmans, went through many editions in the closing months of 1874. Tyndall, however, had "polished" this version considerably, toning down some parts, cutting out some, and adding others. This version ends with the famous lines from Wordsworth's "Tintern Abbey," beginning "For I have learned/To look on nature; not as in the hour/Of thoughtless youth." Tyndall was accused of thus falsifying for public consumption what he had actually said at Belfast, but his defense, in the "Apology for the Belfast Address," is unconvincing. His purpose may have been the innocent one of changing passages which affronted many feelings, but there is no doubt it was a tactical and polemical blunder. It is significant that it was the original version which he reprinted in *Fragments of Science* and which thus became a part of his complete works.

[4] *Fragments of Science,* II, 204–25.

[5] Reprinted in *Fragments of Science,* II, 226–52.

And Martineau revived his criticism in a more closely reasoned final rejoinder, "Modern Materialism: its Attitude toward Theology," published in the *Contemporary*.[6]

However surprising the heat engendered by Tyndall's address may seem to us today, it is important as revealing the extent to which the fundamental disagreement between the theists and empiricists in the Metaphysical Society was of wide public concern in the middle years of the seventies. Two opposed and equally presumptuous cosmologies were in conflict; each was striving to discover an appropriate role for the other; but each feared, with what may seem justification even to many moderns, that the final supremacy of the other would lead to moral and intellectual chaos. The wider struggle, of which this controversy is only a notable instance, weakened the intellectual authority of religion and the moral authority of science; religion retired to the mysterious cave of faith, while science arrogantly scaled the crystal citadel of reason.

The Society for Psychical Research

The scientific and agnostic attack on revelation and supernatural evidences had been largely critical and negative. The power of Tyndall's Belfast Address lay in its startling assertions and positive claims. But the divided spirit of the age was not yet ready for any naturalistic, organic, or poetico-mythical reconciliation. For the scientists—who were as anxious to disown the accusation of "materialism" as many modern liberals to disown "communism" or "socialism," and with similar motives, deeply rooted in the popular mythology of their respective times—were forced into extreme positions, from which they retreated only slowly and for the most part in old age. The new scientific generation, men like Romanes, Crookes, and the brothers Haldane, found themselves in revolt against the mechanism of their teachers, while Clerk Maxwell and Samuel Butler in England, Poincaré and Bergson in France, and Willard Gibbs and William James in America began to develop scientific and philosophical theories which recognized the significance of the concept of energy but which made of dy-

[6] Reprinted in Martineau's *Essays, Reviews, and Addresses,* 4 vols., London, Longmans, 1890–1, IV.

namism something more than the articulation of a machine. New discoveries in electricity, chemistry, genetics, and neurology began, indeed, to give to the law of the conservation of energy the new philosophical implications which Tyndall had dimly foreseen.

But at the very time when the positivism and mechanism of nineteenth-century science were being abandoned in large measure by the most brilliant younger scientists, the public mind, already dominated by the economic materialism of an industrialized middle-class society, was accepting this scientific mechanism and identifying it with the social and economic materialism of the age. This identification, encouraged by a long history of popular education in science, to which men like Huxley and Tyndall had already made great contributions, was perhaps inevitable; we are still dominated by its spirit; but we must remember that it took generations for Victorian science to dominate the public mind. Once mechanistic science had attained a central place in popular education, it became also the central principle of the popular cosmology and, when thus elevated to the dignity of doctrine, was singularly unresponsive to the insights and discoveries of the newer, more dynamic and organic, science. This kind of "cultural lag" remains one of the major problems of a democratic society pledged to universal public education.

However, once the theists and religionists realized that their battle with secular education could never be won on their own terms, and that the spread of middle-class materialism was an inevitable consequence of material progress, they began to see that this popular materialism could be turned to their own purposes. There was nothing conscious or conspiratorial about this discovery; it was a gradual development from the apparent impossibility of any reconciliation between the two cosmologies. The truce between religion and science, under which we still live, is thus the result of a slow acceptance of a new form of the "double truth." The Churches learned once more to take advantage of the paradoxes, inequalities, suffering, and tragedy which were the obvious and increasingly intensified results of industrialization and urbanization; these could easily be pointed to as effects of human greed and thus related to the whole history of the Christian protest against the world as it is, the world of merely human existence and understanding. Science and materialism may be the necessary formulations of man's earthly life, but the Church appealed with new force to the human longing for a heavenly kingdom, another life, where pain and sorrow would be no more and where peace would take the place of the struggle for the survival of the fittest. In a society where evil and greed were rarely punished but in many ways made principles of earthly success, the Church could comfort the masses of men with promises of future retribution for cruelty and sin. Theology began to disappear from the pulpit, and the gospel of love became the Church's weapon in a society dominated by fear, mistrust, and hate. The Christian gospel of love is a powerful doctrine; an hour or two of it on a Sunday morning may serve for large numbers of men as sustenance and support in a troubled world for an entire week. The modern religious dispensation gradually became clear, for by the end of the century the Churches were saying with unction and new assurance, "Render unto science the homage you justly owe, but beseech Christ in your sin and your suffering."

A critical attitude toward this conflict of cosmologies does not presuppose a cynical scorn either of the achievements of science and the scientific spirit or of the role of religion in modern life, but it does necessitate a kind of ironic detachment, especially if we are to weigh justly the relevance of this conflict to our own problems. But to many men in the latter half of the nineteenth century, neither conventional belief nor objective detachment was possible. Both religions, whether of the Christian churches or of science, seemed to many inadequate to the contemporary situation. Those who were thus dissatisfied turned to a variety of new cults and new cosmologies.[7] Some who were neither sceptics nor scientists were content with agnosticism or a Spencerian faith in progress and evolution; but others turned to the substitute rituals and dogmas of Positivism, the Religion of Humanity, or to the neo-Hindu mysticism of Madame Blavatsky's Theosophical Society, founded in New York in 1875. The Church of Christ, Scientist, was established in Boston in 1879 by Mary Baker Eddy; her doctrinal reve-

[7] For what follows, see also Jacques Barzun, *Darwin, Marx, Wagner: Critique of a Heritage,* Boston, Little, Brown, 1941, pp. 110–24.

lation, *Science and Health, with Key to the Scriptures,* marked an extreme denial of scientific materialism, even in the field of medicine, and an assertion of the psychic power of faith to cure all ills, physical, mental, and moral.

Those who had earlier looked to evangelical humanitarianism or utilitarian liberalism for a solution of the evils of society and the problems of the individual had been repeatedly disillusioned by the political compromises of the sixties and seventies. Christian Socialism, the Workingmen's College, Ruskin's St. George's Guild, and the Y.M.C.A. were all attempts to justify an altruistic social ideal in an increasingly scientific world. The missionary work of the early years of the century was now criticized in terms of domestic needs, and although "foreign missions" have remained until our own day one of the most characteristic activities of English and American Protestantism, in all large centers of population home missions and settlement houses sprang up to mitigate the spiritual and material lot of the urban poor. But the most effective and most redeeming of these efforts was the Christian Mission, established by William Booth in Whitechapel in 1865, with no theology, no official church affiliation, and no doctrine but Christian assistance to the broken and needy on their own level of spiritual understanding. In 1878 this mission changed its name to the Salvation Army and has since become one of the most active forces in one kind of religious revival among the downtrodden all over the world. In great cities it still speaks with social and evangelical power.

But there were many, both Christians and agnostics, who were not content with religious efforts to cure social ills by hymns, soup kitchens, and the Word. Organizations like the Social Democratic Federation, the Socialist League, and the Fabian Society sprang up in the eighties in consequence of the failure of mid-Victorian liberalism to maintain its vitality in the face of the Primrose League and the new Tory imperialism. This is not the place to examine these tendencies, which has recently been done admirably by Mrs. Lynd.[8] But it is the Fabian Society, founded during the winter of 1883–4, that inherited the social interests of Victorian liberalism and to which the modern Labour Party

[8] Helen Merrell Lynd, *England in the Eighteen-Eighties: Towards a Social Basis for Freedom,* New York, Oxford, 1945.

owes its true origin. By concerning themselves "not with 'the Poor' but with 'Poverty,' " [9] the Fabians emphasized social and governmental responsibility for both spiritual and material evils and reasserted the empirical and scientific method in sociology and economics as the instrument of reform. Here, once more, the men of religion were confronted by the prestige of science and the authority of a purely secular faith.

A significant consequence of the battle between religion and science was a notable increase of interest in various psychical phenomena which seemed to resist scientific explanation. On every hand there was a multiplication of miraculous occurrences, at the very time when miracles were being subjected to constant rationalistic criticism. The facts of hypnotism had long impressed the learned world, but although hypnotism was feared, its authenticity was no longer seriously doubted, and psychiatrists had already begun to use it in mental therapy. But from time to time since the beginning of the century, a new kind of manifestation, the forms of which we now lump together under the name of "spiritualism," had attracted public attention. D. D. Home, who convinced Sir William Crookes and many other Englishmen that his psychic powers were genuine, held many séances, both public and private, from 1855 on, and it is perhaps to the great public curiosity about his powers that the Metaphysical Society owed the concern with spiritualism which was one of its original and unrealized purposes. Home himself was immortalized in Browning's poem "Mr. Sludge, the Medium," but a host of followers and imitators began to earn a more doubtful immortality by becoming intermediaries between the living and the world of departed spirits. While science was denying to men their age-old faith in personal immortality and a life after death, countless persons were being convinced of the reality of another world by spirit-rappings, messages, and uncanny reminiscences transmitted through strange "mediums" who, like many visionaries who have become saints, seem to have had few virtues but the psychical. Frauds there were in abundance, and some of them were unmasked and punished, but

[9] *Ibid.*, p. 398.

a sufficient number of instances stood up well enough under criticism to justify confirmed and even passionate belief in many minds.

The Christian tradition had always asserted the reality of miracles, visions, and a world of spirits. A belief in ghosts is still common in many parts of the world, even though it is often, as in *Hamlet*, not clear whether ghosts serve God or the Devil. It is probably hard to convince a man who has seen a ghost that ghosts do not exist; but it is equally hard to convince a sceptic who has never seen one that they do. It is interesting to observe, however, that in a world dominated by a spiritual cosmology, the world of spirits makes itself known to us by ghostly apparitions, mere unsubstantial wraiths, possessing only the faintest trace of visible substance. But in a world which has adopted some form of man-centered materialism, at least as a weekday philosophy, it is perhaps natural that the spirits should manifest themselves through a human voice and by physical phenomena—by noises, music, levitations, "ectoplasm," "apports" (the moving of objects, often quite large, from one place to another), and similar sensory manifestations. A world which has accepted hypnotism is similarly open to further conviction through trances, telepathy, second sight, extrasensory perception, and the like. These latter phenomena, however, we do not necessarily label "spiritualistic," but dignify with the adjective "psychical."

It is certain that most men are by temperament inclined to agree either with Shakespeare's Glendower, who claimed he could "call spirits from the vasty deep," or with Hotspur, who replied, "But will they come when you do call for them?" And it is equally true that in the Victorian period, as in our own day, men of the most exemplary honesty and disinterested objectivity have been divided between willing belief and casual scepticism in their appraisal of psychical phenomena. Among the members of the Metaphysical Society, Huxley and Tyndall were strongly sceptical, Sidgwick and Tennyson more actively open-minded. Many other members attended séances and acquired varying degrees of interest and conviction. None that I have discovered was ever a true believer. But Sidgwick had been interested in the phenomena since his college days and with his customary thoroughness maintained a vigorous critical interest throughout his life. And it was Sidgwick who was the most important single figure in the foundation of the Society for Psychical Research in 1882.

The Metaphysical Society had never examined the spiritualistic and psychical phenomena which interested many of its founders. But Sidgwick's own early curiosity had been revived by the experiments on "thought transference" carried on in 1881 by Professor W. F. Barrett of Dublin. At a conference called by Barrett and held January 6, 1882, the Society for Psychical Research was planned, and it was finally constituted in February, with Sidgwick as its first president, and F. W. H. Myers as secretary. Its declared object was to make "an organised and systematic attempt to investigate that large group of debatable phenomena designated by such terms as mesmeric, psychical, and spiritualistic." In his first Presidential Address, delivered July 17, 1882, Sidgwick asserts the purpose of the Society to be the establishment of some kind of scientific agreement "as to the reality of these marvellous phenomena,—of which it is quite impossible to exaggerate the scientific importance, if only a tenth part of what has been alleged by generally credible witnesses could be shown to be true." [10]

The new society thus disclosed the same concern with evidences which had so dominated many of the discussions of the Metaphysical Society and for a number of years performed its most significant function as a clearing-house for reports and records of psychical manifestations. It also made a reasoned effort to establish canons of procedure in the investigation both of thought-transference and mediumistic spiritualism. Its most distinguished members were scientists, sceptics, agnostics, and "freethinkers" of various complexions. They were all dissatisfied with the psycho-physical materialism of their day and were vaguely uneasy about the world of souls and spirits which had recently been so cavalierly dismissed by the new science. The Society, to be sure, included a number of convinced spiritualists, and many of the sceptics, men like Sidgwick himself and Edmund Gurney, were more than willing to be convinced. But practicing mediums were not encouraged,

[10] *Presidential Addresses to the Society for Psychical Research, 1882–1911,* Glasgow (for the Society), 1912, p. 2.

and the Society itself never held séances. It was interested in the detection of fraud, but even more eager for any positive evidence which would produce conviction in the scientific mind. Sidgwick himself eventually became assured of the reality of thought-transference, but always remained sceptical of mediums and their world of extraterrestrial spirits. Other important members were more convinced by spiritualism itself, and these included F. W. H. Myers, Sir William Crookes, Alfred Russel Wallace, Sir Oliver Lodge, and Sir Arthur Conan Doyle. But all insisted, at least to begin with, that the Society was a scientific society and not a spiritualistic cult.

The foundation of the Society for Psychical Research reflects the failure of the Metaphysical Society to bridge the gulf between the intuitionist and empiricist positions and the admitted inability of the scientists to relate the "facts of consciousness" to their material hypotheses. The eighties saw the scientists, including Huxley, very much more on the defensive in all questions involving the psychological, moral, and spiritual implications of their discoveries. Huxley asserted in 1894, in *Evolution and Ethics,* that "the influence of the cosmic process on the evolution of society is the greater the more rudimentary its civilization. Social progress means a checking of the cosmic process at every step and the substitution for it of another, which may be called the ethical process; the end of which is not the survival of those who may happen to be the fittest, in respect of the whole of the conditions which obtain, but of those who are ethically best." [11] W. K. Clifford had attempted a reconciliation of matter and consciousness, moral and psychological, in his vitalistic theory of "mind-stuff." But it was Clifford who also asserted before the Metaphysical Society that "No real belief, however trifling and fragmentary it may seem, is ever truly insignificant" but leaves "its stamp on our character for ever."

Sidgwick, in his second address (December, 1882) as president of the Society for Psychical Research, commented upon a recent attack on spiritualism in the *Pall Mall Gazette,* which had observed that "owing to the many generations of our ancestors who

[11] *Evolution and Ethics,* London, Macmillan, 1894, p. 81.

believed in spirits, we retain, it seems, in our nervous mechanism, 'innumerable connections of fibers' which will be developed into superstitious beliefs if we give them the slightest opportunity. . . . 'The scientific attitude can only be maintained by careful abstention from dangerous trains of thought.'" But Sidgwick points out that this view is "the exact counterpart of the dissuasions which certain unwise defenders of religious orthodoxy, a generation ago, used to urge against the examination of the evidences of Christianity." He remarks "how the whirligig of time brings round his revenges and how the new professor is 'but old priest writ large' in a brand-new scientific jargon."[12] He sees, more clearly than many of his contemporaries, that those whom science had deprived of their faith in a spiritual world were now in danger of losing their faith in science. But it remains curious and revealing that so many men of science turned to "psychical research" as a means of ascertaining the truth of supernaturalism by the methods of science, hoping in this way to justify both their science and their faith, their knowledge and their ignorance.

Sidgwick delivered eight presidential addresses between 1882 and 1890. By 1901 six other presidents had served: Balfour Stewart, Arthur Balfour, William James, Sir William Crookes, F. W. H. Myers, and Sir Oliver Lodge, all men of great distinction. Within two years of its founding the society had 192 members, 185 associates, and a number of honorary and corresponding members. Beginning in February, 1884, it published, "for private circulation among members and associates only," the *Journal of the Society for Psychical Research,* originally edited by Sidgwick, and which still appears. By 1886 its membership had grown to 600. Among the former members of the Metaphysical Society who later joined the Society for Psychical Research, I have traced, in addition to Sidgwick, A. J. Balfour, Shadworth Hodgson, R. H. Hutton, and Roden Noel; there were probably others. Nicholas Murray Butler of Columbia University became a member in February, 1884, and William James in November of the same year. The prestige of the society, which was very low in the beginning, began to rise, as more and more men of intellect and position

12 *Presidential Addresses,* pp. 8–9.

showed an interest in its purposes. Believing Christians, who had at first feared the society as a formal alliance between science and a world of evil spirits, began to recognize the possible usefulness of its attempted demonstrations of the separate existence of an immortal soul. But the more authority the society acquired, the more sceptical it became in all truly spiritualistic matters, until in 1930, when Sir A. Conan Doyle resigned from it in his old age, he felt obliged to say that "the Society, originally intended to be a sympathetic and fair centre for inquiry, seems to have become simply an anti-spiritualist organisation. . . . For a generation . . . the Society has done no constructive work of any importance, and has employed its energies in hindering and belittling those who are engaged in real active psychical research." [13]

Conan Doyle came to be highly prejudiced in favor of the world of spirits, but his remarks reveal what is perhaps the inevitable fate of an organization which attempts to discover the "truth" of a spiritual realm by the methods and in the vocabulary of science. "Spirit" dissolves, leaving only material phenomena, chiefly of a petty and even shabby nature, startling and eccentric symbols of little earthly meaning, pallid voices from either a dreary or a chucklingly euphoric "other world," which in the end seems as "material" as our own. This has been the great stumbling block, even for the open-minded: granting the difficulty of communication between the worlds of the living and the dead, what possible lesson can there be for men in the messages we have thus far received? How much more meaningful any number of religious visions, how much more moving the great myths and symbols of Christian tradition. What is spirit, indeed?

The Aristotelian Society

We have seen how the temper of the Metaphysical Society made itself felt in its lifetime through a number of periodicals, and how in Tyndall's Belfast Address the fundamental conflict which divided its members was publicly dramatized in his assertion of the cosmological claims of empirical science. The founding of *Mind*

[13] Arthur Conan Doyle, "Letter of Resignation from the Society for Psychical Research," three-page printed folder, issued by Doyle. Copy in the Columbia University Library.

in 1876 marked a further stage in the Society's history, as it began to become clear that professional philosophy would have to undertake the reconciliation of metaphysics, psychology, and scientific method.[14] And at a time when many scientists and psychologists seemed to be abandoning an interest in the mysteries of spiritual immortality, the establishment of the Society for Psychical Research continued the examination of supernatural evidences which had often characterized both the theistic affirmations and the sceptical denials of the Metaphysical Society.

But the questioning spirit of the Society was carried on most effectively after its dissolution by the Aristotelian Society, founded by Shadworth Hodgson in 1879, when the Metaphysical was approaching exhaustion.[15] The Aristotelian Society for the Systematic Study of Philosophy, to give it its full name, was designed to attract men and women of all shades of opinion and all degrees of distinction to the close and conscientious study of all the questions on which philosophy or metaphysics could be said to bear. Frederic Harrison, who had as wide an experience of clubs and societies as any thinker of the day, was Hodgson's adviser in preparing the first list of invitations, and himself soon joined the Society. Hodgson became the first president and served in that capacity for fourteen years, making it the chief business of his life. He gave his first presidential address, on "Philosophy in Relation to History," October 11, 1880, and throughout the years attended regularly and took an active part in its discussions. Like Knowles, he was a skillful impresario. He had been one of Croom Robertson's most active supporters in the establishment of *Mind;* and throughout the years he maintained a close connection between *Mind* and the Aristotelian Society.

The Society met fortnightly, from October or November to June or July. At each meeting one or more papers, prepared in

[14] It is interesting to note that the important scientific weekly, *Nature,* was established in 1869, the year of the founding of the Metaphysical Society.

[15] A debased version of the Metaphysical Society, called the "Zetetical Society" (whether named after "Z," *zeta,* or Zetes, one of the Argonauts, I have been unable to discover) was founded in 1878 "to furnish opportunities for the unrestricted discussion of Social, Political, and Philosophical subjects." The annual subscription was *5s.* and the honorary secretary was a certain J. M. Fells of Brixton. George Bernard Shaw attended its meetings and indeed used it to train himself in public debate.

advance by the members, were read and discussed, and every member was expected either to contribute a paper or to initiate a discussion at least once each session. At the end of each year plans were laid for the following year under two heads: the historic development of philosophy, and its methods and problems. It is perhaps natural that the bylaws of the society (or of any similar society) resemble those of the Metaphysical. But the Aristotelian was never as "exclusive" as the Metaphysical, and its members were not all men of established intellectual position. It welcomed young minds just out of the university as well as older amateur philosophers with serious interests and purposes. But many distinguished men were faithful members, and not the least virtue of the society has remained, even to the present day, the opportunity it affords for different intellectual generations to meet in an atmosphere of reasoned and responsible discussion. Alexander Bain, Bernard Bosanquet, S. H. Butcher, F. C. Conybeare, W. R. Dunstan, R. B. Haldane, G. J. Romanes, and W. R. Sorley, were all members during the early years, and among the first foreign members were four Americans, the philosophers William James, Thomas Davidson, and William T. Harris, as well as the young psychologist, J. M. Cattell. From later generations of English thinkers came J. H. Muirhead, L. T. Hobhouse, C. B. Upton, Bertrand Russell, A. N. Whitehead,[16] and G. E. Moore, most of whom joined when quite young, as well as many lesser-known men and women of considerable later achievement.

The Executive Committee for the twelfth session of 1890–1, however, was obliged to raise a question which, as we have seen, dominated the last years of the Metaphysical Society. Psychological and methodological problems had bulked large in the discussions, and the committee's report complains of "the comparatively small space which the subject of philosophy proper fills in [the papers read before the Society]. . . . Yet this is avowedly the primary purpose of the Society, without fulfilling

[16] Whitehead's important paper on "Space, Time, and Relativity," read before the Aristotelian Society in 1915, marks an important stage in his progress from mathematical to philosophical and cosmological interests. See Victor Lowe's admirable essay on "The Development of Whitehead's Philosophy" in *The Philosophy of Alfred North Whitehead,* edited by P. A. Schilpp, Evanston and Chicago, Northwestern University, 1941.

which, we have no justification for continuing to meet." [17] But the society did continue, and later in 1891 began the publication of its *Proceedings*, still one of the most important of modern philosophical journals, in which certain selected papers are reprinted for a wider circle.[18] A little later the committee proposed that the papers should be circulated among the members before being read. This method, which had been so necessary to the success of the Metaphysical Society, was tried and found desirable. In 1900 it was decided to hold meetings monthly instead of fortnightly, and thereafter proofs of papers were distributed to the membership two weeks in advance of each meeting. This procedure has been followed with little change ever since.

From 1918 until the present, interrupted only by the recent war, the Aristotelian Society has met once a year in a symposium with the *Mind* Association in various British university centers, often in collaboration with local university philosophical clubs. These symposia, whose papers are also regularly published, have brought before a wider public the problems of the society and have thus continued, however indirectly, the spirit of the Metaphysical Society and the method which Knowles had found so successful in the "Modern Symposia" with which he launched the *Nineteenth Century*. It is outside the purpose of the present study to examine the history of the Aristotelian Society in detail, but it is significant as one of the most vital and longest surviving offspring of the Metaphysical Society and a direct link with its distinguished parent. The continuing vigor of the younger society, however, seems to indicate that the Aristotelian's principle of admitting young, unknown, and as yet philosophically unformed minds to an active collaboration with their teachers and masters is the secret of its longer life and its proved ability to translate the problems of one generation into the vocabulary and intellectual temper of the next.[19] For it is not only the philosophical "professionalism"

[17] *Proceedings of the Aristotelian Society* (1891), I, 134.

[18] Many of the papers read in the early years had already been published in *Mind*. From 1896 to 1900 there was a brief hiatus in the publication of the *Proceedings*, during which period many of the papers were again published in *Mind*. But with the volume of 1900–01 a new series was begun, which still appears.

[19] In illustration of the importance of youth to such a society, it is interesting to observe that in 1880, at the time of the dissolution of the Metaphysical Society,

of the Aristotelian Society which has assured the unity of its history and its purposes, but also a devotion to the principle of social discourse and what may well be called "collaborative meaning."

The Aristotelian Society, like the Metaphysical, shared Spinoza's conviction that there is nothing more useful to man than man. Ever since the founding of the French Academy in 1635 and of the Royal Society in 1662, academies, learned societies, and clubs had, in many and various ways, played a large part in the molding and development of the European tradition. But the more specialized these societies, the more certain they have become that at least some kind of truth was attainable through their efforts, and the more persuaded that the wisdom of many men has greater general validity than the wisdom of one or a few. Bacon was certainly one of the first moderns to see the applicability of this principle to the advancement of science, and in his *New Atlantis* imagined a "Salomon's House," which combines the characteristics of the later Royal Society (whose members looked to Bacon as its spiritual founder) with those of a modern research laboratory.

Whatever the motives and consequences of the declaration of papal infallibility by the Vatican Council of 1870–1, the Church Councils had themselves manifested a similar conviction in their assumption of the superior wisdom of a majority, an assumption which had prevailed since the very earliest days of Christian history. But there is considerable difference between rule by a majority in questions of politics, problems to which most men have never expected answers absolute or "true," and the determination by vote of questions of dogma, questions involving entire cosmologies and with implications affecting the minds of many men. This is especially clear when the majority answers are imposed as true in an absolute sense, and presumed to have divine sanction. Only revelation or, if you will, insight, can justify this kind of truth, and even here it is assumed that the insights of the majority are more *true* than those of the minority. "Truth," which is cer-

of its members or former members, eight were dead; six were over seventy; eighteen were over sixty; fourteen were over fifty; ten were over forty; and only six were in their thirties, and five of these six had been elected during the last year of the Society, of whom three may never have attended a meeting.

tainly not only a difficult word to define, but hard to understand in a philosophical sense, has thus perhaps always been relative and has never meant more than "that which is conformable to the cosmology of the majority." But it is equally clear that this is a definition which, however psychological and naturalistic, would be unacceptable to any philosopher or any natural scientist.

The learned societies, the discussion clubs, and the various academies of arts and sciences which have sprung up all over the world represent a recognition of this relativism, but with a further emphasis on the cultural and intellectual values of a pluralism of intellectual ends and means. Many kinds of truth are attainable by many kinds of men, but if we are to escape the solipsistic dangers implicit in the most rigorous relativism, or the disparate private worlds resulting from vastly multiplied knowledge in highly specialized fields, we must cultivate even more than we have in the past the arts of discourse, the poetry of intellect. Failing this, we shall echo the despair of Job answering his comforters, and say with him, "No doubt but ye are the people, and wisdom shall die with you," or the cynicism of Pilate, who said to Jesus, "What is truth?"—and did not stay for an answer.

The Synthetic Society

The problem uppermost in the minds of the founders of the Metaphysical Society had been the relation of religion and science, and their original intention had been to form a society to combat scepticism and the philosophical pretensions of the scientific spirit. This purpose had been modified, largely owing to Martineau's refusal to join a group of theists pledged only to combat disbelief, and the Society finally met with hopes of achieving an ultimate reconciliation of the two cosmologies. But we have seen how these hopes of *rapprochement* were frustrated by the critical temper of the agnostics and the failure of the Society to discuss religion except in terms of miraculous evidences and the ethics of belief. The polemical victories of mechanistic science, not only in the Society but in the public mind, had eventually led to the gradual withdrawal of the theistic members from open controversy and the acceptance of a *modus vivendi* between them and the scientists which ignored their still unresolved differences.

We have already remarked on the change in the intellectual atmosphere of England in the late seventies and early eighties. But the decade of the nineties saw even more striking shifts in critical and philosophical emphasis, as the great figures of the mid-Victorian period began to disappear more and more rapidly, and a younger generation which had been brought up in the atmosphere of positivistic science, middle-class prosperity, and a widening imperialism, began to turn against the tradition of their fathers. In 1890 a group of eleven High Churchmen, six of them connected with Keble College at Oxford, published *Lux Mundi*, a volume of twelve theological essays, which deserves to be compared with *Essays and Reviews*, although on the more secular public mind of the nineties it made no such dramatic impression. The importance of these essays lies in their acceptance of virtually all the findings of the higher criticism and their commitment to a formulation of religious meanings and scriptural authority largely in terms of myth and symbol—in a spirit not unlike that of Renan. Most of the writers were known as Ritualists, but now the characteristically High Church tendency of Ritualism was claiming a theological justification hardly distinguishable from the attitude of the Broad Church. The Anglican heirs of the Oxford Movement had at last begun to vindicate all the fears of Newman and had taken a position that must have caused Pusey to turn over in his grave. Those who had remained in the English Church had at last succumbed to the most tempting dangers of Liberalism, and only in the Roman Catholic Church, where the Modernist position was being slowly but firmly annihilated, was the divine authority and the literal truth of scriptural revelation still held inviolate as an article of faith. During these last years of the century the Catholic Church acquired new prestige in England, and even many non-Catholic Christians, including R. H. Hutton, came to regard her dogmatic impregnability as one of the surest guarantees of the survival of Christian theism.

This was the religious attitude which led in 1896 to the foundation of the Synthetic Society, an explicit imitation of the Metaphysical Society in form and method, although differing from it as much as possible in composition and central purpose. Frederic Harrison and Cardinal Manning had been unable to agree on the precise nature of the theological society which they hoped in 1889 might succeed the Metaphysical,[20] but it was their desire to found a society to discuss with "dry light" the problems that lie "*inter apices Theologiae*," which finally bore fruit in the Synthetic. It was not until January 24, 1896, that Wilfrid Ward, son of W. G. Ward, finally met at the Carlton Club with Arthur Balfour and two of the contributors to *Lux Mundi*—the editor, Canon Gore, later Bishop of Birmingham, and Dr. Talbot, later Bishop of Winchester—to determine the name and purpose of the Synthetic Society. Since the new society was intended "to aim more definitely at construction" than the old Metaphysical, membership was restricted to those who truly *desired* to find "a working philosophy of religious belief." [21] Spencer's "Synthetic Philosophy" had already largely lost its popular appeal in England, and the name of the society must therefore be understood, in a more Hegelian sense, as an effort to create a new synthesis of religious positions and convictions. Balfour's *Foundations of Belief* had appeared the year before and had removed any question as to the true position of the author of *A Defence of Philosophic Doubt.* Wilfrid Ward, in thanking Balfour for his adherence, spoke of the scheme as "an experiment" and as furthering the spread of his own conviction "that the introspective method is *not* a *practical* guide to truth, and thus helping people to doubt the value of their doubts." [22]

Earlier suggestions to call the new organization the "Philalethic," or the "Philosophical Discussion Society," may have reflected an original desire to establish a society with the breadth of interest and the variety of intellectual positions which characterized the old Metaphysical Society, but by the time of the actual founding of the Synthetic any such scheme had been abandoned, and the society was from the first restricted to Christian theists. But some continuity with the elder society remained.

[20] Shane Leslie, *Henry Edward Manning, His Life and Labours,* London, Burns, Oates, and Washbourne, 1921, p. 324.

[21] Maisie Ward, *The Wilfrid Wards and the Transition,* London, Sheed and Ward, 1934, I, 354. The whole of Chap. XX, "From the Metaphysical to the Synthetic," as well as App. B, is of great importance to a history of the Synthetic Society.

[22] *Loc. cit.*

Wilfrid Ward himself, now just turned forty, had often heard of the Metaphysical from his father. In 1893 he had published *William George Ward and the Catholic Revival* and had devoted a chapter to the Metaphysical Society and his father's share in its debates. Seven former members of the Metaphysical became members of the Synthetic. James Martineau, although nearly ninety-one, had been asked to join and had accepted, reminding Ward, however, of his original doubts about a society from which agnostics would be excluded. He justified his present decision, nevertheless, by saying:

> The really misplaced people in the old Society were those who had no belief in metaphysics at all, and could only treat their problems with impatience and derision. To these members the end which the Society had in view was not only unattainable but unreal; and an evening spent in quest of it was a futile waste of life.
>
> I certainly feel that we could have prospered better without this class of members, to whom the questions discussed were closed before the attempt to answer them. . . . Those of us who are already in agreement on a fundamental epistemological question, may help each other by comparing our several views of what the ulterior Reality is, which is delivered to us in aspects so various.[23]

Henry Sidgwick had attended the first meeting, although he did not finally become a member until 1898. Bishop Gore, in a memorial address delivered after Sidgwick's death in 1900, spoke warmly of his contributions to the Synthetic:

> At once he became the life and soul of that Society, so much so that his death makes us wonder whether we had not better die too. We were all, or most of us, men who had reached, or were getting beyond, middle life; we had our positions settled, we knew what we thought and what we were unable to think. To most of us it was quite apparent that we should not change our views, and we had ceased to believe that other people would change theirs. Therefore, though we were interested, we were not hopeful. It was extraordinary the difference which appeared in the treatment of questions by Henry Sidgwick. . . . That was what was so remarkable in Henry Sidgwick—the perpetual hopefulness of his inquiry. . . . There was in him an extraordinary belief in *following reason*—a belief and a hopefulness which continued up to the last. This is, I venture to

23 From Martineau's letter to Wilfrid Ward, reprinted in James Drummond and C. B. Upton, *Life and Letters of James Martineau,* New York, Dodd, Mead, 1902, II, 375–6, and in Maisie Ward, *op. cit.*, p. 355.

think, a quality which is exceedingly rare in our time, for mostly when we have settled down to our positions we lose any real hope of obtaining any strikingly new light on the deepest matters. It was quite otherwise with Sidgwick.[24]

Gore's remarks are not only a commentary on the character and temper of the Synthetic's members; they mark the change in intellectual climate since the fervid days of the seventies, when all things were possible. Sidgwick had himself slowly returned to a theistic position and had admitted this in the conclusion to his first paper read before the Synthetic, February 25, 1898, "On the Nature of the Evidence for Theism":

It seems to me, then, that if we are led to accept Theism as being, more than any other view of the Universe, consistent with, and calculated to impart a clear consistency to, the whole body of what we commonly agree to take for knowledge—including knowledge of right and wrong—we accept it on grounds analogous to those on which important scientific conclusions have been accepted; and that even though we are unable to add the increase of certitude derivable from verified predictions, we may still attain a sufficient strength of reasoned conviction to justify us in calling our conclusions a "working philosophy." [25]

But the tone of this utterance is still essentially agnostic and even empirical. Through Sidgwick the questioning spirit of the Metaphysical Society asserted itself once more in this new atmosphere of accepted certainties. In reply to a letter of Ward's about this first paper, he remarks, "I am glad too that the discussion seemed to [Lodge] to 'make for approximation to agreement': the phrase exactly expresses what I think we ought to aim at; it would be idle to expect more." [26]

The only Catholic member of the Metaphysical Society to join the Synthetic was the Reverend Father Robert Clarke, who had joined the Metaphysical in 1879 and could hardly have known much about its best years. He was a Scot, a former doctor and physiologist, who had taught metaphysics and psychology at the short-lived Catholic University at Kensington, where he had trained Wilfrid Ward. Ward later characterized him as "the most learned

[24] Arthur and Eleanor Sidgwick, *Henry Sidgwick, a Memoir,* London, Macmillan; New York, The Macmillan Co., 1906, p. 557.

[25] *Ibid.,* p. 559. [26] *Loc. cit.*

man I ever met, not even excepting Baron von Hügel."[27] C. B. Upton, Martineau's younger colleague at Manchester New College, who had become a member of the Metaphysical in 1879, also now became one of the founding members of the Synthetic. And R. H. Hutton and Shadworth Hodgson who, with Martineau and Sidgwick, had been original members of the Metaphysical, now joined the Synthetic and helped to continue the tradition of the older society. Thus, of the twenty-five surviving members of the Metaphysical, seven joined the Synthetic and became active participants in its discussions. Of the eighteen survivors who did not become members of the Synthetic, only five could be considered convinced theists: Gladstone, who was 85; Grove, who was 76, and more deeply than ever involved in music; Argyll, who was 73, and had retired from active life; Alfred Barry, who was 70, and a confirmed Broad Churchman; and Gasquet, who although only 50 was busy at historical scholarship in the archives of the British Museum and the Vatican.

But the Synthetic Society included, among its total membership of fifty-four, a number of younger and equally distinguished men, although its roster is nothing like that of the Metaphysical either in the accomplishments of its members or in its representative quality. Among those who are still remembered were Lord Hugh Cecil, James Bryce (afterwards Viscount Bryce), A. V. Dicey, Lord Rayleigh, Baron von Hügel, F. W. H. Myers, Hastings Rashdall, Oliver Lodge, A. S. Pringle-Pattison, R. C. Jebb, James Ward, Father Tyrrell, William Temple, G. Lowes Dickinson, and G. K. Chesterton.[28] Wilfrid Ward himself became the honorary secretary, sharing his duties for a time with George Wyndham, and presumably saw to it that "all shades of constructive opinion should be represented in the Synthetic."[29]

The first meeting of the society was held on February 28, 1898, under the chairmanship of the Bishop of Rochester. The society resolved to dine together (usually at the old Westminster Palace

27 Maisie Ward, *op. cit.,* p. 48.

28 For the "Rules of the Society," a complete list of members, and a group of interesting "Concessions and Questions," see Maisie Ward, *op cit.,* App. B, pp. 417–20.

29 *Ibid.,* p. 363.

Hotel) in January, February, March, April, and May, on the last Friday of the month, and that "after dinner a Paper shall be read and discussed, having been previously printed and circulated among the members." Papers were to take not more than half an hour in the reading, and seven minutes were allowed to each member for discussion. The chairman was to be elected annually. Two guests could be invited to the dinner and meeting, "provided that their names are submitted to the Chairman and approved by him at least a fortnight before the meeting to which they are asked." New members must be elected unanimously. The first two rules assert that the "objects of the Society are to consider existing Agnostic tendencies, and to contribute towards a working philosophy of religious belief"; and that "should any question in controversy between different communions be raised in discussion, it should be borne in mind that the Society aims at mutual understanding among its members, with a view to the maintenance of those beliefs which they hold in common."

A brief history of the early years of the Synthetic Society has been already undertaken by Mrs. Maisie Ward Sheed in her study of Wilfrid Ward. From her account and from the correspondence of many members with her father which she gives, it is clear that the Synthetic suffered from many of the difficulties and shocks which eventually weakened the Metaphysical. The Hegelians often disturbed the more orthodox Christians, and F. W. H. Myers, who had become a true convert to spiritualism, so astonished many of the members by his intransigent convictions that Wilfrid Ward came to believe that they "ought not to have taken him in." The number of Catholic members was large, and there was occasionally a suspicion of proselytism. The preparation of a series of "Concessions and Questions" aroused considerable disagreement among some of the members, and only Ward's tact and skill at compromise eased the minds of men like Haldane, who wrote, "So long as the Society is not looked on as a serious enterprise I am quite ready to remain a member." The death of Sidgwick affected his brother-in-law Balfour even more than Gore, and he wondered "whether we ought not to take the occasion of Henry Sidgwick's death for winding up our Society while it is yet in full strength, and before the inevitable period of senile decay sets in—I have an idea that no such Association can last usefully for more than a limited period." [30] The members voted against dissolution but resolved to suspend for a year. At the end of this period many of the members did not wish to resume but, owing to Ward's efforts, new members were found (although the membership never reached forty at any time) and the society continued until 1908. The Synthetic thus enjoyed a life only slightly longer than the Metaphysical, although if we count the year of suspension, it too, like the Metaphysical, had an active life of about eleven years. After the dissolution of the society, Balfour had sets of the papers bound up and presented a copy to each of the members.[31]

Maisie Ward remarks that "the Synthetic, like the Metaphysical, was in danger of suffering from a general diffused friendliness and the absence of sufficiently 'close' discussion," and records that her father once mentioned to Balfour the impression of the hotel waiters "that we are called 'The Sympathetic Society.' " [32] But in a group so firmly pledged to some kind of theism, such a fundamental intellectual and emotional sympathy was both more natural and more deeply felt than in the Metaphysical. The "love," too much of which Huxley blamed for the death of the Metaphysical, was a love consequent upon complete intellectual freedom under the privilege of a magnificent courtesy, not the pre-ordained agreement on a central principle which characterized the Synthetic. Paradoxically enough, this "Synthetic" agreement made possible not only a general sympathy, but the public and private airing of conscientious scruples. In this sense the Synthetic could not prove as interesting an intellectual experiment as the Metaphysical, although it is possible that its religious and philosophical achievement may have been greater. The unified purpose of the society naturally tended to give its dominantly churchly majority the appearance of a pressure group, but its greatest concession —"that for the purposes of our debates no arguments should be based on the assumption of either a supernatural inspiration of

[30] *Ibid.*, p. 379.

[31] A full study of these papers might prove an interesting key to the relation of Victorian and modern religious thought.

[32] Maisie Ward, *op. cit.*, p. 368.

the Bible or a supernatural authority residing in the Church"[33] —must have deprived many theological arguments of a good deal of their presumptive force.

By refusing to discuss the very questions which had loomed so large in the debates of the Metaphysical Society, the Synthetic strengthened its own narrow polemical purpose—to find a non-naturalistic justification for theism—but apparently discovered in the end that some kind of faith in what had been eliminated from discussion at the beginning constituted the essential core of the Christian faith, not only for most of its members but also for all men who are willing to call themselves believers in any of the historical forms of Christianity. This was inevitable in a society most of whose members were either Roman Catholics or High Church Anglicans; Sidgwick once wrote, "We have no pure-blooded Protestants";[34] but this implicit limitation deprived the society of the opportunity it possessed of once more criticizing the implications of religious authority and religious belief in a world still dominated by science and the critical spirit. For science continued to lust after strange gods, and, like St. Paul, many men of science preached the Unknown God to the superstitious Athenians of the present, who, gathered in the free air which is the Areopagus of the modern spirit, were all still anxious to hear some new thing.

[33] *Ibid.*, p. 419.

[34] *Ibid.*, p. 356.

Chapter 13

THE PROMISE AND THE HOPE

JOHN STUART MILL once said that England could be reproached by Continental thinkers for an "indifference to the higher philosophy." This was perhaps true of English thought in the first half of the nineteenth century, owing in large measure to the close relation of the universities to an established church which was suspicious of speculation. Besides, the practical demands of the new industrialism and the immediacy of the social and economic problems to which this wave of material progress gave rise absorbed the fullest energies of the best minds among a people never given to system-making and never convinced that intellectual consistency or a rigorous agreement on first principles was either a necessity or a virtue. England has had no revolution since the seventeenth century, during a period when the rest of the western world saw so many revolutions and changes in governments and national boundaries, and this fact is as important to an understanding of the English mind as the influence of all that happened across the narrow Channel. English insularity, however, has had the virtues of its defects. For in the absence of revolution, England has established a political system and a social attitude which, however grudging and inconsistent its processes, represents the finest achievement of one great tradition in political philosophy, and which continues to influence more than half the world.

England, Germany, and France

We have all learned from the social and military struggles of recent years what we have known theoretically since the eighteenth century, that the cultural life of a people is inextricably bound up with its social, political, and economic forms and institutions. What has happened in Germany and the rest of Europe, including

Russia, since the first World War is proof that the meaning of any system, the force of any philosophical ideal, must be measured, not only by its industrial or military consequences, but by what it does to the hearts and minds of men. The astonishing vitality of Continental thought, art, and literature during the nineteenth and early twentieth centuries has been succeeded in our own time by a spirit, a culture, and a political civilization in many ways markedly inferior to the European tradition of the past. The profound philosophical and scientific contributions of Germany, the subtly passionate political and intellectual life of Italy, the rich and varied insights into the relations of mind and spirit which France has given to the world in politics, art, and literature, have indeed created a body of historical and literary tradition which in many respects has never been surpassed in the history of man and which we rightly and proudly call European culture. Even after the first World War, this tradition was still in possession, but it had long been the ornament and prerogative of the upper classes, and now served less and less the contemporary needs and aspirations of the great mass of the people. It was more and more concerned with the maintenance of its own now diminishing vitality and became a kind of inherited *noblesse,* obliged to defend itself against the encroachments of popular democracy, in the name of a false spiritual eugenics and a tired legitimacy.

The tradition of liberalism on the Continent, throughout the nineteenth century, was weakened by the repeated splitting of the middle class along religious, professional, and economic lines, at the very time when the urban and industrial workers were rediscovering the philosophic and revolutionary base of that liberalism. The only bonds among the different segments of the middle class were on the one hand economic self-interest, and on the other the European cultural tradition, which, because of its very sophistication, elegance, and intellectual depth, could only be fully shared by the class which enjoyed considerable leisure and economic self-sufficiency. The European masses had long desired a fuller participation, not only in social and political benefits, but in these cultural fruits of their own civilization. When these fruits, in the forms of education and opportunity, were not obtained by revolution or political change, largely owing to the intransigent fears of the dominant middle class, the workers were forced either into a closer alliance with that class in the hope of becoming middle class themselves, or into parties which came to teach the inevitability of proletarian revolution and the destruction of this older culture. The leadership and rationale of this revolutionary movement came inevitably from the middle class itself, from those who perceived the paradox presented by a civilization which denied its highest enjoyments and the fulfillment of its noblest aspirations to the great masses of men when the economic prosperity and continued existence of that civilization was most dependent on the productive capacity of these very masses.

The bankruptcy of the European "intellectual," wherever it has manifested itself, is not merely the moral bankruptcy of corrupt politics, the not letting the right hand know what the left hand doeth, but the psychic bankruptcy of a divided intellect. This state of mind led in recent years to the most violent attempt at cure in the history of mankind, the enforced unification of a divided social fabric in a new organism of the State—Fascism in Italy, Nazism in Germany, the Falange in Spain, and similar movements all over the world. In Russia, where the problem, for a variety of reasons, had manifested itself much sooner, the process took a different form—the complete destruction of the old middle and upper classes—with complex consequences which we are only now beginning to understand, as we try to rebuild our world on the ruins left by a second World War.

The failure of the European mind to solve the problems of the twentieth century appears at this moment to be complete. No Voltaire, no Rousseau, no Jefferson, no Marx has yet appeared in this century to give critical understanding or philosophic meaning to the travail of our time. Spengler indeed has shown with learning and systematic thoroughness that the West is in decline. Other historians have studied our social and political history with such care that much I have said here is almost commonplace. But since the recent war began and, even more significantly, since its victorious conclusion, no true successor to Lincoln, Mazzini, or Lenin has appeared in continental Europe to bring the deepest aspirations of our tradition and our civilization into political light and into the social consciousness of the people. Leaders and thinkers have arisen and will arise, but whether they will be able to revitalize what we call the European tradition is as yet an unanswered question. Perhaps France will once more give a new heart and a new mind to Europe, as she has done so many times in the past, and, if so, we may find hope that the European vision will not be forever dimmed. But even this hope must be tempered by the realization that after the first World War Paris and Berlin were the Athens and Sparta of a modern Peloponnesian War. Berlin is already, after this second World War, a second Carthage; and Paris may be tragically forced to become a second Alexandria, where the refinement and wisdom and intellectual subtlety of an age long past will endure while new Caesars usher in One World.

Continental thinkers have never been indifferent to the higher philosophy; but they have often been indifferent to its consequences. To be sure, philosophy, like God, must be loved for its own sake; knowledge has always been its own justification. But man is both knower and known, and man as knower must never forget that knowledge is not merely the ordering of experience and consciousness in the pattern of laws and systems, but also the representation of thinking, acting, living man as a thing known, not only the self understanding and reacting to the world of phenomena, but also other selves engaged in the same process. The transcendentalism and idealism of German philosophy, together with the critical reactions to it, have often seemed oblivious of this primary empirical truth. The consequence has too often been that the "truth," whether in philosophy or science, has become a means of individual salvation, not a means of grace to all men. During the political and social turmoil of Germany in the eighteenth and nineteenth centuries there was no nation, no community, no consensus which men of intellect and imagination could share with their fellow men. Goethe and Nietzsche, a century apart, both manifest this lack and this need.

During this period in Germany, the universities, and the universities alone, offered not merely the atmosphere of *Aufklärung* and intellectual progress, but also the comforting envelopment of common purpose and common satisfactions. There was no Germany, but there were "the German universities"; there were no Germans, but there were German professors, German philosophers, and German scientists. The failure of the revolutions of 1848 put an end to the hope that the tradition of the German Enlightenment could create a nation in its own image. And when the successful rise of Prussia had at last created a single German state, the social, political, and artistic insights of German philosophy, of Kant, Fichte, Schelling, Hegel, and Schopenhauer, were often, by a kind of neurotic elective affinity, perverted to the service of the new state. It was not the state which German thought had looked for and fought for, but it was *a* state, and at last they had it: a state, but not yet a nation; subjects, but as yet no citizens; Germany, but still no Germans. Lassalle, Bismarck, Wagner, and H. S. Chamberlain all hammered away at a new myth, hoping to create a nation out of tribal memories and political dreams. Only Nietzsche, so critical of the "higher philosophy," knew that Germans were lost because they had never found themselves or each other and so urged upon them the ideal of the good European, transfigured beyond all the limitations of nation, class, and even self in the most supreme of self-assertions.

German thought and German science, in the search for a true German culture, had taken the world and all mankind for their province and, through the nineteenth century, gradually spread their influence all over Europe, into England, and even across the Atlantic to America itself. But there was still no German nation, only a German enlightenment; victorious armies, but no society of men; an intellectual and philosophical tradition of the most transcendental ingeniousness and a science of the most effective practicality; much soul but no body. What was to be done? If there was as yet no German nation, there must still be some corporate Germania more tangible than the structure of the state. Surely the answer lay in the idea of a German *race;* a systematic and organic answer, fulfilling so many of the unrealized dreams of generations of philosophers and thinkers. But what had kept this talented and glorious race from final realization of itself?

Some disease, some canker, eating at its noble heart? Yes, other races, other nationalities, not German, which must be purged from the system before Germany could be herself. And all around the boundaries of the new German state there were other states and other races, nations who had found themselves or would soon arise, shaming the colossus of central Europe with their individuality and unity, but all fearful of German power and German logic, all fearful of that impulse to aggression which is as characteristic of divided and unhappy nations as it is of insecure and neurotic individuals. German failure to create a nation at home and German aggression abroad are thus parts of the same picture, a picture which is a fierce and humorless caricature of the great German philosophical and scientific tradition: the search for a system of Reason in Nature and Nature in Reason; an Absolute which transcends human limitations but which can be known by the human mind; a science which is at the service of man, but which man in the end must serve with passionate devotion, whatever the consequences.

England presented her own paradoxes, but they were not those of nineteenth-century Germany. She was a remarkably homogeneous nation; she had no revolutions and no great social upheavals; she was never invaded; and she embarked on no wars with her near Continental neighbors after the Napoleonic period. Perhaps in consequence of the Six Acts, the Reform riots, and the Chartist agitations, her parliamentary system became stronger and stronger during the nineteenth century and in the end presented the typically English paradox of a firmly entrenched monarchy combined with an increasingly complete political democracy. Her indifference to the higher philosophy was characteristic of her own intellectual tradition; but it was also the essence of her political and religious pluralism, without which the gradual extension of political and social reform would have been impossible. The English fear of dogma, authority, and system led to all kinds of compromises, in politics, in morals, in religion; but these compromises were in the end accepted by Englishmen of all classes as an expression of the national temper and diverse symbols of a fundamental national homogeneity. But compromise first implies argument, debate, and struggle; no country in the world endured so many battles over social, political, and religious issues as England in the nineteenth century. Not only did she fight these battles at home, but in diplomacy, journalism, and war waged them in all the corners of the earth. England has never been much given to battle over first principles, but no nation has ever been more willing to fight for principles sometimes great, sometimes shallow or perverse. Her diplomacy has often been the envy of the world, if only because what looks opportunistic abroad has been often accepted as principle at home; and what seems the enforcement of a principle abroad has always had to be justified in the light of the national interest at home.

English homogeneity in diversity, and the will to compromise and coöperation, derive from a recognition of the rights as well as the obligations of the individual. They are the fruits of a relatively simple philosophy, and a practical, empirical, and man-centered psychology, both fearful of the transcendental and the absolute, and as appropriate to a nation of shopkeepers, factory workers, and farmers, as to industrialists and statesmen; but no less useful to poets, novelists, and all practitioners of the arts of discourse so important to a democratic nation. Matthew Arnold could call the English a nation of Philistines, but if he had looked more closely at his contemporaries he would have seen that every Englishman could also be a Samson when the need arose.

Germany was the home of "the higher philosophy" in the nineteenth century, building upon the achievements of the *Aufklärung,* which itself grew out of the French tradition of the age of reason and out of the English empirical philosophy and psychology of the seventeenth and eighteenth centuries. In France, the Revolution and the Napoleonic wars interrupted the development of the critical and rationalistic materialism of the *philosophes,* by largely illusory promises of social and political fulfillment of their aims. However, in biology, medicine, and mathematics, France continued to lead the world during the period between 1789 and 1830, when in that country science and philosophy had to be nonpolitical in order to survive. During the Restoration and the July monarchy,

French romanticism owed nearly as much to England and Germany as German philosophy had owed to England and France and, for the first half of the century, manifesting itself in both history and literature, continued to be the principal activity of the French mind.

French philosophy, in this period, produced only two philosophers of European reputation, Cousin and Comte, although a number of social, political, and religious thinkers, among them Tocqueville, Saint-Simon, Fourier, and Lamennais, exercised considerable influence for brief periods both in France and abroad. Cousin was primarily a teacher, and in his courses at the Sorbonne and at the École Normale taught an entire generation the necessity of a revolt against the rationalism and materialism of the Enlightenment. His philosophy was one of "eclecticism" and as such never acquired the form or substance of a system, but in his emphasis on selecting from past philosophy all that subordinated the senses to the spirit, and by teaching the use of reason as a means of increasing the moral stature of man, he placed a stamp on French philosophical education which has endured till our own day. He became Director of the École Normale and Minister of Education, and in these two posts was to apply the methods of his philosophy to the whole plan and temper of French education.

Much of what is best in his thought derives from Pascal, whom he greatly admired and whose works he did much to make available to the modern mind. In his own words, his philosophy taught "the spirituality of the soul, the freedom and responsibility of human actions, moral obligation, disinterested virtue, the dignity of justice, the beauty of charity, and, beyond the limits of this world, a God both author and type of mankind, Who, having evidently made man for an excellent purpose, will not abandon him, whatever the mysterious development of his destiny." [1] This is not only the voice of Pascal, but also the voice of a great tradition of French moral sensibility. He shared with Comte the honor of influencing the young Renan, and his interest in the psychology of man's moral nature was reflected in the work of both Paul and Pierre Janet. Through the latter, who first propounded a general

[1] *Du vrai, du beau, et du bien,* Preface of 1853. My own translation.

theory of neurosis, he helped break down the abstract mechanism of much earlier psychology and paved the way, somewhat paradoxically, for the pyschic materialism of Freud. Cousin's "meditative interrogation of the consciousness," following upon the work of Cabanis, Destutt de Tracy, and Maine de Biran, is thus another step toward Freud's vivid representation of the unconscious through psychoanalysis of the conscious mind.

Cousin's spiritualistic psychology also paralleled the increasing concern with psychological problems seen in Stendhal and continued by realistic novelists like Flaubert, and in its criticism of shallow and adulterated materialism warned the French mind against the misplaced scientific enthusiasm of the later naturalists. Through his influence on younger philosophers like Lachelier and Boutroux, who devoted their thought and their teaching to the problem of the limits of science, the best French minds were prepared in the seventies and eighties to question many of the fundamental social and philosophical assumptions of the "naturalist" school, including the pretensions of the "experimental novel." Thus Cousin, whose eclecticism and lack of system have caused him to be compared unfavorably with his contemporary Comte and the great German philosophers of the Enlightenment and the Romantic period, can be seen to have had a considerable influence on the thought and culture of his century. His philosophic method is also typical of that moral and psychological rationalism which we today associate with so much of French tradition.

Cousin was a product of the École Normale; his philosophical rival Comte was a student and for a short time a teacher at the École Polytechnique. The intellectual tone of these two schools has pervaded the whole of French cultural history in the last hundred years; the modern French mind owes as much to the one as to the other; Cousin and Comte are striking symbols of their influence. Comte, at first a disciple and collaborator of Saint-Simon, became the founder of the one great French philosophical system of the century, the "Positive philosophy." For a long time its prestige was greater abroad than in France, thus paralleling the later history of his English admirer and near-disciple, Herbert Spencer. In England, interest in Comte dated from Mill's early contacts with Saint-Simon and his school; Mill himself, who corresponded with Comte and helped to support him, devoted one of his most important books to an examination of Comte's philosophy. Harriet Martineau, George Eliot, George Henry Lewes, and Frederic Harrison were all proud to be called "positivists," and although none of them, nor for that matter few men anywhere, ever accepted the whole of the doctrine in all its ramifications, we have seen how important were some of its major assumptions in many of the discussions of the Metaphysical Society.

Comte's "law of the three states" was the chief doctrine of his philosophy, although an overemphasis upon the centrality of this general thesis has sometimes tended to obscure his more detailed contributions to psychology and sociology. Comte believed himself to have discovered "a great fundamental law" of the development of human intelligence: "that each of our principal conceptions, each branch of our knowledge, passes successively through three different theoretical states: the theological or imaginative state; the metaphysical or abstract state; the scientific or positive state." In the first state (the theological), the mind searches for the nature of being, first and final causes, and absolute knowledge, and "represents to itself all phenomena as produced by the direct and continuous actions of more or less numerous supernatural beings, whose arbitrary intervention explains all the apparent anomalies of the universe." In the second state (the metaphysical), which is only a simple and general modification of the first, "supernatural agents are replaced by abstract forces, veritable entities or personified abstractions, within the multifarious existences of the world. These entities are conceived as capable of originating in themselves all observed phenomena, the explanation of which then consists in attributing to each phenomenon its corresponding entity." Finally, in the third state (the positive), "the human mind, recognizing the impossibility of attaining absolute ideas, renounces the search for the origin and purpose of the universe and the knowledge of the inmost causes of phenomena in order to devote itself solely to the discovery, by the joint use of reason and observation, of their real laws, that is to say their invariable relations of succession and resemblance. The explanation of events reduced in this way to their actual limits is henceforth no more than the conjunction established between various particular phenomena and whatever general facts or actualities there may be, the number of which, however, the progress of science tends more and more to reduce." [2]

It is more than possible that this "law of the three states" is a historical truism, but it is none the less important for so being. It bears certain resemblances to the "thesis, antithesis, and synthesis" of Hegel, a relation often pointed out by Comteans and Hegelians alike. And in the history of philosophy it has many striking parallels: Socrates, Plato, and Aristotle; Augustine, Aquinas, and Descartes; even Leibnitz, Berkeley, and Hume. But such identifications are perhaps more entertaining than profitable, satisfying our own historical prejudices and no more convincing than the effort to place every Frenchman or even every member of the Metaphysical Society on the level of one of the three categories. The true importance of the law lies in the emphasis it places on social and cultural change and development and the explicit assumption that the positive and scientific stage is the most advanced, the most permanent, and the most worthy of the greatness and power of the human mind. Comte's conviction that civilization was entering the positive stage was easily assimilated both to the new theories of biological evolution and to the idea of progress—an idea which had its roots not only in the tradition of the age of reason, but in the material and technological achievements of the nineteenth century. And in this form it has become also the explicit assumption of the great majority of modern educated men, whatever their Sunday religion or their weekday politics. Comte was thus an effective prophet and the influence of his main thesis of unquestionable importance, however ambiguous our judgment of its truth or ultimate value.

Whatever England learned from Germany and France in the nineteenth century—and the influence of both Hegel and Comte was widespread after 1860—she rediscovered, perhaps most sig-

[2] The quotations from Comte (*Cours de philosophie positive,* I, i) are in my own translation. There are several important sentences in this famous passage which offer more difficulty than has often been recognized.

nificantly of all, the value and continued usefulness of her own empirical and psychological tradition. Thus, although the voices of Hegel and Comte echo from time to time through the debates of the Metaphysical Society, the major themes and their variations are heard primarily in the language and in the spirit of the English empiricists, the Scottish critics of Hume, and the Germanized synthesis of Sir William Hamilton, reformulated and made both more English and more widely known in England by Mansel. Victorian thought, like Victorian politics, was often attuned to the Lydian music of Continental philosophy and Continental statecraft, but resistance was even more common than acceptance, and what we call the Victorian period would have been less "Victorian" and perhaps less great, had England not made a virtue of her insularity. This has been done by other nations in their own great periods, by Greece, by France, by the United States, perhaps now by Russia. But insularity does not mean isolation, and few cities have ever been less isolated than Athens of the fifth century B.C. or London of the nineteenth A.D.

Certainly, the members of the Metaphysical Society who met nine times a year in London felt no narrow nationalism and manifested few insular prejudices. The most amazing aspect of their discussions is how entirely absent are the qualities of softness, sentimentality, easy moralizing on English virtues, and hypocritical idealism so often and so wrongly attributed to the Victorians by a generation of earlier critics. The Victorian period did not lack these qualities—what age in history ever has?—but the great spirits, with few exceptions, were far more free of them than modern politicians, journalists, or social reformers. And the Metaphysical Society can be called representative of the great spirits.

Metaphysics and Psychology

In the very passage in which Mill admitted an English "indifference to the higher philosophy" he went on to say: "But England did not always deserve this reproach, and is already showing, by no doubtful symptoms, that she will not deserve it much longer. Her thinkers are again beginning to see, what they had only temporarily forgotten, that a true Psychology is the indispensable scientific basis of Morals, of Politics, of the science and art of Education; that the difficulties of Metaphysics lie at the root of all science; that those difficulties can only be quieted by being resolved, and that until they are resolved, positively if possible, but at any rate negatively, we are never assured that any human knowledge, even physical, stands on solid foundations."[3]

The Metaphysical and Psychological Society, to give it the name it bore at its founding, recognized from the first the profound truth of Mill's methodological assertions. But, even without his warning, the history of European philosophy from the pre-Socratics to the present day shows a continued concern with the importance of the relation of man's knowledge to the nature and limitations of the knowing instrument, the human mind. Especially since the time of Descartes, every responsible European thinker has been obliged to grapple in some measure either with the relation of method and epistemology, or of psychology and metaphysics. The distinctively English contribution to these problems lay in the gradual development through the seventeenth and eighteenth centuries, in the philosophies of Hobbes, Locke, Berkeley, and Hume, of the empirical approach. But until the critiques of Kant, empiricism was not brought into full or coherent relationship with the methods and insights of other philosophical traditions.

In the nineteenth century the Scottish philosophers[4] represent the principal British attack on a narrow empiricism. Like Kant, whom Hume "awakened from his dogmatic slumbers," they owed much to the tradition they criticized. But, unlike Kant's, the moral and metaphysical system which they built upon the results of their criticism has neither logical and systematic persuasiveness nor deep psychological insight. Kant, far more than Sir William Hamilton, himself brings together and organizes the epistemological conclusions of empiricism and the a priori elements in human knowledge so dear to the Scottish philosophers. Kant's categories, in their relation to the a priori conceptions of time and

[3] *An Examination of Sir William Hamilton's Philosophy,* 2 vols. in one, New York, Holt, 1884, pp. 10–11 (original edition published in 1865).

[4] Thomas Reid, Dugald Stewart, Thomas Brown, and Sir William Hamilton.

space, remind us in both logical and psychological terms of Spinoza's twin attributes of thought and extension, while his "transcendental unity of apperception" is perhaps a more psychological expression of Spinoza's third kind of knowledge (*scientia intuitiva*). This is important in view of the fact that many of the empirically minded members of the Metaphysical Society, who were unable to accept much of Kant's transcendentalism, found in Spinoza a doctrine much more to their liking. But it is also worth noting that the members of the Society who found most value in either the philosophy of the Scottish intuitionists or the German transcendental tradition were those who wished to preserve an element of mystery in the world, either as a defense of their theistic beliefs, or in fear of what they conceived as the harsh mechanism of the empiricists. The empiricists, on the contrary, however much they eschewed intuition or any a priori faculties, were often driven by their own inability to accept a complete and deterministic mechanical materialism toward various forms of "vitalism," such as that manifested by Clifford's "mind-stuff." Thus, while the intuitionists like Ward continued to be interested in epistemology as the safest means of justifying their a priori metaphysics, empiricists as different as Huxley, Hodgson, and Sidgwick, who accepted in large measure the theory of knowledge of Hume and Mill, turned away from epistemology toward psychology and were, for example, more concerned with criticism of the nature and grounds of belief than with what man *could* be persuaded to believe.

If psychology is "the study of mental functionings considered in themselves and in their mutual relations," including patterns of behavior, and epistemology is "the theory of the nature of and sanction for our knowledge of the external world," it is clear that the empiricist will consider psychology the more important, and the intuitionist, metaphysics, whether ontological or epistemological. Whitehead, who more than any other modern philosopher has attempted to bring mathematics, physics, and speculative reason into the synthesis of a philosophy which is organic in its emphasis on process rather than on mechanical sequence and relation, has said that preoccupation with this "uneasy division" of metaphysics and psychology has created confusion and brought ruin to modern philosophy. Certain it is that this division in essential interests was one reason for the failure of the Metaphysical Society to find a common ground on which intuitionists and empiricists, theists and scientists, could truly meet.

Since the time of Descartes psychology and epistemological metaphysics have, thus, shown a tendency to separate, however closely related and interdependent they have been recognized as being throughout the greater part of the European intellectual tradition. The great strength of the English empirical philosophy of the eighteenth century lay in its insistence on keeping them together; but the critical reactions to that philosophy have invariably continued the process of separation. The French disciples of Locke were also admirers of Bacon, and the *philosophes* of the Encyclopedia, who became materialists and even rationalistic mechanists, abjured epistemological metaphysics. They have continued to be important as psychologists, social critics, and cosmological theorists who base their hypotheses on empirical evidence rather than on intuitive faculties or revealed absolutes. Rousseau, Diderot, and Holbach, and even, in many respects, Voltaire, all illustrate in different ways this abandonment of metaphysics in favor of an empirically tested psychology.

The modern scientist, whether psychologist or not, who claims that he does not need a theory of knowledge is merely saying that what was good enough for Diderot is good enough for him. But he is also saying that whether he accepts Locke, Berkeley, Hume, or Hartley, his methods and his conclusions will be substantially the same. To the Christian intuitionists, however, an acceptance of Locke may require also an acceptance of his doctrine that revelation cannot be admitted against the clear evidence of reason; an acceptance of Berkeley may mean acceptance of a Deity reconcilable only by a very sceptical kind of faith with the Christian God of scriptural revelation; and an acceptance of Hume would inevitably lead either to religious scepticism or a pallid Deism, for even if Hume might permit some contingent faith in revelation, he would tend to deny the greatest and most significant Christian miracles. How much safer to rely on the sceptical and even empirical evidence for faith and revelation offered by Pascal, himself a scientist and mathematician, or to turn to the Practical Reason of Kant and the unknown certainty of a noumenal world?

The intuitionist may even turn to Goethe's philosophy of moral striving as the great lesson of experience, with its Spinozistic relativism of good and evil and its characterization of Mephistopheles as a power who wills evil but works the good. For this doctrine may seem to him more compatible with the providence of a Christian God and with the tradition of an immortal soul than the purely man-centered philosophies of empiricism. To the intuitionist, a scientific materialism which limits man's knowledge and experience to a world of phenomena, possesses unity but no spiritual meaning and no moral direction. However, the empiricist may turn also to Goethe and, ignoring the disordered theology of the poem, regard Mephistopheles and the rest of its mythology and allegory as symbolic projections of a thoroughly naturalistic mind. He finds in the variety and multiplicity of Faust's quest for experience the essential quality of the modern mind—a desire for Bacon's Experiments of Light as well as Experiments of Fruit, and a confidence that the empirical method, with whatever modifications may, from step to step, be required, is the only means for the understanding of the mysterious as well as the more clearly comprehensible aspects of the human mind and human history. The confusion and profusion of the second part of *Faust* has made the poem a text for both kinds of critic, but the rest of Goethe's work, including his conversations with Eckermann, seems to justify the naturalistic empiricist rather than the Christian believer in intuition. The modern scientist may be able to get along without a clearly formulated theory of knowledge, but he is more dependent on some kind of cosmological myth than he is always ready to admit, and the myth most clearly justified by the fruits of his empiricism is that which expects not only the scientist himself, but all mankind, to manifest the intellectual and moral heroism of Faust.

Whitehead, in speaking of Wordsworth, has observed that it is to the poets that we must look for the concrete outlook of humanity,[5] and although we look in vain to either Goethe or Wordsworth for a coherent metaphysical system, we find in them both that kind of poetic validity which draws its strength from psychological insight. Whitehead's cosmological metaphysics, which once more brings together epistemology and psychology in a philosophy of nature utilizing all the resources of logic, mathematics, and physics, has as its prime subject matter the ideas which have always been the concern of the greatest poets: "change, value, eternal objects, endurance, organism, interfusion." The Metaphysical Society failed to integrate these central problems or even ever to see them all together, for the intuitionists felt that their own preoccupation with value, eternal objects, or interfusion was constantly threatened by the scientist's assertions of change, endurance, or organism. If this division seems too arbitrary, the charge can be admitted, for no two theists or scientists in the Society began with the same prepossessions or ended with the same cosmology. But in the senses in which their quests were different they often slipped past each other in debate and illustrated once more that if the variety of metaphysical convictions reflects the variety of temperaments, the truth and utility of any metaphysics can be tested only in the light of an adequate psychology.

Evidence and the Supernatural

The desire of the Christian intuitionists to preserve an element of mystery in the relations of man to the universe affected not only their cosmology and their theory of knowledge but even the logic of their historical method and its fundamental premises. Newman's *Grammar of Assent*, with great subtlety, illustrates this tendency. Catholics, Anglicans, and Nonconformists, even including the Unitarians, all insisted on some direct communion of man with God, either through the sacraments, hallowed by the Gospels and church tradition, or by some divine grace or spiritual visitation which would enable man to hear the voice of God through the often ambiguous and contradictory words of scripture. However, without

[5] A. N. Whitehead, *Science and the Modern World,* New York, Macmillan, 1925, Chap. V, "The Romantic Reaction."

a long tradition of symbolic and allegorical interpretation of biblical language, stretching far into the pre-Christian era of the Old Testament prophets, the historical criticism of the Bible as divine revelation would have proved much more damaging to the faith of most intelligent Christians than was actually the case. Every step in the development of the higher criticism, from the sixteenth-century humanists through Spinoza and the German textual scholars of the eighteenth and nineteenth centuries, was thus met by new interpretations of the sacred nature of the scriptures; these interpretations admitted in many instances the force of the new historical and philological evidence, but they elaborated equally new theories of symbolic continuity and of the role of divine grace in the earthly history of the church and its theological beliefs.

John Henry Newman's theory of development in church doctrine was only one of the means by which human inconsistencies in theology were conceded, at the same time as the authority of a continuing ecclesiastical tradition, guided and empowered by divine grace, was asserted in refutation of scepticism and the scientific or "liberal" spirit. Even the liberal Protestant theologians were not slow to use the varied insights of the Enlightenment and of nineteenth-century scholarship—the social spirit of Montesquieu, Chateaubriand, and Renan, as well as the historical vision and the higher criticism of Semler, Herder, Eichorn, Schleiermacher, and Strauss. Thus, "the seven against Christ" of 1860, the authors of *Essays and Reviews*, were attempting to invigorate the Church by the correction of historical errors and the abandonment of intellectually untenable dogmatic positions. But even more important, because more emotionally acceptable to believers, was the effort to understand the Christian revelation in terms common to all religions, an historical and even anthropological defense of the religious spirit as an a priori faculty representing not only a human need but a divinely supported power of the human mind. The importance and human validity of myth is thus once more recognized, and religion becomes the living and active poetry of life itself. By the time the higher criticism had done its work this was, in effect, the only position left to any Christian thinker who had accepted its conclusions.

Thus it has long been difficult for some to understand the logic by which the Christian Bible is asserted by many to be "the one and sole competent Book of Witness," when similar scholarly methods or speculative insights can justify other great world religions of equal antiquity and equally wide acceptance. It is possible to compare Christianity favorably and to its own advantage with many other religions, merely in terms of certain selected moral and social qualities. But such a comparison is a very human value judgment, the essential character of which has been criticized for centuries by More, Montaigne, Swift, and Montesquieu, all of whom were believing Christians, and by men like Voltaire, more questionably devoted to Christianity. Max Müller's monumental editing of translations of the great Eastern religious books revealed to sceptic, scientist, and believer alike a vast wealth of sacred and moral wisdom previously little known in the West, at the very time when Christian thinkers were being forced to find new sanctions for their belief in the Christian revelation. These sanctions they have since found either in new mysticisms or in new philosophical and poetic interpretations of Christ's gospel of love. Both kinds of modern theology have been able to establish historical and philosophic continuity with earlier Christian tradition, but the vitality of the work of Ritschl, Kierkegaard, von Hügel, and their more recent successors in England, Scotland, Switzerland, and America, lies in their attempt to see religion in modern terms and to relate the individual and social consequences of Christian belief.

However, a contemporary figure like Aldous Huxley, who has cut himself off from the Christian tradition after a period of reëxamination of its values in the terms of Quaker pietism, has turned to Buddhism in a personal revolt against naturalism and modern sensual egoism. Apparently, the critical method which deprived him of Christian faith does not function in the alien context of the mysterious East. Here the eclectic but positive moral philosophy of his friend Gerald Heard has exercised a great influence. But Huxley's position, as well as Heard's, can also be understood in the light of the repeated failure of a religion with the social values of Christianity to make those values more directly felt in the modern world. More will be said on this question in the next section of this chapter, but there is at least a logical justification for a modern sceptic's turning to an Eastern religion which avows no social responsibility save guidance toward *Nirvana*, a state realizing complete loss of individuality and identification with the supreme spirit. In this sense Huxley's acceptance of the Buddhist conviction that suffering is an inevitable corollary of existence (existence itself being an evil), and that suffering can only be mitigated by the cessation of desire, is not only a doctrine with a long history in western philosophy but is also an interesting modern complement to neo-Calvinist efforts to revive the doctrine of original sin as a key to our own social and political problems.

Certain it is that criticism of the evidence for Christian revelation has led to a far wider religious pluralism even among believers than would have been possible a hundred years ago. Thus, a general recognition of the private or limited "truth" in each of a number of different religions and sects has become even more characteristic of modern religious life than was dreamed of in the seventeenth and eighteenth centuries by those who first propounded the principle in order to gain freedom for their own often highly dogmatic beliefs. But this accepted pluralism of faiths and dogmas also parallels the modern secularization of many aspects of life, especially education, with the result that even in their totality religious myths and beliefs can no longer be recognized as expressing a central social and moral consensus. This tendency was already clear in the seventies and constituted not only one of the major problems which the Metaphysical Society faced, but was, as we have seen, one of the causes of its failure to develop a common philosophical method. When no religious revelation is accepted as literally true, and every form of religious belief can be justified or understood in terms of its psychological sanctions, social values, and anthropologically analyzed origins, an adherence to one religious position rather than another seems either a gratuitous act or a form of psychic therapy, or both. This was long ago recognized as a danger by the Roman Catholic Church, which has continued to resist any "liberal" concessions to the pluralistic spirit. The logic of this argument, however, has always been one of the most powerful incentives to conversion, and the Catholic Church, by opposing the absolute to the relativistic, has weaned many great souls away from this prevailing modern position. But it remains almost impossible to conceive of a common philosophical ground which will reconcile the naturalistic explanations of religious pluralism with the authoritarian and dogmatic assertions of any form of Catholicism.

However, an even more significant consequence of this religious pluralism has been the multiplication of the "varieties of religious experience," to use the phrase James used as the title of his Gifford Lectures of 1901. The empirical method had been used in justification of religion since the time of Pascal; every mystic has also in effect appealed to experience. But the now concentrated attack of the empiricists upon all supernatural explanations of events had the paradoxical consequence we have already remarked of multiplying on every hand the "evidences" of supernatural power. Many of these were nonreligious in any theological sense and were merely reputed "psychic" communications between the living and the dead. It was such startling and often seemingly convincing manifestations that led, as we have seen, to the founding of the Society for Psychical Research. But the specifically religious experiences which were pointed to as evidences of supernatural powers also increased on every hand. They were particularly numerous in Catholic countries, but Protestants enjoyed their share. William James has illustrated and examined these phenomena in his *Varieties of Religious Experience;* it is unnecessary to recapitulate them here. But they resulted in a considerable number of new Catholic saints, the establishment of many new centers of healing through faith (such as Lourdes in France and Ste. Anne de Beaupré in Quebec), and, outside of the Catholic fold, a rapid increase in new sects and even new religions enjoying their own revelations and special mystical ties with the Deity. Thus, throughout the nineteenth century, while the empirical spirit of scientific method was criticizing all revelation and all supernatural explanations, religious freedom and the empiricists' own emphasis upon the validity of experience were stimulating on every hand the evidences of supernatural powers. It has often been remarked how effectively Hume's argument against miracles can be used to justify them.

The higher criticism was never a subject of debate in the Metaphysical Society, partly because of the convention which forbade references to the authority of Christian doctrine and Christian revelation, but perhaps even more because theists and agnostics alike accepted by this time most of its fundamental conclusions. The nature and authority of belief, however, attracted the constant attention of many of the best minds of the Society. The ardently believing Christians, men like Manning, Dalgairns, and Martineau, contented themselves with polemical defenses of their theistic postulates; the agnostics and sceptics, however, not only criticized the grounds for belief in any supernatural power, but also leveled their sharpest attacks at miracles, including the central Christian miracle of the Resurrection. Huxley, Sidgwick, Bagehot, Froude, Pattison, Ruskin, Hodgson, Clifford, and the two Stephens all examined the foundations of a faith in the miraculous from the point of view of scientific, historical, legal, or psychological evidence; and even Carpenter, always attempting a mediation between Christian belief and scientific rationalism, devoted one paper to "The Fallacies of Testimony in Relation to the Supernatural" (No. 57; December 14, 1875).

But the English fear of transcendental explanations, which we have already noted, seems to have kept the members of the Society from any very immediate debt to Romantic philosophy. The influence of Coleridge and German thought on Maurice and even, to a certain degree, on Hutton is clear; Noel and Russell owe a great deal to Hegel; Hodgson and Hinton both make rather paradoxical use of Kant; while Bagehot, Ruskin, Sidgwick, Clifford, and, especially, Hinton, all highly endowed with the critical imagination, are those most conscious of the importance of the relation between social and individual emotional patterns in any understanding of belief. The psychological insights of Freud and the metaphysical solutions of Bergson, which have had so great an influence on modern religious thinking, were still to come; but Bagehot, Ruskin, Sidgwick, Clifford, and Hinton are all, though in different ways, aiming at a method of imaginative understanding which will bridge the gulf between the intuitionists and the empiricists by enlarging the scope of both intuition and experience. Each is groping for a new formulation, according to which the totality of experience would be the most fundamental of intuitions, and the validity of intuition could be tested and guaranteed by experience. This is a ground on which theist and scientist could have met, provided both had been willing to see both religion and science as forms of poetry, in the old Greek sense of ποίησις, that which man *makes* or *creates*. But the time was not ripe for this kind of admission from either camp.

Meanwhile, any phenomenon in explanation of which divine or supernatural power was invoked drew the philosophical and argumentative fire of the empiricists. Sometimes, scientific "law" was spoken of as if it were in itself a supernatural power, but this was rare; and the difference between scientific laws as hypothetical organizations of observed data and human laws (which compel obedience in proportion to their authority and their acceptance as ways of constituting and arranging patterns of action) was as clear to most members of the Society as to us. The empiricist attack on miracles was not merely a criticism of the theory of knowledge by which they attempted to establish the truth of their evidences; it was also an assault on the morality of believing in any miracle at all as a sign of divine or supernatural power and interference. Men like Fitzjames Stephen and W. K. Clifford regarded every such belief as disingenuous. They would have admitted the empirical fact that many an honest simpleton believed in miracles and received from them comfort in his ignorance; but that any man of trained intelligence could accept them as in any rational sense "true" was to them incredible. In consequence, they and their allies in the Society, as well as many of their more modern successors, insisted over and over again that man's reason is ultimately adequate to a sufficient and effective understanding of every phenomenon and every pattern of events which the human senses can perceive.

Failures there will be, and complete knowledge may be difficult to achieve; some of the secrets of nature may long resist human mastery; but the conviction remains firm among the critics of supernatural revelation that what man does not understand cannot be useful to him until known by reason. The constructive power of the human imagination is at work in every myth and every religious belief, but it is the deepening knowledge of both nature and human nature which demands that man criticize every belief and every imaginative insight in terms of the constantly changing values of "truth" and usefulness. Revelation there may be, but it is the revelation of the human mind, the human imagination, the human gift for seizing on what is useful and necessary to man in the complex chaos of nature—and not a divine or supernatural revelation by a power outside nature. It is not surprising that the seventies saw a wide revival of interest in Spinoza among scientists, philosophers, and theologians. For Spinoza, besides being one of the most naturalistic of thinkers, realized that knowledge of all things true and excellent is as difficult as it is rare, and that there is nothing more useful to man than man. Spinoza identified substance with both God and nature; the most agnostic members of the Society tried to do the same. The fact that Huxley, the author of "The Physical Basis of Life," was unwilling to be called a determinist or a materialist reflects the moral and imaginative passion with which the agnostics and scientists of the seventies strove to deny all supernatural evidences in the name of a humanistic "religion" of nature. Christ himself was the Son of Man, whatever the divine or supernatural explanations of his greatness and power.

Religion and Authority

During the latter half of the nineteenth century all religious authority—non-Christian and Christian alike—was on every hand subjected, more intensively than ever before, to searching criticism in the light of a secular philosophy and in the spirit of an essentially naturalistic or materialistic science. In one sense this criticism was a belated extension into a wider public consciousness of the spirit of the Enlightenment, but it was equally rooted in the Protestant Reformation and the latter's appeal to individual and group judgment rather than to centralized ecclesiastical authority.

In countries like England and some of the German states, where Anglicanism or Lutheranism became the established church, there was a considerable retention of many of the forms and dogmas of a previously universal Catholicism. But the authority of the Papacy and of the Roman Catholic hierarchy was once and for all denied, and the problems of the relation of church and state became henceforth not only a theological but also a political problem. Roman Catholics in England, as well as Protestants in France, Spain, and Italy, not only suffered from religious prejudice and persecution but also often endured various civil disabilities. The dissolution of the bonds of any strong authority inevitably involves revolutionary consequences; the replacement of Catholic absolutism by a growing religious pluralism and relativism proved to be no exception.

The political and religious history of Europe from 1500 to the present is so full of illustrations of this truth that many modern thinkers, as well as many political leaders, have become convinced that only by a return to a unified, hierarchical, and authoritarian system—religious, political, or both—can Western man attain peace, order, and true civilization. Since it is extremely doubtful whether Europe has ever in any period enjoyed these blessings, and certainly obvious that our present civilization, whatever its essential character, is the fruit of religious, political, and intellectual freedom, this appeal to an authority which man has already cast off, out of fear of a liberty whose fruits the majority of men have not yet tasted, constitutes the major problem of the modern mind. It is a moral as well as political truth that there is no liberty without law, and no law without authority. The aim of all modern political theory is to ask, in Rousseau's words, whether, "in the civil order, there can be any sure and legitimate rule of administration, men being taken as they are and laws as they might be."[6] But there is an authority in the individual as well as in the group and in the state; the problem of politics is their relative value and how they should be weighted for the attainment of diverse and not always closely integrated ends. The more we know about man as he is—his needs, his desires, his abilities—the harder it becomes to make fully adequate and effective "laws as they might be." But the difficulty cannot be avoided merely by hypothesizing a least common human denominator and accepting an authority and laws appropriate to this social abstraction. Such a view in religious philosophy manifests the cynicism of Dostoevsky's Grand Inquisitor and, in politics, leads either to various forms of the class or race myth, or to the synthetic imagining of a mass-man, a proletarian integer.

The growth of political democracy in England during the nineteenth century was paralleled by a corresponding increase in religious pluralism. The Oxford Movement itself convinced even those who were not touched by its doctrines that Catholicism was no longer politically dangerous in England. Some Englishmen, indeed, took the eminently practical position, since shared by many Anglicans, that the Established Church had been strengthened rather than weakened by the defection of dissident elements to the discipline and authority of Rome. The gradual removal of Catholic civil disabilities helped make possible the abolition of all religious tests at the universities; and the failure of the prosecution of *Essays and Reviews*, as well as the Colenso controversy, guaranteed that religious and doctrinal liberty would be as secure as the right to vote. The politically untenable prerogatives of the Anglican church in Catholic Ireland were abolished, although Gladstone, who had obtained Irish disestablishment, remained a firm supporter of the Established Church at home, a policy in which he had the support of the vast majority of the people, including many Nonconformists. But the victories of the liberal spirit within the church had made impossible any narrow or highly dogmatic definition of Anglican doctrine. The important principle of Multitudinism, enunciated by H. Bristow Wilson in his contribution to *Essays and Reviews*, had become by 1880 the prevailing temper of

[6] J.-J. Rousseau, *The Social Contract,* prefatory paragraph to Book I.

the national church. For Anglicans, there would be no dogma of infallibility, however seriously successive Lambeth Conferences have taken the problems of faith and morals.

Matthew Arnold's grave attempt to purge Protestantism of its theological sectarianism and metaphysical paradoxes was not only an effort to find in the Bible itself a justification of an almost naturalistic morality, but also reflects his desire to see that morality established in terms which recognize the authority of Eternal Order as man's only means of knowing God.[7] Here his debt to Spinoza is clear. It is also evident that when Arnold makes religion function as a popular interpreter of philosophic truth and as poetic symbol of the sanctions of morality, he deprives it of the "power of the keys," that authority of eternal dispensation which has from the first been claimed by the Catholic Church and has always in large measure been the most forceful moral assumption of every Christian sect. For, once morality is deprived of the authority of divine revelation and the supernatural provision of eternal rewards and punishments, it becomes essentially a series of social, psychological, and even political problems, in solution of which religious insights and institutions may be useful, but the source of whose authority, to use Arnold's own phrase, lies in the "possible Socrates" in each man's breast. However, any appeal to a "possible Socrates" invites not only the political liberalism and moralistic social authority to which Arnold was inevitably attracted, but also a religious pluralism not very different from H. Bristow Wilson's Multitudinist ideal.

The Catholic fear of "Liberalism" and "Modernism" is even older than the Syllabus of Errors of 1864 and perhaps antedates the Reformation itself. The loss of the "power of the keys" would not only deprive the Papacy of its own central power and authority over Roman Catholics, but would also destroy that element of unity in diversity, of the general in the particular, which has always constituted the major claim of Catholicism to the name of a universal religion. It is clear that the loss of the temporal power was an important factor in the decision to promulgate the dogma of

[7] See Lionel Trilling's brilliant chapter, "Joy Whose Grounds are True," in his *Matthew Arnold,* New York, Norton, 1939.

papal infallibility. Manning, who had so great a share in this decision, was in England almost a missionary bishop *in partibus infidelium.* He realized that the authority of an infallible church is without question a potent weapon against scepticism and schism. Doubt may be an indispensable prerequisite to faith for the strongest minds; but faith is never, in the last analysis, a weighing of possibilities; it is a positive embracement of certainty, however difficult to achieve. Infallibility in questions of faith and morals was thus inevitably recognized as a corollary of those primary theological assumptions which the higher criticism and the historical relativism of nineteenth-century religious thought had laid so open to attack. Without the one it is impossible for an ecclesiastical authority to maintain the other, a fact which Protestants, whatever the degree of their belief in private judgment of scripture, had long recognized.

The multiplicity of Protestant sects, each claiming to possess the truth, is a paradoxical reminder that theological infallibility requires ecclesiastical infallibility; schism is the natural consequence of the right of individual or group judgment. A religious attitude which abjures infallibility and embraces diversity must substitute for a central moral and theological authority either the social and political authority of a state establishment, or the psychological unity of a common faith in freedom and variety. But in the modern world such uniformities of social and moral tradition are only possible in national terms; such terms accepted, gone once more is the Catholic ideal.

The moral role of the Papacy in our own day, whatever its political and diplomatic motives, is clearly to assert its superiority to the variety of national ideals and to claim for itself the authority of moral arbiter in the One World which all hope may some time be. But here, once more, the Catholic Church is faced by the spread of secular, naturalistic, and man-centered philosophies; and in these, now as ever, lies the greatest danger to the fundamental supernatural and theological premises of the Catholic faith. The Catholic dream of a social, moral, and psychological world unity can thus be achieved only at the expense of those diverse critical, emotional, and scientific freedoms which have created

both the opportunities and the responsibilities of modern society. Manning, when he proposed a return to the scholastic tradition, knew its relevance to the problems of his day; but so did those members of the Society—by far the majority—who could not accept a supernaturally sanctioned authoritarianism.

Gladstone's fear of the political consequences of the Vatican decrees "in their bearing on civil allegiance" was reflected in his controversy with Newman, undertaken after the fall of his government in 1874. At the time Newman had the best of it, and Gladstone's anxiety seemed without foundation. But the problem of religious authority continued to dominate many of the discussions of the Metaphysical Society, and, in more recent times, the question has often posed itself once more. The many problems of the relations of church and state, the political implications of religious freedom or the lack of it, and the nature and extent of the moral authority of religious groups, all bid fair to be major preoccupations of the coming age. We have seen the danger of national moralities based on race or class myths, moralities which have provided the satisfaction of specious and temporary unity to countries torn by economic and political civil war. But we have also seen the rise of new secular moralities based not so much on class myths as on social and economic functions in a society. Trade unions and manufacturers' associations, professional groups and coöperative organizations, have not only been acquiring increasing authority but have also developed their own codes of individual and social behavior.

We have accepted in the secular world the principle of popular sovereignty, but we have interpreted the principle in terms of rule by the majority. In consequence we are faced with the fact that the true "children of light," by the very nature of their critical and intellectual function, are almost inevitably forced into the minority. The majority always wins—in a democratic society—but we have no guarantee that the majority will always include the wisest men, for although in our political philosophy might, measured by numbers, makes right, the happiest, most peaceful, and most productive society cannot set somewhat more than half the population against somewhat less than half without running the risk of

revolutionary consequences. Here lies the value of the concern shown by the Metaphysical Society with the problem of authority and the nature of the popular judgment in politics. Unless we are prepared to accept a completely egalitarian or classless culture, in which many of the values we consider essential aspects of our common humanity might be lost, we too must see the wise and equitable division of social and political authority as the principal problem of our time. For only in a pluralistic society, where not merely the privilege but the function of discussion and disagreement is recognized, can the minority, however right or wrong, escape the tyranny of the majority, however powerful.

The members of the Metaphysical Society were committed to rational discourse. Their attitude toward man and his universe, whether expressed in intuitional or empirical terms, demanded that all analysis of human problems be in a form communicable to one another. There was no obscurantist or anti-intellectual prejudice in the method of their discussions, even though some members defended positions which seemed obscurantist to others. The form of the Society and, especially, the adherence of the Catholic members, constituted an admission that even religious authority is subject to critical examination. Personal compromises are always possible in religious belief as well as in acceptance of and obedience to ecclesiastical or theological authority. But there is no question that since the great movement of ideas in the nineteenth century and the development of the critical, rationalistic, and scientific spirit—an intellectual revolution culminating both in England and on the Continent in the questionings of the seventies—"man thinking" has been unable to accept any so-called "legitimate authority" as in itself an evidence of truth,[8] whether in religion, science, or politics. Thus far has empiricism been victorious, for although the greater part of our knowledge of the world and of our fellow men is vicarious, in the sense of being accepted on the authority of others, we all now recognize that we live under the dispensations of multiple authorities. We have, therefore, a fundamental obligation to examine the nature and

8 Compare Manning's paper, "That Legitimate Authority is an Evidence of Truth" (No. 26; May 14, 1872).

the motives of these authorities, accepting or rejecting their dictates as they accord with our view of our own functions and of human destiny. Nothing more can be expected of any man, however wrong his judgment may prove; nothing less than a response to such examination can be demanded of any authority, however imposed.

The Problem of Language

"In the beginning was the Word, and the Word was with God, and the Word was God." Thus the Gospel of John expresses the ambiguous and mystical relation between the Logos, or Word, and the divine nature.[9] Men seem always to have attributed to words mysterious and magical powers, from the earliest days of human history and in the most primitive societies. For mankind has always recognized language not merely as a means of direct communication (which can perhaps be done almost as effectively by the "languages" of signs or of pictures), but as the primary and even the only instrument for the grasp as well as the expression of relation, significance, and value. These are the aspects of human rationality which are concerned not only with the present and the immediate, but with the relevance to the present of the past and the future.

We may never know the precise nature of the relation between communication by means of signs and linguistic symbols and the development of human rationality. We may never know with certainty what kind of reason may exist independently of language. But the complex mental, neurological, and affectively responsive organization which to us marks man's superiority to the rest of the animal world is inconceivable without the development of language and the transmission of human knowledge and experience

[9] The Greek λόγος, *logos,* is used by Homer only in the sense of "word," or as meaning, in the plural, "language" or "talk"; in this use it signifies "the word or outward form by which the inward thought is expressed," and with this emphasis Plato uses it also for the *statement* of a proposition, a principle, or a definition. But by the fifth century the word had acquired a further meaning, which can only be translated as "the power of the mind which is manifested in speech, that is, reason or thought." It is so used by Herodotus, Sophocles, and Plato, as well as by Aristotle. See Liddell and Scott, *A Greek-English Lexicon,* 8th edition, New York, American Book Co. (no date).

which language makes possible. Language is the very body of thought, and philosophers have been concerned for centuries with the relation of words to things. If words are indeed symbols for things and actions, and are thus representations of spatial reality —then grammar, or the art of relating words to each other by inflection or position, is a representation of relationships in temporal reality. Language is thus not only the body of thought but the indispensable skeleton of its articulation. So complex is this question of the origin of language and so circular any argument over the connection of language and human rationality that it is not strange that the Greeks identified "the word" and "reason." Most religions, furthermore, have hypothesized a Creator who is presumed not only to have established hierarchies of being, but to have placed in man a spiritual soul or mind with the specific function of rational discourse and understanding, and to have revealed to that mind by His divine Word both His own nature and the nature of man. The great myths are all cosmological, and religion is originally the formulation of a primitive metaphysics, an attempt to express the relation of man to man, and man to nature, in codes, revelations, and scriptures, whatever the social or subjective nature of the parallel forms of totem and taboo.

It is only recently that historical, psychological, and philological knowledge has made possible a more truly adequate study of significant meaning under the name "semantics." But from the Greek sophists, through Plato and the scholastics, and especially in the English empirical tradition, the problem of language has been inseparably connected with the search for an adequate theory of human knowledge. The French Academy from the first concerned itself with definition, devoting its scholarly efforts to the compilation and maintenance of an authoritative dictionary of the French language. The Royal Society, formed in 1662 for the extension and promulgation of scientific knowledge, included from the beginning a number of literary men and exacted from all its members close attention to the improvement of English and the development of a clear, compact, positive, and meaningful prose. John Wilkins, a founder of the Society, was one of the first men to attempt the construction of an artificial scientific language, and in 1668 published *An Essay towards a Real Character and a Scientific Language*, printed by order of the Council of the Royal Society.[10] Many other little-known men made notable contributions to the study of semantics before Michel Bréal popularized the word in his *Essai de sémantique* of 1897, even though the widespread contemporary interest in the subject has encouraged in many the illusion that no one before the twentieth century had been seriously concerned with the "meaning of meaning."

The great development of the higher mathematics in the last three hundred years has paralleled the growth of natural science and the more philosophical analysis of language and universal grammar. Mathematics has in consequence become the "language" not only of physics, but also, in varying degrees, of chemistry, biology, and even psychology. In many other fields mathematical formulations and the use of the "laws" of mathematical probability have proved to be the most effective methods of recording and integrating complex data; under the name of statistics, a new art to which Francis Galton, cousin of Darwin, made great contributions, this method of organizing knowledge and deriving conclusions has become a new fetish of the modern mind. But it is perhaps in the field of symbolic logic that the most significant attempt has been made to correlate the abstract symbols and operational certainty of mathematical language and the particular signs or words which in their logical relationships constitute the meanings of verbal discourse. But symbolic logic, like semantics, mathematics, or statistics, is a special language or method of interpreting language and, as such, seems destined to remain an esoteric accomplishment of highly specialized minds. The fundamental language of religion, philosophy, literature, and politics must inevitably remain the exoteric language of the Word, the language of life itself.

The nature of the problems to which the Metaphysical Society addressed its attention, as well as the personalities and interests of the members, guaranteed that the problem of language should occasionally be treated in their papers. One who is convinced that

[10] See the interesting essay on Wilkins by Lancelot Hogben in *Dangerous Thoughts*, London, Allen and Unwin, 1939.

all metaphysical or abstract speculation is pathologically verbal, or one who believes strongly that all argument is essentially a futile consequence of the inability or unwillingness of the opponents to define and agree upon basic premises, will be surprised and perhaps annoyed that the Society did not devote itself more consistently to questions of meaning and definition. But only a believer in a universal and absolute truth attainable by man will seriously maintain that a common understanding of absolute and essential meaning is possible. All communication by language implies compromise, and every language symbol has a particular and complex meaning to each person who uses it and each who reads or hears it. Whatever the unities or patterns in human groups, however large or small, the mental and psychological patterns of each individual are necessarily distinct. Generalizations of these individual patterns are practicable, but each such generalization is in itself a compromise. The miracle of human communication is the degree of common understanding which *is* attained, even when personal presuppositions and private meanings are present. Imagination is present in all discourse, and makes possible not only mutual sympathy but collaborative meaning.

It was largely in consequence of the Metaphysical Society's critical reëxaminations of its attitude toward the problems of definition, that the history of the society divided naturally into three periods. During the early years, when the members were discovering one another's prejudices and predispositions, there is more concern with the statement and criticism of fundamental premises than later. Almost every paper of these years is in large part devoted to an exposition of the author's own central philosophical position. But there are no papers dealing with the problems of language and definition per se. F. D. Maurice's paper, "On the Words 'Nature,' 'Natural,' and 'Supernatural,'" (No. 20) is only in a measure semantic. J. A. Froude's, "Are Numbers and Geometrical Figures Real Things?" (No. 24), is an epistemological attack on the intuitive truth of mathematics rather than a study of the "language" of mathematical symbols. Frederic Harrison's paper, "On the Supposed Necessity of Certain Metaphysical Problems" (No. 28), is an appeal for a consideration of intellectual problems in relativistic terms, in their "gestalt" or contemporary bearing; but a criticism of irrelevant and antique verbalisms is implicit in his own positivistic approach. Shadworth Hodgson's "Five Idols of the Theatre" (No. 29), an elaborate analysis of major metaphysical questions, was undertaken in the spirit of Bacon's own linguistic criticism. But G. Croom Robertson's "The Action of So-Called Motives" (No. 35) is the only paper read before the Society which discusses the difficulties in the use of common language to express the data and conclusions of science, difficulties made all the greater in psychology by the subjective nature of so many of the phenomena with which it deals.

Archbishop Manning's paper "A Diagnosis and Prescription" (No. 36), was, as we have already seen, a criticism of the Society's successes and failures in the first four years of its history. In spite of the fact that most of the members had made a conscientious effort to make clear their premises and their prejudices, Manning found that the Society's discussions had suffered from three wants: the lack of a common terminology, the lack of a common method, and the lack of formal, logical definition. But Manning's desire to press upon the members the common terminology of the scholastic philosophy is clearly another instance of the long quest for a universal scientific language. His demand for a common method could have been repeated by the scientists, who would have claimed that in empiricism and its experimental techniques the sciences had already found such a method, however difficult of application to metaphysics. And Manning's final desire to see more attention devoted to formal definition is an example of the tendency to oversimplification which can be seen in all his papers. If the puzzling problems of language could be solved merely by more rigorous definition, dictionaries would presumably be better and even more important than they are. But since imagination was not one of Manning's gifts, he could not have known how close to the function of poetry are the crucial questions of meaning and communication.

During the middle period of the Society's history Manning's advice was largely ignored. In these years the chief subjects of discussion were the grounds of belief and the evidence both for miracles and for a faith in the supernatural. As a corollary, the Society devoted considerable attention to the varying sanctions for intuitive and utilitarian morality. But except for the controversy between J. Fitzjames Stephen and W. G. Ward on "Necessary Truth," [11] and John Morley's "Various Definitions of Materialism" (No. 72) which touch on language problems very directly, there are no papers which reflect the influence of Manning's prescription. However, Mark Pattison's paper "Double Truth" (No. 74; February 12, 1878), the last paper of the middle period, is the most ingenious analysis of the linguistic problems of the Society ever presented.

Only two papers of the final years have any bearing on the problems of language. Henry Sidgwick, in his "Incoherence of Empirical Philosophy" (No. 80), is chiefly concerned with a criticism of empirical epistemology. But his acceptance of empirical science at the same time as he rejects empirical metaphysics presents an interesting analogy with Pattison's paper on "Double Truth." Frederick Pollock's "Generic and Symbolic Images" (No. 88) is primarily psychological in its emphasis, but the problems of generalization with which it deals have important linguistic and semantic implications to a modern reader. He observes that however much the use of words permits us "to symbolize with comparative impunity generic images of any degree of complexity, . . . the use of words has dangers all its own; it is a long time before men recognize that the word is only a symbol; they assume that there is an intimate and mysterious connection between the name and the thing named."

This observation of Pollock's raises the whole problem of linguistic symbolism. The Metaphysical Society had never really coped with it, and at this late date in its history it is unlikely that the remaining members were prepared to discuss its relevance to all of the Society's principal preoccupations. It is even doubtful whether Pollock himself realized its importance. Yet there is no doubt that a closer attention to the problem of language might have broken down much earlier the distinction between "intuition" and "experience" which so dominated the Society's discussions.

11 Stephen, No. 42, March 10, 1874; Ward, No. 46, July 14, 1874.

For the distinction, however crucial, is indeed a difference in the manner of expressing the relation between subject and object or the relation of an internal and an external world, analogous in many ways to the two Greek uses of "logos." But whatever errors and failures may be charged against the Metaphysical Society, it cannot be accused of paralyzing discourse by quixotic efforts to create a universal language. Moreover, the members never forgot that an understanding of meaning, in all the senses of the word, is the highest function of the human mind.

We are less interested in metaphysics than were the members of the Metaphysical Society, and more interested in psychology. We are less interested in the supernatural, and therefore less troubled by questions of "evidence." We are, however, although on the whole less religious, even more deeply involved than they in the problem of authority, whether in religion or politics, or both. And, like all men, we too maintain our faith in discourse and proximate communication as the chief symbol and public witness of our claim to rationality.

Chapter 14

LIBERALISM AND PLURALISM

THE VICTORIAN intellectual tradition, with its emphasis on freedom, dignity, courtesy, and mutual respect, is the tradition of a class, but of a class of men who would protest any name but that of "gentlemen." They belonged to a privileged group and they knew it, but rarely in history have the intellectual professions taken the responsibilities of privilege more seriously. The social homogeneity of their class, and the dominating and unifying power of life in or near London, gave them indeed the sense of being freemen of a great city-state. And the cultural authority of the elder universities continued to encourage this feeling in their sons. In such a society of peers the complex implications of the subtle relationships between mind and personality become the source of the deepest moral and political insights. Matthew Arnold is one of the most notable examples of this characteristic of the Victorian spirit, but a society like the Metaphysical illustrates it even more dramatically.

This pattern of unity in diversity, of social homogeneity encouraging intellectual heterodoxy, has continued typical of the English mind. Nowhere, perhaps, has it been more beautifully expressed than in Goldsworthy Lowes Dickinson's little classic, *A Modern Symposium,* first published in 1905 and many times reprinted since. Not only the relation of Victorian minds to our own, but the very atmosphere and spirit of the Metaphysical Society itself are brought to life in a philosophical "dialogue" among men of the most varied personalities and representative of the most diverse social and political opinions. The opening passages, and the care with which Lowes Dickinson, in a few deft phrases, draws personal portraits of the speakers, recall Hutton's "Reminiscence" of the Metaphysical Society. And the setting of the dialogue in a pleasant English country house, as well as the eminence and distinction of the participants, is a reminder of the more satiric success of W. H. Mallock's *New Republic.* Even the title is a probably accidental repetition of the name Knowles gave to the series of symposia with which he opened the *Nineteenth Century.*

Lowes Dickinson begins by saying:

> Some of my readers may have heard of a club known as the Seekers. It is now extinct; but in its day it was famous, and included a number of men prominent in politics or in the professions. We used to meet once a fortnight on the Saturday night, in London during the winter, but in the summer usually at the country house of one or other of the members, where we would spend the week end together. The member in whose house the meeting was held was chairman for the evening; and after the paper had been read it was his duty to call upon the members to speak in what order he thought best. On the occasion of the discussion which I am to record, the meeting was held in my own house, where I now write, on the North Downs. The company was an interesting one. There was Remenham, then Prime Minister [Gladstone], and his great antagonist Mendoza [Disraeli], both of whom were members of our society. For we aimed at combining the most opposite elements, and were usually able, by a happy tradition inherited from our founder, to hold them suspended in a temporary harmony.

There were also Lord Cantilupe, a Tory; George Allison [Sidney Webb], a socialist; Angus McCarthy, an anarchist; Henry Martin [Henry Sidgwick], a professor; Charles Wilson, a man of science; Arthur Ellis, a journalist; Philip Audubon [Ferdinand Schiller], a man of business; Aubrey Coryat, a poet; Sir John Harington, a gentleman of leisure, recently returned from years in Italy; William Woodman, a member of the Society of Friends; and Geoffry Vivian [George Meredith], a man of letters.[1]

Cantilupe, according to Dickinson, was to have read a paper, but came unprepared; in consequence, he was asked to start the discussion with a personal confession, telling "why he has been a politician, why he has been, and is, a Tory, and why he is now retiring in the prime of life." And with this beginning the dialogue

[1] The identifications are my own, apart from Gladstone and Disraeli, who are obvious, and Meredith and Schiller, whom E. M. Forster identifies in his *Goldsworthy Lowes Dickinson,* New York, Harcourt, Brace, 1934, pp. 76 and 113. The quoted passage is by permission of Doubleday and Co.

unfolds, each member in turn commenting on his predecessor's positions and presenting his own point of view. It becomes a masterly philosophical and dramatic analysis of the significance of background, personality, and fundamental social premises to any understanding of the variety and conflicting values of the modern mind. And in its entirety as well as in its conclusion it bespeaks the quality and saving power of a cultural and intellectual pluralism.

Lowes Dickinson himself wrote of the book: "But still it does not solve the problem, which is perhaps insoluble, of making the bridge between speculation and art and that side of life, and what is called practical politics. For practical politics involves fighting, and the object of such a book as mine, as it was Plato's object long ago, is to raise the mind above the fighting attitude. There lies here obscurely the great problem of the relation of ideals to passions and interests which I do not seem able clearly to formulate. It seems impossible to go into active life of any kind without being ready to kill or lie or cheat." [2]

However, Lowes Dickinson, a scholar, philosopher, and university teacher, devoted many of the best years of his life to fighting for world peace; he was one of the instigators and founders of the League of Nations; were he alive today he would be working in the same cause. His father was an artist, a man who had himself been fired with enthusiasm for the Christian Socialism of Maurice and Kingsley and who had taught at the Workingmen's College. The son had studied at Cambridge in the early eighties, during a period when discussion clubs like the Apostles [3] and Sidgwick's Eranus Society dominated the intellectual life of the university. *A Modern Symposium* is dedicated to such a society, probably the one which Lowes Dickinson maintained for many years in his college rooms. He later fell under the influence of the Webbs and the

[2] E. M. Forster, *op. cit.*, p. 112.

[3] A. N. Whitehead, who was at Cambridge in the same period, has paid tribute to the share of the Apostles in his education: "That was the way Cambridge educated her sons. It was a replica of the Platonic method. . . . It was a wonderful influence." He adds, however, that "the Platonic education was very limited in its application to life." From "Autobiographical Notes," contributed to *The Philosophy of Alfred North Whitehead,* P. A. Schilpp, ed., Evanston and Chicago, Northwestern University, 1941.

Fabian Society, and although he never became a statistically minded reformer, he called himself a socialist throughout his life.

A paper which Lowes Dickinson once read to an earlier Cambridge discussion society is still interesting and significant. It was called "Shall We Elect God?" and imagines Goethe, Hegel, Turgenev, and Victor Hugo, all gathered to discuss the election of God to their society. They are all against him, each for different reasons. God himself walks in, in a great cloak and with his face hidden by his collar and a broad-brimmed hat. He tells them that they cannot exclude Him; He is in the face of every passerby they meet, He is all they struggle against, He is all they believe in; He is even the founder of their society. They question His identity, and beg Him to uncover, to reveal Himself. He does so. Goethe cries out "Das Schöne!"; Turgenev, "La Vérité!"; Hugo, "L'Idéal!"; and Hegel, "Das Absolut!" [4] Here is cosmological relativism with a vengeance, but it is also perhaps a witty key to the indispensable correlation of true liberalism and cultural and philosophical pluralism.

The successes and failures of the Metaphysical Society, its temper and its method, are alike characteristic of the hopes and the pretensions of the liberal intellect. The critical and inquiring spirit of liberalism in all its confusions and temptations was not only the lifeblood of the Society but also the source of all the greatest accomplishments of the Victorian Age. But by the very nature of that spirit no problem is ever "solved": every "solution" or every compromise brings new insights and new questions. This became increasingly clear to the Victorians; it is even more clear to us as we struggle with the terrible consequences of a second World War.

The alleged "failure" of the nineteenth century to effect a philosophical or cosmological reconciliation of religion and science may prove one of its boldest affirmations, for it was not so much a failure as a refusal, a refusal to accept either as a sufficient explanation of man's relation to the universe or the world about him. The conviction that their realms of discourse are distinct, and that the difference in their ends presupposes a difference in

[4] My version of Forster's paraphrase, *op. cit.*, p. 74.

means, had, however, even larger consequences. For an acceptance of distinction and difference between the spheres of science and religion encouraged not merely a renewal of the scholastic doctrine of "the double truth," but also a fresh realization of the multiplicity of "truths" and the complex variety and interrelation of all values. The great movement of the human spirit which we call Romanticism had recognized this principle and given it almost universal validity in the arts, long before the terms of the nineteenth-century conflict between religion and science had become clear.[5] And in politics the applications of this principle had throughout the century constituted the forms of what became the liberal tradition.

The critical spirit, with its suspicion of absolutes and its passion for the analysis of paradoxes and contradictions, is thus both the source and the product of what we have come to call liberalism. And although the word "liberalism" has come to have as many meanings as "romanticism" and to be as widely misused and misunderstood, its essential meaning still constitutes our major debt to the nineteenth century. It is now the fashion for men who still, or but a short time since, called themselves "liberals"—in politics, religion, or even science—to belittle liberalism and to attribute to what is called its compromising spirit the evils, weaknesses, and inadequacies of modern thought and modern social and political life. Such a turn upon itself is, however, a natural consequence of liberalism's fundamental emphasis on free criticism and unhampered analysis, extending even to a criticism of its own dogmas. For in this insistence on a critical justification of values the liberal spirit has found the most characteristic principle of life itself and the symbol of all growth and all change. This is the lesson of history, of science, of religion, and of all social and moral development; this has always been the function of the "free spirit," of the artist, who sees and hears strange harmonies, creates new orderings of chaos, and by his vision enriches our experience of the multifarious wonder of the world. But the danger in this self-denigration, to which modern liberals are so subject, has perhaps

[5] See Jacques Barzun, *Romanticism and the Modern Ego,* Boston, Little, Brown, 1943.

always besieged the liberal spirit. It seems to be a consequence of the liberal tendency to mistake the hope for the reality, a confusion of purposes and instruments which often creates new dogmatisms and may even persuade men to the tempting security of powerful absolutes.

The problems of the continued struggle of the liberal mind with a seemingly inevitable pluralism of values can be seen in the discussions of the Metaphysical Society and in the many controversies which were initiated by these discussions or influenced by them. And other societies, as we have seen, inherited the method and tradition of the Metaphysical, even when they imperfectly realized its spirit. The tendency of the new science to create its own dogma even while resisting dogmatism is typically represented by Tyndall's Belfast Address, with its assertion of a new criterion of "truth." The Society for Psychical Research manifests a curious effort to test the avowed phenomena of a supernatural world by the logic and methods of natural science, in the hope of demonstrating the existence of "spirit." The professional philosophers in the Aristotelian Society quietly assumed the task of reconciling science and metaphysics, of determining, in whatever senses discourse can make acceptable to the human mind, solutions to the age-old problem of reality and the nature of "matter" or substance. And the foundation of the Synthetic Society marked a renewed attempt by believing Christians to defend the theistic postulate against the negative presumptions of the critical and scientific spirit; by a use of the forms and methods of that spirit, they thus endeavored once more to prove by means of reason the necessary existence of God.

These societies all mark in varying degrees a continuation of the open conflicts of the seventies, but they also constitute a more specialized effort to find new or to restore old cosmologies. They manifest a new faith in organization and even a desire on the part of many individuals to "escape from freedom." A passion for certainty and commitment lies deep in the human mind and clearly motivated all the great minds of the seventies. But even those members of the Metaphysical Society who were most certain of their methods or their conclusions, men like Huxley, Fitzjames

Stephen, W. K. Clifford, and W. G. Ward, all still lived, during that decade, in an atmosphere of crisis, of crucial issues, of life-involving judgments and decisions. Such an atmosphere is not comfortable; it may not be abstractly desirable; it may even paralyze certain forms of creative activity and misdirect others. But because men in such a world are seeking for meanings and expect to find them, their lives seem to them full of meaning. Every great critical period presents this same sense of vitality and vigorous delight in purposive conflict.

The liberal promise and the liberal hope have somehow survived temporary failure. Even today millions of men look to the liberal tradition for economic salvation and moral security. The Western mind has perhaps never been more conscious that there is a close relationship between the responsibilities of intellect and political progress, between philosophy and government. It is at least possible that psychology can help us to understand more fully our often credulous metaphysical assumptions. We are still striving to achieve the use of reason in any examination of evidence. We are as concerned as any of the Victorians with moral and religious freedom and the conflicts of religious and political authority. Finally, the problem of language in an increasingly literate world is, more than ever before, central to any solution of our difficulties which is dependent on a faith in rational discourse.

The fact that the problems and crises of the seventies were largely intellectual and individual may make them seem distant from our own, which are more emotional and political. We long for security where the Victorians sought for certainty. And there is little question, it seems to me, that the Victorians' concern with the problems of the individual in a rapidly changing culture blinded them to the true nature of the social and political decisions facing the liberal mind. This can be clearly seen even in so powerful a thinker as John Stuart Mill. But it seems equally true that it is to the individual compromises, adjustments, and partial reconciliations of the late nineteenth century that we owe whatever we possess of freedom from spiritual trauma, and whatever willingness to subordinate our individual interests to the larger welfare that may characterize our social and political judgments.

Our increased concern with the psychological problems of the individual, and the parallel development of the science and art of psychiatry, illustrate the modern conviction that true freedom requires an inward as well as an outward security. Here, too, we may learn from the inner doubts and uncertainties of the Victorians how varied are the needs of the human spirit.

This examination of the Metaphysical Society and its central place in the intellectual history of the seventies has now carried us far afield, and we have seen the spirit and example of the Society spreading its influence even into our own times. My true subject, however, has not been the Society, but the faith in discourse of which it is merely a noble symbol. The once almost anonymous figure of James Knowles has been swallowed up in his achievements, the Metaphysical Society and the journal to which he gave the presumptuous and challenging name of the *Nineteenth Century;* Lowes Dickinson, in turn, has brought us back to the oldest and most perennial of human questions. Even if we do not "elect God," we must still strive to understand Nature and our own nature. And however much we long for a commonwealth of the human spirit, we must remember that no League of Nations, no United Nations, can do more than men can do; and that only when discourse is as free, as responsible, and as committed to a unity of spirit in a diversity of tongues as the Metaphysical Society at its best, can the liberal hope become not merely a workable political principle, but a philosophy worthy of man's greatest gifts and accomplishments. We must, however, also recognize the use and inevitability of both philosophical conflict and political compromise, for it is when discourse fails that men resort to war. The great problems will constantly recur, and only the fullest and widest exercise of the critical spirit will preserve us from false prophets and the tyranny of absolutes.

Appendix A

THE MEMBERS OF THE METAPHYSICAL SOCIETY

List of Members of the Metaphysical Society from its Foundation in 1869 to its Dissolution in 1880

FOLLOWING is the list of members of the Society which was printed and distributed, along with a list of the Papers read, to the members after the dissolution of the Society in 1880: "The descriptions of members are in every case given as they stood at the date of election." Those marked with an asterisk (*) died during the life of the Society. The information in brackets has been added; it is intended to characterize the members briefly in all the variety of their occupations and interests.

1869

The Very Rev. the Dean of Westminster [A. P. Stanley; historian and religious writer].

Professor J. R. Seeley [Professor of Modern History at Cambridge; historian of the growth of the British Empire].

The Hon. Roden Noel [poet and critic].

Rev. James Martineau [Principal of Manchester New College; philosopher and theologian].

Dr. W. B. Carpenter, F.R.S., F.G.S. [Professor of Physiology and Registrar of the University of London].

*Mr. James Hinton [aural surgeon and philosopher].

Professor T. H. Huxley, F.R.S. [Hunterian Professor, Royal College of Surgeons; Fullerian Professor at the Royal Institution; zoölogist and comparative anatomist].

Mr. C. Pritchard [Savilian Professor of Astronomy at Oxford, 1870].

Mr. R. H. Hutton [editor of the *Spectator;* critic and theologian].

Mr. W. G. Ward [editor of the *Dublin Review;* Catholic philosopher].

*Mr. Walter Bagehot [editor of the *Economist;* literary critic and political thinker].

Mr. J. A. Froude [editor of *Fraser's Magazine;* historian and biographer].

Mr. Alfred Tennyson [Poet Laureate].

Professor J. Tyndall, D.C.L., L.L.D., F.R.S. [Professor of Physics at the Royal Institution].

Rev. Alfred Barry, D.D. [Principal of King's College, London; Primate of Australia, 1883–9; theologian].

Mr. Arthur Russell, M.P. [political observer, traveler, philosopher].

The Right Hon. W. E. Gladstone, M.P., D.C.L. [Prime Minister, 1868–74, 1880–5, 1886, 1892–4].

Rev. Dr. Manning, Archbishop of Westminster [H. E. Manning; Cardinal, 1875; ecclesiastical statesman and controversialist].

Mr. James T. Knowles, Jr. [editor of the *Contemporary Review,* 1870–7; founder and editor of the *Nineteenth Century,* 1877–1908].

Sir John Lubbock, Bart., M.P. [banker, anthropologist, entomologist, and public health reformer].

The Very Rev. the Dean of Canterbury [Henry Alford; preceded Knowles as editor of the *Contemporary Review;* textual scholar and poet].

Sir Alexander Grant, Bart. [Principal of Edinburgh University; philosopher].

*The Right Rev. the Bishop of St. David's [Connop Thirlwall; philosopher, theologian, historian].

Mr. Frederic Harrison [Professor of Jurisprudence and International Law at the Inns of Court, 1877; critic, philosopher, Positive "religionist"].

*Father J. D. Dalgairns [of the Brompton Oratory; theologian and philosopher].

Mr. George Grove [editor of *Macmillan's Magazine;* compiler of the *Dictionary of Music and Musicians*].

Mr. Shadworth H. Hodgson [philosopher].

Mr. Henry Sidgwick [formerly of Trinity College, Cambridge; philosopher and educational reformer].

Mr. Edward Lushington [Professor of Greek at the University of Glasgow; Tennyson's brother-in-law].

The Right Rev. the Bishop of Gloucester and Bristol [C. J. Ellicott; textual scholar].

The Rev. Mark Pattison, Rector of Lincoln College, Oxford [philosophical critic and essayist].

1870

The Duke of Argyll [George Douglas Campbell, 8th Duke; statesman and amateur scientist].

Mr. Ruskin [Slade Professor of Fine Arts at Oxford, 1870–84, with interruptions; critic and political thinker].

The Right Hon. Robert Lowe, M.P. [Chancellor of the Exchequer, 1868–74].

Mr. M. E. Grant Duff, M.P. [Lord Rector of the University of Aberdeen, 1866–72; politician, philosopher, and traveler].

1871

Mr. W. R. Greg [essayist and critic of politics].

Professor A. C. Fraser [Professor of Philosophy at the University of Edinburgh].

Dr. Henry Acland, F.R.S. [Professor of Medicine at Oxford, Director of the Radcliffe Museum].

*Professor F. D. Maurice [Professor of Casuistry, Moral Theology, and Moral Philosophy at Cambridge].

The Archbishop of York [William Thomson; theologian and logician].

*Dr. J. B. Mozley [Canon of Worcester; Regius Professor of Divinity at Oxford, 1871].

1872

The Very Rev. the Dean of St. Paul's [R. W. Church; historian and biographer].

The Right Rev. the Bishop of Peterborough [W. C. Magee; ecclesiastical statesman and controversialist].

Professor G. Croom Robertson [Professor of Mental Philosophy and Logic at University College, London; founder and editor of *Mind,* 1876].

1873

Mr. J. Fitzjames Stephen [Professor of Common Law at the Inns of Court, 1875].

Professor J. J. Sylvester [Professor of Geometry at Oxford; Professor of Mathematics at Johns Hopkins University, 1876].

Dr. J. C. Bucknill, F.R.S. [Lord Chancellor's Medical Visitor of Lunatics, 1862–76; well-known alienist].

1874

Dr. Andrew Clark [leading London physician; at his death President of the Royal College of Physicians].

*Professor W. K. Clifford [Fellow of Trinity College, Cambridge, 1868–71; Professor of Applied Mathematics at University College, London].

Professor St. George Mivart, F.R.S. [zoölogist and comparative anatomist].

Mr. Matthew Boulton [philosopher, amateur physicist, and translator of Greek and Latin poetry].

1876

The Right Hon. Lord Selborne [Roundell Palmer; Lord Chancellor, 1872; jurist and theologian].

Mr. John Morley [editor of the *Fortnightly Review;* critic, political thinker, and statesman].

1877

Mr. Leslie Stephen [editor of the *Cornhill Magazine;* after 1882, editor of the *Dictionary of National Biography;* literary critic and historian].

1878

Mr. Frederick Pollock [philosopher and barrister; lifelong correspondent of Mr. Justice Holmes].

Dr. Gasquet [F. N. Gasquet; later Abbot, then Cardinal; historian].

Professor C. B. Upton [Professor in Manchester New College from 1875; philosopher].

Sir William Gull, M.D., F.R.S. [physician].

Rev. Professor Robert Clarke [Catholic priest, doctor, physiologist, philosopher, and teacher].

1879

Mr. A. J. Balfour, M.P. [philosopher and statesman].

Mr. James Sully [psychologist].

Mr. A. Barratt [philosopher; Secretary to the Oxford University Commission, 1880–1].

Alphabetical Index to Members of the Metaphysical Society

Acland, Sir (Dr.) Henry Wentworth (Aug. 23, 1815–Oct. 16, 1900). Elected 1871.

Alford, Henry (Dean of Canterbury) (Oct. 10, 1810–Jan. 11, 1871). Elected 1869.

Argyll, George Douglas Campbell, 8th Duke of (April 30, 1823–April 24, 1900). Elected 1870.

Avebury, 1st Baron: see Lubbock.

Bagehot, Walter (Feb. 3, 1826–March 24, 1877). Elected 1869.

Balfour, Arthur James (later 1st Earl of Balfour) (July 25, 1848–March 19, 1930). Elected 1880.

Barratt, Alfred (July 12, 1844–May 18, 1881). Elected 1880.

Barry, Alfred (Jan. 15, 1826–April 1, 1910). Elected 1869.

Boulton (sometimes spelt "Bolton"), Matthew P. W. (Sept. 22, 1820–June 30, 1894). Elected 1874.

Bristol, Bishop of Gloucester and: see Ellicott.

Bucknill, Sir (Dr.) John Charles (Dec. 25, 1817–July 19, 1897). Elected 1873.

Campbell, George Douglas: see Argyll.

Canterbury, Dean of: see Alford.

Carpenter, Dr. William Benjamin (Oct. 29, 1813–Nov. 19, 1885). Elected 1869.

Church, Richard William (Dean of St. Paul's) (April 25, 1815–Dec. 9, 1890). Elected 1872.

Clark, Dr. Andrew (Oct. 28, 1826–Nov. 6, 1893). Elected 1874.

Clarke, Rev. Dr. Robert (?–April 21, 1906). Elected 1879.

Clifford, William Kingdon (May 4, 1845–March 3, 1879). Elected 1874.

Dalgairns, Rev. Father John Dobree (Oct. 21, 1818–Feb. 11, 1876). Elected 1869.

Duff, M. E. Grant: see Grant Duff.

Ellicott, C. J. (Bishop of Gloucester and Bristol) (April 25, 1819–Oct. 15, 1905). Elected 1869.

Fraser, Alexander Campbell (Sept. 3, 1819–Dec. 2, 1914). Elected 1871.

Froude, James Anthony (April 23, 1818–Oct. 20, 1894). Elected 1869.

Gasquet, Francis Aidan (later Abbot and, still later, Cardinal) (Oct. 5, 1846–April 5, 1929). Elected 1879.

Gladstone, William Ewart (Dec. 29, 1809–May 19, 1898). Elected 1869.

Gloucester and Bristol, Bishop of: see Ellicott.

Grant, Sir Alexander, 8th Bart. (Sept. 13, 1826–Nov. 30, 1884). Elected 1869.

Grant Duff, Sir Mountstuart Elphinstone (Feb. 21, 1829–Jan. 12, 1906). Elected 1870.

Greg, William Rathbone (1809–Nov. 15, 1881). Elected 1871.

Grove, Sir George (Aug. 13, 1820–May 28, 1900). Elected 1869.

Gull, Sir (Dr.) William (Dec. 31, 1815–Jan. 29, 1890). Elected 1879.

Harrison, Frederic (Oct. 18, 1831–Jan. 14, 1923). Elected 1869.

Hinton, James (1822–Dec. 16, 1875). Elected 1869.

Hodgson, Shadworth (Dec. 25, 1832–June 13, 1912). Elected 1869.

Hutton, Richard Holt (June 2, 1826–Sept. 9, 1897). Elected 1869.

Huxley, Thomas Henry (May 4, 1825–June 29, 1895). Elected 1869.

Knowles, Sir James T., Jr. (Oct. 13, 1831–Feb. 13, 1908). Elected 1869.

Lowe, Robert (later 1st Viscount Sherbrooke) (Dec. 4, 1811–Nov. 3, 1892). Elected 1870.

Lubbock, Sir John, Bart. (Baron Avebury) (April 30, 1834–May 28, 1913). Elected 1869.

Lushington, Edmund L. (Jan. 10, 1811–July 13, 1893). Elected 1869.

Magee, William Connor (Bishop of Peterborough and later briefly Archbishop of York) (Dec. 17, 1821–May 5, 1891). Elected 1872.

Manning, Henry Edward (Archbishop of Westminster and later Cardinal) (July 15, 1808–Jan. 14, 1892). Elected 1869.

Martineau, Dr. James (April 21, 1805–Jan. 11, 1900). Elected 1869.

Maurice, Frederick Denison (Aug. 29, 1805–April 1, 1872). Elected 1871.

Mivart, St. George (Nov. 20, 1827–April 1, 1900). Elected 1874.

Morley, John (later Viscount Morley) (Dec. 24, 1838–Sept. 23, 1923). Elected 1876.

Mozley, James Bowling (Sept. 15, 1813–Jan. 4, 1878). Elected 1871.

Noel, (Hon.) Roden (Aug. 27, 1834–May 26, 1894). Elected 1869.

Palmer, Roundell: see Selborne.

Pattison, Mark (Oct. 10, 1813–July 30, 1884). Elected 1869.

Peterborough, Bishop of: see Magee.

Pollock, Sir Frederick (later 3rd Bart.) (Dec. 10, 1845–Jan. 18, 1937). Elected 1879.

Pritchard, Charles (Feb. 29, 1808–May 28, 1893). Elected 1869.

Robertson, George Croom (Mar. 10, 1842–Sept. 20, 1892). Elected 1872.

Ruskin, John (Feb. 8, 1819–Jan. 20, 1900). Elected 1870.

Russell, Lord Arthur J. E. (June 13, 1825–April 4, 1892). Elected 1869.

St. David's, Bishop of: see Thirlwall.

St. Paul's, Dean of: see Church.

Seeley, Sir John Robert (Sept. 10, 1834–Jan. 13, 1895). Elected 1869.

Selborne, Roundell Palmer, 1st Earl of (Nov. 27, 1812–May 4, 1895). Elected 1876.

Sherbrooke, Viscount: see Lowe.

Sidgwick, Henry (May 31, 1838–Aug. 28, 1900). Elected 1869.

Stanley, Arthur Penrhyn (Dean of Westminster) (Dec. 13, 1815–July 18, 1881). Elected 1869.

Stephen, Sir James Fitzjames (Bart.) (March 3, 1829–March 11, 1894). Elected 1873.

Stephen, Sir Leslie (Nov. 28, 1832–Feb. 22, 1904). Elected 1877.

Sully, James (March 3, 1842–Nov. 1, 1923). Elected 1880.

Sylvester, James Joseph (Sept. 3, 1814–March 15, 1897). Elected 1873.

Tennyson, Alfred, 1st Baron (Aug. 6, 1809–Oct. 6, 1892). Elected 1869.

Thirlwall, Connop (Bishop of St. David's) (Feb. 11, 1797–July 27, 1875). Elected 1869.

Thomson, William (Archbishop of York) (Feb. 11, 1819–Dec. 25, 1890). Elected 1871.

Tyndall, John (Aug. 2, 1820–Dec. 4, 1893). Elected 1869.

Upton, Charles Barnes (Nov. 19, 1831–Nov. 21, 1920). Elected 1879.

Ward, Dr. William George (March 21, 1812–July 6, 1882). Elected 1869.

Westminster, Archbishop of: see Manning.

Westminster, Dean of: see Stanley.

York, Archbishop of: see Thomson; Magee.

Appendix B

THE MINUTE-BOOK

The Minute-Book of the Metaphysical Society, "with the documents thereto belonging," was presented to Dr. James Martineau, the Society's last chairman, at the conclusion of the final meeting "as a token of the Society's thanks for his services during the past year." (See Appendix D.) A note dated August, 1895, by "F. P." (probably Frederick Pollock) on a copy of the circular announcing the dissolution of the Society, now in the library of Manchester College, Oxford, states that the *Minute-Book* "has lately been given by Dr. Martineau to Mr. James Knowles, the founder of the Society." Mrs. Frewen Lord of London, a daughter of James Knowles, was not aware that the book had ever been out of her family's hands. In any case it remained in the possession of the Knowles family until 1926 when it was sold to a London bookseller, since deceased. His son, who has inherited the business, remembers that the book was sold, but does not know to whom.

Mrs. Frewen Lord has found among her father's papers and made available to me proof-sheets of the *Minute-Book* from the first meeting, April 21, 1869, through June 13, 1871, showing that Knowles was in 1904 considering publishing the *Minute-Book* in the *Nineteenth Century;* it was, however, never published. It is possible that proof-sheets of more of the book may turn up, but it is equally likely that none were ever set in type. In any case those which do exist give invaluable information about the early meetings of the Society, and show that for the later meetings the disappearance of the *Minute-Book* is not crucial, except for the record of attendance, which is always interesting and sometimes important in an understanding of the future course of a particular argument.

Appendix C

THE PAPERS OF THE METAPHYSICAL SOCIETY

The Papers of the Metaphysical Society (*1869–1880*) are not, so far as I know, anywhere available in their entirety. I possess a photographic record of 90 papers, which probably includes all the papers actually printed for the Society. This collection of photographs is made up of papers from: (1) the nearly complete file owned by Miss Diana Russell of London (the daughter of Lord Arthur Russell, a member of the Society from the beginning); (2) the almost as complete file now in the Bodleian Library, Oxford (from the file formerly belonging to Mark Pattison, filled out with some papers from the file formerly owned by Sir Frederick Pollock—both were members of the Society); and (3) the collection of thirteen papers now owned by Mr. W. D. Paden of the University of Kansas (purchased from Blackwell in Oxford, and formerly belonging to Sir Frederick Pollock). These I have called the Russell, Bodleian, and Paden papers, respectively.

The Bodleian Library, which, through the kindness of Miss Russell, photographed for me her father's volume of the papers, has been generously permitted by her to make photographic copies of those papers in the Russell collection which are not in its own; the addition of photographs of one paper from the Paden collection will make the Oxford collection as complete as my own. There is also an incomplete file of 86 papers formerly belonging to Dr. James Martineau in the library of Manchester College, Oxford. Mr. Raymond V. Holt, the librarian of the College, has kindly sent me a list of the papers in that collection, which has been useful for purposes of bibliographical analysis, although neither the numbering adopted by the Bodleian nor that used by Manchester College seems satisfactory for purposes of reference. Other sets of the papers may also exist, but these are all I have been so far able to trace. Since each paper was printed in a small edition (probably seldom many more than 50) and *never* bore the author's name, except in the case of one paper by Ruskin, they must often, owing to this anonymity, have been regarded as philosophical or theological ephemera by most booksellers and collectors, and even by libraries. The British Museum itself does not possess a set.

I have been able to trace the republication of 39 of the Papers, often in somewhat expanded form, in periodicals, 28 of them in the *Contemporary Review,* of which the secretary of the Society, James Knowles, was editor from 1870 to 1877, when he founded the *Nineteenth Century.* At least 6 others can probably eventually be traced to other periodicals. Thirty-five of the papers (and perhaps more) were republished, reprinted, or paraphrased in collected volumes, privately printed pamphlets, or biographies, 16 of them for the first time. Thus more than half of the papers (55) are obtainable in whole or in part in available printed sources.

The four papers of which no original versions printed for distribution to members have been found, include the first two papers read before the Society: R. H. Hutton's paper, "On Mr. Herbert Spencer's Theory of the Gradual Transformation of Utilitarian into Intuitive Morality by Hereditary Descent"; and Dr. W. B. Carpenter's paper, "The Common Sense Philosophy of Causation." In the numbering of the papers which I have adopted in an effort to put an end to earlier bibliographical confusion, these papers are: No. 1, June 2, 1869; and No. 2, July 14, 1869. Hutton's paper was fortunately republished in *Macmillan's Magazine,* and Carpenter's long paper is probably paraphrased and perhaps reprinted as the final chapter of his *Principles of Mental Physiology* (1874). There is reason to believe that neither of these papers was printed in advance of the meeting, because it was not until the second regular meeting (July 14, 1869) that Hutton was appointed chairman of a committee to arrange for the "supply" of papers and their printing and distribution to members.

The two other papers of which no *original* printed versions seem to exist are: G. Croom Robertson's paper, "How Do We Come by Our Knowledge?" to which I have given the number 63x, November 14, 1876; and J. Fitzjames Stephen's paper, "The Effect of a Decline of Religious Belief on Morality," to which I have given the number 63y, December 12, 1876. Although both of these papers appear in the list of papers read before the Society, neither of them is to be found in any of the three nearly complete files. This in itself does not prove that they were not printed; but the paper read at the meeting of July 11, 1876 (the last meeting before Robertson's No. 63x) bears the printed number "63"; and the paper read at the meeting of January 9, 1877 (the next meeting after J. Fitzjames Stephen's No. 63y) bears the printed number "64." Therefore, since there is no numerical hiatus in the number series of existent printed papers, it is a fair deduction that these two papers also were never printed. A change of printer or a committee error of some sort may have been responsible for the failure, which came at the very beginning of a new year; for the Society's year began with the November meeting, and no meetings were ever held in the months of August,

September, and October, during the parliamentary recess. Fortunately, G. Croom Robertson's paper, "How Do We Come by Our Knowledge?" (No. 63x; November 14, 1876), was published in the *Nineteenth Century* for March, 1877; and J. Fitzjames Stephen's paper (No. 63y; December 12, 1876) probably appears as part of the "Modern Symposium" in the *Nineteenth Century,* April and May, 1877. Thus, except for Bishop Ellicott's "Oral Communication on Euthanasia" (see below), which was possibly delivered extempore, *every paper* delivered before the Society has been found in some form.

The first 23 papers printed for the Society bore no numbers. Manning's paper of May 14, 1872, "That Legitimate Authority is an Evidence of Truth," was the first paper to be numbered; it was given the apparently erroneous number "xxiii" which I have corrected to 26. If the first two papers were never printed, and Huxley's paper (No. 3; November 17, 1869), "The Views of Hume, Kant, and Whately upon the Logical Basis of the Doctrine of the Immortality of the Soul" (which is the first paper of which an original printed version exists), was not counted as a paper because so obviously a mere outline of what Huxley actually said, then the Manning paper was correctly numbered in terms of papers *printed* up to that time. In this argument, of course, lies a further indication that the first two papers were never printed. However, when Manning in his paper, "A Diagnosis and Prescription" (No. 36; June 10, 1873), listed all the papers previously read, he established a new and corrected numbering, not of papers *printed,* but of papers *read,* including his own paper of that date. This correct numbering continued with only a few minor errors until the end of the Society.

From the erroneous No. "xxiii" (26) through No. "lxxix" (79), the papers were numbered in small Roman numerals; from No. 80 through No. 90 (the last paper), Arabic numerals were used. In my bibliography below I have used Arabic numerals in parentheses; the number (when there was one) printed on the original source for the paper immediately follows my own numbering. In my text of this book I have used my own numbering throughout.

At the meeting of July 8, 1873, the month after Manning had established the corrected numbering, there were two "papers." One of these was an "Oral Communication on Euthanasia," by C. J. Ellicott, Bishop of Gloucester and Bristol, of which we have no further record, except some slight evidence that it may exist in some form in the library of Manchester College, Oxford. To this "paper" I have given the number 37b. The second is a reprinted paper, numbered "37," on "Euthanasia," offered by R. H. Hutton to fill a gap; to this paper I have given the number 37a.

In 1875 J. Fitzjames Stephen's paper of November 9 was given the printed number "55," which repeated the number of Sidgwick's paper of July 13; this number I have corrected to 56. In consequence of this error, Carpenter's paper of December 14, was wrongly numbered "56"; this I have corrected to 57. The next paper (No. 58; January 11, 1876), by Huxley, bears the proper printed number and corrects the series.

The printed numbering then continues without interruption [ignoring No. 63x and No. 63y, which I have already shown may never have been printed; and except for No. 78, which through some oversight bears no printed number] until the three papers read on May 27 (Manning), June 10 (Harrison), and November 25 (Manning), 1879, all of which bear the same number, "84." These I have numbered (as has the Bodleian): 84a, 84b, 84c. There may have been no meeting in July of this year; in any case there is "no paper recorded" for July 15, 1879. No. 85, December 9, 1879 (Hutton) resumes the correct numbering, which continues until the last paper, No. 90, May 11, 1880 (Upton).

It will be seen that my purpose in establishing a careful numbering of the *Papers of the Metaphysical Society* has been to preserve wherever possible the original printed numbering, correcting or supplementing it only where necessary. This numbering not only makes my own task in referring to the papers much easier, but, if generally adopted, will simplify and correct the Oxford catalogues.

To summarize, the Metaphysical Society met regularly once a month, for nine months of the year, June 2, 1869, through May 11, 1880, with only a few interruptions. No meetings were held in August, September, or October, during the parliamentary recess. There was no meeting in May, 1870. On February 15, 1876, there was no new paper, but the discussion on Huxley's paper of the previous month, "The Evidence of the Miracle of the Resurrection" (No. 58; January 11, 1876), was continued, the only paper ever so honored. On March 12, 1878 there was no paper, but a "Report" was offered by a "Committee on Definitions," a report which was unfortunately not printed. The following month Mr. Matthew Boulton read his paper, "Has a Metaphysical Society any *Raison d'être?*" (No. 75; April 9, 1878); the next month, May, 1878, there was no meeting. On July 15, 1879 there was "no paper recorded" and perhaps no meeting worthy of the name. These were the only interruptions in the regularity of the Society's monthly proceedings. There were no meetings in June or July of 1880, and the Society was dissolved at the first meeting of its new year, November 16, 1880.

In the following bibliography, the libraries and collections where original copies of the Papers may be found are indicated by a letter or letters following the title, according to this key:

B — In the Bodleian Library, Oxford.

M — In the Library of Manchester College, Oxford.

P — In the possession of Mr. W. D. Paden of the University of Kansas.

R — In the possession of Miss Diana Russell of London.

RB — The papers in Miss Russell's collection which have been photographed for the Bodleian.

The attendance at each meeting is also given, whenever known, together with any other "business" transacted. For the first nineteen meetings, this information comes from the incomplete proof of the *Minute-Book of the Metaphysical Society,* loaned to me by Mrs. Frewen Lord, the daughter of James Knowles (see Appendix B).

April 21, 1869, *Organization Meeting.*

No paper was read.

Present, 13: Carpenter, Hinton, Hutton, Huxley, Knowles, Lubbock, Martineau, Noel, Pritchard, Seeley, Stanley, Tennyson, Ward.

(1) June 2, 1869, *R. H. Hutton:* "On Mr. Herbert Spencer's Theory of the Gradual Transformation of Utilitarian into Intuitive Morality by Hereditary Descent."

This paper does not exist in an original printed form; but it was published in *Macmillan's Magazine,* XX (July, 1869), 266, under the title, "A Questionable Parentage for Morals."

Present, 13: Alford, Barry, Carpenter, Hinton, Hutton, Huxley, Knowles, Lushington, Manning, Russell, Stanley, Tyndall, Ward.

(2) July 14, 1869, *Dr. W. B. Carpenter:* "The Common Sense Philosophy of Causation."

This paper does not exist, either in an original or in a republished form. The main course of its argument, however, is clear from the final chapter of Carpenter's *Principles of Mental Physiology,* New York, Appleton, 1875, pp. 691–708.

Present, 12: Alford, Carpenter, Grove, Hinton, Huxley, Knowles, Lubbock, Manning, Noel, Russell, Sidgwick, Ward. Hodgson proposed. Thirlwall proposed and elected.

(3) November 17, 1869, *T. H. Huxley:* "The Views of Hume, Kant, and Whately upon the Logical Basis of the Doctrine of the Immortality of the Soul" (R, RB).

This is the first printed paper of the Society, but it is a mere outline and would therefore scarcely deserve republication in its original form. The argument is summarized in Huxley's *Hume,* London, Macmillan, 1894, pp. 201 ff.

Present, 14: Alford, Carpenter, Dalgairns, Froude, Gladstone, Grove, Hutton, Huxley, Knowles, Lubbock (first chairman of the Society, who served for the year 1869–70), Noel, Pritchard, Russell, Sidgwick. Hodgson elected; Ellicott, Harrison, and Pattison proposed.

(4) December 15, 1869, *W. G. Ward:* "On Memory as an Intuitive Faculty" (R, RB).

Present, 17: Alford, Bagehot, Carpenter, Dalgairns, Froude, Hinton, Hodgson, Hutton, Huxley, Knowles, Lubbock, Martineau, Noel, Russell, Sidgwick, Stanley, Ward. Ellicott, Harrison, and Pattison elected.

(5) January 12, 1870, *Sir John Lubbock:* "The Moral Condition of Savages" (R, B, M).

Apparently not republished; but the drift of the argument can be seen in his book, *The Origin of Civilization,* London, Longmans, 1870.

Present, 16: Alford, Barry, Carpenter, Dalgairns, Ellicott, Grove, Harrison, Hinton, Hodgson, Hutton, Knowles, Lubbock, Martineau, Sidgwick, Stanley, Ward. Ruskin proposed.

(6) February 9, 1870, *Roden Noel:* "What is Matter?" (R, B, M).

Published in *Contemporary Review,* XVIII (October, 1871), 362.

Present, 14: Alford, Carpenter, Ellicott, Harrison, Hinton, Hodgson, Hutton, Knowles, Lubbock, Martineau, Noel, Pritchard, Tyndall, Ward. Ruskin elected; Lowe proposed.

(7) March 16, 1870, *Father J. D. Dalgairns:* "On the Theory of a Soul" (R, B, M).

Published in *Contemporary Review,* XVI (December, 1870), 16.

Present, 17: Alford, Bagehot, Carpenter, Dalgairns, Froude, Hinton, Hodgson, Hutton, Huxley, Knowles, Lubbock, Martineau, Noel, Russell, Sidgwick, Tyndall, Ward. Lowe elected.

(8) April 27, 1870, *Henry Sidgwick:* "The Verification of Beliefs" (R, B, M).

Published in *Contemporary Review,* XVII (July, 1871), 582.

An expansion of this paper appears in the appendix to his essay, "Criteria of Truth and Error," in *Lectures on the Philosophy of Kant,* London, Macmillan, 1905.

Present, 16 plus 1: Alford, Dalgairns, Ellicott, Grant, Harrison, Hinton, Hodgson, Hutton, Knowles, Martineau, Noel, Pattison, Russell, Sidgwick, Stanley, Tennyson; and Baboo Keshub Chunder Sen, member and missionary of the Brahmo Samaj, a reformed Hindu theistic society. He was the only visitor to the Society of whom I have found any record. (Only "foreigners" were allowed as guests by the original rules of the Society.)

(No meeting in May, 1870.)

(9) June 15, 1870, *James Martineau:* "Is There Any 'Axiom of Causality'?" (R, B, M).

Published in *Contemporary Review,* XIV (July, 1870), 636. Reprinted in his Essays, Reviews, and Addresses, 4 vols., London, Longmans, 1890–1, III.

Present, 14: Alford, Bagehot, Carpenter, Ellicott, Harrison, Hinton, Hutton, Huxley, Knowles, Martineau, Noel, Russell, Sidgwick, Tennyson (in the chair).

(10) July 13, 1870, *Frederic Harrison:* "The Relativity of Knowledge" (R, B, M).

Published in an expanded form in *Fortnightly Review,* N.S. VIII (August, 1870), 184, as "The Subjective Synthesis." Reprinted in Harrison's *The Philosophy of Common Sense,* New York, Macmillan, 1907, pp. 21–41.

Present, 9: Alford, Carpenter, Harrison, Hinton, Huxley, Knowles, Lubbock, Russell, Tennyson. Duke of Argyll proposed and elected.

(11) November 8, 1870, *T. H. Huxley:* "Has a Frog a Soul; and of What Nature is That Soul, Supposing it to Exist?" (R, RB, M).

Summarized in the *Life and Letters of Thomas Henry Huxley,* by his son Leonard Huxley, London, Macmillan, 1903, I, 458–9.

W. G. Ward chairman for the year 1870–1.

Present, 19: Alford, Argyll, Bagehot, Carpenter, Dalgairns, Ellicott, Hinton, Hodgson, Hutton, Huxley, Knowles, Lowe, Lubbock, Manning, Pattison, Ruskin, Russell, Stanley, Ward. Grant Duff proposed and elected.

(12) December 13, 1870, *Walter Bagehot:* "On the Emotion of Conviction" (R, B, M).

Published in *Contemporary Review,* XVII (April, 1871), 32. Republished in *The Works and Life of Walter Bagehot,* edited by Mrs. Russell Barrington, London, Longmans, 1915.

Present, 13: Alford, Bagehot, Dalgairns, Ellicott, Froude, Grant Duff, Harrison, Hinton, Hutton, Knowles, Sidgwick, Tennyson, Ward (in the chair). Greg proposed.

(13) January 11, 1871, *Archbishop Manning:* "What is the Relation of the Will to Thought?" (R, B, M).

Published in *Contemporary Review,* XVI (February, 1871), 468. An answer to Huxley's "Has a Frog a Soul?" (No. 11; November 8, 1870).

Present, 18: Argyll, Carpenter, Dalgairns, Froude, Grant Duff, Grove, Harrison, Hodgson, Hutton, Huxley, Knowles, Lubbock, Manning, Martineau, Ruskin, Russell, Stanley, Ward. Greg elected; Fraser proposed.

(14) February 8, 1871, *Sir Alexander Grant:* "On the Nature and Origin of the Moral Ideas" (R, B, M).

Published in *Fortnightly Review,* N.S. IX (March, 1871), 363; reviewed by Henry Holbeach in *Contemporary Review,* XVII (May, 1871), 299.

Present, 18: Argyll, Bagehot, Dalgairns, Ellicott, Froude, Grant, Greg, Hinton, Hodgson, Hutton, Knowles, Lubbock, Manning, Martineau, Pattison, Ruskin, Russell, Ward. Fraser elected.

(15) March 14, 1871, *Lord Arthur Russell:* "On the Absolute" (R, B, M).

Published in *Contemporary Review,* XVII (June, 1871), 338. Reprinted in the privately printed volume, *Papers Read at the Meetings of the Metaphysical Society by Lord Arthur Russell,* 1896. A paper prepared by Frederic Harrison as his contribution to the discussion of this paper of Russell's was published as "The Absolute" in Harrison's *Philosophy of Common Sense,* New York, Macmillan, 1907, pp. 126–36.

It is interesting to note here that beginning with Lubbock's paper (No. 5; January 12, 1870), every paper printed for the Society except the last four carried the following note: "Any member unavoidably absent from the Meeting can, if he think proper, make written remarks on the foregoing Paper, and forward them to the Secretary. No such remarks should exceed ten minutes in length of delivery viva voce." Harrison was, however, present at this meeting and delivered his "remarks" in person.

Present, 12: Carpenter, Grant Duff, Greg, Harrison, Hinton, Hutton, Huxley, Knowles, Manning, Russell, Ruskin, Tyndall. Acland proposed.

(16) April 25, 1871, *John Ruskin:* "Theorem: The Range of Intellectual Conception is Proportioned to the Rank in Animated Life" (R, B, M).

Published in *Contemporary Review,* XVII (June, 1871), 424. Republished in the collected edition of his *Works,* edited by Cook and Wedderburn, London, G. Allen (New York, Longmans), 1903–12, XXXIV, 107–11. In part an ironic answer to Lord Arthur Russell's previous paper (No. 15; March 14, 1871).

Present, 15: Barry, Carpenter, Ellicott, Grant Duff, Harrison, Hinton, Hutton, Huxley, Knowles, Manning, Ruskin, Russell, Stanley, Thirlwall, Ward. Acland elected; Maurice proposed and elected.

(17) May 16, 1871, *J. A. Froude:* "Evidence" (R, B, M).

Present, 16: Acland, Bagehot, Barry, Carpenter, Froude, Greg, Hinton, Hodgson, Knowles, Lubbock, Manning, Martineau, Pattison, Ruskin, Russell, Ward. (William Thomson, Archbishop of York, was probably proposed at this meeting.)

(18) June 13, 1871, *R. H. Hutton:* "Mr. Herbert Spencer on Moral Intuitions and Moral Sentiments" (R, B, M).

Published in *Contemporary Review,* XVII (July, 1871), 463. An answer to Spencer's article in the *Fortnightly,* N.S. IX, (April, 1871), 419, which was a reply to Hutton's paper (No. 1; June 2, 1869), published in *Macmillan's Magazine,* XX (July, 1869), 266.

Present, 13: Carpenter, Ellicott, Fraser, Hinton, Hodgson, Hutton, Huxley, Knowles, Manning, Martineau, Noel, Sidgwick, Ward. This is the last meeting for which we have the incomplete proof of the Minute-Book. (Thomson, Archbishop of York, probably elected at this meeting.)

(19) July 11, 1871, *Bishop C. J. Ellicott:* "What is Death?" (R, B, M).

Published in *Contemporary Review,* XVIII (August, 1871), 56.

Present, unknown: Tennyson, Ellicott, and others (see *Tennyson, a Memoir,* II, 171).

(20) November 21, 1871, *F. D. Maurice:* "On the Words 'Nature,' 'Natural,' and 'Supernatural' " (R, B, M, P).

Present, unknown: Tennyson, Maurice, and others (see *Tennyson, a Memoir,* II, 171).

(21) December 19, 1871, *A. P. Stanley:* "Do We Form Our Opinions on External Authority?" (R, B, M).

(22) January 17, 1872, *W. B. Carpenter:* "What is Common Sense?" (R, B, M).

Published in *Contemporary Review,* XIX (February, 1872), 401.

(23) February 13, 1872, *W. R. Greg:* "Wherein Consists the Special Beauty of Imperfection and Decay?" (R, B, M).

Published in *Contemporary Review,* XX (October, 1872), 692, as "The Special Beauty Conferred by Imperfection and Decay."

(24) March 12, 1872, *J. A. Froude:* "Are Numbers and Geometrical Figures Real Things?" (B, M).

(25) April 9, 1872, *Mark Pattison:* "The Arguments for a Future Life" (R, B, M).

(26) xxiii, May 14, 1872, *Archbishop Manning:* "That Legitimate Authority is an Evidence of Truth" (R, B, M).

Briefly paraphrased in: Shane Leslie, *Henry Edward Manning,* London, Burns, Oates, and Washbourne, 1921, p. 321.

(27) xxiv, June 11, 1872, *Father J. D. Dalgairns:* "Is God Unknowable?" (R, B, M).

Published in *Contemporary Review,* XX (October, 1872), 615.

(28) xxv, July 9, 1872, *Frederic Harrison:* "On the Supposed Necessity of Certain Metaphysical Problems" (R, B, M).

Published in *Fortnightly Review,* N.S. XII (November, 1872), 517. Reprinted with modifications in his *Philosophy of Common*

Sense, New York, Macmillan, 1907, pp. 1–20. A privately printed copy of this paper is in the Bodleian Library.

Present, 9: Ellicott, Greg, Harrison, Hodgson, Huxley, Knowles, Russell, Sidgwick, Tennyson. (Note by Russell.)

(29) xxvi, November 12, 1872, *Shadworth Hodgson:* "Five Idols of the Theatre" (B, M).

Developed from Harrison's paper at the previous meeting.

Present, unknown: Dalgairns, Hodgson, Knowles, Manning, Tennyson, and others (see *Tennyson, a Memoir,* II, 117, 118, 171). Archbishop Manning chairman for the year 1872–3.

(30) xxvii, December 10, 1872, *W. G. Ward:* "Can Experience Prove the Uniformity of Nature?" (R, B, M).

A brief paraphrase of this paper is found in "The Metaphysical Society: a Reminiscence," by R. H. Hutton in *Nineteenth Century,* XVIII (August, 1885), 177 ff., paraphrased in Chapter IV, above.

Present, 10: Bagehot, Dalgairns, Hinton, Huxley, Manning, Martineau, Ruskin, Stephen, Tyndall, Ward. (According to Hutton's "Reminiscence.")

(31) xxviii, January 14, 1873, *Lord Arthur Russell:* "Darwinians and Idealists" (R, B, M).

Reprinted in the privately printed volume, *Papers Read at the Meetings of the Metaphysical Society by Lord Arthur Russell,* 1896.

(32) xxix, February 11, 1873, *John Ruskin:* "The Nature and Authority of Miracle" (R, B, M).

Published in *Contemporary Review,* XXI (March, 1873), 627. Republished in the collected edition of his works, edited by Cook and Wedderburn, London, G. Allen (New York, Longmans), 1903–12, XXXIV, 115–25. A pamphlet version of this paper (of which there is a copy in the Harvard Library) is strongly suspected of being a forgery by J. Carter and G. Pollard in *An Enquiry into the Nature of Certain Nineteenth Century Pamphlets,* pp. 242–3. Ruskin's paper is an effort to define more clearly some of the terms used in the discussion of Ward's paper (No. 30; December 10, 1872).

Present, 14: Dalgairns, Ellicott, Fraser (?), Froude, Grant (?), Greg, Hutton, Knowles, Magee, Manning (in the chair), Noel,

Ruskin, Russell, Ward. (J. C. MacDonnell, *Life of William Connor Magee,* I, 284.)

(33) xxx, March 11, 1873, *Henry Acland:* "Faith and Knowledge" (R, B, M).

Published in *Contemporary Review,* XXI (April, 1873), 719. A privately printed pamphlet version, published by Oxford in 1873, is in the Yale University Library.

(34) xxxi, April 8, 1873, *Roden Noel:* "On Will" (R, B, M).

Published as "On Causality in Will and Motion," in *Contemporary Review,* XXIII (February, 1874), 380.

(35) xxxii, May 13, 1873, *G. Croom Robertson:* "The Action of So-Called Motives" (R, B, M).

"This paper expands some remarks made in the course of our last discussion, with the object of reviving the debate upon a rather more definite issue."

Present, 16: Carpenter, Dalgairns, Ellicott, Greg, Hodgson, Hutton, Huxley, Knowles, Manning, Noel, Robertson, Ruskin, Russell, Stanley, Tyndall, Ward. (Note by Russell.)

(36) xxxvi, June 10, 1873, *Archbishop Manning:* "A Diagnosis and Prescription" (R, B, M).

The definitions of this paper are paraphrased in part in: Shane Leslie, *Henry Edward Manning,* London, Burns, Oates, and Washbourne, 1921, pp. 321, 322.

This paper establishes the correct numbering, not of papers *printed,* but of papers *read,* which continues with minor errors until the dissolution of the Society.

(37a) xxxvii, July 8, 1873, *R. H. Hutton:* "Euthanasia" (R, B, M).

Note at head of the paper as printed: "As there has been a double failure in the promise to write a Paper on Euthanasia for this Society, it is thought that the following remarks, which recently appeared, by one of our members, in a weekly periodical [the *Spectator*], may furnish a certain basis of discussion, in case the Bishop of Gloucester and Bristol [C. J. Ellicott], who has kindly given the Committee some hope that he will orally fill the gap, should not be able to do so."

(37b) July 8, 1873, *Bishop C. J. Ellicott:* "Oral Communication on Euthanasia" (possibly M).

No further trace has been found of this communication. Further checking may identify this paper in some form in the Library of Manchester College, Oxford.

(38) xxxviii, November 18, 1873, *James Hinton:* "On the Relation of the Organic and Inorganic Worlds" (R, B, M).

(39) xxxix, December 16, 1873, *Henry Sidgwick:* "Utilitarianism" (R, B, M).

Present, 11: Carpenter, Dalgairns, Hodgson, Hutton, Huxley, Knowles, Manning, Ruskin, Russell, Sidgwick, Tennyson. (Note by Russell.)

(40) xl, January 13, 1873, *Lord Arthur Russell:* "The Speculative Method" (R, B, M).

Published in *Contemporary Review,* XXIII (April, 1874), 814. Reprinted in the privately printed volume, *Papers Read at the Meetings of the Metaphysical Society by Lord Arthur Russell,* 1896.

(41) xli, February 10, 1874, *Walter Bagehot:* "The Metaphysical Basis of Toleration" (R, B, M).

Published in *Contemporary Review,* XXIII (April, 1874), 765. Reprinted in *The Works and Life of Walter Bagehot,* edited by Mrs. Russell Barrington, London, Longmans, 1915, VI, 219 ff.

Present, 20: Bagehot, Huxley, Manning, Russell, and others unknown. (Letter of Lord Arthur Russell to his brother Lord Odo Russell, February 11, 1874.)

(42) xlii, March 10, 1874, *J. Fitzjames Stephen:* "Some Thoughts on Necessary Truth" (R, B, M).

Published in *Contemporary Review,* XXV (December, 1874), 44. Ward's reply is No. 46. Ward had circulated among the members of the Society several papers on Mill which he had also recently published in the *Dublin Review.* Stephen, finding them unconvincing, took up the cudgels in this paper.

Present, 16: Acland, Bagehot, Bucknill, Clifford, Greg, Harrison, Hinton, Hodgson, Hutton, Knowles, Martineau, Robertson, Russell, J. Stephen, Sylvester, Tyndall. (Note by Russell.)

(43) xliii, April 14, 1874, *R. H. Hutton:* " 'Latent Thought' " (R, RB, M).

Published in *Contemporary Review,* XXIV (July, 1874), 201.

(44) xliv, May 12, 1874, *Father J. D. Dalgairns:* "The Personality of God" (R, B, M).

Published in *Contemporary Review,* XXIV (July, 1874), 321.

Present, 12: Clifford, Dalgairns, Ellicott, Hodgson, Knowles, Lubbock, Martineau, Noel, Robertson, Russell, J. Stephen, Tyndall. (Note by Russell.)

(45) xlv, June 9, 1874, *W. K. Clifford:* "On the Nature of Things in Themselves" (R, B, M).

Published in *Mind,* III (January, 1878), 57. Reprinted in his *Lectures and Essays,* edited by Leslie Stephen and Sir Frederick Pollock, London, Macmillan, 1901 (1st ed. 1879), II, 52–73.

Present, 12: Bucknill, Carpenter, Clifford, Dalgairns, Greg, Knowles, Manning, Martineau, Noel, Robertson, Russell, Ward. (Note by Russell.)

(46) xlvi, July 14, 1874, *W. G. Ward:* "A Reply on Necessary Truth" (R, B, M).

Published in *Contemporary Review,* XXV (March, 1875), 527. A reply to Stephen's paper (No. 42; March 10, 1874).

(47) xlvii, November 17, 1874, *W. B. Carpenter:* "On the Doctrine of Human Automatism" (B, M).

Published in expanded form in *Contemporary Review,* XXV (February, 1875), 397, and XXV (May, 1875), 940. Delivered as a lecture, before the Sunday Lecture Society, March 7, 1875, of which there is a pamphlet version (London, 1875) in the Harvard Library.

W. E. Gladstone chairman for the year 1874–5.

(48) xlviii, December 8, 1874, *W. R. Greg:* "Can Truths be Apprehended Which Could not Have Been Discovered?" (B, M).

Published in *Contemporary Review,* XXV (February, 1875), 431. Reprinted in his *Miscellaneous Essays,* London, Trübner, 1882.

(49) xlix, January 12, 1875, *J. Fitzjames Stephen:* "On a Theory of Dr. Newman's as to Believing in Mysteries" (R, B, M).

(50) l, February 9, 1875, *Archbishop Thomson:* "Will and Responsibility" (R, B, M).

(51) li, March 9, 1875, *W. K. Clifford:* "The Scientific Basis of Morals" (R, B, M).

Published in slightly expanded form in *Contemporary Review,* XXVI (September, 1875), 650. Reprinted in his *Lectures and Essays,* edited by Leslie Stephen and Sir Frederick Pollock, 2 vols., London, Macmillan, 1901 (1st ed. 1879), II, 74–95. There is also a pamphlet version in the Harvard Library. This paper, as published in the *Contemporary Review,* was the first part of a discussion "On the Scientific Basis of Morals." All three parts appeared in the September, 1875, issue. The second contribution was by "P. C. W." (the initials, in reverse order, of "W. C. Peterborough," William Connor Magee, Bishop of Peterborough) and presents his paper (No. 52; April 13, 1875). The third part is by Frederic Harrison, and represents his contribution to the discussion of these two papers before the Society; it was republished by him as "The Basis of Morals: A Symposium at the Metaphysical Society," in *The Philosophy of Common Sense,* New York, Macmillan, 1907, pp. 137–51.

(52) lii, April 13, 1875, *Bishop W. C. Magee:* "Hospitals for Incurables Considered from a Moral Point of View" (R, B, M).

Published in *Contemporary Review,* XXVI (September, 1875), 661, as Part II of a discussion "On the Scientific Basis of Morals." (See No. 51, March 9, 1875, by W. K. Clifford, to which paper it was an ironic rejoinder.) Reprinted in J. C. MacDonnell, *The Life and Correspondence of William Connor Magee,* 2 vols., London, Isbister, 1896, II, 24–32.

Present, 14: Carpenter, Clark, Ellicott, Grant Duff, Harrison, Hutton, Knowles, Lubbock, (Magee), Mivart, Ruskin, Russell (in the chair), Tyndall, Ward. (Note by Grant Duff in *Notes from a Diary, 1873–1881,* 2 vols., London, Murray, 1898, I, 90–1.)

(53) liii, May 11, 1875, *John Ruskin:* "Theorem: Social Policy Must Be Based on the Scientific Principle of Natural Selection" (R, B, M).

Published in his volume, *"A Joy for Ever,"* London, G. Allen, 1880, pp. 209–20. Reprinted in the collected edition of his *Works,* edited by Cook and Wedderburn, London, G. Allen (New York, Longmans), 1903–12, XVI, 161–9. A further ironic discussion of Clifford's and Magee's two previous papers above.

(54) liv, June 8, 1875, *Lord Arthur Russell:* "The Right of Man over the Lower Animals" (R, RB, M).

Reprinted in the privately printed volume, *Papers Read at the Meetings of the Metaphysical Society by Lord Arthur Russell,* 1896.

Present, 11: Clifford, Fraser, Gladstone (chairman for the year), Greg, Hutton, Knowles, Martineau, Mivart, Pattison, Russell, Sylvester. (Note by Russell.)

(55) lv, July 13, 1875, *Henry Sidgwick:* "The Theory of Evolution in its Application to Practice" (R, B, M).

Published in *Mind,* I (January, 1876), 52.

(56) lv, November 9, 1875, *J. Fitzjames Stephen:* "Remarks on the Proof of Miracles" (R, B, M).

Discussed from the point of view of a lawyer examining evidence.

Present, 12: Clifford, Gladstone (in the chair), Hodgson, Hutton, Huxley, Knowles, Martineau, Mivart, Pattison, Russell, J. Stephen, Ward. (Note by Russell.)

(57) lvi, December 14, 1875, *W. B. Carpenter:* "On the Fallacies of Testimony in Relation to the Supernatural" (R, B).

Published in *Contemporary Review,* XXVII (January, 1876), 279. A reply, by James Gairdner, appeared in *Contemporary Review,* XXVII (February, 1876), 440. This paper continues the discussion of the previous meeting, December 14, 1875, from the point of view of a scientist using "scientific methods."

Present, unknown: Carpenter, Manning, Mivart, Harrison, Russell, and others. (Letter of Lord Arthur Russell to his brother Lord Odo Russell, December 15, 1875.)

(58) lviii, January 11, 1876, *T. H. Huxley:* "The Evidence of the Miracle of the Resurrection" (R, B, M, P).

Huxley and Morley decided not to publish this paper in the *Fortnightly Review,* although some of Huxley's friends had urged him to do so (*Life and Letters of Thomas Henry Huxley,* 3 vols., by his son, Leonard Huxley, London, Macmillan, 1903, II, 196–7). Huxley's contribution to the discussion of miracles and supernatural evidences was undertaken to meet Ward's suggestion at one of the two previous meetings that "those who fail to perceive the cogency of the evidence by which the occurrence of miracles is supported, should not confine themselves to the discussion of general principles, but should grapple with some particular case of an alleged miracle." (Huxley's version of Ward's suggestion.)

Present, 13: Bagehot, Clifford, Froude, Greg, Harrison, Hodgson, Hutton, Huxley, Knowles, Mivart, Russell, J. Stephen, Ward. (Note by Russell.)

February 15, 1876. No paper. Discussion of Huxley's paper of January 11, 1876, "The Evidence of the Miracle of the Resurrection," continued, the only paper read before the Society ever so honored.

(59) lix, March 14, 1876, *Shadworth Hodgson:* "The Pre-Suppositions of Miracles" (R, B, M).

This paper is a professional philosopher's contribution to the subject discussed at the four previous meetings.

About this time Harrison proposed John Morley for membership, and he and Lord Selborne were elected by acclamation. (F. W. Hirst, *Early Life and Letters of John Morley,* 2 vols., London, Macmillan, 1927, II, 7.)

(60) lx, April 11, 1876, *W. K. Clifford:* "The Ethics of Belief" (R, B, M).

Published as part of an essay with the same title in *Contemporary Review,* XXIX (January, 1877), 289; answered by Prof. Wace in *Contemporary Review,* XXX (June, 1877), 42. Reprinted in Clifford's *Lectures and Essays,* edited by Leslie Stephen and Sir Frederick Pollock, 2 vols., London, Macmillan, 1901 (1st ed. 1879), II, 163–76. This important paper extends the field of debate of the previous five meetings. "No simplicity of mind, no obscurity of station, can escape the universal duty of questioning all that we believe."

(61) lxi, May 9, 1876, *Lord Arthur Russell:* "The Persistence of the Religious Feeling" (R, B, M).

Reprinted in the privately printed volume of *Papers Read at the Meetings of the Metaphysical Society by Lord Arthur Russell,* 1896. A brief contribution to one of the questions raised by Clifford at the previous meeting.

(62) lxii, June 13, 1876, *St. George Mivart:* "What is the Good of Truth?" (R, B, M).

This paper, and No. 68, May 8, 1877, contributed to the substance of Mivart's "Force, Energy, and Will," in *Nineteenth Century,* III (May, 1878), 933.

(63) lxiii, July 11, 1876, *J. Fitzjames Stephen:* "What is a Lie?" (R, B, M).

An attempt at definition, which led to Stephen's paper, No. 81, February 11, 1879, which in its turn answered Mivart's papers, No. 62 and No. 68.

Present, unknown: Ellicott, Grant Duff, Russell, Stephen, and others. ("A very small party."—Grant Duff, *Notes from a Diary, 1873–1881,* 2 vols., London, Murray, 1898, I, 199.)

(63x) November 14, 1876, *G. Croom Robertson:* "How Do We Come by Our Knowledge?"

Published in the first number of the *Nineteenth Century,* I (March, 1877), 113. However, this and the following paper have not been found in any original form. They were probably never printed, perhaps owing to a committee error or some printing difficulty at the beginning of the Society's new year. In any case, the paper of January 9, 1877, is numbered "lxiv" and resumes the regular numbering of papers.

(63y) December 12, 1876, *J. Fitzjames Stephen:* "The Effect of a Decline of Religious Belief on Morality."

There is every reason to believe that this paper appeared in the *Nineteenth Century,* I (April, 1877), 331, as the initial contribution to Knowles's first Modern Symposium on "Morality and Religious Belief," which began in April with the second number of the new journal. Stephen's rebuttal appeared in the May, 1877, issue, I, 545. (See Chapter X, above.) This likelihood is increased by the fact that Harrison's two articles which initiated the second Symposium on "The Soul and Future Life" appeared in the *Nineteenth Century,* June and July, 1877, and were expansions of his paper, "The Soul before and after Death" (No. 64; January 9, 1877). However, no original printed version of Stephen's paper has been found. (See note on No. 63x.) But if the above presumptions are sound, and the assumption made in the note on Carpenter's paper, No. 2, July 14, 1869, is accepted, we possess a printed or published version of every paper read before the Society except Ellicott's "Oral Communication on Euthanasia" (No. 37b), of which, however, some form may exist in the Library of Manchester College, Oxford.

(64) lxiv, January 9, 1877, *Frederic Harrison:* "The Soul before and after Death," Part I (R, B, M).

Published in *Nineteenth Century,* I (June, 1877), 623, and I (July, 1877), 832. These articles became the starting point for Knowles's second Modern Symposium on "The Soul and Future Life" (see Chapter X, above), September and October, 1877. Reprinted in Harrison's *Philosophy of Common Sense,* New York, Macmillan, 1907, p. 184–p. 193, par. 2; p. 212, par. 1–p. 218, par. 2; p. 222, par. 1–p. 224.

Present, 12: Bucknill, Carpenter, Clifford, Harrison, Hodgson, Huxley, Knowles, Manning, Martineau, Russell, J. Stephen, Tyndall. (Note by Russell.)

(65) lxv, February 13, 1877, *Cardinal Manning:* "The Soul before and after Death," Part II (R, B, M).

Not published in Knowles's second Modern Symposium in the *Nineteenth Century,* although a contribution to this argument in the meetings of the Society. Since the paper would invoke theological and dogmatic dispute, and Manning had discussed the subject in purely metaphysical terms, he was probably unwilling to take part in a public debate on this subject. (See note on Manning's share in the debate recorded in Hutton's "Reminiscence," Chapter IV, above.)

(66) lxvi, March 13, 1877, *J. Fitzjames Stephen:* "Authority in Matters of Opinion" (R, B, M).

Published in *Nineteenth Century,* I (April, 1877), 270, as "Mr. Gladstone and Sir George Lewis on Authority." Gladstone had published, in the *Nineteenth Century,* I (March, 1877), 2, an attack on Sir George Cornewall Lewis, under the title, "On the Influence of Authority in Matters of Opinion." It was the first article in the new review, immediately following Tennyson's prefatory sonnet.

(67) lxvii, April 17, 1877, *James Martineau:* "The Supposed Conflict between Efficient and Final Causation" (R, B, M, P).

Present, 9: Acland, Bucknill, Carpenter, Ellicott, Hutton, Huxley, Martineau, Robertson, Russell.

(68) lxviii, May 8, 1877, *St. George Mivart:* "Matter and Force" (R, B, M).

This paper, and No. 62, June 13, 1876, contributed to the substance of Mivart's paper, "Force, Energy, and Will," in *Nine-*

teenth Century, III (May, 1878), 933; reprinted in his *Essays and Criticisms,* 2 vols., Boston, Little Brown, 1892, II, 226–49.

(69) lxix, June 12, 1877, *Leslie Stephen:* "Belief and Evidence" (R, B, M).

A further contribution to the questions raised by Clifford in No. 60, April 11, 1876, which, however, Leslie Stephen had not heard at the Society, for he was not then a member. But he had probably read it in its expanded form in *Contemporary Review,* January, 1877; or he could have seen either the manuscript or the version printed for the Society.

(70) lxx, July 10, 1877, *Lord Arthur Russell:* "On Ideas as a Force" (R, B, M).

This very brief paper was reprinted in the privately printed volume, *Papers Read at the Meetings of the Metaphysical Society by Lord Arthur Russell,* 1896. It continues to raise questions deriving from Martineau's paper (No. 67; April 17, 1877) and Mivart's (No. 68; May 8, 1877).

(71) lxxi, November 13, 1877, *R. H. Hutton:* "On the Relation of Evidence to Conviction" (R, B, M).

A reply to Leslie Stephen's paper (No. 69; June 12, 1877).

Present, 10: Carpenter, Ellicott, Hodgson, Hutton, Huxley, Mivart, Ruskin, Russell, Tyndall, Ward. (Note by Russell.) Lord Selborne chairman for the year 1877–8.

(72) lxxii, December 11, 1877, *John Morley:* "Various Definitions of Materialism" (R, B, M).

(73) lxxiii, January 15, 1878, *Henry Sidgwick:* "The Relation of Psychogony to Metaphysics and Ethics" (R, RB, M).

The word "psychogony"—the origin and primitive condition of the mind—is borrowed from G. H. Lewes.

Present, 7: Clifford, Knowles, Martineau, Pattison, Robertson, Russell, Sidgwick. (Note by Russell.)

(74) lxxiv, February 12, 1878, *Mark Pattison:* "Double Truth" (B, M).

A magnificently characteristic modification of the argument of Mivart's paper (No. 62; June 13, 1876) and J. Stephen's reply (No. 63; July 11, 1876). It is also relevant to Hutton's more recent paper (No. 71; November 13, 1877).

Present, unknown: Tennyson, Pattison, and others. (*Tennyson, a Memoir,* II, 171.)

March 12, 1878. No paper, but there was submitted a "Report of the Committee on Definitions."

The secretary's list of papers read before the Society says that this report was "not printed."

(75) lxxv, April 9, 1878, *Matthew P. W. Boulton:* "Has a Metaphysical Society any *Raison d'être?*" (R, B, M).

Present, 11 or 12: (Boulton), Gladstone, Grant Duff, Greg, Harrison, Hodgson, Hutton, Knowles, Martineau, Mivart, Russell, Sidgwick. Boulton may not have been present at the reading of his own paper; and there is a slight possibility that this attendance is for the meeting of June 11, 1878. (Note by Russell; not clear on these points.)

(No meeting in May, 1878.)

(76) lxxvi, June 11, 1878, *Bishop W. C. Magee:* "The Ethics of Persecution" (R, B, M).

See notes on attendance at meeting of April 9, 1878, above, and of July 9, 1878, below.

(77) lxxvii, July 9, 1878, *J. C. Bucknill:* "The Limits of Philanthropy" (R, B, M).

Present, 7: Bucknill, Carpenter, Huxley, Knowles, Mivart, Russell, L. Stephen. It is very unlikely, but this may possibly be the attendance for June 11, 1878. (Note by Russell; not clear on this point.)

(78) November 12, 1878, *Shadworth Hodgson:* "Is Monism Tenable?" (R, B, M).

Present, 5: Harrison, Hodgson, Knowles, Martineau, Russell. Russell to attend a committee meeting November 26. (Note by Russell.)

(79) lxxix, December 17, 1878, *R. H. Hutton:* "Is 'Lapsed Intelligence' a Probable Origin for Complex Animal Instincts?" (R, B, M, P).

This paper is a reply to the lecture on "Animal Intelligence" which had been delivered by G. J. Romanes to the meeting of the British Association at Dublin and printed in *Nineteenth Century,* IV (October, 1878), 653.

(80) 80, January 14, 1879, *Henry Sidgwick:* "Incoherence of Empirical Philosophy" (R, B, M, P).

Published in *Mind,* VII (October, 1882), 533. Reprinted in his *The Philosophy of Kant and Other Lectures and Essays,* London, Macmillan, 1905. "We cannot get along without the empirical sciences. But we might perhaps make a shift to dispense with Empirical Philosophy."

Present, 8: Huxley, Knowles, Mivart, Pattison, Russell, Sidgwick, J. Stephen, L. Stephen.

(81) 81, February 11, 1879, *J. Fitzjames Stephen:* "On the Utility of Truth" (R, B, M, P).

An answer to Mivart's "Force, Energy, and Will," in *Nineteenth Century,* III (May, 1878), 933, which in its turn derives from Mivart's papers before the Society (No. 62; June 13, 1876) and (No. 68; May 8, 1877). "Our Secretary having asked me to get him out of a difficulty, by writing something which the Society could discuss, I have tried to do so, at very short notice indeed."

(82) 82, March 11, 1879, *Leslie Stephen:* "The Uniformity of Nature" (R, B, M, P).

"I must begin by an apology which is not, I fear, unprecedented in this Society, for the roughness of the following remarks. I have been unexpectedly called upon to honour a bill, before I have provided the necessary funds."

Present, 11: Acland, Bucknill, Hodgson, Hutton, Huxley, Knowles, Lubbock, Martineau, Russell, L. Stephen, Tyndall. (Note by Russell.)

(83) 83, April 8, 1879, *St. George Mivart:* "The Religion of Emotion" (R, B, M).

Springs from or contributes to his review article "The Psychology of the Emotions," in his *Essays and Criticisms,* 2 vols., Boston, Little Brown, 1892, I, 423–72.

(84a) 84, May 27, 1879, *Cardinal Manning:* "The Objective Certainty of the Immaterial World" (M, P, and probably in B).

Probably never published or reprinted. Very briefly paraphrased in: Shane Leslie, *Henry Edward Manning,* London, Burns, Oates, and Washbourne, 1921, p. 323.

(84b) 84, June 10, 1879, *Frederic Harrison:* "The Social Factor in Psychology" (R, B, M).

Published in his *Philosophy of Common Sense,* New York, Macmillan, 1907, pp. 118–25.

July 15, 1879. No paper.

Perhaps no meeting worthy of the name. The secretary's list says, merely, "No paper recorded."

(84c) 84, November 25, 1879, *Cardinal Manning:* "What is Philosophy?" (R, B, M, P).

A series of brief definitions, presenting paradoxes, probably never published or reprinted. A very brief paraphrase appears in: Shane Leslie, *Henry Edward Manning,* London, Burns, Oates, and Washbourne, 1921, p. 323.

Present, 12: Bucknill, Clarke, Gasquet (?), Gull, Hutton, Manning, Martineau, Mivart, Robertson, Russell, Tyndall, Upton. (Note by Russell.) Knowles resigns the secretaryship of the Society. Martineau elected chairman for the year 1879–80. Four of those present, Clarke, Gasquet, Gull, and Upton, were new members.

(85) 85, December 9, 1879, *R. H. Hutton:* "Is Causation or Power in Nature a Reality, or a Mere Anthropomorphic Fancy?" (R, B, M).

This paper had its origin in the discussion after the previous paper (No. 84c; November 25, 1879).

Tennyson resigns (*Tennyson, a Memoir,* II, 170). Martineau has been serving as secretary pro tem; Frederick Pollock elected secretary at this meeting.

(86) 86, January 13, 1880, *Sir William Gull:* "What Are the Elements of a Sensation?" (B).

The year is wrongly printed on this paper as 1879.

(87) 87, February 10, 1880, *Henry Sidgwick:* "The Scope of Metaphysics" (R, B, M, P).

The heading of the papers was changed with this number. The new heading also gives the new place of meeting, the Grosvenor Gallery Restaurant in New Bond Street. "Some time ago, an attempt was made to introduce somewhat more regular progress into the discussions of our Society, by providing definitions of the principal terms used in Metaphysics. I had much sympathy with this attempt, but it seemed to me a matter of considerably more labour and difficulty than Mr. Knowles, who started it, appeared to think; since complete agreement in definitions cannot, I conceive, be expected until we have also reached complete agreement as to doctrines. At the same time, I am quite of opinion that we might gain a good deal from a serious endeavour to agree, as far as we can, on the meaning of our cardinal terms; and it seems natural to begin with the term that denotes the whole subject of our discussion, that is, with a definition of 'Metaphysics.' "—Henry Sidgwick.

(88) 88, March 9, 1880, *Frederick Pollock:* "Generic and Symbolic Images" (R, B, M, P).

The starting point of this paper is an article by Francis Galton, "Generic Images," *Nineteenth Century,* VI (July, 1879), 157.

(89) 89, April 13, 1880, *F. A. Gasquet:* "The Relation of Metaphysics to the Rest of Philosophy" (R, B, M, P).

A brief reply to some of the points made by Sidgwick in No. 87, February 10, 1880.

(90) 90, May 11, 1880, *C. B. Upton:* "The Recent Phase of the Free-Will Controversy" (R, B, M, P).

"The discoveries of Science and the evidence of statistics do not seem to him [the believer in Free Will] to be incompatible with the view that our nature is so constituted as to afford rational ground for the ascription of personal merit and demerit, and that at the same time our actions are sufficiently correlated to character and open to prediction to furnish a solid basis for moral discipline and ethical science."—Final words of final paper.

November 16, 1880. *Final Meeting.*

No paper was read. Martineau in the chair. The Society was dissolved at this meeting. (See Appendix D.)

Present, 8: Bucknill, Gasquet, Hodgson, Martineau, Noel, Pollock, Robertson, Upton. Letters read, concurring in the plan for dissolution, from Ellicott, Hutton, and Russell.

It is interesting to note that after Knowles resigned the secretaryship of the Society, four out of the six remaining papers were read by newly elected members, and that apparently none of the six found publication in periodicals. Nor have I discovered any other form of publication for these final papers.

In the case of nearly all the papers which were published in periodicals or elsewhere, the authors necessarily made a number of changes in wording, punctuation, and paragraphing in the published versions. They also frequently expanded the papers, by the addition of further examples, more extensive quotation, or the further elaboration of an argument or an idea. Certain kinds of changes in the published versions of some authors' papers (Frederic Harrison's, for instance) seem to have been the result of the discussions at the Society's meetings. But on the whole, it is astonishing, not how many changes were made for the public eye, but how few.

Index to Papers, by Author

(The numbers are those which I have given the papers.)

Appendix D

NOTICE OF THE DISSOLUTION OF THE METAPHYSICAL SOCIETY

METAPHYSICAL SOCIETY

Copies are sent herewith of the Minutes of a Meeting, held on the 16th of November, 1880, at which it was determined to dissolve the Society.

The third Resolution of the Meeting, as to the disposal of the ultimate surplus of the Society's funds, is a recommendation only, and neither is, nor purports to be, binding on Members absent from the Meeting. Any Member who does not approve of the proposal is entitled to have his share of the ultimate surplus paid out to him. It will be assumed, however, that any Member who does not, on or before the 31st of December, signify to the Society's Bankers his dissent from the proposed application of the fund, does not dissent from the same.

The probable net balance, after payment of all the Society's debts and calling in of outstanding subscriptions, is roughly estimated at from £30 to £40; a sum insufficient, in any case, to return or remit the subscription for the current year.

In order to facilitate the winding-up of the Society's affairs, it is particularly requested that Members who have not paid their Subscriptions for the current year, 1880, will as soon as possible pay them into the account of the Society, with Messrs. Robarts, Lubbock, and Co.

James Martineau, late Chairman.
F. Pollock, late Secretary.

December 4, 1880

The Minutes of the Final Meeting

At a Meeting of the Metaphysical Society, held at No. 35 Gordon Square, on the 16th of November 1880, Dr. Martineau in the Chair,

The following resolutions, of which notice had been given by special circular to all who were Members at the date of the last meeting, was proposed by the Chairman, and seconded by the Secretary:—

"That, having regard to the difficulty lately found in keeping up this Society's meetings and the extent to which this Society's original objects have, since its foundation, been provided for in other ways, it is expedient that this Society be dissolved, and its affairs wound up."

Letters having been read from Lord Arthur Russell, M.P., the Bishop of Gloucester and Bristol, and Mr. Hutton, expressing concurrence in the resolution, the resolution was put, when the following members voted for the same:—

James Martineau.
F. Pollock.
[F. A.] Gasquet.
Shadworth H. Hodgson.
G. Croom Robertson.
Charles B. Upton.

Dr. Bucknill and the Hon. Roden Noel attended the meeting, but did not vote.

The Secretary reported that a balance of £17 *5s. 9d.* was standing to the Society's credit with Messrs. Robarts and Co., and that divers subscriptions were believed to be outstanding.

The following resolution was proposed by Professor Croom Robertson, and seconded by Mr. Roden Noel:—

"That a list of all the Papers read at the Society's meetings, with dates, and the names of the writers, be printed and sent to all persons who at any time have been Members of the Society, together with a copy of the Resolutions passed at this meeting; the expenses of such printing and circulation to be paid out of the Society's funds."

Which resolution was put and carried.

It was moved by the Secretary, and seconded by Dr. Gasquet:—

"That, subject to the assent of the existing Members of the Society, the Treasurer be authorised to pay over the ultimate net surplus, if any, of the Society's assets, to the Publishers of *Mind,* for the use of the Proprietors."

Which resolution was put and carried.

It was moved by the Secretary, and seconded by Dr. Bucknill:—

"That the Chairman be requested to accept the Minute-book, with the documents thereto belonging, as a token of the Society's thanks for his services during the past year."

Which resolution was put and carried unanimously.

The Minute-book was accordingly delivered to Dr. Martineau, and the meeting broke up.

Selected Bibliography

Handbooks, Histories, and Reference Works

Alfred William Benn. The History of English Rationalism in the Nineteenth Century. 2 vols. London, Longmans, 1906.

Dictionary of National Biography, including Supplements.

Walter James Graham. English Literary Periodicals. New York, Nelson, 1930.

Harley Granville-Barker, ed. The Eighteen-Seventies. New York, Macmillan, 1929.

Stanley J. Kunitz and Howard Haycraft. British Authors of the Nineteenth Century. New York, H. W. Wilson, 1936.

J. T. Merz. A History of European Thought in the Nineteenth Century. 4 vols. Edinburgh and London, Blackwood, 1907–14.

Presidential Addresses to the Society for Psychical Research, 1882–1911. Glasgow, 1912. (For the Society.)

Proceedings of the Aristotelian Society. Vol. I, Nos. 1–4. London, 1891.

Proceedings of the Royal Society of London. Vol. LXXV ("Obituaries"). London, 1905.

H. V. Routh. England Under Victoria. London, Methuen, 1930.

——— Towards the Twentieth Century. New York, Macmillan, 1937.

D. C. Somervell. English Thought in the Nineteenth Century. London, Methuen, 1929.

George Macaulay Trevelyan. British History in the Nineteenth Century, 1782–1901. London, Longmans, 1936.

Hugh Walker. The Literature of the Victorian Era. Cambridge, Cambridge University Press, 1931.

Andrew D. White. A History of the Warfare of Science with Theology in Christendom. 2 vols. New York, Appleton, 1897.

Esmé Wingfield-Stratford. The Victorian Sunset. New York, Morrow, 1932.

General Bibliography, principally relating to the Metaphysical Society

Walter Bagehot. The Works and Life of Walter Bagehot. Mrs. Russell Barrington, ed. 10 vols. London, Longmans, 1915.

Alexander Bain. Mental and Moral Science, a Compendium of Psychology and Ethics. London, Longmans, 1868.

A. J. Balfour. Retrospect, an Unfinished Autobiography, 1848–1886. Blanche E. C. Dugdale, ed. Boston, Houghton Mifflin, 1930.

Mrs. Russell Barrington. Life of Walter Bagehot. London, Longmans, 1915.

G. F. Barwick. "The Magazines of the Nineteenth Century," Transactions of the Bibliographical Society. Vol. XI, Oct., 1909–March, 1911. London, 1912. (For the Bibliographical Society.)

Jacques Barzun. Darwin, Marx, Wagner: Critique of a Heritage. Boston, Little Brown, 1941.

——— Romanticism and the Modern Ego. Boston, Little Brown, 1943.

Merle M. Bevington. The Saturday Review, 1855–1868: Representative Educated Opinion in Victorian England. New York, Columbia, 1941.

Charles and Frances Brookfield. Mrs. Brookfield and her Circle. New York, Scribner's, 1905.

Mrs. Frances M. Brookfield. The Cambridge "Apostles." New York, Scribner's, 1907.

W. B. Carpenter. Nature and Man: Essays Scientific and Philosophical. With an introductory memoir by J. Estlin Carpenter. London, K. Paul, Trench & Co., 1888.

——— Principles of Mental Physiology. New York, Appleton, 1875.

John Carter and Graham Pollard. An Enquiry into the Nature of Certain Nineteenth Century Pamphlets. London, Constable; New York, Scribner's; 1934.

W. K. Clifford. The Common Sense of the Exact Sciences. New York, Appleton, 1885; New York, Knopf; 1946.

——— Lectures and Essays. Leslie Stephen and Sir Frederick Pollock, eds. 2 vols. London, Macmillan, 1901. (1st ed. 1879.)

W. G. Collingwood. The Life and Work of John Ruskin. 2 vols. Boston, Houghton Mifflin, 1893.

Francis Darwin. The Life and Letters of Charles Darwin. 2 vols. New York, Appleton, 1888.

G. Lowes Dickinson. A Modern Symposium. New York, McClure Phillips, 1906.

James Drummond and C. B. Upton. The Life and Letters of James Martineau. 2 vols. New York, Dodd Mead, 1902. (With a Survey of his Philosophical Work by C. B. Upton.)

Edith M. O. Ellis (Mrs. Havelock Ellis). James Hinton, a Sketch. Preface by Havelock Ellis. London, S. Paul, 1918.

Edwin Mallard Everett. The Party of Humanity: "The Fortnightly Review" and its Contributors, 1865–1874. Chapel Hill, University of North Carolina Press, 1939.

E. M. Forster. Goldsworthy Lowes Dickinson. New York, Harcourt Brace, 1934.

A. C. Fraser. Biographia Philosophica: a Retrospect. Edinburgh and London, Blackwood, 1904.

Mrs. Adrian Grant Duff (nee Ursula Lubbock). The Life-Work of Lord Avebury (Sir John Lubbock), 1834–1913. London, Watts, 1924.

Sir Mountstuart E. Grant Duff. Notes from a Diary, 1873–1881. 2 vols. London, Murray, 1898.

——— Out of the Past: Some Biographical Essays. 2 vols. London, Murray, 1903.

Charles Larcom Graves. The Life and Letters of Sir George Grove, C.B. London, Macmillan, 1903.

W. R. Greg. Miscellaneous Essays. London, Trübner, 1882.

Frederic Harrison. Autobiographic Memoirs. 2 vols. London, Macmillan, 1911.

——— The Creed of a Layman. New York, Macmillan, 1907.

——— The Philosophy of Common Sense. New York, Macmillan, 1907.

——— Realities and Ideals: Social, Political, Literary and Artistic. New York, Macmillan, 1908.

[Frederick H. Hedge. American editor.] Essays and Reviews, 2d American ed., from the 2d English ed. Boston, Walker, Wise, 1861.

Maurice Hewlett. Letters of Maurice Hewlett. Lawrence Binyon, ed. London, Methuen, 1926.

F. W. Hirst. Early Life and Letters of John Morley. 2 vols. London, Macmillan, 1927.

J. A. Hobson. John Ruskin, Social Reformer. London, Nisbet, 1898.

John Hogben. Richard Holt Hutton of "The Spectator," a Monograph. Edinburgh, Oliver and Boyd, 1900.

Lancelot Hogben. Dangerous Thoughts. London, Allen and Unwin, 1939; New York, Norton, 1940.

Ellice Hopkins. Life and Letters of James Hinton. Introduction by Sir William Gull. London, Kegan Paul, 1878.

Horace G. Hutchinson. Life of Sir John Lubbock, Lord Avebury. 2 vols. London, Macmillan, 1914.

Arthur Wollaston Hutton. Cardinal Manning. London, Methuen, 1894.

Richard Holt Hutton. Aspects of Religious and Scientific Thought. London, Macmillan, 1899.

——— Criticisms on Contemporary Thought and Thinkers, Selected from the "Spectator." 2 vols. London and New York, Macmillan, 1894.

——— Theological Essays. London, Strahan, 1871.

Leonard Huxley. The House of Smith, Elder. London, privately printed, 1923.

——— Life and Letters of Thomas Henry Huxley. 3 vols. London, Macmillan, 1903.

T. H. Huxley. Evolution and Ethics. London, Macmillan, 1894.

——— Hume. London, Macmillan, 1894.

——— Science and Christian Tradition. London, Macmillan, 1894.

A. W. Jackson. James Martineau, a Biography and Study. Boston, Little Brown, 1901.

Frances Wentworth Knickerbocker. Free Minds: John Morley and his Friends. Cambridge, Harvard University Press, 1943.

Shane Leslie. Henry Edward Manning, His Life and Labours. London, Burns, Oates, and Washbourne, 1921.

Sir John Lubbock. The Origin of Civilization. London, Longmans, 1870.

Helen Merrell Lynd. England in the Eighteen-Eighties: Towards a Social Basis for Freedom. New York, Oxford, 1945.

J. C. MacDonnell. Life and Correspondence of William Connor Magee. 2 vols. London, Isbister, 1896.

F. W. Maitland. Life and Letters of Leslie Stephen. London, Duckworth, 1906.

William Hurrell Mallock. The New Republic, or Culture, Faith, and Philosophy in an English Country House. New York, Scribner and Welford, 1878.

Henry Edward (Cardinal) Manning. Miscellanies. 2 vols. London, Burns and Oates, 1877.

Henry L. Mansel. The Limits of Religious Thought. 5th ed. London, Murray, 1870.

Leslie M. Marchand. "The Athenaeum," a Mirror of Victorian Culture. Chapel Hill, University of North Carolina Press, 1941.

A. Patchett Martin. Life and Letters of the Right Honorable Robert Lowe, Viscount Sherbrooke. 2 vols. London, Longmans, 1893.

James Martineau. Essays, Philosophical and Theological. 2 vols. Boston, Spencer, 1868–70.

——— Essays, Reviews, and Addresses. 4 vols. London, Longmans, 1890–1.

Frederick Maurice. The Life of Frederick Denison Maurice. New York, Scribner, 1884. (Chiefly told by his son, using Maurice's own letters.)

John Stuart Mill. An Examination of Sir William Hamilton's Philosophy. 2 vols. New York, Holt, 1884. (First published 1865.)

St. George Mivart. Essays and Criticisms. 2 vols. Boston, Little Brown, 1892.

John Morley. Critical Miscellanies. London, Macmillan, 1921. (Vol. VI of The Works of Lord Morley.)

——— The Life of William Ewart Gladstone. 3 vols. New York, Macmillan, 1903.

——— On Compromise. London, Macmillan, 1910.

——— Recollections. 2 vols. New York, Macmillan, 1917.

Henry S. Nash. The History of the Higher Criticism of the New Testament. New York, Macmillan, 1906.

Harold Nicolson. Tennyson, Aspects of his Life, Character and Poetry. Boston, Houghton Mifflin, 1923.

Roundell Palmer (Lord Selborne). Memorials: Part II, Personal and Political, 1865–1895. London, Macmillan, 1898.

Houston Peterson. Huxley, Prophet of Science. London, Longmans, 1932.

Sir Frederick Pollock. For My Grandson, Remembrances of an Ancient Victorian. London, Murray, 1933.

Ada Pritchard. The Life and Work of Charles Pritchard. London, Seeley, 1897.

G. W. Prothero. "Memoir" of J. R. Seeley, prefixed to Seeley's Growth of British Policy, an Historical Essay (2 vols., Cambridge, Cambridge University Press, 1895).

E. S. Purcell. Life of Cardinal Manning. 2 vols. London, Macmillan, 1896.

John Ruskin. "A Joy for Ever." London, G. Allen, 1880; also in Works, ed. Cook and Wedderburn. Vol. XVI.

John Ruskin. Letters of John Ruskin to Charles Eliot Norton. 2 vols. Boston, Houghton Mifflin, 1905.

——— Works. ed. E. T. Cook and A. Wedderburn. London, G. Allen; New York, Longmans, 1903–12.

Lord Arthur Russell. Papers Read at the Meetings of the Metaphysical Society. [Edinburgh], privately printed, 1896.

Lady St. Helier (Mary Jeune). Memories of Fifty Years. London, Arnold, 1910.

P. A. Schilpp, ed. The Philosophy of Alfred North Whitehead. Evanston and Chicago, Northwestern University, 1941.

Wilfrid M. Short. The Mind of Arthur James Balfour. New York, Doran, 1918.

Arthur and Eleanor Sidgwick. Henry Sidgwick, a Memoir. London, Macmillan; New York, The Macmillan Co., 1906.

Henry Sidgwick. Lectures on the Philosophy of Kant and other Philosophical Lectures and Essays. London, Macmillan, 1905.

Warren Staebler. The Liberal Mind of John Morley. Princeton, Princeton University Press (for the University of Cincinnati), 1943.

James Fitzjames Stephen. Liberty, Equality, Fraternity. London, Smith Elder, 1873.

Leslie Stephen. The Life of Sir James Fitzjames Stephen. London, Smith Elder, 1895.

Lytton Strachey. Eminent Victorians. New York, Putnam's, 1918.

Alfred Tennyson. Works. London, Macmillan, 1893.

Hallam Tennyson. Alfred Lord Tennyson, a Memoir. 2 vols. New York and London, Macmillan, 1898.

——— ed. Tennyson and his Friends. London, Macmillan, 1911.

J. C. Thirlwall, Jr. Connop Thirlwall: Historian and Theologian. London, Society for Promoting Christian Knowledge. New York, Macmillan, 1936.

William Beach Thomas. The Story of the "Spectator," 1828–1928. London, Methuen, 1928.

Miriam M. H. Thrall. Rebellious "Fraser's." New York, Columbia University Press, 1934.

Lionel Trilling. Matthew Arnold. New York, Norton, 1939.

John Tyndall. "The Belfast Address," in Fragments of Science (6th ed., 2 vols., London, Longmans, 1879).

Maisie Ward (Mrs. Maisie Ward Sheed). The Wilfrid Wards and the Transition. Vol. I: The Nineteenth Century. London, Sheed and Ward, 1934.

Wilfrid Ward. The Life of John Henry, Cardinal Newman. 2 vols. New York, Longmans, 1912.

——— Ten Personal Studies. London, Longmans, 1908.

——— William George Ward and the Catholic Revival. London, Macmillan, 1893.

Arthur Waugh. "The English Reviews: a Sketch of their History and Principles," The Critic (New York), Vol. XL (Jan., 1902).

Alfred North Whitehead. Science and the Modern World. New York, Macmillan, 1925.

Index